THE
UNIVERSITY OF
CAMBRIDGE

G.R. Evans is Professor Emeritus of Medieval Theology and Intellectual History in the University of Cambridge, is a graduate of the University of Oxford and holds higher doctorates of both Oxford and Cambridge. She has written many well-received books in the fields of medieval and ecumenical theology, intellectual history and public policy in higher education and also serves as editor of the *I.B.Tauris History of the Christian Church* series.

THE
UNIVERSITY OF
CAMBRIDGE

A NEW HISTORY

G.R. EVANS

I.B. TAURIS

LONDON · NEW YORK

Published in 2010 by I.B.Tauris & Co Ltd
6 Salem Road, London W2 4BU
175 Fifth Avenue, New York NY 10010
www.ibtauris.com

Distributed in the United States and Canada Exclusively by Palgrave Macmillan
175 Fifth Avenue, New York NY 10010

ISBN: 978 1 84885 115 3

A full CIP record for this book is available from the British Library
A full CIP record is available from the Library of Congress

Library of Congress Catalog Card Number: available

Printed and bound in Great Britain by CPI Antony Rowe, Chippenham

Ideals pass into great historic forces by embodying themselves in institutions
> – Hastings Rashdall, *The Universities of Europe in the Middle Ages*, ed. F.M. Powicke and A.B. Emden (Oxford, 1936), Vol. I, p.3

PREFACE

The punt glides past the smooth green lawns which it has taken college gardeners generations to manicure to perfection; are you an admiring tourist or thinking critically that it is all very well for some and no one from your family has ever gone to Cambridge? Do you feel an insider, recollecting the tensions of cycling late to lectures with a flock of others who overslept their alarms, or an outsider, for whom the sunshine falls on ancient walls which are beautiful but forbidding, keeping you out of the 'real' Cambridge ('College Closed' and every porter able to distinguish a genuine member of the University from a mere 'visitor' at a hundred yards). The aim of this book is to give everyone a chance to be an insider, and see what has been going on for centuries in Cambridge and what it is up to now.

Unless you are very old indeed you will not remember the seventh centenary of Cambridge in 1909, but as the story of the University through the twentieth century is told in the opening chapter of this book, there will certainly be flashes of recognition and recollection. Cambridge – like Oxford – lingers powerfully in the memories of those who have spent some of their most deeply experienced years there. Cambridge revisited has the capacity to make an atmospheric clutch at the heart as one turns a corner, or walks again through streets and alleyways where the strong emotions of youth have been felt. A consciousness of 'membership' remains real, particularly for one's College. But you do not have to have been a Cambridge student to feel the connections with your own life. Cambridge has had its fingers in many of the twentieth century's pies, in Britain and throughout the world.

So this book has a tale to tell whose realities have many levels. Endless anecdotes survive in which Cambridge confidently caricatures itself. There is much that is topical today in the controversies of its earlier centuries. *Is* Cambridge privileged and élitist? Is it exclusive? Is it full of wealth and self-indulgence (all those six-course college feasts with fine wines)? Should that sort of thing be 'allowed' any longer? Why have Oxford and Cambridge been allowed to be 'different'? Should the pursuit of knowledge for its own sake be paid for out of public money, or is it exactly what should be protected in the public interest, when commercial research funders are only pursuing their own advantage and private benefactors just want their names going down to posterity on a building?

Dip in, and get to know Cambridge through the ages.

ACKNOWLEDGEMENTS

I am grateful to Professor Ross Anderson, Dr. Douglas De Lacey, Professor A.W.F. Edwards, Dr. William Griffin for reading this book in draft and making innumerable helpful suggestions. The mistakes are my own. I would especially like to thank Alex Wright and Victoria Nemeth of I.B.Tauris, in particular for their help with the illustrations, and Anula Lydia who copy-edited with immense skill and patience.

ABBREVIATIONS

Cambridge University Transactions	*Cambridge University Transactions during the Puritan controversies of the sixteenth and seventeenth centuries,* ed. James Heywood and Thomas Wright (London, 1854), 2 vols.
Camhist	*A history of the University of Cambridge,* general editor C.N.L. Brooke (Cambridge, 1988–93), 5 vols.
Cooper, *Annals*	Charles Henry Cooper, *Annals of Cambridge* (Cambridge, 1842–1908), 5 vols.
CR	*Corpus Reformatorum* (Brunswick, 1834–1908).
Heywood, *Transactions*	Heywood, James and Thomas Wright, eds., *Cambridge University Transactions during the Puritan controversies of the sixteenth and seventeenth centuries* (London, 1854).
Rashdall	Hastings Rashdall, *The universities of Europe in the Middle Ages,* ed. F.M. Powicke and A.B. Emden (Oxford, 1936), 3 vols.
Williamson, 'The plague'	Raymond Williamson, 'The plague in Cambridge', *Medieval History,* 1 (1957), 53–4.
William Wordsworth	Wordsworth, William, *The prelude,* ed. Stephen Charles Gill (Cambridge, 1991).

CONTENTS

LIST OF ILLUSTRATIONS

Plate sections located between pages 112 and 113, and between pages 240 and 241

Every effort has been made to contact the owners of images, and the publishers will be pleased to rectify any omissions in future editions and printings of this book.

List of Illustrations

1 CAMBRIDGE IN LIVING MEMORY: THE LAST HUNDRED YEARS

Where is the University?

It is a standing joke that tourists ask to be told where the University is, because it seems to be scattered everywhere in the city. The central area of Cambridge, where the Old Schools and the Senate House now stand, was first occupied in the fourteenth century by the University's 'schools', buildings designed for lecturing and holding teaching-disputations. These were allocated by subjects to students working for their first degrees in Arts or to the sometimes much older graduate students studying for 'higher degrees' which were then taught courses and not at all like modern research degrees. On March 1459, the land known as Thornton's Ground was leased to the University for 99 years by Corpus Christi College. The rent was to be two shillings a year. The School of Civil Law seems to have stood there at the time. The University Church of Great St. Mary's was hard by and on the other side the old market place. An adjacent piece to the west was leased to the University in 1421 for two silver pennies. The record shows a good deal of acquiring and exchanging from this period as Henry VI sought land for the ambitious construction of King's College in the fifteenth century. It was going to take up a sizeable chunk of the centre of the small town and start a rivalry for land between the University and the colleges.

The tiny centre of Cambridge is full of corners and alleyways that evoke memories, but students of earlier centuries might not have had the same picture of the place at all. The shops and pubs of the twentieth century were for the most part not the ones medieval students went to. Few of the buildings of Cambridge which will be familiar to any student or resident or traveller now alive met medieval eyes, though the medieval churches are still there and portions of medieval walls still stand, though some of them are now built into quite different structures. But the very streets have moved, as bargains were struck and land was leased or bought to provide a footing for the ambitions of those who began to build the great colleges. Land

and property-hungry colleges and their would-be founders have been making deals for land throughout the history of the University. For example, Robert Willis, who made a painstaking study of the 'architectural history' of the University of Cambridge, published in three volumes in 1886, notes that

> [t]he site of Peterhouse is bounded on the east by Trumpington Street; on the south by an estate bequeathed to Caius College by the Lady Ann Scroope, called Lammas Leys; on the west by Coe Fen; on the north by the churchyard of St. Mary the Less, anciently St. Peter, and by some dwelling-houses. The southern portion of this extensive ground...originally belonged to the White Canons of S. Edmund of Sempringham, whose house...was directly opposite it on the east side of Trumpington Street...[and] purchased by Peterhouse in the reign of Elizabeth, at which time it was laid out as a garden.[1]

The controversy over Butt Close, involving Clare Hall and King's College illustrates the intensity of the jostling for space. Butt Close is now part of the College garden just across the river. At the beginning of the seventeenth century, what was then Clare Hall was planning some substantial rebuilding and reorganization of its limited space in the town centre. Its old quadrangle was right up against King's College Chapel. Clare Hall wanted to move it to its present position; it asked King's College for permission to use a piece of King's land as a passageway so that Clare's members could conveniently get across the river.[2] The King himself wrote to King's College, to ask it to grant a lease to Clare. A complex arrangement of renewable twenty-year leasing was thrashed out from 1651, with a yearly rent of £5 to be paid by Clare to King's. In return, the narrow piece of land alongside King's College Chapel which belonged to Clare was to be leased to King's, both for twenty years. The intention was that these leases would be renewed. In 1823, Clare exchanged the White Horse Inn, which it owned and which is now the site of the part of King's College next to St. Catherine's College, for Butt Close, so there were still battles being fought between the colleges over these and other scraps of city-centre land at the beginning of the nineteenth century.

Schemes were not always carried through even where there was a splendid vision, a positive Master Plan on offer from a well-known architect. The famous library of Trinity College was first conceived quite differently by Christopher Wren (1632–1723) from the way in which it was eventually built.[3] He thought of laying down a square foundation and then making the building circular with a dome or cupola – not unlike the appearance of the Radcliffe Camera in Oxford. Still, King's was not to be outdone. It commissioned one of Wren's pupils, Nicholas Hawksmoor, (c. 1661–1736), to produce designs in 1714, but they did not win approval and the College invited James Gibbs to try instead in 1723. His ideas for buildings, forming the sides of a rectangle but not joined at the corners, coupled with inadequate funds, left King's looking distinctly unfinished in the early nineteenth century.[4] St. Catherine's was to have had a library, too, which would have closed the quadrangle opening onto King's Parade.[5]

Other schemes were vastly more ambitious still. Nicholas Hawksmoor thought of rearranging the whole of the centre of Cambridge to provide it with wide streets and demolishing St. Edmund's Church to make way for them and to create a site for a brand new University Church. He planned a Senate House for this Roman forum, all to be classical and spacious and dignified. St. Mary's, left standing, would do for the townspeople.[6]

The Senate House was eventually built, but not for nearly a century after the idea was first floated in 1640. James Burrough, Master of Caius and designer of a number of college buildings, put forward the plan which was eventually adopted for a Senate House facing a mirror building on the opposite side of what is now Senate House Yard, though that was not built in the end because it was thought that it would spoil the view of King's College Chapel. The Senate House itself was built between 1719 and 1730, to the design of James Gibbs,[7] and standing at the head of King's Parade, it became one of Cambridge's most iconic buildings, after King's College Chapel.

> On my right the Senate House, sitting set-square and slide rule, topped by its mathematical pots, logically placed on the corners of the equilateral triangles that alone break the even balustrade of its roof. Behind me, the rows of stone griffins, checked eternally in mid-leap by the jealous walls of Caius. A flat water of a sky…I wanted to stick around Cambridge for a spell. I didn't want to go down that day,[8]

wrote Andrew Sinclair (b.1935) in his student novel *My Friend Judas* in 1959, suddenly realizing that the place held for him the record of an enormously important period of his life.

From place to context

> May was brilliant with sunshine. They sat on the Mill bridge with their tankards and their Players' Number Three and talked of doing some serious work the next day. They lay on the

Backs with their books face down on their chests and promised themselves that relaxation was the best way of preparing for an approaching examination. One day they took a punt and went with Barbara and Helga, up to Granchester for tea.[9]

That was in the 1950s, too, in a Cambridge showing the preoccupations of its times. We shall find throughout this last century a sharpening of its 'perennial character' with changing contemporary notes and emphases.

John Cowper Powys remembered how his father took him to the shops when he brought him up to Corpus Christi College in 1891 'and the particular type of purchases he made, wherewith to start me in my first experience of housekeeping'.[10] He was deeply affected by things he saw and experienced, if not by the course itself:

In reading for the Historical Tripos – in which I ultimately obtained a very moderate Second Class – I must confess I was only once really thrilled by any of the University teachers. This was by Professor Seeley, a far-sighted and indeed a rather Goethean person...but I shall never forget – as he gave one particular lecture upon the Athenian view of life – the reverberating unction with which...he uttered the word 'Ecclesia'.[11]

The beauty of Cambridge was what caught at his throat, and he was powerfully affected by a historical nostalgia. John Powys's rooms at Corpus Christi College were

part and parcel of one of the most romantic relics of medieval scholasticism that I have ever seen...I hardly realized what I was enjoying as I swam about in this bottomless pool of antiquity. The Corpus Old Court had the look...of some enchanted Ruin in a fairly-like forest of Old Romance. 'Over the ancient roofs of the interior of the Old Court there rose a church Tower that was older than William the Conqueror'.

When he dined in Hall, 'it was wonderful to be eating my meal in so medieval a manner'.[12]

He later wrote with a wry sense of the absurdities when as a young graduate he

dined on Saturday and Sunday at the high table, and drank port afterwards with the Dons in what they call the Combination Room. The Tutor sits in an armchair on one side of the fireplace and the Dean on the other, and by means of a sort of pulley they cause the Decanters to move of themselves backwards and forwards along the chimney piece, which is an odd sight.[13]

The privileged young who were his fellow students were not all charming companions. They could be thuggish. He writes of 'Third Year Rapscallions' and how

at the beginning of our Chapel services – these were compulsory then – they lounged in, swollen with insolence, pale with dissipation, brimming over, in fact, with what Homer calls 'hybrus', and with the barest relics of their undergraduate gowns hanging in weary effrontery from their drooping shoulders.[14]

He became a bit of a rapscallion himself. John Powys left Corpus after he had taken his degree to keep an assignation with a 'pretty person' in London at the Haymarket Theatre. He was expecting a letter from his father 'containing money wherewith to pay my College bills'. Impatient to be off, he gave instructions to the College Porter to open this letter and distribute the money and to send his luggage after him. It may be guessed what happened.[15]

His mixed experience was not going to put off other members of the family from going to Cambridge. This was an era when a College might be 'in the family'. The cost of being a Cambridge student at the beginning of the twentieth century can be quantified at about £160. A Professor would be paid about £500.[16] So to send more than one son (and John Powys came from a large family) would cut a considerable hole in a family's resources.

He wrote to his brother Llewelyn in 1903 from Cambridge. 'We were talking about you last night; Pearce of course thinks you would be unpatriotic to the family College if you did not come to Corpus. He says that Pembroke is overcrowded and Clare very rowdy'. In such subtle ways, the genius of place and the sense of membership and of ownership were interconnected in the experience of Cambridge.

* * *

Running their own show

The 'little world' of Cambridge in 1908

The Great Court is the centre of the universe and King's Parade is Paradise and the backs the Elysian Fields – Lytton Strachey[17]

More readers will be former students or non-students than will have been Cambridge dons. But what the dons did spun the plot. So they will carry one of the main story-lines and we shall begin with Francis Cornford's little classic, published close to the year of Cambridge's last centenary, the *Microcosmographia Academica*, where Cambridge is indeed a world of its own, hot with internal politics. That habit of seeing itself as the centre of the universe did not have the negative connotations for Lytton Strachey (1880–1932) that it has now.

Francis Cornford (1874–1943) was a successful student of Classics at Trinity, coming near the top of the list in both parts of Cambridge's two-part degree examination, the Tripos (so-called because it is taken over three years) in 1895 and 1897. Within two years of graduating, he had become a Fellow of Trinity College. It was in the light of the observation of these few years of donnish life that in 1908, he wrote his elegant 20-page satire full of the paradoxes of Cambridge society.

It was an important feature of the academic democracy which had always run Cambridge that the youngest members had the same vote as the older ones and could join in with the fun and controversy as soon as they felt inclined. Indeed, in earlier centuries, the Regent Masters had all been young, recent graduates, doing their required stint of teaching in completion of the requirements for their degrees:

> The Principle of Sound Learning is that the noise of vulgar fame should never trouble the cloistered calm of academic existence. Hence, learning is called sound when no one has ever heard of it; and 'sound scholar' is a term of praise applied to one another by learned men who have no reputation outside the University, and a rather queer one inside it. If you should write a book (you had better not), be sure that it is unreadable; otherwise you will be called 'brilliant' and forfeit all respect.[18]

This is a description of a world in which scholarship was taken very seriously but it was important not to admit it, when the very nature and purpose of scholarship was under radical review. Cornford was having a not very sly dig at the habit of respecting obscure and what would now be called 'irrelevant' learning. This intellectual self-consciousness has persisted. A little affectation was still expected in Frederic Raphael's post-war Cambridge. ('Adam was eating cornflakes and reading *Brideshead Revisited* when Donald returned from Mass.'[19]) But the flavour has changed and with it the character of the wit-sharpening rivalry with Oxford. One might be deprecating about one's learning, but not when it came to outpointing Oxford.

Two of Frederic Raphael's '1950s' characters 'had agreed to meet and go to the Moral Sciences Club together. An Oxford theologian was due to be roasted on the slow spit of Cambridge linguistic ingenuity'.[20]

It would be a pity to lose sight for a moment of the fact that Cambridge's life is and always has been an intellectual life. Its quirks and excesses bear the stamp of that life of the mind. H.A.L. Fisher, taking stock of the state of the universities of Britain in 1927, suggested that the greatness of a university 'does not lie in the number of its students or in the lavishness of its buildings or the smartness of its administration or in the renown of the men and women who give it support from outside'.[21] He favoured taking the quality of its inner intellectual life as a university's defining characteristic. Yet a university's institutional stability, its reliability as a continuing 'place' in which knowledge is protected, extended and transmitted are important. They give that life a lodging and they protect those who seek to live it. Cambridge has had stability and durability and a nice place to be.

When he said this, Fisher was looking back in 1927 over a century of development in higher education which had ended for ever the English monopoly of Oxford and Cambridge. The new institutions of the nineteenth century were the civic universities and the colleges which were providing a technical and scientific education for factory workers and secretarial workers. The old universities were increasingly thrown on the defensive and had to argue fiercely for the legitimacy of their own teaching and research in a modern world, which said it now most urgently needed skilled workers, future employees and entrepreneurs. It is not far from the adoption of a pragmatic view of the purposes of higher education to the accusation that anything else is élitist and ought to be discouraged, and that there are better uses for the money.

Francis Cornford espied scientists who thought like that inside Cambridge's own 'bastion of privilege'. His satirical term for them was 'Adullamites', after the resentful dwellers in the caves of Adullam described in the Old Testament (1 Samuel 22.1):

> The Adullamites are dangerous, because they know what they want; and that is, all the money there is going. They inhabit a series of caves near Downing Street. They say to one another, 'If you will scratch my back, I will scratch yours; and if you won't, I will scratch your face'. It will be seen that these cave-dwellers are not refined, like classical men. That is why they succeed in getting all the money there is going.[22]

Cornford had teasing words for businessmen, too:

> Or, perhaps, you may prefer to qualify as a Good Business Man.
> He is one whose mind has not been warped and narrowed by
> merely intellectual interests, and who, at the same time, has not
> those odious pushing qualities which are unhappily required
> for making a figure in business anywhere else. He has had his
> finger on the pulse of the Great World – a distant and rather
> terrifying region, which it is very necessary to keep in touch
> with, though it must not be allowed on any account to touch
> you. Difficult as it seems, this relation is successfully maintained
> by sending young men to the Bar with Fellowships of £200 a
> year and no duties. Life at the Bar, in these conditions, is very
> pleasant; and only good business men are likely to return. All
> business men are good; and it is understood that they let who
> will be clever, provided he be not clever at their expense.[23]

Democracy and internal politics

Cornford wrote his book to brief the young 'academic politician'. It
is still a handy guide for the reader who has been a student – or
wonders what it is like to be a student – at Cambridge, but cannot
easily find out what really goes on behind the scenes in the common
rooms and committee rooms. Cornford himself had only just found
out as he made the transition from student to don. The great thing was
the fact that the place was run by the academics and the graduates,
and everyone had an equal vote. In Cambridge, as in Oxford, the
ancient democratic constitution survived. It was a direct democracy;
it did not work by electing representatives. A hundred years ago,
even graduates who had long ago left the University and now lived in
remote parts of the country had a right to vote in its affairs as members
of the Senate. The vote is now restricted to the academic and senior
administrator community who actually work in the University and it
is conducted by post. At the beginning of the century, voting meant
turning up in person in the Senate House where the 'Senate' divided
to either side of the Senate House to be counted.

That did not prevent those who actually lived and worked in the
University from doing most of the 'fixing'. Cornford describes the
practice of strolling up and down King's Parade each afternoon so as
to engage in a little horse-trading:

> This most important branch of political activity is, of course,
> closely connected with Jobs. These fall into two classes, My
> Jobs and Your Jobs. My Jobs are public-spirited proposals,

which happen (much to my regret) to involve the advancement of a personal friend, or (still more to my regret) of myself. Your Jobs are insidious intrigues for the advancement of yourself and your friends, speciously disguised as public-spirited proposals. The term Job is more commonly applied to the second class. When you and I have, each of us, a job on hand, we shall proceed to go on the Square. Squaring can be carried on at lunch; but it is better that we should meet casually. The proper course to pursue is to walk, between 2 and 4 p.m., up and down the King's Parade, and more particularly that part of it which lies between the Colleges of Pembroke and Caius. When we have succeeded in meeting accidentally, it is etiquette to talk about indifferent matters for ten minutes and then part. After walking five paces in the opposite direction you should call me back, and begin with the words, 'Oh, by the way, if you should happen ...' The nature of Your Job must then be vaguely indicated, without mentioning names; and it should be treated by both parties as a matter of very small importance. You should hint that I am a very influential person, and that the whole thing is a secret between us. Then we shall part as before, and I shall call you back and introduce the subject of My Job, in the same formula. By observing this procedure we shall emphasise the fact that there is no connection whatever between my supporting your Job and your supporting mine. This absence of connection is the essential feature of Squaring.[24]

These early twentieth-century 'Job'-seekers were shortly to oust the wider community and take over the democratic conduct of most of Cambridge's affairs themselves.

Cambridge was shortly going to have to address itself to the problem that the democratic governance of the resident Masters was being weighed down by the continuation of the convention that all Masters of Arts had a vote although a high proportion of them lived away from Cambridge, might not have visited it for years and no longer had any active engagement with the University's affairs. This question lurks in the wings of the *Microcosmographia* too. Cornford's young academic politician is to learn to be an 'operator' within the local community, but he is well aware that the whole body of graduates thinks itself entitled to be consulted:

By vesting the sovereign authority in the Non-placets (technically known as the 'Senate' on account of the

9

high average of their age), our forefathers secured that the final decision should rest with a body which, being scattered in country parsonages, has no corporate feeling whatever, and, being necessarily ignorant of the decisive considerations in almost all the business submitted to it, cannot have the sense of any responsibility, except it be the highest, when the Church is in danger. In the smaller bodies, called 'Boards', we have succeeded only in minimising the dangerous feeling, by the means of never allowing anyone to act without first consulting at least twenty other people who are accustomed to regard him with well-founded suspicion. Other democracies have reached this pitch of excellence; but the academic democracy is superior in having no organised parties. We thus avoid all the responsibilities of party leadership (there are leaders, but no one follows them), and the degradations of party compromise. It is clear, moreover, that twenty independent persons, each of whom has a different reason for not doing a certain thing, and no one of whom will compromise with any other, constitute a most effective check upon the rashness of individuals.[25]

Cornford warns the could-be activist in this direct democracy that he is entering a competitive world:

If you persist to the threshold of old age – your fiftieth year, let us say – you will be a powerful person yourself, with an accretion of peculiarities which other people will have to study in order to square you. The toes you will have trodden on by this time will be as the sands on the sea-shore; and from far below you will mount the roar of a ruthless multitude of young men in a hurry. You may perhaps grow to be aware what they are in a hurry to do. They are in a hurry to get you out of the way.[26]

He warns the ambitious young man that it will be no good merely having a sound case to put. 'You think (do you not?) that you have only to state a reasonable case, and people must listen to reason and act upon at once?' If you are to succeed, young man, he advises, 'you must address your arguments to prejudice and the political motive'. He outlines for him the categories of movers and shakers in the University and those who will always try to stop any moving and shaking, the Conservative Liberals and the Liberal Conservatives and the Non-placets. These are the people who will call for a vote against it when any proposal is put that might change anything:

> The *Non-placet*... is a man of principle. A principle is a rule of inaction, which states a valid general reason for not doing in any particular case what, to unprincipled instinct, would appear to be right. The Non-placet believes that it is always well to be on the Safe Side, which can be easily located as the northern side of the interior of the Senate House (II).

The young academic politician himself may be in danger of becoming one of the Young Men in a Hurry, who are 'afflicted' with consciences. He will do little harm, suggests Cornford, because the underlying rules of the game are resilient:

> He may be known by his propensity to organise societies for the purpose of making silk purses out of sows' ears. This tendency is not so dangerous as it might seem; for it may be observed that the sows, after taking their washing with a grunt or two, trundle back unharmed to the wallow; and the purse-market is quoted as firm.

With uncomfortable accuracy, Cornford identifies the patterns of argument and the principles on which the democratic business of Cambridge was conducted – and to a large extent still is. Cornford's Cambridge was a University of pusillanimous academics of an essentially cautious and conservative bent. In the later twentieth-century University and the modern one, many of the same patterns of behaviour can be observed, although the default position is probably more liberal. Thanks to the Hansard-like record of the debates or Discussions in the *Cambridge University Reporter* from the 1870s, we can observe in this chapter the moves Cornford describes as going on in real life, especially in the arguments put in the regular Discussions of the Senate. Discussions were published in reported speech until the 1950s, at which point they began to appear verbatim, with the added sharpness that ensued. Occasionally a few words have been omitted from the record, in case the University was sued for defamation, but not often.

Without some understanding of this 'Cambridge' way of running its affairs, the stories in this book will make little sense. It is the engine of the Cambridge way of life, giving every academic that sense of having a personal share in the enterprise in which he or she works which is probably more responsible than anything else for

11

the way Oxford and Cambridge keep their places at the top of the league-tables.

*   *   *

Shall we let women in?

Widening access for girls

This was still an almost wholly male society, though clever girls and indignant older women were beginning to knock at its doors. The first residential college for women had been established in 1869 at Hitchin, though it soon moved to Girton, just outside the city of Cambridge, a vigorous uphill cycle ride. Tea parties might be allowed at which the young women met undergraduates, but only with chaperones.

Henry Sidgwick (1838–1900), an energetic backer of the admission of women, was something of a maverick. He had been a student at Trinity College and a member of the Cambridge Apostles, still flourishing from its nineteenth-century beginnings,[27] but his academic career was threatened by his discovery that he could not in conscience any longer call himself a practising member of the Church of England. The abolition of the Test Acts came in time for him to return to Trinity as a Fellow and he became Knightbridge Professor of Moral Philosophy in 1883. Sidgwick helped to arrange the Lectures for women which began in 1870. He was concerned that girls for whom a daily commute was not practical might not be able to benefit. So he rented a house in which five of them could live during the course. The five may have been emboldened by the tea parties which Mrs. Henry Fawcett used to hold at 18, Brookside, where educational projects seem to have been often discussed.[28] It was necessary to provide a chaperone and Anne Jemima Clough (1820–92) agreed to act as a 'warden'. She had experience running a school. Four years later, this venture developed into Newnham Hall and eventually in 1880, it became Newnham College.

Anne Clough was the sister of Arthur Clough (himself consciously an Oxford man). She was strongly interested in education and especially in the education of women. She was a friend of Emily Davies (1830–1921), founder of Girton (and the chief instigator of the practice of allowing girls to take secondary school examinations); she was a friend too of Frances Buss (1827–94), a leader of the movement to win a serious secondary education for girls. She set up the training college for teachers in Cambridge which became Hughes Hall. These women were suffragettes as well as educationalists.

The first concession came in 1881 when women were allowed, on a Senate vote, to take the examinations for honours degrees, though the results were published in a separate list from those of the men from 1882. The women were not allowed to proceed to degrees even if they would have been qualified to do so by their examination passes if they had been men.

Young women growing up in Cambridge families, with father and brothers involved in the University, could achieve a fair level of shrewdness and intellectual sophistication without formal study. Gwen Raverat's *Period Piece* contains sharp insights. She realized that she was a new kind of 'Cambridge child':

> From 1878 onwards, the revised Statutes, which allowed Fellows of colleges to marry without losing their fellowships, came into force in one college after another. Until then…the children of the university remained few in number. But after 1878 families began to appear…I belong to the first hatching of Fellows' children, and was born into a society which was still small and exclusive. The town, of course, did not count at all.[29]

She was not easily impressed. 'We must have seen a good many Great Men in our youth, but most of them seemed to me very uninteresting':[30]

> The regular round of formal dinner-parties was very important in Cambridge…Everybody of dinner-party status was invited strictly in turn. The guests were seated according to the Protocol, the Heads of Houses ranking by the dates of the foundations of their colleges, except the Vice-Chancellor would come first of all. After the Masters came the Regius Professors in the order of their subjects, Divinity first; and then the other Professors according to the dates of the foundations of their chairs, and so on down all the steps of the hierarchy. It was better not to invite too many important people at the same time, or the complications became insoluble to hosts of only ordinary culture. How could they tell if Hebrew or Greek took precedence, of two professorships founded in the same year?…and their wives were…easily offended.[31]

She enjoyed the full ruthlessness of Cambridge gossip:

> Nearly every day we could watch the Master of St. Catherine's riding by on his small black pony. He was a little old man, and made an antique and lonely figure in his clerical clothes. Even we children knew that he had been cut by all the university,

ever since the rumours about the election to the Mastership in 1861, thirty years before; and it is said that he had been passed over when his turn came to be Vice-Chancellor. It was believed that, at the college election, he and another Fellow each promised to vote for the other...but when it came to the point, Dr. Robinson voted for himself, thus becoming Master by two votes,[32]

and

[t]he Jebbs spent only the winters in Glasgow, and kept on their Cambridge house for the summers, while they waited hopefully for old Dr. Kennedy to retire, so that Uncle Dick might succeed him in the Cambridge professorship. This was the Dr. Kennedy who wrote the Latin Grammar...and he had not the slightest intention of retiring.[33]

Yet, despite the living evidence that at least some women were not to be intellectually trifled with, until at least the end of the nineteenth century, there was a gap between what it was believed could reasonably be expected of women, intellectually speaking, and what was routinely required of men. Girls had to overcome the comparative limitations of the available secondary education or the still greater limitation of no education at all. Campaigners for the education of women were fierce on the subject of content and standards ('Is it really necessary that women should be shut out from the knowledge of physical sciences?') and insisted that girls be allowed to prove themselves in equal competition in the same examinations and not given special easy courses and certificates. 'We do not want certificates of proficiency given to half-educated women.' Emily Davies, the author of these ideas, expressed them in 'The influence of university degrees on the education of women', in *The Victoria Magazine*, July 1863, reprinted as *Thoughts on some questions relating to women 1860–1908*, ed. E.E. Constance Jones (1910).[34] Here was a category of potential new student in a world of 'widening access' whose appearance posed dilemmas which were not primarily to do with class, or the bridgeability of class divisions by getting an education.

The Syndicate of 1897

The most dare-devil action they ever take is to move for the appointment of a Syndicate 'to consider what means, if any, can be discovered to prevent the Public Washing of Linen, and to report, if they can see straight, to the Non-placets'. The result is the formation of an invertebrate body, which sits for two years, with growing discomfort, on the clothes-basket containing the linen. When the Syndicate is so stupefied that it has quite forgotten what it is sitting on, it issues three minority reports, of enormous bulk, on some different subject. The reports are referred by the Council to the Non-placets, and by the Non-placets to the wastepaper basket. This is called 'reforming the University from within'.[35]

The Syndicate most likely to have been in Francis Cornford's thoughts is probably the one responsible for the failed attempt to allow women not only to take the examinations but also to 'proceed to degrees' as did the male students who passed the same examinations.

It was all happening in the year Cornford graduated. The *Report of the Degrees for Women Syndicate* – on which Frederick Maitland served[36] – was published on 1 March 1897 in the *Reporter*.[37] Even Maitland said its members were the dullest in Cambridge.[38] The Syndicate was as thorough as Cornford the satirist could have wished. It enquired in detail into the 'present position of women', which seemed to depend a good deal on the goodwill of individual lecturers and Professors, who might or might not admit them to lectures or laboratories as they chose. Lecturers had been asked to comment on 'any inconveniences or advantages to which the informal admission of women might have led' (p.596) and 'whether the admission of women had been found to necessitate any change in the subject-matter or mode of treatment' (p.596). Comments from History suggested that the presence of women was 'enough to prevent anything like boisterous amusement' and thus improved behaviour. It was also noted that 'many of the best students in each year have been women' and that they set an example by assiduously taking notes 'and pains taken with essays' (p.598). Biology lecturers noted that certain topics caused embarrassment, but they tried to soldier on. Woman after woman who had been a student at Girton or Newnham described the disadvantages she had suffered professionally from the fact that women did not have actual degrees, for example, 'among parents of pupils in a manufacturing or country town' (p.604). 'Miss Eleanor Purdie had 'experienced difficult in getting her Tripos certificates accepted as substitutes' when she had sought 'admission to the examination for PhD' at the University of Freiburg (p.608).

Several of these points were taken up in the ensuing discussion. Mr. Cartmell feared that 'the admission of women to membership would also destroy the homogenousness of our student-body and this is a serious matter. You will find that some of the lecturers complain of difficulties cause by the heterogenousness of classes to which female students are admitted'.[39] Professor Marshall noted – in terms striking close to modern observations about the examination performance of girls – the loss suffered by letting in women, which distracts undergraduates, and 'it tends to make the teacher adapt his teaching to minds which, though splendid for examination purposes, in some respects better than most men's, are receptive rather than constructive'.[40] The adjourned discussion from the Saturday had continued on the following Monday, when it was admitted (p.763), as the Syndicate itself had stressed, that women 'educated at Cambridge are at some disadvantage in competing for professional appointments'.

It was strongly felt in some quarters that it was one thing to allow women to attend lectures, quite another to let them matriculate and become members of the University, take examinations – the same examinations as men – and actually graduate so as eventually to become M.A.s. There were speeches, some from distant non-resident M.A.s, though still members of the Senate, to the effect that God had so arranged creation that women were intended for home life and that they lacked the intellectual capacity to compete with men. The Bishop of Durham's remarks making this point were read for him by the Master of Selwyn. 'A perfect woman is distinct in type from a perfect man,' wrote the Bishop. 'I gratefully recognize the intellectual gain which women have found in the Cambridge course, but I believe it has been secured at a high cost, and not without loss'.[41] He favoured a separate university just for women, the 'Queen's University' proposal, and he thought it definitely ought to cater for passwomen and not concentrate on honours graduates. There was strong awareness that Oxford was going through its own process of deciding what to do about women. Maitland himself spoke feelingly of the waiting room at Bletchley station where (until the Oxford–Cambridge line was closed by Beeching in the 1960s), one might take a train one way for Oxford and the other for Cambridge. Maitland said, 'I do not believe there is any man in Cambridge who has a deeper respect for Oxford opinion than I have'.

Perhaps, it was proposed as a compromise, women might be allowed the titles of degrees though not the substance.[43] But that took the debate back to the territory of real equality, onto which the majority were not yet prepared to venture. Dr. Allbutt thought that

> So long as women were coming up here mainly for general
> culture and for the disinterested love of knowledge they were

very welcome, for the thing was easy to manage ... The change of principle now is that women are to come up here as we come up here, for professional purposes; a very different thing indeed. We hear that the denseness of the British father will be a sufficient barrier against any great flood of women hither.

But as soon as it is clear that the girls will be able to earn their livings with degrees, he thinks these fathers will stand in the way no longer.[44] Some speakers thus glimpsed the social importance and some of the implications of equality of opportunity between the sexes. Master of Trinity Hall: 'Let us look to the higher education of the women of England as a whole ... Behind what we see there may be a greater movement than we think of'.[45]

The Syndicate's recommendations were not unanimous, and they were extremely lengthy, creating a natural concern in their readers that wool might be pulled over their eyes. The students were no more certain than their elders that this was the way to go. An unofficial student poll had shown a big majority against letting the women in on the same basis as the men.[46] The day of the vote – and voting was done in person not on paper – had the students out in the streets in huge numbers carrying placards ('no Gowns for Girtonites'). A dummy of a woman in cap and gown was displayed and a figure on a bicycle was suspended from a window.[47] The recommendations were defeated on a huge vote of the Senate (1,707 to 661).

The issue subsided, as is the way with Cambridge controversies (and as Cornford would have predicted), to come to the surface again during the First World War. The period leading up to the war had seen the beginnings of an exchange of intellectual equals among the young. The poet Rupert Brooke (1887–1915) went to King's College on a scholarship and became a member of the Cambridge Apostles, the still-flourishing nineteenth-century student debating society.[48] Frances Cornford (wife of Francis), a granddaughter of Charles Darwin, depicts him in her own poems as 'Youth', 'Young Apollo, golden-haired'.[49] Exchanges of letters on the writing of poetry between Rupert and Frances survive.[50] The same circle of friends engaged in literary reflection included E.M. Forster, to whom Rupert Brooke was writing in 16 October 1909,[51] and Hugh Dalton, to whom he wrote on 21 September 1909, 'Isn't originality only unconscious plagiarism?'[52] Brooke wrote for the *Cambridge Magazine* and the *Cambridge Review*,[53] and he read a paper to the Cambridge University Fabian Society in 1910 in which he rejected the claim that 'When Everyman has reached a decent amount of leisure and education, the whole community will foster and patronize and delight in the Arts'. That seems unlikely, he wryly notes, on the evidence of the behaviour of those who already have these advantages.[54] He had friendships among the mixed-sex Bloomsbury Group too, which had its roots in Cambridge and among the Apostles.

Of that group, the home-educated Virginia Woolf (1882–1941) was realistic enough to see that not all women who wanted to learn wanted to go to Cambridge (or Oxford). She notes in *The early journals*, for 16 January 1905, how she

> '[w]rote all the morning on my "lecture" for the Working women, & chose Prose as my subject, which does not commit me to anything. It amuses me to write, as I can say what I like, without fear of criticism, and the subject interests me – but Heaven knows if it will interest them'... 17 January, 'Finished my Prose lecture, which must still be written out, as I cant trust myself to speak from memory – & with writing before me I cant go far wrong'.[55]

She was still preparing material for the working women a few days later. On 21 January, she notes that she '[w]rote a lecture – an odd kind of lecture! – upon our journey in Italy, for the working women'. This was a journey which had been undertaken by the family in 1904, after their father's death, in company with Violet Dickinson. 'This is the kind of thing they really enjoy I know – whether there were fleas in the beds at Venice. I shall have to invent some – &c&c. It is easy, though not instructive to write', and it filled '12 pages'.[56] If her judgement of what would please these women was accurate, this was the stuff of the popular lecture geared to her notion of feminine tastes.

But there were other women teaching more ambitiously. Exciting dramas were possible in their lectures. One of the first women classics lecturers, Jane Harrison (1850–1928), Fellow of Newnham, used to arrange for bull-roarers to be swung at the back of the room, first darkened for the purpose, to give the students an idea of the Aeschylus reference to invisible bull-voices roaring.[57]

Leonard Woolf, later to be Virginia Woolf's husband, described the 'adolescent mind' with which he entered Trinity College, Cambridge, in the winter of 1899:

> I had intense intellectual curiosity; I enjoyed intensely a large number of very different things: the smooth working of my own brain on difficult material...omnivorous reading and in particular the excitement of reading what seemed to one the works of great writers.[58]

One of his great friends was to be Saxon Sydney-Turner. Woolf describes him as 'immensely intelligent and subtle' but says he 'had little creativeness':

> When, years later, crossword puzzles were invented and became the rage, he was a champion solver. And it was characteristic of him that he was a champion solver, never an inventor, of crossword puzzles and other mental gymnastics, including the art of writing. He had an immense knowledge of literature, but he read books rather in the spirit in which a man collects stamps.[59]

In G.E. Moore he found quite another sort of mind. He got to know him in 1902:

> Moore was not witty; I do not think that I ever heard him say a witty thing; there was no scintillation in his conversation or in his thought. But he had an extraordinary profundity and clarity of thought, and he pursued truth with the tenacity of a bulldog and the integrity of a saint. And he had two other very rare characteristics. He had a genius for seeing what was important and what was unimportant and irrelevant, in thought and in life and in persons, and in the most complicated argument or situation he pursued the relevant and ignored the irrelevant with amazing tenacity. He was able to do so because of the second characteristic, the passion for truth ... which burned in him.[60]

This critical observation of the qualities of mind of others was a feature of the community of scholarship in which Woolf consciously lived during his time as an undergraduate. He too joined 'The Apostles'. Their spirit, he says, gradually 'absorbed and dominated' him:

> I can only describe it as the spirit of the pursuit of truth with absolute devotion and unreserve by a group of intimate friends, who were perfectly frank with each other, and indulged in any amount of humorous sarcasm and playful banter, and yet each respects the other, and when he discourses, tries to learn from him and see what he sees. Absolute candour was the only duty that the tradition of the society enforced ... It was rather a point of the apostolic mind to understand how much suggestion and instruction might be derived from what is in form a jest – even in dealing with the gravest matters.[61]

However, able women such as Frances Cornford and Virginia Woolf seem to have blended in without difficulty and without the advantages of these academic experiences.

The argument that carried the day for doing nothing hasty about the women in Cambridge, when the matter was raised again during the war, was that it was not a decision which could be taken while so many men were at the Front. The matter was held over and debated again in 1921.[62] The Discussion took place on 14 October. One proposal was still that there should be a separate women's University, perhaps twinned with Oxford, with arrangements to be negotiated about use of laboratories and libraries; or possibly a federal scheme in which 'the conditions of education and discipline of male undergraduates shall be primarily determined by men, and that conditions of education and discipline for women undergraduates shall be primarily determined by women graduates'. Mr. Damier Whetham pointed out that the argument that men and women needed different kinds of education fell at the hurdle of 'learning and research'.[63] There could be no distinction 'between the training required by men and women respectively for advanced learning and research'. Cornford could have predicted that in the intervening decades when the question was in abeyance, the University would quietly have moved on in its thinking; the proposal carried was the one formerly defeated, that women should be given the titles of degrees but not the actual degrees. A mob of excited undergraduates rushed off to Newnham to break the news and broke down the gates as well.[64]

Inside the two colleges for women there was now a world where serious ambitions could be followed. Virginia Woolf sketches a character in a fictional 'women's college': 'Angela...realized – how could she express it? – that after the dark churning of myriad ages here was light at the end of the tunnel; life; the world. Beneath her it lay – all good; all lovable. Such was her discovery'.[65]

* * *

Meeting national needs: putting Cambridge in the spotlight

A Professor of Reinforced Concrete would have seemed to Dean Gaisford a very weird and indigestible dish in any academic menu. Now we absorb him without a murmur; he is about as conventional as a Professor of Glass Technology or Metallurgy or of the Chemistry of Brewing...There is no end to the requirements of modern technology.

H.A.L. Fisher, in his centenary oration at University College on 30 June 1927, reflected (p.18) on the growing 'range of subjects comprised within the compass of University education'. Factories needed industrial chemists and men who could supervise production lines. Should areas of knowledge which had formerly seemed inappropriate for study at degree level become degree-subjects so as to equip graduates to make themselves useful in this world? One Education Act had been passed in 1902 and another was to come in 1918, both inspired in part by the aim of creating a 'national system of education'. Under the heading 'Higher Education', s. 2 of the 1902 Act spoke of 'the supply of education other than elementary' and 'the general co-ordination of all forms of education'. Oxford and Cambridge began to come under the spotlight. Could they be left out and allowed to carry on their independent way of life?

The House of Lords considers the situation

In July 1907, the House of Lords[66] debated the future of Oxford and Cambridge, taking care to rely on precedent in claiming that the state had a right to interfere. 'The principle of the right of the nation to inquire by means of a Commissions may be regarded as having been established by the [Royal] Commissions of 1855 and 1877'.[67] These Royal Commissions had led to Acts of Parliament radically affecting Oxford and Cambridge,[68] so this was a significant reminder.

The concern now being expressed was that social change was again radically altering what society needed from the two ancient universities. Charles Gore, Bishop of Birmingham, had plenty of ideas. He wanted to facilitate widening access. 'It has always been the honour and pride of the old universities that they trained the governing classes of the country' but that class has recently 'received a very wide extension'.[69] Time must no longer be wasted in coaxing the dim offspring of the well-to-do through their courses. Tutors are spending too much time digesting knowledge for unbookish young men to get them through examinations.[70] Among the Workers Educational Association and Ruskin College students, by contrast, 'are signs and evidences that among the working classes there is a very considerable body of people who desire to be students and are capable of becoming students'.[71]

He also had views on the importance of making it possible for students assisted in this way to go on to professional training. Funds which could provide 'post-graduate endowments should be used to subsidize either those who are to be teachers or those who are engaged in researches such as are worthy of advanced students'. There should be no more prize Fellowships.[72]

A new Commission, he thought, should look again at the 'balance between the wealth of the colleges and the poverty of the university',[73] the theme of the Commission which had led to the 1877 Act. The balance was not right yet. 'Let the Universities have a little time to set their house in order?' Not too long, this speaker thought.[74]

The Bishop of Bristol intervened to say that in his view all this mostly applied to Oxford. Cambridge did not need an inquiry. 'Cambridge has adapted itself to modern conditions'. 'The University of Cambridge is independent of its colleges'. 'I cannot conceive that it is possible to adapt ourselves more to modern conditions than we have done.'[75] There were, however, one or two embarrassing matters which other peers did not allow him to forget. In response to the argument that it was not satisfactory for Cambridge to continue to be run by a Senate many of whose members were not resident and had no real understanding of the current affairs of the University, the Bishop of Bristol said he believed it was seldom that any voting was done by non-residents (the larger Senate of all the graduates). He (though not seeing a need to make a declaration of interest at this point) had himself drafted 'every regulation with regard to the external work of the University' for 21 years and never a vote had there been.[76]

Lord Ellenborough disagreed that all was in hand. He spoke against compulsory Greek and the dominance of non-residents in a single argument. All those graduates who are now schoolmasters teaching the classics throughout England have a vested interest in maintaining a requirement that university entrants study Greek. It should be no business of theirs:

> If I am rightly informed compulsory Greek is required at Cambridge – against the wishes of the more enlightened graduates who reside there – by the Boeotians of the University, by men who earn their living by teaching Greek in other places, and who, as protectionists of their own trade, are desirous of seeing the study of that fetish enforced on all undergraduates so as to prevent their wares becoming unsaleable.

Warming to his theme, he claimed that this 'universal study of dead languages' was doing damage to education 'far beyond the limits of Oxford and Cambridge'.[77] The problem was that it was discouraging the introduction of useful subjects. He cited a letter in *The Times* of 3 March 1905 whose author had written:

> We were approached at Cambridge by a gentleman who wished to found a Professorship of Naval Architecture and endow it liberally, with the fullest equipment for experimental

work. Such a Chair would have been an element of strength in the University. It would have been a great national possession. But he withdrew it,

on learning that the students would all have to do compulsory Greek.[78] 'Think,' continues Lord Ellenborough,

how our food supply, our commerce, and all that makes us an independent nation, is contingent upon our finding the right solution of many problems of naval architecture! Is it a study to be discouraged at Cambridge for the sake of those non-resident Boeotians, who are too groovy to allow people to learn anything new? Are they afraid of the students of naval architecture describing dead languages as the 'barnacles' of education?[79]

'It would seem more reasonable to make a knowledge of shorthand compulsory instead of a knowledge of Greek'... 'How can we expect to be able to hold our own in the twentieth century in industry, war or commerce, if we educate all the sons of the well-to-do on theories based on the dreams of ancient tragedians.' He asks how Britain can hold its own against the Japanese 'if we deliberately waste the time of our youth'.[80]

Speaker after speaker rose to say that he only knew about Oxford, or only about Cambridge, but the shared character of the big underlying issues was undeniable. They all turned on the fact that there was now a new world of higher education and Oxford and Cambridge could not hope to carry on unchallenged as though it did not exist. The Bishop of Hereford,

Probably the most important work the Commission would have to do would deal with the relations to be established between the old Universities and the new City Universities which have sprung up, and, through them, with the new democracy.

He credited Joseph Chamberlain with having broken the pattern of creating 'federal' universities, as in the north of England so that the great cities, Manchester, Liverpool, Leeds, Sheffield and Bristol, have all become keen to have their own universities.

Mr. Chamberlain has done very great service to the nation by creating in English cities this new interest in higher education...but these new city Universities are still in their infancy. We have not yet had time to know with any certainty

23

what sort of relationship they ought to bear towards the older Universities. I have a vision of all these city Universities being connected by an open high road of communication, and of students passing from one to the other, following some famous teacher, or to study some special subject...I hold that this relationship is by far the most important part of what would be the work of the new Commission.[81]

Speakers noted that Oxford and Cambridge were declaring themselves short of money. It was already easy to see that this was dangerously likely to expose them to state interference, since if Government money was to be provided there would need to be assurances about the way it was spent. It was urged that Oxford and Cambridge should be given time to raise money privately; there could be no hurry for another Royal Commission. The Earl of Crewe stressed that it was essential to be clear 'exactly what the Universities cannot do of their own motion and for what purpose legislation would be required on the recommendation of a Commission, and...whether there does exist at the Universities anything like a deadweight of obstruction against reforms which is of a character which could only be removed by statute'.[82] The gauntlet of state interference had been thrown down and Cambridge, with Oxford, was on notice that it needed to reform itself to meet modern needs.

* * *

The First World War and the spectre of state inspection again

War and a deserted Cambridge

War intervened. Rupert Brooke was one of the First World War poets old enough to have completed his Cambridge degree before the war began. In Berlin, he wrote with painful nostalgia of the world he had known there:

> Just now the lilac is in bloom,
> All before my little room;
> ...And clever modern men have seen
> A Faun a-peeping through the green,
> And felt the Classics were not dead,
> To glimpse a Naiad's reedy head,
> Or hear the Goat-foot piping low:...
> I only know that you may lie
> Day long and watch the Cambridge sky,
> And, flower-lulled in sleepy grass,

Hear the cool lapse of hours pass,
Until the centuries blend and blur...
Dan Chaucer hears his river still
Chatter beneath a phantom mill.
Tennyson notes, with studious eye,
How Cambridge waters hurry by...
And oft between the boughs is seen
The sly shade of a Rural Dean...
And Cambridgeshire, of all England,
The shire for Men who Understand;

...

Say, do the elm-clumps greatly stand
Still guardians of that holy land?
The chestnuts shade, in reverend dream,
The yet unacademic stream?...
Stands the Church clock at ten to three?
And is there honey still for tea?[83]

Whatever the current state of the broken clock on the church tower at Grantchester, Cambridge itself was deserted as he wrote. A dramatic effect of the First World War was the drop in the number of undergraduates in residence, from more than 3,500 in 1910 to 575 in the summer of 1916. Fellows of Colleges joined up too, further depleting the population of the University. Arthur Quiller-Couch (1863–1944), who was to become one of the outstanding exemplifications of the approach to literary criticism that F.R. Leavis was to seek to discredit, described the scene:

We came up in October to find the streets desolate indeed. The good soldiers who had swarmed in upon town and college in August – a Commander of Cavalry occupied my rooms; too busy, I hope, to curse the dull contents of my shelves – had all departed for France...A Head of House stopped me [in front of a group in a photograph] and ticked off the cheerful resolute faces of those fallen, by the Marne or the Aisne, since he had entertained them a few weeks ago. In one row of a dozen West Yorks, he could find two survivors only.

These had come and gone like a summer cloud: and October in Cambridge might have passed for the Long Vacation turned chilly...no men passed on their way to lecture 'with the wind in their gowns'...a suspended Cambridge...The Belgian refugees from their Universities had found harbour with us...A notice-board at the entrance of Burrell's Walk advertised the 1st Eastern

General Hospital, and on any afternoon you might see the Red Cross motor ambulances bringing in the wounded. A whole block of King's had been handed over to house the nurses.[84]

For young officers, the Front could seem at first – until the war revealed itself as the horror it really was – like a club where all their former Cambridge friends were also members.[85] Meanwhile in Cambridge itself, the empty classrooms and lecture rooms were used to provide training courses for soldiers, with military encampments on the open spaces around the city and officers invited to become honorary members of Senior Common Rooms and to dine at High Tables in the colleges. There was even billeting on the colleges.

Some of Cambridge's routine 'public service' provision was adversely affected. The 'Annual Report of the Foreign Service Students' Committee' (*Reporter*, 18 December 1917, p.280), tells a depressing tale of shortage of students. No student interpreters or probationers for the civil services of Egypt or the Sudan had been in residence during the year, nor any Indian Civil Service probationers. The War Office had sent ten cadets to study Persian in 1916. They completed their course and were sent to Aldershot for 'further military training', but it is thought that only five ever went to Persia. A second class of 20 were sent in February 1917, 'superior candidates from a military point of view perhaps, but in linguistic ability they were markedly inferior, though they worked with diligence and attention'. The proposed Turkish class for wounded officers was eventually 'secured' by the London School of Oriental Studies and lost to Cambridge.

The University still took its public service duties very seriously, in the Victorian spirit of providing graduates to go out and govern the Empire, and candidates for the Civil Service examinations which had been instituted in the middle of the century, and now soldiers to fight for their country. Those who expressed conscientious objections, such as Bertrand Russell (1872–1970), who held a College lectureship at Trinity, could find themselves ostracized. He was deprived of his post by the College after he had been found guilty under the Defence of the Realm Act of 'statements likely to prejudice the recruiting and discipline of His Majesty's Forces'.

The spectre of state inspection again

The nervousness caused by the pre-war pressures to adapt to the modern world was reawakened by the return of peace-time. There was general review of the Needs of the University.[86] A Discussion of the Senate was held in 1918 about the lengths of terms, since it was realized that elsewhere they lasted ten weeks and in Cambridge only eight.[87] Mr. Glover said it was important to balance the needs of teaching with those of research. 'There were some in the University who were engaged in research and the extension of knowledge, and he asked what research could be done in term-time'. ... the vacation ... was not wasted time, but real working time.'[88] In a similar spirit of concern to keep up with the times and meet new needs, a Report was published on the Pass degree, which had long been a convenience for the less-talented students from wealthy families who could not aspire to an honours degree.[89] There was discussion of plans to form collaborative arrangements with universities overseas,[90] involving affiliations with Madras and Patna. Research students' work was approved.[91]

Yet no one would know from reading the *University Reporter* of 1918–19 that a new Royal Commission was about to begin work. Cambridge had other things on its mind as it emerged from the war, as J.B. Priestley describes from his own recollections of arriving there after he was demobilized in 1919:

> Men who had lately commanded brigades and battalions were wearing the short tattered gown and broken mortar-boards of the undergraduate. Freshmen who had just left school, nice pink lads, rubbed elbows with men who had just left Ypres and Scapa Flow. All the colleges were crammed full. (I spent a year in a disused porters' lodge.) The older dons hurried from one crowded lecture room to another with a bewildered air. The pubs did a roaring trade. Nearly all meetings were riotous. College rooms were loud with argument until dawn.[92]

The Asquith Commission

The Royal Commission which sat from 1919 to 1922 made recommendations which were eventually to be embodied in the Oxford and Cambridge Act of 1923, under which statute both universities still stand. This was the last stage of what had turned out to be a series of Royal Commissions on Oxford and Cambridge which had begun in the 1850s and continued in the 1870s. There has been none since, at least not specially for Oxford and Cambridge; the Commissioners of 1988 were to address themselves to all the then existing universities alike in their task of making provisions to remove old-fashioned tenure for academics.[93]

There was an 'Oxford Committee' and a 'Cambridge Committee'.[94] On the Cambridge Committee sat individuals with family connections to prominent Cambridge figures such as the Sidgwicks and the Cloughs; G.M. Trevelyan and M.R. James (author of manuscript descriptions and ghost stories); and Sir Hugh Anderson, Master of Caius from 1912 to 1928, who had begun his academic research career in the study of the physiology of the nervous system.

The Commission this time had the preoccupations already hinted at as urgent before the war. One was with the need to open up Oxford and Cambridge to a wider social spectrum of students. Another was the call to recalibrate their relations with the outside world.

Aspects of the modern problem of 'widening access' were already visible. 'Does the difficulty arise from the expenses at the University or from the fact that they have not reached the University standard?' it was asked. If the preparation given in ordinary secondary schools was not adequate to get students into Cambridge, was it fair to other schoolchildren to make it so? Is it the 'principal task' of secondary schools to prepare students for university?[95] There was some discussion of the question whether a single curriculum could be appropriate both for boys who were going on to University and to those who 'are going straight into business'.[96] This question has not gone away.

Was it in the interests of the average schoolchild or the nation to encourage more to aspire to be graduates? In Germany, it was suggested:

> the number of students who have been given a University education has led to rather serious results, because it has practically over-stocked the professions for which University education was a good training, the result being they found the utmost difficulty in obtaining a living.[97]

The record of discussion of these concerns suggests that they had been prompted in particular by the Labour Party's submissions to the Asquith Commission.[98]

There was also vigorous debate about the implications of making public money available to assist poor students. Should free places be awarded on 'an intellectual standard' or on need? Cambridge was already greatly broadening the range of subjects taught. Among the memoranda is one from 'The literary departments of the University of Cambridge', which included 'Architectural Studies, Classics, Divinity, Economics and Politics, Foreign Service Studies, History and Archaeology, Indian Civil Service Studies, Law, Medieval and Modern Languages, Military Studies, Moral Science, Music, Psychological Studies, Oriental Studies, Training of Teachers'. The point is made that a good proportion of these are 'instituted for the service of the state', 'professional', or have application 'to the practical life'.[99] 'There is an almost continuous demand for new teaching and new appliances...Cambridge...is falling behind...other universities which are situated in industrial and wealthy centres of population.'[100] Some subjects are booming, for example 'economics and politics'. They need more money. Some are being neglected. "Nothing has been done for the Historical School by the University since the Statutes of 1882'. They need more money too.[102] A memorandum was also submitted by 'the scientific departments' including some, such as Astrophysics, Agriculture and Forestry, which 'receive grants from the Government'. Research is 'subsidised by the Government through the 'Scientific and Industrial Research Committee'.[103]

Should a newly interventionist State 'do anything tending to make the people who come up to the universities, adopt one course rather than another'?[104] Was there a future for Pass candidates in a new Cambridge where entrance was to be on merit? Should there be new practical courses? (What of the new Agricultural Pass Course arrangements at Cambridge?[105]) Should the state take an interest in the 'coordination of teaching' and determine the role of colleges, and who should decide the curriculum, the University or the colleges, as well as questions of student fees and staff salaries?

The Labour Party and trade union submissions were hot on some of these questions. Mr. Young made a statement 'from the point of view of the Labour Party'. He explained that the Labour Party was very interested in Education. 'Our Trades Unions and our Cooperative Societies, as you understand, have been giving their support to University Extension lectures, to the Workers' Education Association' with unions contributing to the cost of sending students to Ruskin College, 'that being the only College open to them at the time'. He himself had been one of them and had thus had a taste of Oxford though not of Cambridge.[107] He argues that there is a need in higher education 'for a wider knowledge of industrial, economic and sociological subjects'.[108]

Cambridge was seen as needing to catch up with Oxford in its provision for adult education.[109] A group of Cambridge dons had suggested that the Workers' Educational Association (WEA) and the trade unions might choose me 'between the ages of 25 and 30 who were coming to the front in the labour world', who could come to Cambridge for a year's study so as to 'come into contact with the best economic teaching at Cambridge, and would mix with the bourgeoisie, shall we say'.[110]

Getting started

The Commission began its work in November 1919, by designing questionnaires to be sent to the Universities. Its remit was to

> inquire into the financial resources of the universities and of the colleges and Halls therein, into the administration and application of those resources, into the Government of the universities, and into the relations of the colleges and Halls to the universities and to each other, and to make recommendations.

Replies by Cambridge University to Preliminary List of Questions in Paper no.1 covered numbers and stipends, tenure (asserting that there were no Professors or other University Officers drawing their pay without taking an active and regular part in Teaching, Research, or Administrative Work), lists of expenses, student statistics and costs.[111]

The wider world was actively interested in what was going to happen, both educationally and politically. The Commission was also sent submissions by the Headmasters' Conference, the Association of Headmistresses and other bodies interested in schools, such as the National Union of Teachers, the Labour Party, the WEA, as well as a variety of comments from parts of the University itself such as those just touched on.

The Commission 'sat' at Cambridge in August 1920 and took evidence from many individuals and officers. One of the key questions was whether if public funding was to be given to the civic universities it should also be provided for Oxford and Cambridge, and if so, on what terms. There were, however, eventually recommendations for Cambridge, including the notion that it should adjust its governing body so that it was no longer the whole Senate, but a House of Residents only, and also that it should organize its teaching provision so as to ensure that University teaching officers had time for research. (The concomitant matters of the need for more teachers, better pay, and whether posts were to be linked to Fellowships were differently resolved in Oxford and Cambridge.)

Custard and prunes: rich and poor colleges

The concern hung in the air that colleges of the Cambridge sort were an expensive luxury in the running of a University, and that there was a consequential exclusion of prospective students whose families could not afford the cost. It had to be emphasized to the Commissioners that

> the University cannot say to the Colleges: You shall keep 25 per cent of your place free; nor can it carry out the changes

required in regard to the scholarships or exhibitions, nor has it power to carry out reforms in regard to the cost of living and education. In all these cases the consent of the Colleges would be necessary.[112]

A memorandum was submitted by Sir Napier Shaw on 'The relation of the University to the Colleges at Cambridge'.[113] The problem of the comparative poverty of University and the wealth of some of the Colleges, makes fund-raising very difficult. 'So long as the colleges speak with seventeen voices, more or less discordant, and are each on the look out to guard its peculiar interest, no common appeal is possible.'[114] In the evidence sessions too, this matter was prominent:

> Q. 'The control of the Colleges by the University is to be obtained first by financial provisions, Colleges are only to be allowed a certain amount of control; and in the second case by the University having control over the Fellows who may be elected by the College.'[115] A. 'I think some people would be annoyed.'[116]

It was pointed out to the Commissioners that the whole question was complicated by the fact that the Colleges felt themselves to be in competition. 'They say: If we lower our standard of living today, the people who come to us from Rugby, Charterhouse and so on will go to Trinity.'[117] 'I do not think any Women's College would agree if you told them they could make their charges cheaper by allowing the richer members to entertain freely.'[118]

Virginia Woolf provides a graphic description of the difference a diner used to the finer fare of a rich college would notice at a poor college's table (the fictional 'Fernham' for Newnham):

> Dinner was being served in the great dining-hall...Here was the soup. It was a plain gravy soup. There was nothing to stir the fancy in that. One could have seen through the transparent liquid any pattern that there might have been on the plate itself. But there was no pattern. The plate was plain. Next came beef with its attendant greens and potatoes – a homely trinity, suggesting the rumps of cattle in a muddy market, and sprouts curled and yellowed at the edge, and bargaining and cheapening and women with string bags on Monday morning. There was no reason to complain of human nature's daily food, seeing that the supply was sufficient and coal-miners doubtless were sitting down to less. Prunes and

custard followed...Biscuits and cheese came next, and here the water-jug was liberally passed round, for it is the nature of biscuits to be dry, and these were biscuits to the core. That was all. The meal was over. Everybody scraped their chairs back; the swing-doors swung violently to and fro; soon the hall was emptied of every sign of food and made ready no doubt for breakfast next morning. Down corridors and up staircases the youth of England went banging and singing.[119]

Her point was that this was not an atmosphere to prompt good conversation. But:

Happily my friend, who taught science, had a cupboard where there was a squat bottle and little glasses – (but there should have been sole and partridge to begin with) – so that we were able to draw up to the fire and repair some of the damages of the day's living.[120]

She found the comparison with better-endowed colleges pressing irresistibly on her mind:

Briefly, then, I told Miss Seton about the masons who had been all those years on the roof of the chapel, and about the kings and queens and nobles bearing sacks of gold and silver on their shoulders, which they shovelled into the earth; and then how the great financial magnates of our own time came and laid cheques and bonds, I suppose, where the others had laid ingots and rough lumps of gold. All that lies beneath the colleges down there, I said; but this college, where we are now sitting, what lies beneath its gallant red brick and the wild unkempt grasses of the garden? What force is behind that plain china off which we dined, and (here it popped out of my mouth before I could stop it) the beef, the custard and the prunes?[121]

Following on a discussion of the reasons why colleges are so expensive to run, with concomitant expense to students, W.G. Balfour asked for comment on the submission that

the proportion of children of working-class parents who now reach a University is incomparably smaller than the proportion of children of a wealthier class, and...the proportion of girls of all classes who reach a University is incomparably smaller than the proportion of boys.[122]

In France or Germany, it was argued, you 'find a democratic university...representing a fair cross-section of the population'.

The 'power of the purse'

The discussion about the need for state funding to make up the deficits led naturally to the consideration of the possibility that Cambridge (and Oxford) should submit to allowing 'external' members of their Councils and thus to a measure of outside control. Balfour asked outright whether 'the control of the University by the nation is to be secured by external representation?' This might be quite a large proportion, though not necessarily a majority 'on the Council which is probably the most important administrative body you would have 25 per cent from outside'.[123]

The neat solution to the problem of returning the running of the University to those who actually worked there and removing it from the diffuse and enormous Senate was the suggestion that non-resident members of the Senate might do very well as such 'external' representatives. That was not smiled upon. 'Whenever public money has been granted to educational institutions, it has always been assumed with that grant will go a certain measure of public control.'[124] Some thought state control through finance ought to go much further:

> Dr. Anderson: 'Is it your deliberate and considered opinion that the best way to really dictate the policy is to dictate it through finance?' A. '...The most effective power... is the power of the purse, and one does need to reserve that finally in the hands of the representatives of the public... I do not imagine Parliament would sanction a proposal for large grants of money to Oxford and Cambridge without some measure of public control.'[125]

Questions of control by funding and how far it should go became prominent in the work of the Commission. Benefactors might save the state money, but there was a long history of benefactions at Cambridge being tied up decades, even centuries, beyond the time when their terms had ceased to be appropriate. That had been addressed in part in the 1877 Act, which made it possible to get the terms of trusts changed. No longer was a large sum to be restricted to the left-handed sons of red-headed clergymen in the West Riding of Yorkshire even if that had once seemed a good idea to some benefactor. There was again discussion of the need to be able to use benefactions for changing needs and the fear that benefactors would begin to tie up the terms very tightly if that was allowed.[126]

A summary survives of the proceedings of the Commission Meeting on 16 July 1920 discussing Balfour's memorandum on Government.[127] It was felt that reform of the composition of Oxford's Convocation and the Cambridge Senate were needed, for 'No really important changes have been made in the Government of the University since 1882'.[128] The key thing was to be the creation of a House of Residents along the lines proposed in the Reform Committees of 1910–11. The residual veto of the Senate must be restricted, it was argued, and 'some kind of "ornamental" functions would have to be devised for it' or no one would pay to proceed to M.A. 'with consequent financial loss to the University'.[129] There was concern about 'control' even of this reduced body of Regents, and it was even suggested that the veto might be vested in the Chancellor. But that was thought likely to lead to 'inconvenience and difficulty'.[130]

The question what to do about the women was not ignored. 'It is evident, I think, that the position of women is very unsatisfactory at Cambridge…Cambridge has lagged very much behind.'[131] But the topic was not central to the concerns of the Commission in the way the widening of access socially proved to be, and the best the Commissioners were able to achieve was to stipulate that women could hold teaching offices but not become members of a college.[132]

The Oxford and Cambridge Act 1923

The method of proceeding adopted by the Oxford and Cambridge Act 1923 was the same as that of the Acts which followed the two nineteenth-century Commissions. It involved the creation of a short-term body of Commissioners. Cambridge as well as Oxford was to draft new statutes by the end of 1924 and lay them before the Commissioners, with opportunity for objection and reconsideration provided for. The duty to have regard 'to the interests of education, religion, learning and research' laid down in the 1877 Act was continued. A Universities Committee of the Privy Council was to provide an avenue of recourse if someone wished to object to a proposed statute after it had been forwarded to the Privy Council for approval. From this exercise emerged the Cambridge Statutes of 1926 which have been amended and adjusted but never comprehensively overhauled since.[133] These laid down the constitutional structure which persists to this day in essentials, despite some high profile and dramatic 'governance' reforms at the end of the century and since.

* * *

Between the Wars

The Cambridge Spies

'What seduced Philby and the rest of the Five, however, was not the reality of the Stalinist régime but the myth-image of the world's first worker-peasant state courageously constructing a new society for the benefit of all.'[134] The 'Cambridge Spies', who included Anthony Blunt, Guy Burgess, John Cairncross, Donald Maclean and Kim Philby, had all become Communists while they were studying in Cambridge in the 1930s. This was a reasonable position for an intellectual with a conscience about class disadvantage to adopt, and they were certainly naïve about the realities of Soviet Russian life and were in for a shock when they went to Russia to live.

These were serious-minded young men. Burgess and Blunt belonged to the Cambridge Apostles, and other Apostles may have been involved with the ring and its satellites, as members or recruiters. There was active cross-recruiting of likely individuals who would be able to 'penetrate the corridors of power' and thus make useful spies. Donald Maclean graduated from Trinity Hall in 1934 with a first class degree in modern languages. He had been recruited as an undergraduate and accordingly set about entering the civil service through the Foreign Office.[135] Guy Burgess was at Trinity, where he was half way through a piece of post-graduate research. He was attracted by the idea of fighting fascism in the service of the Communist International.

> Burgess was one of the most flamboyant figures in Cambridge: a brilliant, gregarious conversationalist equally at home in the teetotal intellectual discussions of the Apostles, the socially exclusive and heavy-drinking Pitt Club, and the irreverent satirical revues of the Footlights.[136]

The 'five' used their wits and contacts to penetrate Whitehall.

These were young men of a type who might easily have been recruited to the diplomatic service or British Intelligence and asked to spy for Britain, but during the War some at least were apparently spying for the Russians, with aspirations to defect to the Soviet Union. Maclean and Burgess did so, and then Philby eventually did the same in 1963. Cairncross confessed to spying in 1951.

Some of the Cambridge Spies of the mid-twentieth century were recruited predominantly through Bletchley Park, which ran 'signals' in the Second World War and was looking for clever men who could crack codes. The Fellows of King's were numerous there during the war, including Alan Turing. Younger recruits were actively sought in Cambridge. Harry Hinsley, a grammar school boy who later became Master of St. John's College and Vice-Chancellor, was recruited at the beginning of the War in 1939 in the middle of his Tripos studies in History,[137] enlisted by two Cambridge dons for the Government

Code and Cypher School at Bletchley Park. So inter-war Cambridge unknowingly made a contribution in another area which was to be of huge importance during and after the Second World War.

Splitting the atom

> Yes, the atomic bomb gave everyone a shock
> – Gerard Bullett, 17 November 1945[138]

At the end of the First World War, Ernest Rutherford became Cavendish Professor in Cambridge and offered a job to his former pupil James Chadwick. Gonville and Caius College gave Chadwick a home and a Studentship, and in 1921 a Fellowship. The Departments of Scientific and Industrial Research made him an Assistant Director of Research in the Cavendish Laboratory. That freed him from any teaching obligations, which suited Rutherford because Rutherford wanted Chadwick to work with him on the nucleus of the atom.

The pair 'found' the neutron in 1932 and Chadwick won a Nobel Prize for Physics in 1935 on the strength of the importance of the discovery. What was needed now was a particle accelerator which could split the nucleus of the atom. Cambridge owned Cockcroft and Walton's accelerator, but it was not going to be adequate for the work that was now needed. In the end, Rutherford lost Chadwick to a job at the University of Liverpool because he would not seek funding for a more powerful model.

Meanwhile, the designers of a better accelerator were working their way up. John Cockcroft became the Jacksonian Professor of Natural Philosophy at Cambridge from 1939 to 1946. His collaborator Ernest Walton was a recent recruit, a young graduate from Trinity College, Dublin, who had come to join the Cambridge team in 1927. The Royal Society provided funding for Cockcroft to build his new accelerator, the cyclotron. Rutherford was still hostile to this method of taking the research forward and it is possible to see in this episode an example of the difficulties Cambridge scientists have sometimes faced when the patronage of senior scientists is withdrawn over a disagreement. The contrast with the world of William Whewell is striking, for as we shall see, he and his colleagues were as free as those in the art and humanities to let their research take them where it would. When Rutherford died, Cockcroft did not get the Cavendish Chair.

At the beginning of the Second World War, the Liverpool cyclotron was in operation. It was already apparent that it might be possible to generate a nuclear chain reaction and the Secretary of the Department of Scientific and Industrial Research, E.V. Appleton, asked whether that meant it would be possible to create a 'nuclear' bomb. It was unclear at first how much uranium would be needed to make an explosion but it seemed by the end of 1940 that it might be only some kilograms. A committee of British physicists known as the Maud Committee worked on a feasibility study and claimed that a bomb could be produced, with cooperation from the USA and Canada, by 1943. The Quebec Agreement on Anglo-American collaboration was signed in August 1943 on behalf of the British and USA Governments. The result was the bombing of Nagasaki.

Chadwick returned to Cambridge in 1948 and became Master of Caius. He was even chosen as Vice-Chancellor, but lacked the energy to take it on. In the late 1950s he went to live his life in North Wales, in retreat from the fierceness of College politics, and he died in 1974.

The discovery of the double helix lays the foundations of the human genome project

On 21 May 1987, there appeared an issue of the *New Scientist* to celebrate the 40th anniversary of the Molecular Biology Laboratory, which formed part of Addenbrooke's Hospital rather than the University. It was as well that this alternative avenue could be constructed for the work which laid the foundation for the human genome project, for in its early stages it ran up against the brick walls of the divisions between the recognized scientific disciplines as the University was organized to study them in the 1930s. 'Molecular biology' seemed to some to be neither biology nor physics, nor was it, properly speaking, chemistry either. Max Perutz from Vienna and J.D. Bernal were working on crystallography against the grain of the Cavendish Laboratory's then priorities. But Lawrence Bragg was Cavendish Professor of Physics from 1938 to 1953 and he himself had won a Nobel Prize in 1915 at the age of 25 for work undertaken with his father on x-rays and the structure of crystals. He could see the potential of this work, especially when he was shown x-ray photographs of haemoglobin; he made room for it but he was unable to persuade the University to create a permanent post for these scientists.

Two Cambridge geneticists, James Watson and Francis Crick, took the project forward. They determined the structure of the molecules of DNA (deoxyribonucleic acid) in an article published in 1953. Rosalind Franklin (1920–58), who had compiled the preliminary data by means of x-rays, and who contributed essential pieces of the puzzle, did not live to share the Nobel Prize they were eventually awarded, though Maurice Wilkins, who had also been involved in the compilation, did. The 'geometry' of the molecules, it turned out, was that of a double helix, two spirals entwined about one another. It proved possible to 'map' this structure so as to determine the order of the nucleotides in the double helix, and thus describe the basic structure of the protein. Ironically, this was the year when Bragg left Cambridge and his successor took the view that the team had no proper place in the Cavendish Laboratory. So the work moved out of the University to the Molecular Biology Laboratory which was now to be funded by the Medical Research Council.

When Watson made his speech of thanks for the Nobel Prize, he spoke for both Crick and Wilkins, hinting at the struggle with conventional attitudes about the boundaries of scientific disciplines at Cambridge which had gone with the hard work of the science:

> Our discovery was done using the methods of physics and chemistry to understand biology. I am a biologist while my friends Maurice and Francis are physicists. I am very much the junior one and my contribution to this work could have only happened with the help of Maurice and Francis. At that time some biologists were not very sympathetic with us because we wanted to solve a biological truth by physical means. But fortunately some physicists thought that through using the techniques of physics and chemistry a real contribution to biology could be made. The wisdom of these men in encouraging us was tremendously important in our success. Professor Bragg, our director at the Cavendish and Professor Niels Bohr often expressed their belief that physics would be a help in biology. The fact that these great men believed in this approach made it much easier for us to go forward. The last thing I would like to say is that good science as a way of life is sometimes difficult. It often is hard to have confidence that you really know where the future lies. We must thus believe strongly in our ideas, often to point where they may seem tiresome and bothersome and even arrogant to our colleagues. I knew many people, at least when I was young, who thought I was quite unbearable. Some also thought Maurice was very strange, and others, including myself, thought that Francis was at times difficult.[139]

No Depression in Cambridge?

Keynesian economics was framed to make sense of the Great Depression in retrospect. Some at least in Cambridge avoided confronting the realities of the slump which began at the end of the 1920s with a certain insouciance and an approach to the whole problem which has a distinctly topical ring in 2009:

> May we suggest...that members of the University should not rush heedlessly into extravagant economies, and so add

to our existing difficulties? Ostentatious expenditure may at the moment be more than usually undesirable, but wise expenditure is a patriotic duty that we ought to show good cause for refusing.[140]

John Maynard Keynes was born in Cambridge and became an undergraduate at King's College in 1902. The family continuities with the world of recent Cambridge were strong. His mother had been one of the early students at Newnham and became a considerable social activist. His father was a lecturer in economics and a friend of Henry Sidgwick. The younger Keynes developed the same line of interest as his father and became an economist too, with a strong mathematical bent and a leading interest in probability. He was to be both academic and practitioner, advisor to Governments and theorist.

In the 1920s, he began to make a name with challenging pieces in the national press. Observing the Great Depression first hand as it unfolded, he formulated a theory to explain such cycles. A new generation of academics in Cambridge began to form a Keynesian 'school' in sympathy with his ideas. In his *General Theory of Employment, Interest and Money*, published in 1936, he advocated active Government intervention to stimulate an economy in crisis. He was still actively involved with Cambridge life. He opened the Arts Theatre in 1936, and, confident that there would not be a war, he spent some of 1938 in Cambridge helping to get the theatre on its feet.

Throughout the inter-war period, this still tended to be an inward-looking Cambridge, settling back upon its haunches after the disturbances of war and Royal Commission. Shortly before the outbreak of the next War there was discussion of discipline in the University, in particular the 'moral code' underlying Statute B, which dealt with such matters as the maintenance of order and student behaviour.[141] Dr. Needham, speaking in the Discussion, was exercised about the idea that members of the University should be 'subject to any laws, or any standard of behaviour or moral code, other than that to which their position as citizens naturally committed them'. If 'some protection was wanted beyond that afforded by the public laws of the land', 'the question … was whether … a line of demarcation could be drawn between conduct which was permissible and conduct which was not'.[142] The painful area concerned the way misbehaving academics should be dealt with. The discussants came back several times to the problem of distinguishing between 'misconduct' and 'grave misconduct', and Mr. Passant was eventually bold enough to admit that they were all really thinking of sexual misconduct, but 'what was normally described as sexual misconduct was by no means necessarily a disqualifications for the performance of University functions'.[143] We are still a long way here from the modern world of concerns about sexual harassment and the conduct thought appropriate between academic staff and their students.

In these inter-war years in Cambridge, there was, however, some awareness of the importance of other matters which were to become much more significant nationally in the 1990s, what might loosely be called 'quality assurance'. This was the era when research degrees were becoming more important, though it was still not necessary, or even usual, for an academic appointee to have a Ph.D. In 1936, the Board of Research Studies produced two reports discussing the need for consistency in setting standards for research and higher degrees. In borderline cases for Ph.D., M.Sc. or M.Litt., the Board had such cases brought to its notice if resubmission was allowed. 'No such procedure exists in connection with applications for higher doctorates'. The Board thought 'that it would be of assistance in the maintenance of the standard throughout the University for these degrees, if they could ascertain on occasion the reasons' for refusal by Degree Committees.[144]

Medical education was being overhauled with an eye to improving its quality too. The Report of a Syndicate on the Medical Courses and Examinations of the University was discussed in November 1932. Dr. Clark-Kennedy was insistent about maintaining standards. 'The education of any medical man must be founded on the rock which only a course of strict scientific study could supply.'[145]

There were stirrings of change in the expectations about provision to meet international needs. Astonishingly, even in July 1939, there was little hint of the imminence of war to be read in the *Reporter* in this connection. With stolid indifference to any such possibility, the Board of the Indian Civil Service seems to have assumed things would run comfortably on regardless. It offered tuition in English Essays and European History, 1763–1914, which was apparently deemed to be essential background for entrants to the Indian Civil Service in 1939, with additional lectures for those going in for the Open Competition. These would include 'Present Day Science (with papers and visits) for the science questions in the "Present Day" paper, and Elementary Economics'.[146] Lecturers identified for these courses were few – Gaskoin, Parsons and Thatcher. The course provided to meet the needs of the Colonial Administrative Service including Criminal Law, Islam, Geography, Social Anthropology, Primitive Law, Economics and Culture Contact, Agriculture, Forestry, Public Health, Education, Native Administration and various 'colonial' languages.[147]

* * *

The Second World War and a new world for Cambridge

On 3 September 1939, Britain declared war on Germany. Cambridge gave the impression that it was elaborately unruffled. On 24 October, the Historical Society heard a paper on 'The taxation of Wool: a study in English constitutional and economic development in the later Middle Ages' from Professor Eileen Power of the London School of Economics.[148]

But the fact of war had its inevitable impact on the daily lives of students and academics. In a *Life* of John Stott, Timothy Dudley-Smith describes how

> he would sing in the choir of Trinity College chapel on Sunday evenings before dining in hall and going on to the CICCU [Cambridge Intercollegiate Christian Union] evangelistic sermon in Holy Trinity, Charles Simeon's old church. On Sunday mornings he would sometimes make his way down Hills Road to St. Paul's, and once or twice to sit under Graham Hobson at the 'Round' Church of the Holy Sepulchre. Academic life was interspersed with fire-drills, ARP training, and occasional night-long vigils on the roof of Trinity chapel... He took half-an-hour's brisk walk for exercise (he played almost no games) and allowed himself by way of recreation to skim briefly through *The Times*.[149]

No one could fail to notice uniforms in the street. Students might sit in one of the five pubs on Green Street or go to the pictures when they needed relief from tensions and gloomy headlines. Even the richer colleges had to bow to the exigencies of rationing. And rationing did not end with the War. When Donald Keene arrived at Corpus in 1948, he explains, 'a gyp (college servant) led me to my rooms, remarking, "Coldest rooms in Cambridge, sir"... That afternoon the gyp brought me my daily ration of milk, about one inch of milk in a jug'.[150]

It was not until internal difficulties became apparent that Cambridge really seems to have given its mind to the implications of the war for the conduct of its own affairs. Research students had had to go off and fight and could not get on with their work. In February 1940, the Board of Research Studies was 'of the opinion that in the period of the present emergency some research Students... will suffer hardship if the existing requirements of residence and research in Cambridge are not modified'.[151] In March, problems with the conduct of the oral examinations in Modern Languages were identified, again because of absence on war service. That was considered to be a barely adequate excuse. 'They might have pleaded that administrative difficulties were greater in war-time than in peace. He did not himself see why, unless Tutors were duller or slacker in war-time than in peace; but that was not alleged', Mr. Harrison is reported as saying in a Discussion on the matter.[152]

There was of necessity a virtual freeze on recruitment of academics during the war. But it was by no means obvious – or agreed – what was the best thing to do. The Vice-Chancellor read a speech for Lord Keynes in a Discussion on what to do about vacant Professorships, 'It would be most regrettable if this University emerges from the period of the War with its higher appointments heavily depleted'. Professor Robertson recognized the problem of 'absence on war service of potential candidates'. Dr. Clapham had asked Oxford what it was doing about this problem. He himself did not think 'that the possibility that some people might be in remote places was a reason for the holding-up the filling of all the vacancies'.[153] It does not seem as though there was much realism about seeking academics from the wider world. 'Unpleasant comments about Americans formed part of the normal conversation of some of the people I met,' notes Donald Keene.

> It was annoying at first to be asked such questions as, 'Is it true that American universities grant doctorates in dishwashing?' I gradually realized that there was generally nothing more than a pleasantry involved in these queries.[154]

In the face of the shortage of administrators, there was debate about the case for keeping on the elderly Registrary Ernest Harrison, who had come into office in 1925 and therefore before the 1926 statutes came into force. He was liked for his approachability. Mr. S.W. Grose said that he himself had

> always felt conscious that they had there someone to whom they could turn for help whatever their difficulties. He was always available and ready to give ... his time, and particularly to help [colleagues] in those difficulties which were not of their own making. [He was replaced in 1943 by Walter Grave.][155]

A land fit for heroes but nowhere to live

After the War a different problem was to emerge, that of lack of accommodation, and even where accommodation was on offer, it might have a utilitarian flavour new to at least some parts of Cambridge tradition:

> Cambridge 1947 was indeed a land fit for heroes to live in. The University was at the forefront of pure and applied science: it had invented and installed in every college room gas fires which drew the heat out of a room and dispersed it out of the chimney without actually raising the temperature of the fenland air outside. The culinary art had been refined to its purest in college halls...: one could... either take or not take both the reconstituted dehydrated potatoes and the mushy peas. Then, at no extra charge, one could carry one's tray to share a table with E.M. Forster.[156]

Concerns about accommodation led to the calling of a Discussion on a Matter of Concern to the University (forerunner of the modern 'Topic of Concern'), by a few individuals who wanted accommodation to be bought 'which could be rented unfurnished or furnished to teaching or administrative members of the University' who cannot find anywhere to live.[157] The chief instigator of this idea, Eric Ceadel, represented the young married appointee and he pointed to the contrast between 'the plentiful housing and easy hospitality of pre-war days and the miserable overcrowding of the present'.[158]

New subjects of study

After the War, new subjects began to present themselves as appropriate additions to the Tripos, but those who were offering them were feeling their way. One of the first students of Japanese at Cambridge from 1947 was William Skillend. He had a place to read Classics but was bored with Latin and Greek and in his time in the army he had been taught Japanese by Eric Ceadel, the very person who was now to be supervisor in Japanese at Christ's College. The text specified for study for the preliminary examination was a history of the First World War, from which the passage set for the examination 'described a German attempt to bomb Sandringham'.[159] Skillend had not been in the army until the end of the war, in 1944. 'I suspect that I probably knew as much Japanese as my teacher/examiner by the end of my first year.'

> We students had no conception of the massive scholarship there was on [the works they studied] in Japan. We were the bold explorers, mapping accurately territory of which there had previously only been sketch maps... I was not conscious that this attitude was arrogant.[160]

Donald Keene commented that in conversational practice it was rather as though a Japanese 'had learned his English conversation from a combination of Beowulf and Ernest Hemingway'. He became lecturer in Korean as well as Japanese although all he knew was what he had picked up from a few prisoners of war. '"Excellent!" was the response. "Nobody will ever want to study Korean, and Korean goes well with Japanese"'.[161] Even in Japanese he usually had only a couple of students. He found the sustained lack of interest in his work discouraging. When he put on a series of five special lectures in a very large lecture room allocated to him, the audience 'ranged from six to ten people, huddled together', among them some of his loyal personal friends.[162]

The 1944 Education Act and a new social mobility

The tide of first-generation undergraduates from ordinary grammar schools which was about to arrive saw Cambridge differently once they got there, with less awe and often with critical eyes. The Education Act of 1944, known as the Butler Act, after R.A. Butler, ensured that all pupils could have free secondary education, in one of three types of school, to which entrance was to be by a competitive examination – known as 'the 11-Plus' because children took it once they had reached the age of 11. The ideology informing this change involved an assumption that children differed innately in 'ability and aptitudes' and that these differences would be apparent by the age of 11, so that it was appropriate to allocate them at that age to a grammar school, a technical school or a secondary modern school. It quickly became apparent that this was socially divisive and limited opportunities for upward social mobility through higher education for the majority of children who did not win places at grammar schools. But it had the immense advantage of opening up opportunity for those who did, and for whom free secondary education could lead to tuition-fee-free university education with maintenance support available through state studentships and other bursaries.

For the even more fortunate there were Direct Grant schools. These were otherwise 'independent' schools which received grants not from the local education authorities which maintained the grammar schools, but directly from the Ministry of Education, with a requirement that in return they should grant a number of free places, again on competitive examination. Able children of modest backgrounds were thus enabled to get the best possible education and the strongest possible chance of university entrance, and in some numbers. Girls were offered the same opportunities as boys, except that places at Oxford and Cambridge were still only available on a rough ratio of 1 to 10. A few decades on the number of those of both sexes who had achieved prominence in public life and the professions who had attended Direct Grant schools was out of all proportion to the numbers they had educated from such backgrounds.

Women get degrees and membership at last

The Women's Appointments Board of 1943 had reported that 36 candidates recommended by the Board had been accepted for the 'Women's Services', 19 in 'research associations, industrial, and engineering firms', 7 were in 'social work', 3 in the 'teaching profession', and 73 in Government Departments.[163] So women had been establishing themselves professionally but still as a race apart. It took another world war to bring to the fore again the unfinished business of the early 1920s about their status in Cambridge.

Discussion of a Memorial (a signed request from voters) on 'the admission of women to membership of the University' took place in December 1946.[164] Sir A.D. McNair confessed in the Discussion that as someone living outside Cambridge 'he had to admit that he had from time to time experienced the greatest difficulty in explaining – let alone justifying – the present system'. The Memorial itself pointed out that by now there were two women Professors and two University Lecturers and two heads of department and lots of women on committees, but none of them 'entitled to take part in the Discussion of a Report'. (In 1998, women of this generation coming to celebrate the 50th anniversary of the admission of women to degrees commented that they had not realized the existence of this disability.)

In November 1947, a Discussion took place of the *Report of the Syndicate appointed to consider the status of women in the University.* This had been prompted by the rebalancing of numbers in residence with the demobilization of those who had been fighting in the war. Some thought the moment had come, with a changed membership of the Senate over the 20 years since the last attempt, and power now in the hands of the Regent House. By now a considerable number of women held senior academic positions but could not vote and the anomalies were multiplying. A *Memorial* was created, with more than 140 signatures, the signatories led by R.B. Braithwaite and K.P. Harrison, but without consulting the women's colleges.

In the discussion, Professor Dickens saw no benefits for women in allowing them proper degrees with full membership of the University. 'They would have to wear gowns presumably' and pay higher fees and they would have to 'give up afternoons to the Senate House unless things should go through which they might not wish should go through'. He knew Oxford had done something similar 'but he had not heard that Oxford was particularly happy about it'.[165] Even in 1948 when the decision was eventually taken to grant degrees to women, some of the discussants tended to the petty-minded. Was precedence to be given to Girton and Newnham? 'When they came new upon the floor of the Senate House' surely they' 'should not be made to displace anyone already there'?[166] The continuance of a 'separate species' approach to women is evidenced by the fact that the Annual Report of the Women's Appointments Board continued to appear.[167]

Compared with the positive riots in the streets and undergraduate enthusiasms of the two former (failed) attempts, this was a comparatively quiet occasion. Some women were able to be present at the vote as guests or wives of members of the Regent House. When the Grace was put no one shouted 'Non Placet'. Women got their degrees.

* * *

Student revolution, eccentric dons and the Swinging Sixties

Class envy and widening access

Andrew Sinclair wrote his early novels *The Breaking of Bumbo* and *My Friend Judas* when he was still a Cambridge student at the end of the 1950s. He thought when he was older that these novels had been rather pretentious, but there are moments of vivid description of student life:

> The thing is, supervisions with Johnson are fun... When you come, he puts you in a chair, and gives you a Tio Pepe in a big glass as an anaesthetic to show you he thinks you're human and he's interested in that. Then he switches on the lamp in his cranium, which must be about four hundred Whats and some Whys. Then he leans forwards, and makes you open up your mouth, so he can have a squint inside. He probes around with a few points from your essay, feeling out your cavities, which he's nice enough to treat as if they were depths. Then out come his pincers.[168]

He describes the way he and his contemporaries were affected by the Hungarian Revolution of 1956. 'All work stopped at the university,' he says; 'fist-fights broke out in the streets; a Tory student even knocked down his supervisor'.[169] Sinclair was highly class-conscious, at least in retrospect. 'My crassness at Eton and in the Brigade of Guards had been scarcely dented by reading political philosophy at Cambridge'.[170] He came from the social class which had for some time been the usual one for Cambridge students, but later saw that he was 'on the slippery Odessa steps down to a failed revolt at the end of the sixties, the débâcle of a whole generation'...'I found myself waved as the red flag of the upper middle classes'. 'Young women wrote to me about fleeing their convent schools to liberty in the Fens...I appeared to be the apostle of elegant mutiny...I dressed *de rigueur* for the period in old corduroy trousers and thick wool polo-necked sweaters and scuffed black suede shoes so rarely cleaned that I had to be hoovered before entering any drawing-room, which I hardly ever did'.[171] Other people (Philip Larkin, Kingsley Amis, John Braine, John Wain), were writing in the spirit of a 'radicalism and socialism' which were 'red rungs to be climbed on the way up the high social ladder', he suggests. Sinclair quotes his contemporary Eleanor Bron on the huge confidence of his generation of young Cambridge intellectuals:

> It may all have been ambition but if so it was adulterated by a lovely exuberance and a perhaps sneaking desire to make things good and interesting and if possible enjoyable. There was an assumption, very arrogant, that if you were any good, things would happen. I think...we felt able to make this assumption just because we were at Cambridge.[172]

He had it too. 'We reckoned we were the top people, if you estimate big noises by the wind they make. We were the publicity boys, the golden kids of our year. We were different and said so.'[173]

Close contemporaries were two other novelists. Margaret Drabble and her elder sister A.S. Byatt both read English at Newnham. Drabble's novel of young student and post-student life *A Summer Bird Cage* was published in 1963. Byatt's *The Virgin in the Garden* (1978) was followed by three other novels, *Still Life* (1985), *Babel Tower* (1996) and *A Whistling Woman* (2002) whose heroine throughout is Frederica, who also studied at Cambridge. For both novelists, in their distinct styles, there was something fundamental to their formation in Cambridge undergraduate life for a girl who found herself in an extreme minority among vastly predominant male undergraduates. Sinclair and these two sisters all came from families that had been able to educate them privately. Byatt and Drabble had been sent to a Quaker boarding school in York.

A new generation was arriving, products of the 1944 Education Act and its dramatic widening of educational opportunity. It was going to look at Cambridge traditions with eyes not educated by family tradition.

Cambridge and its colleges, alert to the need to make adjustments, began uncertainly to experiment with changing traditional ways:

> Porterhouse is famous for its food. There was Caviar and Soupe à l'Oignon, Turbot au Champagne, Swan stuffed with Widgeon, and finally, in memory of the Founder, Beefsteak from an ox roasted whole in the great fireplace of the College Hall. Each course had a different wine ... along the tables a hundred candles ensconced in silver candelabra cast elongated shadows of the crouching waiters across the portraits of past Masters that lined the walls ... the portraits had one thing in common: they were all rubicund and plump ... 'This swan is excellent,' said the Dean. 'A fine bird and the widgeon gives it a certain gamin flavour.'[174]

In *Porterhouse Blue*, published in 1974, Tom Sharpe only slightly over-egged the pudding in his descriptions of college life, understanding very well the deep attachments to traditions which had preserved the eccentricities of the colleges so long.

There is a new Master at 'Porterhouse', a former politician. He makes a speech at the Feast, in breach of the practice of former years. 'I feel,' he says, 'that this is a suitable occasion to put before you some new thoughts about the role of institutions such as this in the modern world'. 'Changes ... must surely be made if we are to play our part in the contemporary world.'[175] Sir Godber Evans was

> an advocate of comprehensive education at no matter what cost, chairman of the Evans Committee on Higher Education which had introduced Sixth Form Polytechnics for the Mentally Retarded, Sir Godber prided himself on the certain knowledge that he knew what was best for the country.[176]

One of the threads of the story which unfolds is the problem of accommodating the different social expectations of a new sort of student. Skullion, the Head Porter, polishing his shoes, recollects a conversation with 'a young pup in a pub' who had described the College's members of the past as 'a lot of rich bastards with nothing between their ears who just exploited you'. Skullion had replied, 'A gentleman stood for something. It wasn't what he was. It was what he knew he ought to be.'[177] The 'forward-thinking' were already able to perceive that fund-raising required some fine-tuning of the balance between preserving tradition and offering something new and up-to-date. 'If the College were only less ... antiquated in its attitudes, I daresay I could use my influence on the city to raise a substantial sum, but as it is ... ,'[178] says Sir Godber to the Bursar.

Student protest

Students of the expanding university system of the 1960s began to express their opinions in demonstrations. Some of their opinions concerned matters of political importance in which students were inclined to be idealistic. In California, from 1964, students were protesting at Berkeley in favour of free speech. By 1968, students were protesting throughout the world, in Germany and Spain and Italy and Egypt and Japan as well as in England. There were demonstrations at the Sorbonne, and at a London School of Economics already very different from the one Eileen Power knew at the outbreak of the Second World War. Protest might focus on abolishing nuclear weapons (the Campaign for Nuclear Disarmament) or preventing the development of chemical weapons; or later, on the Vietnam War, on which a protest banner was suspended from the roof of King's College Chapel in 1967.

Some protests were violent, or at least involved scuffles. There were bids to prevent invited speakers having their say on university property. When Denis Healey, then Minister of Defence, came to speak in Cambridge in 1968, there were battles between student factions. Enoch Powell was due to speak at Queens' College but threats of violence caused the event to be cancelled. There were sit-ins, such as the one in the Old Schools in 1969, to protest about a visit to Churchill College by the American Ambassador.

Much of the protesting was less high-minded and concerned what would now be called 'the student experience', such as demands for changes in the way accommodation was run. Protests about the cost of the meals provided at Emmanuel included refusing to pay College bills promptly in 1965. Fixed overall charges for meals caused protest in the 1970s because students had to pay a block sum for meals they might not actually eat. There were protests about the practice of closing college gates at what were now perceived to be unreasonably early hours. Cambridge was to see a shift from the still faintly Victorian traditions which had led in the 1960s to students being sent down for being found with a member of the opposite sex in their rooms after the College was officially closed for the night. There was going to be less need henceforth for climbing in over the Dean's wall, and in any case, the mixing of colleges from the early 1970s created the need for an entirely new set of overt or implied sexual protocols. By the 1970s it had become a source of indignation that the University did not provide adequate nursery facilities for students or staff and a Nursery Action Group was founded in 1972 with a sit-in of the Senate House on the subject in 1975.

In this new climate the perceived position of students in Cambridge began to change. Student Unions were being established throughout the country. In Cambridge, a Student Union was formed in 1970. Students were indisputably 'members' of the University (though not yet tuition-fee-paying ones) and they now claimed a share in the conduct of its affairs. In 1973 there was a sit-in to protest about slow progress in allowing student representation on the Faculty Board of Economics, and in the reform of the Economics Tripos. There was a sit-in of the University Library in 1976 to press for longer opening hours. Students were given places on committees throughout the University and in colleges, though normally only for unreserved business. If matters of a confidential nature needed to be discussed, especially involving the personal affairs of academic staff, the students would be expected to leave the meeting. Having made their point about being included, the student members rarely objected to that.[179]

The culminating and definitive event of this period was the Garden House Hotel riot of Friday 13 February 1970, which took place when students decided to mount a protest during a Greek Tourist Week in the city. They disapproved of what they considered a fascist government in Greece. Bricks were thrown and a Proctor was taken to hospital. Six students were convicted of riotous assembly and sent to prison and two others were sent to Borstal. In Cambridge, one of the lasting legacies of this episode was the damage it did to the reputation of the Proctors. They gave evidence in court and were resented because they helped identify the 'ringleaders' whose punishment proved to be so draconian.

Student liberation was moving fast now, as was marked by the disappearance of the requirement that they should be instantly identifiable to the University authorities. Students had to wear gowns in the streets after dark until the 1960s (though at the beginning of the century they had had to do so at lectures, examinations, sermons and in the University Library).

New benchmarks in donnish eccentricity

In the era after the Second World War and into the 1960s, some dons were such 'characters' that they sometimes seemed more like caricatures. There is no way of knowing whether they were more colourful than those of earlier generations, but it was not yet a century since allowing the Fellows of Colleges to marry had begun to produce the 'career academic' in some numbers. This meant that more dons stayed in the 'profession' for life and did not have to move out to become clergymen with parishes (the usual route) as soon as they wanted to marry.

The shift was not only to a lifelong career as an academic but away from the presumption that whatever his area of special intellectual interest, a don was essentially a cleric. It was now possible for those academics with strong religious interests to treat them academically in new conjunctions with other subjects than theology. C.S. Lewis (1898–1963) moved from Oxford to Cambridge and from Magdalen College to Magdalene College, in 1954, with his reputation and his hang-ups formed, only to find that Cambridge was, for him, no more restful a place to be.[180] Dom David Knowles (1896–1974) was in Cambridge from 1944 to 1963, Professor of Medieval History from 1947, Regius Professor from 1954. 'He normally wrote his lectures out in full'... 'the contrast of his small figure and slight voice... with the beauty of his language and the depth of his thought made his best lectures memorable and impressive'.[181]

One of the great changes of the twentieth century connected with these changes of expectation was the retreat of theology from its leading position in the intellectual and moral life of Cambridge. Compulsory attendance at College Chapel died away. Cambridge in the 1960s had its share of prominent and eccentric clerics. Several theological revolutionaries felt free to throw down radical challenge. Harry Williams (1919–2006), teaching at Westcott House, the Anglican Theological College, from 1948 to 1951, Dean of Chapel at Trinity from 1958, eventually went off to be a monk in 1969. Before he made that decision he had had a breakdown and a period of psychoanalysis and became outspoken about his own homosexuality and the spiritual lessons to be learned in unlikely corners of life. He became a pastoral rather than an academic leader. His Cambridge sermons were brought together in a book *The true wilderness* (1965). John Robinson (1919–83), later Dean of Trinity, gave evidence as a witness in the obscenity trial of D.H. Lawrence's *Lady Chatterley's Lover* in 1960. He published *Honest to God* in 1963. His thesis was that God should no longer be thought of as 'up there' or 'out there', in the manner traditionally envisaged. Although he was attacking a straw man, for theology had long moved beyond any such crude notions, he was understood to be saying something radical, to be questioning the very existence of God-as-he-had-been-thought-of, and a controversy ensured. He also made a vigorous attack on the quality of twentieth-century New Testament scholarship. Don Cupitt (b.1934) studied both science and theology. He became dean of Emmanuel and theology students were rumoured to be flummoxed when they were sent to him for supervisions by his challenge to the very idea of God. There were tales of the arrival of indignant mothers demanding to be given an explanation of the undermining of their children's faith.

Older academics may well have been dottier academics, having had longer to mature their affectations. Andrew Sinclair writes of 'F.R. Leavis [1895–1978] in his vehement bunker in Downing College, and the Victorian secret society, the Apostles, based in King's College'.[182] Leavis had come into his glory or infamy in the 1940s. In 1943 he published *Education and the University*, in 1948 the ground-breaking *The Great Tradition*. In 1952 appeared *The Common Pursuit*.

> Leavis himself was never fashionable, always at war with the faculty. His was an ideology with a narrow canon of approved reading…one had to be precise in speech and manners, proper in culture and morals, didactic and 'prepared for others to be affronted, or bored, by one's pretensions'. But his followers were truly devotees.

Andrew Sinclair writes too of the period when 'the supreme Wittgenstein [1889–1951] was still lecturing with a bleak wit as acute and rare as James Joyce's in *Finnegan's Wake* or Samuel Becket's in *Waiting for Godot*.[183] Wittgenstein had been appointed to a Chair in Philosophy in 1939. He spent the war years out of Cambridge, working as a hospital porter in London and then as a laboratory assistant in Newcastle, and although he returned after the War he left Cambridge for good in 1947. He never took to the place. Something of his awkward, angular personality is conveyed in the tale of Wittgenstein's Poker. The story was that in 1946 at a meeting of the Cambridge Moral Science Club he got into an argument with the speaker, Karl Popper of the London School of Economics. Popper held that there are 'real' philosophical problems while Wittgenstein maintained that they were actually linguistic. Wittgenstein seized a poker from the fireplace and brandished it as he made his points. He challenged Popper to state a moral principle. 'Not to threaten visiting lecturers with pokers?' ventured Popper. Wittgenstein, defeated, threw down the poker and left.

Wittgenstein was not the most approachable of thinkers, intellectually or personally. His mannerism of allowing a long silence to elapse before replying, his worried expression and the way he would sit with his head in his hands did not make for easy intercourse. Elizabeth Anscombe (1919–2001), who made her name in the field of moral philosophy and the idea of 'intention', used to travel from Oxford to Cambridge every week to hear his lectures. Eccentric herself (there were many stories such as her absentmindedly leaving one of her small children on a library shelf and going home without it), she became Wittgenstein's friend and did a good deal to ensure that his work was known. She was present when he died in 1951 and was one of his literary executors, which gave her the opportunity to do still more to make his work remembered and taken seriously. It was Anscombe who made sense of his ideas and worked them out systematically. She became Professor of Philosophy at Cambridge from 1970 to 1986.

Underpinning all this was a development of surprisingly short duration (a mere few generations), but immense importance, enshrined in Cambridge's Statute D, and deriving from the Oxford and Cambridge Act of 1877. That Act defines the purpose of a university as the encouragement of education, religion, learning and research. Accordingly, the Cambridge Statute requires its University Teaching Officers to do the same, imposing on them a relatively modest burden of the actual hours of work, in the expectation that they will maintain themselves as authorities in their subjects and thus help the University to fulfil its 'purpose.' The expectation is coupled with the recognition that they will need security of tenure and perhaps quite a lot of time to think, years of no great apparent productivity. Some of them will in fact be doing nothing much. Others will win Nobel Prizes. This ideal of the self-regulating and self-motivated independent mature scholar was to be undermined by the loss of academic tenure in the Education Reform Act of 1988 and by the arrival in Cambridge of a line-management approach to the employment relationship which ran alongside the 'holding of a University Office'.

* * *

The Colleges and the University rethink their relationship

On not being left out in the cold

Most of the academic buildings of Cambridge belong to the colleges, not to the University. Cycling down Garrett Hostel Lane from the Senate House to the University Library on a summer evening, the cyclist passes old and new buildings of Trinity College and Trinity Hall, crosses the river with its vistas along the backs of the colleges, and has to go across a road carrying fast traffic before reaching another piece of 'University' building at the Library. The lane itself was provided by Trinity Hall in 1545, to take the place of an older route further south which had been known as Henney Lane. The College wanted to expand to the north and the old lane was in its way. The new lane ran close to the old Town Ditch or King's Stream, which was part of the now vanished straggle of sheds and mooring places for the commercial traffic up the river which brought corn and flax and salt.[184]

The Backs overprinted all that, though not without some argument. Capability Brown (1716–1783) saw the potential of the area in the eighteenth century. In his proposals of 1793, he envisaged a single grand sweep which would have looked like the parkland of a great house, with, at the focus of the vista, the Gibbs Building at the back of King's College. The separate areas belonging to each college, with their distinctive landscaping designs, would have been incorporated into the design and the river would have been widened and its course reshaped to create an elegant meander. The colleges were indignant. They preferred to maintain their own separate avenues from their college buildings and their individual bridges over the river leading beyond; the proposal was thrown out.[185] So the development of this area exemplifies the effective dominance of the colleges on the physical landscape of central Cambridge.

Much the same thing happened in the University's 'human' life. The existence of autonomous bodies in an intimate relationship with a University, yet remaining in charge of their own affairs, remains a structure unique to Oxford and Cambridge. (The relationship of London's Colleges to the University of London was always quite different, and some of them have since broken off and become independent universities in their own right.) Cambridge colleges may not admit anyone to membership (except the 'lay choristers' who sing in the King's College choir), unless they present them at once for matriculation so that they may become members of the University too. That means that every student has to be admitted by a college, but not every academic. Ensuring that every academic who was eligible had the opportunity to become the Fellow of a College became a major problem in the middle of the twentieth century. The colleges can withhold their favours when it comes to the dons.

The relationship between the University and the Colleges had changed several times since the Middle Ages, with the balance of power often going with the balance of wealth. The colleges, especially some of them, had the wealth. That balance had been adjusted in the 1870s, when the Oxford and Cambridge Act of 1877 took powers to alter ancient trusts and ensure that the Colleges handed over funds to the University in both Oxford and Cambridge, with the intention that the two Universities would then be better able to afford to pay Professorial and lecturer salaries.

The discussions of the Asquith Commissioners who took evidence in 1920 had included consideration of the possibility that the University might be made better able to control the colleges in various ways, for example that the state might do so directly or that the state might do so through the University. That came to nothing, although Statute G of the 1926 Cambridge Statutes maintained the '1877' principle that the colleges must make a financial contribution to the University.

The Cambridge way of making arrangements for the appointment of its academics in modern times has been to create University Teaching Offices, whose holders may also hold college Fellowships if the colleges invite them to do so. Meanwhile, the colleges have continued to employ their own lecturers directly. The Oxford way was to create conjoint appointments, in which the University and the College posts were awarded together. This has had the effect of making the colleges proportionately more powerful in Oxford and the faculties in Cambridge. But in both universities there are inequalities arising from the huge differences in the wealth of the colleges. Fellows of the richer colleges were likely to get a better 'deal' financially than those of the poorer colleges, even if the salary for what Cambridge called the University Office was the same.

By the middle of the twentieth century, the Cambridge way was beginning to feel its own special tensions. The question reappeared in the 1960s in the form of a debate about the problems which were being caused by the lack of any system for ensuring that those who had University Teaching Offices also had college Fellowships. A growing number of academics found themselves without Fellowships at all.

Fellowships for women

Women were particularly exercised about the lack of Fellowships. Cambridge was still lagging in the 1950s when it came to provision for women students. Girton and Newnham remained the only women's colleges, to Oxford's five. Hughes Hall could admit women students though it was not yet recognized as a college. In 1954, a new body was founded, to be known as New Hall. It began with 16 students, in premises on Silver St., which were subsequently occupied by Darwin College. The numbers remained small, with a separate admission examination consisting of a single general paper, sometimes taken by girls in the second year of the sixth form. By 1965 funding had been attracted and the College moved to its present site next to Fitzwilliam College on Huntington Rd. It was then able to expand to admit more than 200 undergraduates. In 1972 the College was granted its Charter and became a full College of the University.

Lucy Cavendish College was a foundation of 1965, again for women only. The instigators of its creation were a group of women who had membership of the Regent House but no Fellowships and who formed a dining club to provide themselves with at least something of what they felt they were missing. The call for more collegiate provision for women was eventually taken over by the Third Foundation, which resulted in the founding of New Hall. The dining club, which called itself the 'Dining Group' then formulated a different aim, which was 'to have concern for the problems of academic women in Cambridge, and by providing practical assistance and the stimulus of regular social contact, to encourage academic achievement in teaching, learning and research'. In 1964, the Group asked the University for recognition as the Lucy Cavendish Collegiate Society. This was to be an Approved Society; it was to cater for women graduate students engaged in research and for other women seeking to reequip themselves for professional careers as mature students. When in 1971 the Cambridge Statutes were amended to allow Approved Societies to admit undergraduates as well as graduate students, Lucy Cavendish began to take undergraduates too, from 1972. In 1997 it became a full College.

Colleges for graduate students

At the same time there was a growing awareness that graduate students needed better provision in colleges and that post-doctoral and visiting scholars too could find themselves isolated in Cambridge, and without the focus and social contact provided by college life. Wolfson College was founded by the University in 1965; it took the name Wolfson College in 1973 to honour its benefactor, the Wolfson Foundation (a similar graduate college in Oxford bears the same name).

Darwin, like Wolfson College, was founded exclusively for graduate students in the early 1960s. It was the creation of a joint initiative by St. John's, Trinity and Caius Colleges. Darwin College took its name from the family which owned the house in which it was set up, Newnham Grange. This had belonged to the son of Charles Darwin, who had been Plumian Professor of Astronomy in Cambridge from 1883, and then to his son, another Charles, who died in 1962. Darwin's granddaughter Gwen Raverat (1885–1957) wrote an illustrated account of her childhood world in this house in *Period Piece*. The family declared itself happy to allow the house to be used by the new College and to give it the family name.

Clare Hall was an offshoot of Clare College, designed to provide for the special needs of students and post-doctoral individuals and visiting Fellows who were spending a period in Cambridge with families and for whom family accommodation and a meeting place was needed. Like Lucy Cavendish, it was an experimental variant of the standard college 'model' and created to meet the needs of a new period in Cambridge life.

Would quotas help?

The Bridges Syndicate was set up in 1962 to look afresh at the relationship between University and colleges. Appendix B of its Report proposed a quota system which would ensure that colleges took their fair share of post-holders who were without colleges. There were concerns that the colleges might then find themselves obliged to accept individuals who did not really want a college life and would not pull their weight. The suggestion was that colleges might be obliged to recruit as Fellows only those who 'had put their names on a schedule as signifying their willingness to fulfil the obligations of a Fellowship'.[186]

Statute G,I,1 still stipulates that colleges shall maintain the number – 'quota' – of Professorial Fellowships and other University Teaching Officer (UTO) Fellowships allotted to them. Some traditional links are protected. Even if it upsets the quota, the Dixie Professor of Ecclesiastical History may become a Professorial Fellow of Emmanuel College; the Regius Professor of Greek, a Professorial Fellow of Trinity College; the Downing Professor of the Laws of England, a Professorial Fellow of Downing College; and the Churchill Professor of Mathematics for Operational Research, a Professorial Fellow of Churchill College.

New kinds of college or a University Centre?

Other solutions were being looked at in 1962. One, which had first appeared a generation earlier, was to make separate provision for the needs of those without colleges, a provision which might include something for non-academics. For 'there is in Cambridge no single focus for the Life of the University as distinct from its Colleges'.[187] A Discussion foreshadowing this had been held as long ago as 10 February 1948 (*Reporter*, p.721) on a proposal to establish a Faculty Club:

> Professor Sir J.E. Lennard-Jones said that ... whereas formerly most University teachers were Fellows of Colleges, and were able to take full advantage of their social and corporate life, the situation had now arisen in which about 25 per cent of the University staff had no such College connection.[188]

The needs to be met by this proposal had now been transformed by the presence in Cambridge of a growing crowd of members of staff of various kinds and graduate students, for whom the social facilities historically provided by the colleges were not available, or not sufficient. So another proposal of the Bridges Report was for a non-collegiate solution such as the Centre.

This part of the discussion of the practical needs to be met for graduate students in particular (social meeting places, married accommodation) threw back into the melting pot the very idea of a college which had been forming since the admission of undergraduates at the end of the Middle Ages. The linking of the need for a Graduate College with the need for a University Centre, and the need for 'provision' for 'administrative staff' with the University Centre ('something which we think it needs, but has ever yet had, namely, a focus for the life of the University') was controversial. Those with an existing College affiliation who already enjoyed Senior Common Room college life seemed likely to make little use of such a provision. It was wryly admitted that when members of the Regent House were asked 'to what extent they would make use of club facilities', 'the replies were not at first sight as encouraging as might have been expected'.[189] It would therefore not bring its users inside the system but merely provide them with a convenient meeting place and restaurant facilities. The proposed inclusion of 'administrative staff' became an issue in its own right as their numbers grew with the governance reforms.

Upgradings to collegiate status

The multiplication of colleges from the mid-twentieth century has been in strong contrast with the 200-year gap in college-founding before the arrival of Downing in 1800. One speedy way of adding to the number of colleges was to make full colleges of foundations which had hitherto remained on the fringe. Selwyn had been founded in memory of the Rt. Revd. George Augustus Selwyn (1809–78), who had been the first Bishop of New Zealand (1841–68) and later Bishop of Lichfield (1868–78). The first Selwyn students lived in a hostel with the Master and 12 Fellows from 1882. It became a College in 1958.

This route to a solution to the shortage of places in colleges for academics went back to the dawn of a concern that the collegiate system might be a barrier to the widening of access. A Non-Collegiate Students Board, founded in 1869, was first housed opposite the Fitzwilliam Museum. It was a fruit of the work of the first Royal Commission in 1852. The idea was to make it possible for students to be admitted to the University without having to be accepted by a college. At the time it had the obvious advantage of by-passing the need for the expense of college residence (and the reality that contacts helped), so as to allow more boys from underprivileged backgrounds a change to get in. The Government insisted. As a concession to the existing colleges' indignation, it was agreed that the Board should be composed of members representing the colleges and that it should appoint an executive 'officer' to be known as the Censor. The first Censor was R.B. Somerset of Trinity College. Students thus admitted to the University had to be supervised. They were required to visit the Censor's office on five days of each week and to give a report of their work each year.

Gradually, however, like the Home Students in Oxford who became St. Anne's College, this body of non-collegiate students began to behave like a college. In any case, the Board of Education's recognition that the body had in effect collegiate status was essential in 1919 if students were to be eligible for maintenance grants. The Royal Commission of 1922 feared that to make the body a college would be to defeat its original purpose, which was to provide a route by which a Cambridge education could be had on the cheap. Instead, it made a recommendation that the new University Grants Committee should give what was now to be Fitzwilliam Hall £100 a year. This body languished for a time. It became Fitzwilliam House. Then, in 1966 it became Fitzwilliam College, with buildings on the Huntingdon Rd. This solution developed to meet the needs of male undergraduates. Fitzwilliam did not admit women until 1979.

A shortage of girlfriends: bringing in the teacher training colleges

The male students of earlier ages had had their sexual needs. In the centuries when they were regarded as potential or actual clerics, there was also a requirement of celibacy. There was always a problem for the University in maintaining discipline where the 'women of the town' were concerned, and for some centuries, the Vice-Chancellor had authority to deal with them for the protection of the young men's morals just as he did in the case of licensing of hostelries. In the twentieth century, social norms shifted from the tight requirement that young women students should not be alone with men but should be accompanied by a chaperone to the period from the 1960s when it became acceptable for undergraduates to sleep with their girlfriends. That easing of restrictions did not mean that there was not huge potential for scandal still. 'Cambridge Fellow resigns after claims he had sex with girls in college rooms,' screamed a headline in the *Mail on Sunday* in 2003, after alleged episodes with call-girls.

A shortage of girl undergraduates had post-war students inviting their girlfriends from home:

> After lunch Sheila wanted to see the sights. 'After all, that's what I've come for,' she said… 'I want to see inside… Oh, it's all so lovely. No wonder you're happy. I wish I'd worked harder'… She leaned on the parapet of King's bridge and looked round. 'Golly, you're lucky.'[190]

A good substitute for a fellow-University student, as Frederic Raphael's fictional characters found, was a student from Homerton or Hughes Hall. Homerton and Hughes Hall were originally Cambridge's teacher training colleges. Hughes Hall began in the 1870s with 14 students and a Principal-warden, Elizabeth Hughes, who gave the venture her name; it developed in 1885 into the Cambridge Training College with a purpose-built building from 1895. Miss Hughes was adventurous in seeking to attract international students, even visiting Japan in 1902 for the purpose. After Cambridge finally gave degrees to women in 1948, Hughes Hall developed from a company into an Approved Foundation and in 1985 it voted itself a new structure, with a President and Fellows.

Homerton was older in origin, deriving from a dissenting academy of 1730 which owned a London house in Homerton High St. in 1768. It awarded London University qualifications for a time. It moved to Hills Rd. in Cambridge in 1894 so as to provide a more pleasant environment for its students. Its main work was teacher training for women, and only in 1970 did it accept men students as it had done in its earliest days. In 2001, it became the largest of Cambridge's colleges, broadening its scope beyond the Education Tripos, but it was proposed only in 2008–9 that it should become a full College.[191]

New kinds of college

In the period after the Second World War, Cambridge was expanding in size as well as in the social mix of its students, and wholly new colleges began to appear, some of them experimental in type. Andrew Sinclair was to be one of the founding members of Churchill College. The College was born of a conversation with Winston Churchill in 1955. Like Gordon Brown as Chancellor of the Exchequer in the late 1990s, he had been impressed by what he had seen at the Massachusetts Institute of Technology and wanted to import something like it into British higher education. Churchill's idea was to create a new 'specialist' 'science and technology' college in Cambridge, though one with a sprinkling of arts and humanities to 'civilize' it. Colleges had formerly been 'generalist'. Battles at the beginning over whether the College should have a chapel[192] suggest that there were significant implications of the decision deliberately to gear the work of a college to favour the sciences, when the traditional notion, at least from early modern times, had been that colleges dealt even-handedly in all subjects of study. The college had a site by 1958, though its first students did not arrive for a year or two; it became a full College in 1966. There is still a requirement that it maintain a 70–30 bias in favour of science and technology students among the undergraduate members of the College, and that 30 per cent of its students should be post-graduates.

Mixed colleges

From 1974, individual Colleges took their independent decisions to 'go mixed', slowly at first and then in a rush so as not to lose out. The calculation was that this might enable the old and beautiful Colleges to attract the most able girl candidates, for the women had been on average outstanding in the years when there were ten places for men for every one for a woman.

At the undergraduate level there were practical problems, such as what was to be done about bathrooms. St. John's had carried on with its old system which involved trailing across the courts with bath towel and soap even in winter and in the rain. Girls did not take to that, nor to blushing encounters in the courts half-dressed. A rapid process of social normalizing had to take place. Were the boys to be brothers or lovers? And porters with established habits and a command of the appropriate language for telling off undergraduates who drank too much and misbehaved had to learn how to deal with girls who had had one too many. Conversely, boys had to learn to say 'I am at Girton' to a tide of derisory giggles.

At the level of the Fellowship, the problems were quite different. It was not possible to move to anything like a half and half arrangement with any speed. Existing male Fellows were naturally going to serve out their time and for some years a 'mixed' college might have only one or two woman Fellows. So unsure was anyone what to do with them that it was not unknown for them to be expected to 'retire with the ladies' at the Christmas dinner where Fellows brought in their wives, and not stay with the 'gentlemen and Fellows' who were going to linger for their port and cigars and in some colleges, their snuff. Uneasy male dons sometimes saw young women Fellows as dolls and became indignant when they found they expected to be treated as ordinary colleagues.

* * *

Could Cambridge remain in a world of its own?

Cambridge was not the only University which found it was entering a new world. The Robbins Report was the work of a Commission chaired by Lord Robbins from 1961 to 1964. The Commission said it felt it was working in 'an absence of systematic information' about the way universities are run,[193] and this proved abundantly true for Cambridge. Cambridge had no representation on the committee from among its current staff and Robbins had to call on it to reform itself from within.[194] Little progress seemed to have been made since the 1907 House of Lords debates had suggested that it was urgent to work out the relationship of Oxford and Cambridge to the new 'civic' universities.

The Report suggested that since universities were now in receipt of such large grants from the state and financially dependent on public money, 'it is only natural that the general direction of their development has come to be regarded as a matter of public interest' (para.15). More people, ordinary people, wanted to go to university: 'Many of the detailed proposals are primarily a matter for the academic world, but it is for the Government to take decisions on a number of the most important recommendations.'[195]

During the 1960s, the University Grants Committee smiled on the creation of new universities and Sussex, York, East Anglia, Essex, Lancaster, Warwick, Canterbury, Stirling were founded in the early 1960s, on the clear understanding that they would not be teaching vocational or technical subjects. These were designed with the concept of providing residential accommodation on large campuses outside cities, with the intention that students should go away from home to 'go to university'. There were able students to whom this novelty was attractive. Some of the new universities became sufficiently fashionable to attract students who would otherwise have been probable candidates for Oxford or Cambridge. Cambridge did nothing to counter this threat. It sat tight and waited for what it believed to be its inherently superior attractions to reassert themselves. It was confident that the students would come back.

Cambridge discovers 'administration'

In common with other universities, Cambridge was beginning to find from the middle of the twentieth century that it needed a much more extensive administrative service. The alteration of expectation could be seen in the gradual appearance along the corridors in faculties and departments of first one then several secretaries, and then a series of offices housing specialist sections of an administration, and then, from the 1990s, Faculty Administrators, much more senior figures, with powers as well as duties, though those powers were at first ill-defined. Some of the earliest appointees were heard to ask what exactly it was that they were supposed to do.

It was noted in the *Reporter* in 1968 that

> during the next four years, staff from the Comptroller and
> Auditor General's Office will visit every British University,
> to examine the procedures which are used to authorise
> expenditure from Parliamentary grants. The Comptroller
> and Auditor General has emphasized that his staff are not
> concerned to question policy-decisions made by Universities,
> but only the control which is exercised over expenditure to
> meet these decisions.[196]

There was a tendency, not confined to Cambridge, to overdo
this, appointing additional administrative staff in newly created
administrative divisions, resulting in what the Quality Assurance
Agency was later to call ' "gold-plating" (i.e., bureaucratic features that
may look impressive but add little value)'.[197]

At first, this multiplication of administrators was greeted with some
relief in Cambridge, because it removed from academics some of the
burdens of administration, though there were complaints in Cambridge
that all this new secretarial provision did not include secretarial
assistance in support of their academic work. Indeed, attention was
drawn in 1968 to: 'the need for better typing facilities in connection
with teaching and research by University Teaching officers, especially
in Faculties with no central office and no office staff'.[198] A glimpse
of the way this might be provided draws a sharp contrast with the
present-day needs for IT support. 'The work to be dealt with under
the scheme will be copy-typing, but it may occasionally be possible
by special arrangement for work to be dictated in the Old Schools to
a shorthand-typist.'[199]

There was, however, potentially another dimension to this
development, as Dr. G.C. Evans pointed out in a Discussion in
December, 1967:

> Administrative convenience is a very powerful god. It is a
> jealous god, devouring all other... Among our most notable
> achievement has been the maintenance of a functioning
> democratic system for more than forty years, since the
> Statutes of the last Royal Commission. There can be few major
> institutions in the western world which have such a record.[200]

Not every departmental secretary was Laurie Taylor's 'Maureen',
stoically and unambitiously running its affairs far beyond the calls of
duty.[201] Some were thought to have ambitions to be managers, and
there were fears that a managerial class might be imported into the

University with no real understanding of academic priorities and the old collegiality supported by an administrative 'civil service' be eroded into line-management. A. Hyde had speculated in a Discussion as early 1961 that in

> the next quinquennium it is quite possible, though naturally not certain, that the University Grants Committee will be negotiating with an administration the bulk of whose members have never seen a University, let alone a senior one, are ignorant of critical thought, of the decencies of argument, of the tolerance of day to day intercourse; and with that ignorance will probably go the hostility with which ignorance is usually associated.[202]

The Vice-Chancellor's parting speech on demitting office in 1968 put academic matters first as he stressed was proper, then buildings, and then followed a comment on administrative matters:

> Universities tend to regard academic bureaucracy with suspicion, and there is a risk that in Cambridge at a time of financial stringency our administrative service will not get the funds and accommodation it need to keep pace with the University's growing commitments.[203]

This set of potential difficulties was to lead in two or three decades to the establishment of the modern Unified Administrative Service, the shift from a 'civil service' to a 'management' mindset and the beginning of 'policy-formation'.

Deciding what to do next

The Vice-Chancellor's annual address of 1968 had also noted that 'One weakness in our pattern of administration is that we have had no group of people in the University charged with the duty of reflecting on the future of the University as a whole'.[204] Who should make policy in Cambridge? Was this a task for the growing administration or for the academic community? The academic community was large and although it could debate and vote it was not of a size to facilitate speedy and efficient policy-making. On the other hand, the presumption was still that the administration was a 'service' not a 'management', that the secretaries of academic committees were not members of those committee and took no part in the decision-making, and that the Vice-Chancellor, a Head of House holding office in a two-yearly rotation, was merely a temporary *primus inter pares* with one vote like every other member of the Regent House.

Beneath the surface of that question about policy-making, then, was the problem of fixing the boundary between governance and administration. The legislative powers of the University clearly lay with the Regent House, but there had already been rumblings in response to the suggestion that it should no longer expressly 'Grace' every proposal but be deemed in future to do so by 'default', that is, unless a vote was insisted on.[205] Busy administrators did not want to have to refer decisions to a democratic vote.

The exact 'location' of executive powers remained a grey area. This was not a matter which concerned only Cambridge. The Oxford of the 1960s saw the Franks Commission and the Franks Report tackling similar problems.[206]

The tension between democracy and efficiency, which has since become a repeating theme, already seemed fundamental to Graves: 'The basic problem is to devise arrangements which will ensure on the one hand the maintenance of academic democracy and on the other the adoption of procedures making for efficiency and decision.'[207]

Discussions of the Senate at which criticisms could be voiced and which could lead to voting things down, were not liked by the burgeoning administration, which increasingly felt itself to be engaged in trench-warfare with the academic community. Discussions, it was argued, 'are apt to give prominence to the views of those who are opposed to the recommendations contained in a Report, for it is comparatively rare that a speaker who is in favour of them is at hand, or is willing and able, to reply to criticism'.[208]

William Frend, who was to become a leading patristic scholar, move to a Chair at Glasgow, and return in retirement to appear at Patristic Seminars once more, was in his young days a radical commentator in Discussions. He had a riposte ready:

> They complain that too seldom are speakers in favour of the Council's proposal, Whose fault is that anyway? If there is a good case, then the proposers can take the trouble of organizing themselves... Nor has opposition to Reports in the past been unconstructive.[209]

Dr. U.R. Evans drew attention to the proposal to set an age-limit for contributions to Discussions 'The right to speak does not necessarily imply the right to vote'. And 'a single well-reasoned speech may influence the votes of many voters'.[210] Mr. E.S. Shire, 'Adequate, and, I would stress, willing, communication between the Council and its officers, and the Regent House will, I believe, prove vital'.[211] It is true that Discussions were – and still are – often most actively attended and spoken at when they concern proposals of an essentially minor kind which touch individuals personally.[212]

One idea already afloat at the end of the 1960s was that a Vice-Chancellor might be needed as a voice of the University to Government and in that case, he might need a longer term of office: 'it seems reasonable to assume an increase in Government interest and the need to negotiate with authority, on a national scale, along with other Universities and on occasions in competition with them'. Short-term Vice-Chancellors could not do this as well as a Vice-Chancellor 'with the professionalism of office which stems from continuity of service' (Sir John Baker).[213]

The Regent House was suspicious – quite in the style envisaged by Cornford – about unintended (or worse, intended) consequences. Dr. D. Thomson:

> Steps must be taken to ensure that even when a Grace of the Regent House is not required, full information about any important decisions taken by the Council shall be published well before it could be said that it was now too late to be worth initiating discussion of them in the Regent House … and we may have to accept that reaching good decisions simply does take time in a free society.[214]

William Frend was there again: 'one sees at every point proposals to enhance the status of the administrator and diminish that of the individual don',[215] and

> Assistant Registraries will not only have to be recruited but paid. Once again, money needed for the establishment of posts and recognition of established scholars will be frittered away in projects of administrative finesse. We may lose in permanent loss of scholars more than we gain in any administrative efficiency.[216]

Here the matter rested until the Wass Syndicate made the ambitious proposal to create a Unified Administrative Service, which finally came into being in the 1990s.

* * *

Cambridge dons lose their security

Academic freedom under threat?

After the experiences of the 1960s and 1970s of instances in which invited speakers were prevented by activist student protest from giving lectures on university campuses, it was mooted that there was a need for legislation to protect freedom of speech in universities. Academics young and old have historically been as eager to silence one another as to protect their own right to say what they wish. In the House of Lords, Lord Beloff and several other members drew attention to a number of instances, such as the Guildford College of Law, which 'cancelled an invitation' to the Solicitor-General to come and speak, for fear of the 'demonstrations which would result', a

> host organization being browbeaten into withdrawing the invitations which it has already issued to perfectly innocent academics who have come from a country with an unpleasant government. I refer, of course, to the International Archaeological Conference in Southampton University next year.

There was murmuring to the effect that 'it is hard for some of us to know the difference between soccer hooligans and the type of scruffs who get a subsidy from government to go to universities, and who call themselves students'.

Debate followed on 5 February 1986 in connection with the forthcoming Education Bill. As Baroness Cox insisted, 'Education in a free society should enshrine the principles of freedom of speech, freedom to pursue the truth'.[217]

Education (No. 2) Act 1986 s.43 went on to provide that

> [e]very individual and body of persons concerned in the government of any establishment to which this section applies shall take such steps as are reasonably practicable to ensure that freedom of speech within the law is secured for members, students and employees of the establishment and for visiting speakers.

This was duly embodied in the Cambridge statutes, though in the case of the University of Cambridge, spread as it was throughout the city, it was not easy to define the area of a 'campus'. It is sometimes forgotten what an all-embracing protection this is, since it covers students and all employees and visitors as well as the academic staff.

Academic freedom for academic staff and the loss of academic tenure

A new and far more serious challenge was now coming forward from the Government. In a shrinking national economy Governments were eager to spend less on higher education. One of the most expensive things about universities was – and remains – their salary bills. But academic staff had tenure. They could not be sacked merely to save the University money. Kenneth Baker, then Secretary of State put the Government's position thus:

> The arrangements for strict tenure in some universities... severely circumscribe the flexibility and responsiveness of universities. The Bill proposes that all universities should be able to appoint new permanent staff without offering them strict tenure. Independent commissioners will revise university charters to give effect to this and to safeguard academic freedom.[218]

This would mean the end of 'academic tenure', which had become particularly strong and well-established in Cambridge, making it impossible to sack University Teaching Officers even in some notorious extreme cases of neglect of duties and worse. There was the tale of the son of another Cambridge academic, himself a University Teaching Officer, who went on strike because he felt his father had not been treated properly by Cambridge. The University was said to have responded by setting up a committee to consider what to do, which prudently refraining from meeting, while it waited for him to retire in the natural course of events.

It was pointed out that if academics did not feel safe from losing their jobs, they might be discouraged from the free pursuit of truth (and from challenging Governments). This principle was put succinctly by the Chairman of the Committee of Vice-Chancellors and Principals in January 1988:

> We are arguing vehemently for three fundamental freedoms which we believe to be of lasting value to this country. They are the freedom to research in subjects of as yet unrecognized importance, the freedom to question received wisdom and the freedom to be protected from direct and narrow political interference by the Government of the day. This is what we mean by academic freedom – not a licence to brood comfortably in ivory towers.[219]

The result, after much debate and revision, was the formula which appears in the Education Reform Act 1988 s.202 (1). This sets out the duty to ensure 'that academic staff have freedom within the law to question and test received wisdom, and to put forward new ideas and controversial or unpopular opinions, without placing themselves in jeopardy of losing their jobs or privileges at their institutions'.

The Act also provided that Commissioners should be set up to ensure that the provisions of a new 'Model Statute' were embodied – with minor variations – in each university's statutes, so that there would be 'protections' for academic staff threatened with dismissal to ensure that a fair procedure would be followed. The public law specialist David Williams, and a Cambridge Vice-Chancellor (1989–96), was chosen as one of the Commissioners.

The legislation began to throw into relief in Cambridge the awkward question (still unresolved) why some employees of Cambridge should have the vote and constitute together the supreme authority in the University – the Regent House – while others, sometimes doing much the same work, should remain among the foot-soldiery or peasantry, and lack that right as mere 'assistant staff'.

The removal of academic tenure coincided with the introduction of appraisal for academic staff, as a Government-imposed condition of an increase in academic salaries. The very suggestion that appraisal should be introduced as a requirement for academic staff led to the calling of a ballot (then still a matter of live personal voting, not a postal ballot). One of the flysheets signed by concerned voters points out that 'the proposed scheme will operate in the circumstances created by the Education Reform Act 1988, which makes it possible for Departments to be closed and staff made redundant at a few months' notice'.[220]

So only a few generations after the creation of an academic profession, with lifelong 'academics' in fair numbers, the job security of Cambridge academics began to be threatened.

*   *   *

A business-facing Cambridge?

An efficiency drive

From this point in the story Cambridge began to change in ways more radical even than the social mutations which made the student experience of the post-war period so different from that of earlier generations. It was going to explore its way into a new relationship with the rest of the world, particularly the commercial and industrial world.

The 'Jarratt Report' (*Report of the Steering Committee for Efficiency Studies in Universities*) of March 1985 was the next national review to signal change for Cambridge.[221] In fact it said that all was well in the case of Cambridge. This response met with a critical reception from the University Grants Committee, which claimed that, on the contrary, 'Cambridge stood in need of a fundamental review', and that 'Cambridge has not yet adequately faced these issues'.[222]

Cambridge decided it had better be seen to do so. The Wass Syndicate was established in response to a Memorial dated 5 November 1987, containing proposals for changes to Cambridge's governance to make it more 'efficient'. This was no Cornford-style Syndicate; it had nothing of the *Microcosmographia* about it. It was to be chaired by Sir Douglass Wass, who had been joint head of the Civil Service from 1981. The *Report of the Syndicate appointed to consider the Government of the University*, which appeared in the *Reporter* (1988–9, pp.613–46) said that 'the University of Cambridge must conduct its business efficiently, and it must be prompt and decisive in its dealings with outside bodies'.

To that end it proposed removing some of the direct powers of the Regent House and giving them to a reconstituted Council of the Senate, now to be called just the 'Council'. The Regent House was still to be the legislative body (and was to be able, exceptionally, to initiate legislation), but the Council was to be the 'executive'. The addition of external ('lay') members to the Council, much in fashion on the 1990s and shortly to be imposed everywhere except at Oxford and Cambridge, was not much favoured by Wass himself:

> Sir Douglas Wass expressed the view that a small minority of members from outside the University would not be able to exert much influence on Council decisions, and that lay opinion would be more effectively deployed in an advisory capacity on the proposed Consultative Committee.[223]

The Consultative Committee[224] was to consist of the Vice-Chancellor and two members of the Council with six externals defined as 'not members of the Regent House'.

Subsidiarity was to be encouraged. 'To devolve power from the Regent House to the central bodies will be a partial remedy [for over-centralization] but we also recommend further devolution from the centre to subordinate bodies'. Subtle but significant shifts of power would follow. To balance these, new mechanisms of democratic accountability were proposed.[225] The *Reporter* (21 June 1989, pp.778–80) records an unusual event, an opportunity for everyone, including assistant staff, to consider a proposal to set up a Board of Scrutiny. Sir Douglas Wass was present in person as Chairman of the Syndicate. He explained that the Syndicate conceived of the Board of Scrutiny 'rather as a body which would raise questions on behalf of the Regent House and would direct the attention of the Regent House to issues requiring attention, acting to some extent like a parliamentary select committee'.[226]

This was to have the right to scrutinize all documents of every committee, and a duty to Report to the University once a year so that its observations and recommendations could be Discussed and action taken as appropriate. It was to be elected by the Regent House and include the Proctors. Its success may be measured by the attempts to diminish its powers which were heard on the Council a year or two into its existence.

The Vice-Chancellor as Chief Executive?

It was also suggested by the Wass Syndicate that the role of the Cambridge Vice-Chancellor should be rethought; that the rotating headship of the University by heads of colleges was no longer satisfactory; that 'the University needed a full-time head'.[227] This proposal was to be implemented by appointing a 'full-time' Vice-Chancellor for a term of up to seven years, and requiring that he should not simultaneously be the head of a college (which meant providing him with a house and facilities for entertaining, both of which had previously been given by a Vice-Chancellor's College). This would mean changing the practice of centuries of allowing the office to rotate gently and usually uncontentiously round the Heads of House.

The first of the full-time Vice-Chancellors, from 1989 to 1996, was David Williams. He had been Vice-Chancellor while he was President of Wolfson College, and when the full-time Vice-Chancellorship was introduced it was felt (despite the reservations of some that this scarcely promised a new beginning for the Vice-Chancellorship), to be a sound practical move to allow him to continue to complete a seven-year stint. He was known to be a 'safe pair of hands' and likely to ensure a smooth transition.

Cambridge means business

David Williams' successor, Alec Broers (1996–2003), had also been a Head of House, in his case, Churchill College, but he became Vice-Chancellor without a preliminary running-in period and with little knowledge of the University's history or constitution. An engineer by profession, he spoke the language of technology transfer. On the day he became Vice-Chancellor he made a 'launch speech' to industry. Much energetic activity followed, designed to drive Cambridge towards an engagement with industry and the transformation of its culture to make it more entrepreneurial, and able to produce graduates with the same mindset. This was, to a degree he did not perhaps realise, a continuation of a policy-strand which went back well into the nineteenth century, but now transformed by the arrival of information technology.

His approach raised unprecedented questions for Cambridge. Broers held a non-executive directorship of Vodafone while he was Vice-Chancellor. The Vodafone link opened the way to a scheme under which students would be given free Vodafones in the hope that they might come up with useful research ideas; for a brief period Vodafone operatives stood in King's Parade handing out leaflets which said, 'Great offers for new students', and Colleges offered free Vodafones with their Visa cards.[228] Boers went to China in mid-October at its President's invitation, just as the news had broken on 5 October that Vodafone was moving into China. Meanwhile, the Committee on Standards in Public Life had produced its Second Report in 1996, in which it explored the application to the universities of the seven principles of good conduct in public life which it had set out in its First Report.

Speaking to Government

In February 1999, Broers gave evidence to the Select Committee on Science and Technology. He was surprisingly artless in what he said, setting out his personal 'agenda', seemingly unaware of potential problems of potential conflict of interest or of the limits on his actual power as Vice-Chancellor:

> The things which interest me centrally are more that our advanced research is brought into collaboration with the world's leaders. My attention is spent on making sure that we are working with BP and Unilever and with Microsoft and others. That is my interest: the scientific, the realisation of innovative scientific work (Q.1131).[229]

He was keen on informal networking and trusting of big business in his willingness to work with it. 'We have found several Americans whom I had met and others who are very keen that we realise more of our potential than they see us realising' (Q.1120):[230] 'There is a small team of us. I work with Herman Hauser a lot and David Cleevely but I do not know about their game really. I have always been in big organisations so I am not good at that sort of stuff' (Q. 1139).[231]

He did not feel it essential to be on top of the 'detail', again trusting others to attend to that

> [w]e brought Alistair Morton on board...He offered his services to us and I was on the board of a company with him. He...reported back to us this afternoon on his perception of the way we handle these things. I recognise we are weak

there and not strong, but I am not the expert on the details of how we do that (Q.1131).

He had a strong bias in favour of 'big players' and big business:

Having been in the semi-conductor business I just know that somebody on their own in a room overlooking the Cam with a bright idea and a bit of equipment is going to get nowhere...I have that feeling very strongly and the best start-up companies also come out of large companies and not out of universities if the truth be known...Yes, we need these big companies. The thing I am dedicated towards is making sure that in Cambridge, when we do research in these technologies, we are at the frontier and we are not kidding ourselves that we are at the frontier....Unless you have these big players to talk to and you interact with them and you swop with them, you do not know where the frontier is (Q.1132).[232]

Such individuals overlooking the Cam and thinking their own thoughts independently of commercial funders' wishes and outside the constraints of the 'team project' had been among the great names of Cambridge in earlier centuries. Broers brushed this kind of activity to one side without apparently taking serious thought about the place of 'blue skies' research in the future trajectory of Cambridge intellectual endeavour. The impressive list of Cambridge's 83 associated Nobel Prize-winners, were not obviously the product of the 'technology transfer' mentality and it was unclear how Broers envisaged ensuring the future support of pioneering but non-commercial work.[233]

The Select Committee questioning pressed a point that was going to become immensely important a few years later. What was done about intellectual property rights in Cambridge when an academic made a discovery leading to technology transfer, they asked? Broers explained that

[a]t present it is up to the academic. They are under no obligation...I am sure many of you realise that universities are very democratic places and Cambridge more so than almost any university. The conclusions that Alistair Morton might come to have to be chewed on by our Regent House which comprises our 3,600 academics. So anything I say about Alistair Morton's ideas is very preliminary. His feeling is that we should expand our industrial liaison unit, that we should make it normal that academics are required to share on a third/a third/a third basis, but that is far from a decision of

the university at this stage. Those are his feelings. If he were here I think he would say he was amazingly impressed at the great innovations and creativity he finds in the university. This is a difficult question because you do not know quite what the secret of this is and to put on the controls that many universities put upon intellectual property rights might destroy something (Q.1131).[234]

CMI Ltd.

A new dimension of the Vice-Chancellor's role was speaking to Government. It was rumoured that Broers had a hotline to Gordon Brown at the Treasury and that breakfast calls were not uncommon, for he was usually in his office in the Dome Room in the Old Schools by 7.30. A grand scheme was mooted to create a joint venture with the Massachusetts Institute of Technology, to which Brown eventually gave £68 million of public money. The Cambridge Council was told little or nothing of the approaches to 'big leading players' in connection with this scheme, before a list appeared in the *Sunday Times* including Sir John Browne of BP Amoco, 'which has established a new research institute at Cambridge'; 'Chris Gent of Vodafone Airtouch; Lord Simpson of Marconi; and Martin Sorrell of WPP'.[235]

The Chancellor of the Exchequer held a press conference to launch CMI, and the announcement was made early in November in the *Reporter*[236] that 'the Government is willing to commit up to £68m to CMI over five years against contracts for specific programmes of activity. The private sector in the UK will contribute a further £16m'. There was a small but decisive spat when it was realized that Gordon Brown envisaged that Government control would run to agreeing the funding of particular projects. That idea was dropped.

Moreover, it was not to be all gain. The Office of Science and Technology (OST) in the Department of Trade and Industry (DTI), withdrew nearly £3 million of funding allocated under the Science Enterprise Challenge Scheme to the Cambridge Entrepreneurship Centre (CEC), on the supposition that this would be more than replaced by this gigantic grant for CMI.

There were promises to the University (never fulfilled), of detailed proposals to come and reports to the University on progress.[237] A website was set up for the worried to consult for information, but it proved faulty and hard to access. At an open meeting held in the Babbage Lecture Theatre on 22 February, local businessmen came and asked what was in it for them, but there was little detailed information to be had. The claims, though hot on 'presentation' were of the most general, involving tags such as 'focussed on productivity and competitiveness' and 'emerging fields ... of benefit to the UK economy'. Broers spoke of 'those who go around in their little green suits' in response to a question about the 'massive resentment this has caused around the country'.

At the Discussion of the plan in the Senate which finally took place in March 2000,[238] the Master of Emmanuel College, Professor J.E. Ffowcs Williams, expressed concerns about 'the almost total absence of anything substantial in the information so far released to the University' which 'is raising doubts about the wisdom of the proposal'. In any case,

> [t]here are, of course, great cultural differences between MIT and Cambridge...Here we pay people very low salaries but provide greater freedom to own the intellectual products of academic work. In this Cambridge we value the fact that our University does not pry into our private professional affairs and I think that attitude has been extremely important in the stimulation of the Cambridge phenomenon and the emergent Silicon Fen. Academic freedom is probably more important here and, as long as it is, it must be protected.[239]

It proved impossible to set up CMI as a charity as had originally been intended, and it became CMI Ltd, 'a company limited by guarantee with the status of an exempt educational charity', owned jointly by Cambridge and MIT. There began to be murmurs about the lack of evidence that anything much was happening. Surely if there were triumphs to announce they would have been heard about? In early summer of 2001, *The Times* carried a frustrated letter about the lack of progress and the culture gap, from Professor Vander Sande a Director of the project on behalf of MIT. That prompted an article in *The Times* asking uncomfortable questions. The *Cambridge Evening News* ran an interrogative piece in its pink business pages. There had been rumours that CMI Ltd. money was to go to a project to make virtual reality Shakespearean productions designed to show what they might have looked like in the eighteenth or nineteenth centuries.[240]

The University Press Office became so cross about all this that Professor Windle,[241] the new CMI Ltd. Cambridge Director, was persuaded to agree to speak. On 25 September, the *Cambridge Evening News* published his views. 'Cambridge, according to Professor Windle, has come right round to the view that making money is the goal.' He explains that 'It's no longer the be all and end all to be brilliant'. 'The big difference now is that Cambridge is coming round to applaud commercial success.' He identified among 'projects CMI is supporting' 'using a bug to make a new antibiotic, developing ultra-light metal, the ultimate in polymers'. But the money had not been given for research funding of this kind. 'BT is on side, and wants to get involved in social sciences in a bid to find out how much "over engineering" of consumer products people will tolerate.' It was perhaps open to question how far a University should use public money on research designed to mislead the public for commercial gain, if that was really the intention.

Concerns began to be expressed about what would happen once the five years came to an end. The CMI Ltd. débâcle has since gone very quiet. There is still a website[242] but it does not make it easy to retrieve this narrative. No analysis has ever been published of the achievements or the value for money of the project and the Regent House did not receive even a final Report.

The legacy of the first full-time Vice-Chancellor was, in this respect, a mixed one, but the trends he was riding were running strongly now as tides in the affairs of universities and Cambridge was not going to be able to step off the bandwagon. In the interests of facilitating the forming of relationships with industry (commercial funding of research, technology transfer, spin-outs) it was going to be necessary to change the style of academic activity from the old do-it-yourself approach to something much more regimented.

*　*　*

Intellectual Property Rights and academic freedoms

> Dear author-members of the Poldovian Academy of Literature, as so often in the past few years, the Praesidium of the Academy wishes to bring forward proposals which are simultaneously so minor that they are unworthy of your attention and so important that failure to pass them will lead to unspeakable catastrophe.[243]

The next change, and one directly affecting academics and students and their freedom to follow and discuss their ideas was the plan to control the intellectual property rights of Cambridge's academics:

> As a great Poldovian once said, 'A man who can order someone else to make two blades of grass grow where one grew before will deserve more of humanity than the whole tedious crowd of inventors and intellectuals'. It would be

contrary to the natural order of things to have rich authors and our proposals ensure that the natural order of things will not be disturbed. Suppose, for example, that a book earns 10,000 zorbals a year and the author pays our glorious Poldovian taxes at 40%. In the first year the author will get 5,400 zorbals, in the third year 4,200 zorbals, in the seventh 3,000 zorbals, and so on until in the eleventh year he will see 2,000 of an original 10,000 zorbals. We in the Praesidium feel passionately that an effective rate of tax of 80% reflects the gratitude that all comrades feel to Poldovia and to our Academy. We wish that we too could pay an effective rate of tax of 80% but, unfortunately, we in the Praesidium are not authors and this glorious opportunity must pass us by.

Professor T.W. Körner's memorable satire, which took the form of a speech in a Discussion, may be read in full in the *Reporter*. He went on:

We have not made these changes to increase the short-term revenues of the Academy. Indeed, the cost of expanding the Bureau of Contracts will ensure that there is no short-term gain. However, there is an expectation that in the long term we should get something. As the old Poldovian proverb puts it: 'Better ten zorbals in my pocket than a hundred in yours.'

The 'Bureau of Contracts' was the new Research Services Division, which had been set up in 2000 to take over from the old Research Grants and Contracts Section.

Only a few years earlier, Broers had offered the Select Committee a *laissez faire* personal view of the way Cambridge should handle intellectual property rights created by academics and students. He had correctly asserted that it had always been the convention that any financial rewards of academic research were retained by the Cambridge academic, the usually modest royalties of a book, for example, or the earnings from a patented invention. Copyright law gave the ownership to the employer, the University or the College, but that right had not been enforced.[245]

The Regent House woke up to the fact that something of value to its members as academics was under threat.[246] The proposed shift to an all-embracing seizing of rights put forward in July 2002,[247] led to two rousing afternoons of Discussion on successive Tuesdays with the 'Poldovia' speech delivered at the first. It was clear that there would be no straightforward passage through the Regent House for this proposal. The passions which had been roused did not relate to the financial loss to academic inventors (few sought to exploit their discoveries commercially and pocket all the profits), but from the perceived danger of a fettering of academic freedom.

Down with 'research policies'

Professor Ross Anderson, one of the leaders of the crusade to prevent the intellectual property rules going through, argued that the University's best plan was simply to

> hire the brightest people we can, and let them do whatever turns them on. We must ditch the foolish idea that research is a centrally planned, top-down activity conducted for organizational profit, and get back to curiosity-driven research that bubbles from the bottom up.[248]

Cambridge was now actively moving away from a policy of allowing academics to follow their noses in their choice of research topics to the creation of a 'research strategy'. That could mean that scientists would not be able to get the signatures of heads of department when they sought funding for research which did not comply with the 'strategy', and that researchers in the arts and humanities who did not need project funding to write books as lone researchers might find themselves at the back of the queue for promotion if they did not adapt their work to make it look like a 'team project' and bid for funding. Teaching materials also came into the picture, for these too technically constituted intellectual property.

Then there was the question of student research, mainly that of research students, but also of undergraduates. Student intellectual property did not automatically belong to the University as that of employees did under their employment contracts, but there were moves to require students to sign it away as a condition of admission. P.J. Brinded spoke in Discussion to express concern about that:

> Madam Deputy Vice-Chancellor, I am here today as a representative of Cambridge University Students' Union, and would like to raise some of the issues which are of concern to many students in this University...' Students should be warned of any possible confidentiality clauses with projects as early as possible; in no circumstances should this occur after a project has commenced. Participation in confidential research should not affect assessment of academic performance... A student's future career should not be limited because they choose to work in a confidential research area. The Research Services Division is already getting some students to sign

waivers to their IPR rights when working with patentable ideas involving University employees.[249]

The fear of a commercially driven interference with academics' work was neatly put in the Poldovia speech:

> The Bureau will not normally change current practice under which the author does the actual work of writing the book...However, the Bureau may sometimes take a more active part. The sales of a history of England under the first two Edwards could be much increased by giving it the title 'From Firm Sword to Red Hot Poker'. More intensive work (in which the author might not wish to be involved) could convert a book on 'Adolescent Angst in a Post-Capitalist Society' into a popular and money-spinning television family comedy.

But it had already gone beyond fiction. Dr. M.R. Clark claimed in Discussion that 'agreements were negotiated without the involvement of the inventors and they were approved and signed by the Director of the Research Services Division'. One term, he said, 'offered that if necessary I would be prepared to travel to the USA, yet this was arranged without myself having been a party to this agreement'.[250] The Research Services Division, he complained, also

> promised that for a period of three years from the date of the agreement RSD would offer my relevant publications for review 45 days in advance of any submission date, and that at the company's request I might either have to modify the publications or accept a possible delay of up to two months.

An undertaking was also given which would have had the effect of preventing a student thesis from being examined 'for a period of up to five years':

> It is obvious that these agreements are in direct conflict with academic freedoms and I would assert that they are unreasonable restrictions to place on University research, certainly when these restrictions are applied without the written and informed consent of the individuals that might be affected.[251]

The outcome of this contest between management and academe followed a pattern in Cambridge affairs already noted, the comparative ease with which an objective might be achieved by allowing time to pass and offering a second bite at the cherry, rather as happened over the decision to move the University Library out of its beautiful but confined space in the Old Schools and across the river to a new site and a brand new building. A revised set of intellectual property restrictions got through on a vote.[252]

The Research Services Division comes a cropper

The 'Bureau of Contracts' alias the Research Services Division underwent a Review in 2004 and it emerged that it had been making mistakes and not operating effectively.[253] The Review[254] recommended that Cambridge Enterprise be separated from the Research Services Division.[255] In a damning indictment of incompetence leading to loss of an important opportunity, the internal Technology Appeal tribunal found in May 2007 that 'Cambridge Enterprise' had acted in breach of Regulation 24 of the Intellectual Property Rights rules.[256] The *Times Higher Education Supplement* carried the story on 8 May 2007, relating the loss of a valuable research contract and serious reputational damage for the University. There was a substantial delay before this judgement was published, for this was an embarrassing indication that the new policy was not working in practice.

The Board of Scrutiny took the matter up. Its Thirteenth Report in 2008 pointed out that it had taken nearly a year to publish this finding and noted that:

> The Board has been assured by the current management of Cambridge Enterprise (who arrived in post following [this] débâcle) that they are fully aware of the events and have set up procedures to ensure no repetition occurs and that a successful Technology Transfer function continues taking the inventors' concerns fully into account.[257]

Heads had rolled and new appointments had been made but a number of the concerns expressed by the academic community were proving to have been well-founded.

* * *

The capsize of CAPSA

> I am a sundial, and I make a botch/Of what is done far better by a watch.[258]

In a world of increasing complexity, and with vast sums of money to administer, at the end of the 1990s, the University decided to introduce a new 'commitment accounting system'. This was given the name 'CAPSA' from the Latin for a box or container. Here Cambridge experienced a classic public sector major IT project overspend and delivery failure. It had among its staff all the world-class expertise needed to spot the technical problems and deal with them. Yet their warnings went unheeded.

A Discussion on a Topic of Concern was held in the Senate House on 10 October 2000. The Registrary stood up at the beginning to offer an apology. The hard-pressed staff who had suffered directly were to receive 'a one-off *ex-gratia* payment'.[259] The Discussants let fly. Professor J.R. Spencer spoke of 'the computer equivalent of a cataleptic trance'.[260] 'For blunders on this scale, the buck stops at the top.'[261] So huge was the furore that it was decided to set up a full-scale Inquiry, to be conducted with reference to implications for the way Cambridge was run by Michael Shattock, former Registrar of the University of Warwick.[262] Professor Finkelstein was to examine the way the technical failure had come about.

When the Inquiry reported at the beginning of November 2001[263] and another Discussion was held as the University's constitution required, the Vice-Chancellor presided at a Discussion with the press heavily represented in the Senate-House.[264] In its Seventh Report, the Board of Scrutiny had something important to say about the courage it took to wash the University's dirty linen so publicly: 'The primary task of the University is to seek and disseminate the truth, whether palatable or otherwise, and the work of the Press Office should reflect this spirit.'[265]

Managing the consequences

Shattock, an experienced higher education administrator who had been Registrar at the University of Warwick, was, as Broers had noted, of the view that part of the problem had been an inadequately staffed administrative service. There followed some skilful Old Schools sleight of hand intended to 'manage' the consequences. It was suggested that 'one of the difficulties, against which CAPSA had to be developed and implemented, was that the University's management and administration had not been resourced to keep pace with developments in higher education nationally'.[266] The inference drawn was that more administrators were needed.

But critics had seen the whole débâcle as flowing in part from quite the opposite cause, the reconstruction of the Unified Administrative Service and the importation of professional managers.[267] The administration fought stoutly back, claiming that this had been a governance failure (so governance reform was needed) and that insofar as it was an administrative failure, this was because the administration was under-resourced and more posts and higher salaries for administrators were urgently needed.

The trench-warfare which had been developing in the last half-century between academics and administrators as power in Cambridge shifted from one group to the other had reached a crisis point with the aftermath of CAPSA. The mistakes made in the CAPSA process were claimed to be 'largely a result of the systemic failure of the University to adapt to change'.[268] A report was made to the Higher Education Funding Council for England, and it was reassuringly stated that 'Council have no information which would support the view that either the Funding Council or the National Audit Office intends to institute their own enquiries'.[269] But that did not mean that there were not renewed concerns about possible state interference. Those who wanted to bring about a shift of power claimed that a governance failure was what has had caused CAPSA to go wrong,[270] and 'partnerships and stakeholders,' were 'entitled to expect a modern style of governance'.[271] There was a bid to alter the governance of the University and proposals were put forward for consultation.

* * *

So where are we now?

The Walrus and the Carpenter

Consultation leading up to the publication of the ensuing Report proposing radical changes to the University's historic constitution was by website and 'road shows', both devices new to Cambridge decision-making.[272] A fair objection squarely put to the proposals now before the Regent House was that 'it was not clear how the document's proposals would help to solve the problems it identified'.[273]

The subject of greatest derision were the 'road shows'. These were sessions held peripatetically round the University at which Gordon Johnson, President of Wolfson College and editor of Cornford's *Microcosmographia*, spoke for 45 minutes of the allotted hour advocating the proposals. Malcolm Grant, later Provost of University College, London, took questions for the remaining 15 minutes, a process mainly involving taking notes of the questions on a clipboard. Grant had a small moustache, and after email circulation of one of the original illustrations to Lewis Carroll's poem about the eating of the trusting little oysters, the pair became known as the Walrus and the Carpenter,[274] with the Regent House cast as the oysters:

> The Walrus and the Carpenter
> Were walking close at hand;
> They wept like anything to see
> Such quantities of sand:
> 'If this were only cleared away,'
> They said, 'it would be grand!' ...

> 'O Oysters, come and walk with us!'
> The Walrus did beseech.
> 'A pleasant walk, a pleasant talk, Along the briny beach:
> We cannot do with more than four,
> To give a hand to each.' ...

> 'The time has come,' the Walrus said,
> 'To talk of many things:
> Of shoes – and ships – and sealing-wax –
> Of cabbages – and kings –
> And why the sea is boiling hot –
> And whether pigs have wings.' ...

> 'A loaf of bread,' the Walrus said,
> 'Is what we chiefly need:
> Pepper and vinegar besides
> Are very good indeed –
> Now if you're ready, Oysters dear,
> We can begin to feed.'

> 'But not on us!' the Oysters cried,
> 'Turning a little blue.' ...

> 'O Oysters,' said the Carpenter,
> 'You've had a pleasant run!
> Shall we be trotting home again?'
> But answer came there none –
> And this was scarcely odd, because
> They'd eaten every one.[275]

'Do not ask the frogs before draining the pond'

A significant difference between the way the Wass Syndicate had presented its proposals and those of the new 'governance reformers' was that Wass wished its 'proposals to be seen as an integrated whole', whereas the new ones were offered for separate decisions by the Regent House.[276] In the *Reporter* of 26 June 2002, appeared a series of separate proposals, put forward for Discussion on two occasions, on 9 July and 8 October. Among them was the notion of 'changing the number of signatories required to call for a ballot or for a Discussion on a topic of concern to the University'.[277] This reflected some years of grumbling in the Old Schools that a few individuals could play havoc with proposals requiring the consent of the Regent House, by insisting that they were put to the vote. It was perhaps not realized how difficult it was to obtain the necessary signatures since all the signatories' names were published and even strong supporters of the call for a ballot were often fearful of the career consequences of allowing their names to appear among the dissenters. Körner had referred to this attempt to make it more difficult to trigger a democratic vote in his Poldovia speech: 'As the old proverb goes: "Do not ask the frogs before draining the pond." We consult you now but we remind you of another proverb of our Poldovian folk: "Ten dogs may bark for all I care" (or as we will soon say: "Fifty dogs may bark for all I care")'.[278]

This proposal was held over for entirely separate voting and partly succeeded, with required signature numbers rising to 25.

Letting sleeping dogs lie

Alison Richards succeeded Alec Broers as Vice-Chancellor in 2003 on the clear understanding that she was not going to be a Chief Executive Vice-Chancellor. Though she had a Cambridge degree, she had spent most of her career at Yale and was the first truly full-time Vice-Chancellor to have come from 'outside'. It was perhaps felt to be prudent to let sleeping dogs lie for a while as far as governance went. And although four external members had been allowed onto Cambridge's Council by 2008,[279] it still had its nineteen elected members including three students.

In December 2008, Cambridge seemed to have its face set against further governance change.[280]

The academics have, then, been holding their own against the tidal changes sweeping through the rest of the British – and global – world of higher education, but this part of the story has a distinct air of unfinished business.

Student experience today

Skies threatening to open?... Order one thousand umbrellas... A helter-skelter that won't fit through the gates?... Let down the tyres.

...The menu highlights included ostrich burgers, game sausages with mash, Indian Moghlai chicken fajitas and the traditional steak baguettes and hog roast. There was an overwhelming array of drinks, from champagne in reception to Phil Macartney's own concoction, Victoria's Secret Cocktail, served in an elegant silver fountain...A twenty-foot banner of Queen Victoria was complemented by a fairy-lit miniature of Crystal Palace, maps of the Colonial Empire and painstakingly hand-painted signs...a painted Ferris wheel hung from the tower and a sweet stall even boasted seaside rock imprinted with 'St John's May Ball 2006' (Report of the Ball of 2006).[281]

One might almost be back in the days of 'Porterhouse Blue'. But the students who attended that Ball had come to Cambridge from a wider range of backgrounds and with laptops and radically different ideas about life from the generations of the last decades of the twentieth century. Some of their comments were to be read on the Cambridge website at the beginning of the eighth centenary year. The woman President of the Student Union, 'I was so apprehensive about what I would find at such a historic university that I almost didn't apply; I'm eternally grateful that I didn't make that mistake'. Another woman student: 'there are people from all walks of life, and although people work hard, there's a positive and encouraging work ethos, and the opportunities that present themselves to me are endless.' A boy: 'I was concerned that there may be a divide between state and public school people but was very pleased to find that I couldn't even tell where most people came from and no one really cares – they're more interested in getting to know you.' Other students, including ethnic minority and disabled students, 'Visiting the Colleges I realised that the University was actually full of normal people from normal backgrounds just like me':

> If you are worried about fitting in, don't be – Cambridge is a very diverse place, with people from all kinds of different countries, religions and backgrounds. People accept you for what you are, it doesn't matter whether you're from a state school or public school or whether you are black or white. All that is required is that you are dedicated to your chosen subject.[282]

Cambridge has become highly sensitive to the danger that it will still be seen as exclusive or élitist and it has been working hard to ensure that it is fair to applicants from schools and families which have not sent it students before. The lives of Cambridge students have moved with the times as much as the priorities of the academic community. For the students this has meant that they can enjoy the intellectual richness and the beauty of the place in a thoroughly modern way.

And none can say that modern Cambridge has not made its contribution to the sum total of human amusement. Student dramatics at Cambridge were to reach a high point towards the end of the twentieth century when the Footlights produced a string of inventive comedians and satirists who transformed British comedy. Peter Cook had been President of the Footlights in 1960. He and his contemporaries John Cleese, Spike Milligan and the Python team were beginning to experiment with radically new forms, abandoning the set-piece jokes with punch lines and the comic's standard line of patter. One of the memorable results was the Revue 'Beyond the Fringe'.

Hugh Laurie, somewhat to his surprise, found himself President of the Footlights in 1981:

> I'd gone to Cambridge University to become an oarsman, but I met this woman called Alison in the student bar one night. I'd told a joke or something and she said 'you've got to come with me.' She took me to this club and said 'here are these people doing the Footlights; you've got to audition.' So I did and off it went.[283]

Stephen Fry had been an active student 'entertainments' officer' as and undergraduate at St. Catherine's College ('which largely involved booking myself'). Beginning his doctoral studies in the Cavendish Laboratory he was looking for something more challenging. He tried Shakespeare, but he found that people laughed when he played Iago. So he approached the Footlights:

> Initially it was a disappointment...the Footlights seemed to be at rather a low ebb. There was no bar in the Club Room as in days of yore, when Peter Cook would spend long evenings swilling mint juleps and conversing with an imaginary bee. In fact, there was no longer really a proper Club Room, just a dank, pine-clad hovel in the Union Society's bowels.[284]

They too took off to become national institutions of ironic and sophisticated 'Cambridge comedy'.

2 HOW IT ALL BEGAN

Europe invents universities

An academic, said Henry Sidgwick in 1871, is

> one whose study is the chief interest of his life; and who has that intense and intimate apprehension of its principles and method, that vital sympathy with its constitution and growth, which can only be attained after much independent thought and original research...truly academic teachers...alone can keep the machinery of teaching ever on a level with the advance of knowledge...they alone can properly inspire and regulate the ardent desire to know, and the eager impulse to discover, which ought to be the mainspring of the best work that is done here.
>
> Henry Sidgwick, writing on 'academic teachers' in the *Cambridge University Reporter,* 22 February 1871, pp.203–7

The students of the University of Cambridge did not all become scholars, or lifelong 'academics' (a term in use from the sixteenth century), or 'dons' (a word used from the seventeenth century). But those who did had to discover and define the nature of their work. We shall watch them 'finding their vocation' over the centuries. And it was a vocation, with much of the fire Sidgwick describes.

On the face of it is a puzzle how the educational experiments of these individuals over so many centuries and in such a range of cultures have succeeded in hanging together sufficiently to create, in the concept of a 'university', something which has survived for nearly a millennium. The first universities invented themselves. When they came into being of their own motion, they were recognized from the first to be something new but their persistence is amazing.

France was in the vanguard at the emergence of universities at the end of the twelfth century. It had had, in cathedral schools such as Chartres, Rheims and Laon, some of the most important centres to which outstanding self-appointed 'Masters' (*magistri*) had attracted significant numbers of students (*discipuli*) in the generations before the universities emerged. The cathedral schools had been established – and insisted upon – by the Emperor Charlemagne (747–814) to ensure that cathedral canons were properly educated. These formed a natural geographical focus when ambitious wandering masters of the eleventh and twelfth centuries came to look for fee-paying students. Modern scholars have debated whether there was ever a 'School of Chartres' linked to Chartres Cathedral in the twelfth century, and if there was, in what sense it was a 'school',[1] but in Paris the cathedral of Notre Dame provided a focus alongside the 'school' run by the Canons of St. Victor and the independent schools at St. Geneviève. In the University of Paris, France had one of the first real universities, neck and neck with Oxford in reputation. Yet Oxford became one of the first universities without benefit of an adjacent local cathedral, which it did not acquire until the sixteenth century.[2] Cambridge became a university soon after, relying on Ely fifteen miles away for episcopal 'supervision'.

At their beginning, when the clusterings of 'wandering scholars' were no more than encounters of masters and students, there were no syllabus requirements, no examinations, no graduations, no official 'licences' for teachers. Those came into existence when the lecturers organised themselves into *universitates* or 'guilds' and needed to create routes for admission of new members who would be Masters of a craft like the members of any other medieval guild. A *universitas* did not have to be a particular type of guild. It could be a corporation of Masters (as at Paris) or of students (as at Bologna). It was simply a body of people with a common purpose, acting as a corporate 'person'.

Then universities began to provide 'degree courses' leading up steps (*gradus*) in the arts from the 'bachelor's degree' (at the level of the 'journeyman') to the 'master's degree' (which granted full membership of the guild). The 'higher degree' subjects of theology, medicine and law quickly emerged, with theology the undisputed 'queen' of them all. These led to 'doctorates', with specialist provision at Salerno and Montpellier (medicine) and Bologna (law) and Paris and Oxford (theology). A student would normally not begin on one of these courses until he had completed the arts course, if he did so at all, and few did. Those who returned – and we shall meet some – might spend a few years first in parish ministry. The higher degrees required some years of further study. A doctor of theology would not graduate until middle age, in his mid-forties. These were not 'research' degrees in the modern sense. They were not really 'vocational' either.

Of the three, only law can really be said to have been a preparation for a professional career. The higher clergy were rarely doctors of theology in the Middle Ages. Medicine was actually 'practised' mainly by non-graduates such as the 'barber-surgeons'.

The picture is of a gradual spread of the idea of a university throughout medieval Western Europe, the multiplication of institutions, experimentation in the ways they should be governed, first brushes with a variety of local and European authorities who became anxious to control them. Why, then, did Oxford and Cambridge prove to be uniquely lasting examples of the self-governing academic community independent of the state, and how have they remained so? The answer lies in part in the historical circumstances in which they conducted their battles for independence.

* * *

How it all began in Cambridge

Why here?

> At Trompington, not far from Cantebrig
> There goes a brook, and over that a brig,
> Upon the whiche brook there stands a mill
> Chaucer, *The Reeve's Tale*

> Beside the pleasant Mill of Trompington
> I laughed with Chaucer in the hawthorn shade;
> Heard him, while birds were warbling, tell his tales
> Of amorous passion.
> Wordsworth, *Prelude*, Book III

On the face of it Cambridge was not an obvious choice of a place to create a world-class university which would last for more than eight centuries. It lay on the river Cam, with a hillock from which approaching enemies could be seen. It had a market. But innumerable places in England could say much the same.

Bede (673–735), England's first significant historian, speaks in his *Ecclesiastical History of Britain* of 'a little ruined city called Grantchester', where the monks of Ely had conveniently come upon a Roman stone sarcophagus, suitable to contain the bones of the holy Etheldreda.[3] Etheldreda (d. c.679) had been a princess, daughter of the King of East Anglia in the days when England was still made up of a series of separate kingdoms of Angles, Saxons and Jutes. She was married twice but insisted on keeping her virginity, and in the end, she was allowed to become a nun in a convent run by her aunt Ebbe. She herself then founded a 'double monastery' in 673, an arrangement favoured in the Anglo-Saxon world, in which twin communities of monks and nuns lived in juxtaposition. It was a device which allowed high-born women with intelligence and powers of leadership to establish surprisingly 'learned' communities of women. Etheldreda chose Ely. She restored an even older church on the site of what is now the cathedral and built the abbey church there.

Sixteen years after her death, her sister, who had succeeded her as abbess, gave orders that her bones should be exhumed and that she should be placed in a new coffin in the abbey church. Some of the monks were sent off to look for suitable stone to construct an appropriately dignified coffin. Bede explains that they went by boat, 'for the district of Ely is surrounded on all sides by waters and marshes and has no large stones'. Moving down the river they came to the hill on which was a 'small deserted fortress' (*civitacula*) where they found a beautiful while marble container ideal for their purpose and brought it back as a 'gift of God' for their needs. When the body was dug up, it was found to be uncorrupted. Devils were driven out from those who touched the cloths in which Etheldreda was wrapped and a number of healing miracles occurred. Bede seizes the opportunity to insert a hymn he happened to have written some years earlier in elegiac metre, celebrating virginity.

With such wonders occurring, the remains were therefore clearly to be regarded as those of a saint; they became a tourist attraction for pilgrims, and as a consequence, the abbey became wealthy and important. The great monastic church became a cathedral in 1109, at the centre of a new diocese cut from the huge diocese of Lincoln, which included what is now the diocese of Oxford until the sixteenth century.

But Ely is thirteen miles from Cambridge as the crow flies, and it was at Cambridge not Ely that the University began. Cambridge itself was by the twelfth century an established market town and also a place of some importance in military and administrative terms. It lay on the border between political areas in Anglo-Saxon times; then there was a short-lived Viking occupation about 875. The Danes seem to have stamped some lasting expectations on the area. Courts were held there and there seems to have been a settlement of the 'King's men' of Edward the Elder when the Danes were driven out in 921. An unusual practice is said to have established itself, of local country landholders also holding land within the town. That may have contributed to Cambridge's problems for centuries with filth in the streets as animals were driven in for the night for shelter. A mid-eleventh-century set of rules survives for the Guild of Cambridge Thanes, which seems to have behaved rather like a very early country club for the aristocracy of the surrounding area. This eleventh-century social structure (which had its influence until comparatively recent times) makes it difficult to classify Cambridge as either village or town, for some of the administrative arrangements were rural.

William the Conqueror (1066–87) understood the need to create physical bastions to ensure that his power throughout his English kingdom was obvious to the population. In 1086, the new Norman King, passing on his way from York, made diversions at Lincoln and Huntingdon, where he arranged for castles to be built, and then went on to Cambridge to examine the place and order that a castle should be built there. There was an excellent site on Castle Hill, where the Romans had once built an encampment.[4]

The castle on the hill and the market below provided the makings of a place of lasting importance.

Cambridge runs away from Oxford

Cambridge is probably an offshoot of the University of Oxford. Oxford was itself still a very young university at the time and the never very comfortable relationship between 'town' and 'gown' was already beginning to cause bad feeling there. One of the members of the University killed a townswoman with an arrow. This may have been an accidental consequence of student 'larking about' (the chronicler Roger of Wendover who tells the story speaks of its happening *casu,* by chance). The indignant townspeople took a few students and hanged them publicly outside the city walls to make sure the scholars did not think they could get away with that kind of thing.[5] Matthew Paris tells the story in his chronicle, too, saying that masters and students alike (the *universitas clericorum et scolarium*), left Oxford, giving the improbable number of 3,000.[6]

It had not been unusual in the twelfth century for groups of masters and students to move from one place to another. Masters (*magistri*) might change location to get away from competition with other teachers for fee-paying students. They were, to put it in modern terms, 'self-employed' and their freedom to pursue a teaching career did not yet depend on getting a 'degree' or a 'licence to teach'. But with the settling down of the academic enterprise in northern Europe into a 'guild' structure about 1200, a fixed location became important. When scholars ran away from Oxford in 1209 this was already no longer the old world of freely 'wandering scholars'. A new and more enduring form of *peregrinatio academica* was to emerge, but in a later 'academic world'.

In the mid-nineteenth century, the notion that 'degrees' *(gradus)* are 'steps' on a ladder was touched on by Oxford's Mark Pattison, who understood how long it would take to get as far as a doctorate in the Middle Ages: 'To pass through the whole of this course... whose successive steps were called degrees (gradus), required at least twenty years.'[7] From now on in the thirteenth century, 'degrees' (steps on a ladder or *gradus*) were going to be bestowed by the individual *universitates* and a personal 'licence to teach' *(licentia docendi)* cautiously granted by the Church to graduates of approved institutions. The *universitas* or guild wanted to establish a traditional guild pattern in which the students were apprentices, the Bachelors of Arts 'journeymen' and the Masters of Arts 'were' the Guild, just like the Masters of a Guild of Goldsmiths or Fishmongers. The ecclesiastical authorities granted professional 'licences to practise' because they were anxious to ensure that people were not led astray by individuals who set themselves up as teachers when they had no qualifications, and might turn out not only to be ill-informed, but dangerous demagogues at that. The twelfth century had seen a good few of those, and some of them had been 'academics'. In mid-twelfth century, France Peter Abelard (twice) and Gilbert of Poitiers had been put on trial by the Church for teaching heresy. Neither was under-educated, but they both had disturbing ideas and students liked the exciting things they said. Peter Abelard (1079–1142) deliberately went to hear Anselm of Laon lecture at the cathedral school at Laon in northern France, so that he could outdo him in a performance of his own and seize his students.[8]

One of the prompters of the escape from Oxford is likely to have been not only a natural indignation but the fear that the fragile privileges of the young university were going to be interfered with. The King himself was thought to have given permission for the hanging. Roger of Wendover says as much, and emphasizes that this was done 'in contempt of liberty of clergy (*in contemptum ecclesiasticae libertatis*)'. The defence of the integrity and autonomy of the scholarly 'community' against the attempted take-over by the external authorities, ecclesiastical and secular, is a running thread in the stories of Oxford and Cambridge. And this was a particularly difficult moment in the affairs of Church and State, for, as a result of a quarrel between the King and the Pope over who should be the next Archbishop of Canterbury, England was under an Interdict from 1208, and King John was under a personal ban of papal excommunication from 1209. These ecclesiastical sanctions had serious consequences because it was believed that God would punish the kingdom as well as its King if the Pope was not placated.

The choice of Cambridge as a place to flee to is puzzling, since usually in these early medieval academic centuries, 'wandering scholars', whatever their reason for moving, went to other places where there were already schools; for there they would find ready-made bodies of prospective students. There are hints that there may have been some schools in Cambridge during the twelfth century with pretensions beyond the elementary, though only a fragmentary picture exists of the system of schooling in England at that date. But Cambridge had no settled tradition of being a place to go for advanced or higher education at the time. These refugees were not going to find new students waiting for them. Nor is it certain that all those who ran away went to Cambridge; some seem to have gone to Reading and elsewhere. It seems likely that some of the refugees with surnames which are derived from local place-names such as Foxton and Stortford, originally came from the Cambridge area, which may explain their choice.[9] The early thirteenth-century charters of the Bishop of Ely include extra Masters (*magistri*) as witnesses and these may have been among the incomers.

The period of exile lasted for several years, until the King submitted to the Pope and the bans were lifted. His 'protection' of the townspeople of Oxford by taking their side against the scholar-clerics then became worthless, and in 1214 an ecclesiastical determination of the dispute transmitted by a papal 'legate' in the form of a Legatine Ordinance required the townspeople of Oxford to do penance and pay annual fines. The scholars returned, but not all of them. Some stayed in Cambridge and the University there began.

King John's successor, Henry III, seems to have been well disposed towards any institution which was likely to produce graduates with skills European monarchs were beginning to find they needed. This was the era in which rulers found it useful to have servants who could write a business letter and keep satisfactory records. Prospective members of the growing 'civil service' working for Church and State had to be trained not only in literacy but also in the formal art of administrative letter writing. Student demand for such 'skills' encouraged this trend because here were career openings for the ambitious, in Church as well as in the State, since all clerks were also potential clerics and ordination could easily be arranged. A senior civil servant could reasonably hope for a bishopric at the end of his career. The King encouraged scholars from Paris to come to England

93

in 1229 when the University of Paris had an upheaval of its own to meet this perceived need.

The King also had an interest in ensuring that if there was going to be a 'system' of higher education in his kingdom, it was properly organized from the point of view of state approval of the institution and a requirement of proper institutional record-keeping. He granted 'privileges' to both Oxford and Cambridge *universitates* in a writ of 1231, requiring students to register with a Master within two weeks, so that their names were on the Master's 'list' (*matricula*), on pain of arrest. He also appears to have been instrumental in ensuring that Oxford and Cambridge maintained a joint monopoly of university education in the kingdom, by suppressing a budding 'university' in Northampton in 1265.

The University of Cambridge prudently ensured that it also had 'papal privileges', which it sought and obtained from Gregory IX in 1233. These included the important 'clerical' privilege of being exempt from the jurisdiction of secular courts and helped to balance royal bids for control. The Masters became adept at playing one form of external interference off against another from a very early stage. Within two years, the University was beginning to draw up its own domestic legislation, with its first 'statutes' appearing about 1250. The University had to decide who were to be the University's 'officers', and details of lecture-times. There is nothing in the statutes about the syllabus.

This was much the same approach as is to be found in other universities in Europe. In 1255, the Masters in Arezzo promulgated *Ordinamenta* or ordinances designed to provide structure and order for their own academic community. These Arezzo *Ordinamenta* of 1255 included the provisions that the Masters are to elect their own head (in their case a Rector); to treat one another with respect, in the schools and outside them; not to steal one another's fee-paying students; to meet once a month or pay a fine unless the absentee has permission from the Rector not to attend. Standards are maintained by the rule that no one is to lecture in grammar, logic or medicine unless he has been examined and approved by a committee of all the masters as competent to teach his subject.[10]

This solid-seeming institution seems to have faded away, but a secession of Masters from Bologna's law school[11] revived it after the Interdict of 1338. It was recognized in a letter of the Emperor Charles IV, which sought to restored its lost powers, as a *studium generale* which had 'of old' (*ab antiquo*) had authority to teach the higher degree subject of law and to grant doctorates[12]; but it disappeared again and apparently did not reappear as an established working university, despite a grant of an Imperial Privilege in 1456.[13] These vicissitudes seem to indicate the importance of the active participation of the Masters in keeping a medieval institution in being.

It is known that the Dominicans and Franciscans regarded Cambridge as an appropriate place to have a house as early as 1226 (the Franciscans) and probably about that time or not long after in the case of the Dominicans too. They occupied their sites with an eye to staying long into the future. In the middle of Great Court of Trinity College stands a great fountain. It is fed (now with some assistance from an extra well) by a water pipe more than six centuries old. In 1325, the Franciscans laid themselves a water pipe which ran across land they had succeeded in acquiring from a total of 17 former owners, from a point off the Madingley Rd. to their house on the site of what is now Sidney Sussex College. This useful provision was taken over in 1538 by royal permission and Trinity College tapped the water. The continuation of the pipe to its old destination ceased.[14]

The arrival of these two mendicant Orders was a significant indicator of approval of Cambridge. They had both been founded as teaching orders of 'friars' (*fratres*) barely a generation before. Their members did not live like monks enclosed in their 'houses', leading lives of prayer, manual labour and study; they went out into the world to preach. In the case of the Franciscans the 'mission' of the Order was simply to preach the Gospel and in the case of the Dominicans, to preach against the heresies which were rampant in the south of France and the north of Spain.

These were dangerously persistent heresies which were liable to crop up elsewhere. The 'Albigensians', also known as Cathars or Bogomils, were 'dualists', who believed that the only explanation for the evil in the world was that there were two Gods not one, eternally at war. The 'Waldensians', an anti-establishment movement which would now be regarded as 'left wing', were not unorthodox about doctrine but they did not much like authority. They questioned the need for a priesthood and sacraments (particularly rich bishops who rode about on fine horses), and they called for the Bible to be translated into the vernacular so that lay people could read it for themselves. Orders of preachers need a good education and both Orders established *studia* in university towns. These Orders became powerful, even dominant, throughout the medieval university world. It would have been difficult to 'count' as a university without them. But their early appearance in both Oxford and Cambridge is noteworthy because England was far from being a hotbed of either heresy in the thirteenth century.

Friar-students had the advantage of the loan of 'house' books for their courses, somewhere to live which was not a dubious lodging house, and financial support; their sheer numbers meant that the wishes of the Orders about the sequence of study and the positioning of preliminary training in the 'Arts' had to be taken seriously and sometimes caused dispute with the ordinary Masters or lecturers. Medieval Cambridge probably had a few hundred members at any time, of whom a third or more were friars. Dominicans and Franciscans were also greedy for the prestigious Chairs in universities and had to be allocated an agreed number so as to prevent their seizing them all. Augustinian canons were also present in Cambridge before 1289 and the Gilbertines by 1291. These canons had an outward-looking, active role, too, but they were nothing like as forceful in their influence on the development of the University as the two great mendicant Orders.

In 1240, while all this was far from settled, another batch of refugees from Oxford arrived. Clarity about membership of the *universitas* began to be important to maintaining order. People claiming to be scholars who were nothing of the sort were a potential source of trouble. Unmatriculated 'students' could be disruptive. The principle that you had to register with a Regent Master was not necessarily observed with the care it should have been; the surviving *matricula* lists are not complete, so evidently the Masters were not very thorough in keeping their records.

For this reason, it is hard to be sure about numbers. There were probably twice as many in medieval Oxford as in Cambridge, but still only a few hundred.[15] And there seems to have been a significant medieval 'drop-out' rate. Many came to Cambridge for a while and left without completing their degrees. From 1452, Proctors' accounts for Cambridge show Graces (grants of permission by the University) allowing individuals to take their degrees; so at least the numbers of those who completed degrees are relatively clear from that period. But no complete evidence survives until 1575 about the numbers of those who actually graduated from Cambridge. There were fluctuations, and not until the growth in numbers in the sixteenth century was Cambridge able to match Oxford.

Plague in a famously dirty town

The arrival of the plague had a considerable effect in the little Cambridge community.[16] The disease landed in England in the summer of 1348, probably on a ship which came into a Channel port, and it spread rapidly. Cambridge was growing now in a bend in the river, and many of those in that area died, though probably the mortality was even greater near the Castle mound. A pit full of skeletons which had been hastily tumbled in was found when the Divinity School was being built opposite St. John's College in the nineteenth century.[17] In the statutes Elizabeth of Clare gave to Clare College in 1359 is a mention of the number of men seized by the 'fangs of pestilence', creating an urgent need to recruit more and to fund them and their work.

The important thing is that the numbers were, and remained throughout the Middle Ages, small enough for a form of democracy to be practical. In all the young 'universities' of Europe it needed to be clear how the University could 'act' as a body when it had a constantly changing community. Two forms of governance emerged. One was the type embraced by Bologna, where the students were graduate students and training to be lawyers. In this early form of 'graduate school', they were working towards higher degrees and their lecturers had higher degrees in law themselves and were 'doctors of law'. The students themselves took important decisions such as the hiring and firing of their teachers and chose their Rector. A vestige of this structure survives today in the ancient Scottish universities.

In the 'guild' universities such as Cambridge, it was early established that everyone should be able to meet to debate and vote when the *universitas* had to take a decision on matters of common concern. In Cambridge, the 'everyone' meant at first the Regent Masters. These were recent graduates who were fulfilling the teaching obligation which was a requirement if they were to be granted the University's degree. Normally this expectation involved three or four years of lecturing and a duty to maintain a list of one's registered students. It was not likely, however, that those who had completed this tour of duty but remained in the University would lightly relinquish a right to have a say in its affairs, and by the beginning of the fourteenth century, the Convocation or formal meeting of the members of the University included these 'non-Regents' too. These are early stirrings of a problem which kept recurring but became acute in the early twentieth century, when the whole body of resident teachers and graduate (by now known as the 'Senate') were still allowed to take important decisions even though they might not have been in Cambridge since they took their degrees and had little idea of its current affairs.

The Convocation was summoned by the Chancellor of the University. The Chancellor's was one of the ancient 'offices'. The holder was elected by the Regent Masters and their choice approved by the Bishop of Ely. It will be no surprise that this process of approval by the local bishop could at times be controversial. The Chancellor also presided (in person or through a delegate or Commissary) over the University's domestic 'court'. The court had to deal with internal disputes and also 'clerical' disputes concerning the individuals who had pastoral duties within the town. It was therefore recognized that the University had a jurisdiction which excluded that of the bishop of Ely, who would normally have dealt with 'clerical' cases. More pressing, certainly more noisy, were 'town and gown' disputes, and from the beginning of the thirteenth century, the University's courts dealt with those too.

These could involve an English equivalent of the fights among the *nationes* at Paris, but whereas in Paris there were four 'nations', in England there were only two, the Northerners and the Southerners. Northerners (those who came from the middle-to-northern parts of England loosely defined) were dominant at both universities. Very few recorded foreigners studied in either Oxford or Cambridge in the Middle Ages, and probably most of those were friars. The mid-thirteenth century saw serious trouble of this kind at both universities. There was a major town-gown fight in 1249. This is reported by Matthew Paris who says it took place during Lent and the *discordia* was so great it came to the ears of the King – as it may well have done if he is right in saying that there were lootings and damage to buildings and woundings and even murders (*spoliationes, domorum confractiones, vulnera, homicidia*).[18] Another major disturbance a decade later, a 'Northerners and Southerners' fight which the townsmen joined in, burning and looting, apparently led to some removals back to Oxford. It was this occasion which led to the migration to Northampton and the ruling that there must be no more break-away universities. In 1260 the indignant 'northerners' removed themselves to Northampton and proposed to set up the rival university which was speedily suppressed there.

From 1265, both Oxford and Cambridge made 'inceptors' (those beginning their teaching career on graduation) take an oath not to teach anywhere but Oxford and Cambridge and not to recognize anyone claiming to be a Master who did so. This was a move strongly reflecting the continuing 'guild' character of the *universitas,* for guilds were normally 'closed shops' in this way. Oxford and Cambridge were to retain their dual monopoly for a very long time, however, far beyond the period when it was first insisted on.

Serious attempts to get the situation under control and ensure the maintenance of good order led to the formation of a pact between town and university in 1270, at royal instigation. This contained requirements that there should not be any warlike games such as tournaments within five miles of Cambridge, and that university lodging-keepers should take an oath not to receive any known disturbers of the peace into their houses.[19] It is not difficult to see why the University's Statutes have so regularly been preoccupied with the maintenance of 'order'

The other early 'officers' of the university were the Proctors and the Bedells (who had a mainly ceremonial function). There was not yet a 'professional administration', not even a Registrar until the sixteenth century. The scholars kept their affairs strictly in their own hands and had no hired help of that sort. Two *procuratores* were chosen by vote of the Masters to hold office for a year at a time. These were at first called '*rectores*' but became the *procuratores* ('Proctors'), because they 'took care' of the university's business on behalf of the Masters, including representing it in litigation if that became necessary. In 1275, the University created a statute to give the proctors power to enforce keeping of peace, by suspending those who broke the statutes from their offices; and fixing times for lectures and disputations and other acts of the University so that there need be no argument about them. Provision was even made for the Regent Masters to assemble to deal with a problem themselves if the Chancellor was slow to do his duty.[20]

Proctors carried out a number of duties which were practical necessities for the peaceful transaction of the University's business, such as fixing rents for students' lodgings and dealing with disputes; they draw up timetables for lectures and events occurring through the University year. It is possible that the two proctors were normally expected to be from different 'Nations'. Under the proctors served the 'bedells', a University police force, who rang bells for lectures, ensured good order in lecture rooms, collected the students' tuition fees; they were not themselves academics but secular servants of the University.

The first Cambridge Vice-Chancellor is found in 1412. He was Thomas Ashwell, a friar and he was appointed while Richard Billingford was Chancellor. Billingford held the Chancellorship for two periods, from 1400 to 1402 and again from 1409 to 1413. From that point on, the University found it needed a resident Vice-Chancellor, while the Chancellor became a more distant figure, a kind of backstop. We shall see Chancellors and Vice-Chancellors in correspondence from time to time in what follows. One occasion of setting up this arrangement may have been the Visitation by Arundel, Archbishop of Canterbury, who came himself to ask whether the statutes were being properly observed, whether founders' wills were being respected in the colleges, whether there were any known criminals among the scholars. He had been taking a strong view of the need for Oxford to behave itself in the aftermath of the Wyclif affair, which had led to a confrontation in 1397 over his right to do so. The Cambridge Regents were surprisingly respectful, and held a meeting to offer him their canonical obedience.[21]

The Cambridge Registrary was an invention of 1506, at the end of the Middle Ages. He was entrusted with keeping the University's records and given custody of the University Chest. The Chest provided a storage place for the University's money and also for its books, which could be used as securities against loans. Cambridge still has its 600-year-old Chest, with its 17 locks. The first one was burnt in 1381 during the period of the Peasants' Revolt when there was trouble in Cambridge going beyond the normal town-gown dispute. A gang was formed to go and 'destroy the house of William Wigmore Bedell of the University' and to kill him if they encountered him in person. They looted his possessions and then raided Corpus Christi College 'and took away or destroyed all the books, charters, writings, and effects belonging to that society'. They especially disliked Corpus because it was unpopular as a landlord. The next day they 'compelled the University to execute deeds under their common seal and the seal of every college, renouncing all their privileges'. If this had held it would have given the town the upper hand thenceforth, but this local 'peasants' revolt' was soon and comprehensively crushed and the *status quo* restored, except for the possessions which had been burned.[22]

The other obvious feature of an institution which was here to stay was the building of University buildings. But it was not until the late fourteenth to the fifteenth century that the University began to build for itself in earnest. Great St. Mary's Church had been used for meetings of the Congregation of the Masters (as had St. Mary's Church in Oxford) and for teaching purposes, rooms that could be used as 'schools' had been rented nearby. In the mid-fourteenth-century plans were put in hand to build a more permanent structure, using bequests from Roger Thorp, the Royal Chancellor, and his brother William.

The building – which included a chapel – was ready for use by the end of the century. There were two storeys, a divinity school below and a chapel and meeting room for the Regents above (now the University Combination Room). In the course of the next century, what is now the Old Schools quadrangle was completed with the aid of further benefactions, with teaching space for law and several library areas and a court room.[23]

Cambridge University Library[24] began its physical existence in the fifteenth century as a building and not a mere 'University Chest' which contained some books along with documents and money, which was the form it first took. Now there was to be a 'common library' and the gradual erection of the Old Schools, purpose-built buildings for lectures and library use. The Library had the use of the top storey of part of the buildings. Two wills of 1416 mark a starting point. William Loring and William Hunden both left books which they wished to remain for ever in the University's library for the use of its scholars. Other benefactors joined them. The first register of the University's books includes only 122 volumes, mostly on theology and law, subjects studied by graduate students for higher degrees. An increase of about a hundred books is recorded during the fifteenth century as a result of a single bequest from Walter Crome, a Fellow of Gonville Hall (later Gonville and Caius College), who gave 93 volumes to the University and 7 to his college in his will in 1453. As at Oxford, it was found necessary to keep the Library for the use of graduates since undergraduates proved they could not be trusted. If graduates who no longer lived in Cambridge wanted to use the books they had to arrive in academic dress.

* * *

Student life: the beginning of colleges

In many cases, colleges in European universities remained little more than boarding houses, but the better ones had rules and even bursaries. Italy's early 'colleges' had a history with breaks and discontinuities. Bologna set a fashion here, apparently as a consequence of arrangements made when a Bolognese became Bishop of Avignon and left funds in his will to create a college for eight students from Avignon to study at Bologna. The founder of the college for Brescian students (the Bresciano) had studied and taught at Paris and Padua as well as Bologna and he too therefore had French experience. His will of 1326 set up a college where up to fifty students could study arts, medicine or canon law, to be chosen by the Archdeacon of Bologna, who was to give preference to students from Brescia.

Not all the 'places' were funded to begin with, and anyone who chose to fund one acquired the right to allocate it (*ius presentandi*) thereafter.[25] Pancio of Lucca, who had been a royal physician in England, died in

1340, leaving provision for the foundation of a college for 12 students at Bologna. The plan was never carried through, possibly because some of the money was owed to Pancio by Edward III and perhaps never made available.[26] Other Bolognese colleges were founded in the 1360s, with mixed success. Outstanding was the Spanish College. These colleges constituted a useful test in microcosm of the merits and demerits of various structures of institutional governance which universities were also forced to consider.

In Cambridge, the earliest domestic arrangement was that students lived in lodgings, unless they were members of religious Orders and could therefore reside in a 'house' provided by the Order for the purpose. The lodgings were a perpetual source of trouble, for here town (landlords) and gown (students) had endless opportunities to quarrel. Here began many of the disputes which took the time of the University courts. There also existed more structured 'halls' in which undergraduate students lived under some sort of control.

The religious houses which provided controlled residences for their own monks who were students constituted an altogether safer arrangement than going into lodgings in the town. For example, Magdalene College was originally a 'monks' hostel' for Benedictines from Crowland Abbey near Peterborough, set up with permission from Henry VI, by Letters Patent of 1428. Other Benedictine houses (Ely, Ramsey and Walden) built staircases within the complex with rooms for their own monks opening off each. Such flourishing creations could attract patronage from members of the aristocracy anxious to do charitable acts for the benefit of their souls and (as now) to make a reputation for charitable generosity by attaching their names to their benefactions. Henry Stafford, Duke of Buckingham, made such an arrangement at Magdalene and the title 'Buckingham College' came into use for a time in the 1470s or early 1480s, before its benefactor was executed for treason in 1483.

Proper 'order' was going to emerge only with the invention of real 'colleges' (*collegia*),[27] where a corporate identity and a strong sense of membership could develop. These were communities more than places to live. From the fourteenth century colleges began to be endowed, but it was a slow process. Clare has its origins in the patronage of Elizabeth of Clare in 1336. Corpus Christi was founded in 1352, but it was almost a century before there was to be another, initially called Godshouse, which went through many vicissitudes of changed location and purpose and aborted starts before it settled on a long-term site and became the community which was renamed Christ's College in the sixteenth century.

Queens' College probably began with Henry VI's short-lived foundation of what was known as St. Bernard's College, in 1446, and for only a president and four Fellows. The chosen site was moved at the request of the society, and the King refounded the college in 1447. The Queen then petitioned her husband to be allowed to name it and it became the Queen's College of St. Margaret and St. Bernard.[28] The College was refounded in 1465 by another Queen, Elizabeth the wife of Edward IV (hence the positioning of its inverted comma after the 's'). Until well into the Tudor period, some of the colleges remained unstable creations, liable to change their names, to merge, sometimes to disappear altogether. Nevertheless, these first real 'colleges' were autonomous and more or less financially independent and some of them quickly became wealthy with endowments.

Yet even the most flourishing of these medieval colleges were often very small, with a mere handful of Fellows even in the fifteenth century. In 1473 St. Catharine's College (first called Catharine Hall) was founded for a Master and three Fellows. At first the 'colleges' were for graduate students who were slightly older and working for 'higher' degrees. Such colleges were composed of their Fellows, for whom they provided accommodation and a community. Additional rooms might provide rentable lodgings for pensioner students (those with bursaries), and it was partly by that route that the undergraduates began to have a recognized place in colleges. Students who were not monks came to live in these safer and more stable residences, renting rooms. Where such a house developed into a 'college' – as Magdalene did – these came to be known as 'commoners' (because they shared the 'commons' or meals of the college). They were not members.

Gradually, as they overlapped with 'approved' student lodgings, these residences-cum-communities began ultimately to provide some teaching, especially of a preparatory kind. They could sometimes provide for poor students, the 'scholars' who were also 'on the foundation', in the category defined by the 'founder'. Colleges were able to ensure that students – who were often only in their early teens – were subject to some discipline and could not live all over the town as they chose, disrupting the lives of the townsfolk. This admission of undergraduates to the 'colleges' from the fifteenth century began their transformation to their modern form. Today Oxford and Cambridge colleges remain autonomous charitable corporations but the universities allow them to admit students as well as to house them and to teach them, while the universities set the curriculum, offer 'courses' and grant the degrees.[29]

For junior members of colleges and the residents in 'lay' rooms, financing themselves could be a problem. The later Middle Ages saw a Cambridge intake of yeomanry and lesser gentry seeking careers as *notarii* – notaries, secretaries, civil servants – coming from families of stewards, bailiffs, scribes. Thomas Cranmer and Hugh Latimer, whom we shall meet among the early sixteenth-century students at Cambridge, said none of their fellow-students were 'gentlemen born'.[30]

Colleges, as they became established, could be pleasant places, with grounds which provided for recreation. King's College had a court for ball games by the end of the fifteenth century (it called it a *sphaeristerium*). In the Renaissance the gardens became places for neo-classical strolling and intellectual conversation, but there were also bowling alleys and orchards. The nineteenth century favoured croquet and tennis.[31]

Henry VI founded his school Eton College in 1440, and King's College began in 1441, named St. Nicholas College, as a compliment to King Henry VI, whose birthday was the saint's day. As the 'college' evolved to resemble the modern College with its undergraduates and Fellows, a 'senior' and 'junior' division of privileges began to seem appropriate. The arrangements for student discipline could be elaborate. In 1443 in King's College, students were not allowed to linger in the hall after meals when 'the seniors ... have had their drink'. 'At the hour of curfew, they shall go to their studies or other places, and the juniors shall not be permitted to make any delay'. Sometimes when there was a saint's day a fire would be lit for the Fellows in the hall and everyone could stay for restrained enjoyment, 'for recreation by singing and other honourable pastimes, and to enjoy soberly poetry, chronicles of kings, the wonders of the world, and other things suitable for the clerical estate'.[32]

The students had to dress and behave in a manner appropriate to apprentice clerics not young noblemen.

> All fellows and scholars are forbidden to wear red and green shoes, or secular ornaments or fancy hoods, either inside or outside the university ... or any weapons, offensive or defensive, or girdles and belts adorned with gold and silver ... either publicly or secretly, unless they are given special permission by the provost etc.

They are 'forbidden to let their hair grow' or to keep 'dogs, birds hawks etc.'[33] This was not an era of 'fair admissions'. The royal founder's plan for King's was that the school at Eton should send scholars to the College. Each member of the College would be expected to take an oath not to follow the teachings of John Wyclif, who was causing mayhem in Oxford at the time. It was feared that the ideas current there, leading to Lollardy, a heresy giving an uncomfortable sense of empowerment to a newly literate bourgeoisie, might infect Cambridge too.

Plague-town

King's attracted benefactions from the Lancastrian side in the Wars of the Roses, and by the mid-fifteenth century it was extremely rich, a wealth reflected in the design of its great chapel. The plague was lurking in Cambridge again and the King decided on reflection not to risk himself by actually coming to lay the foundation stone but to send his cousin to take the risk instead. This was not an excessively dainty reaction. Henry III had drawn particular attention to the filthiness of Cambridge in his charter of 1267. The citizens were instructed to clean it up and ensure that the watercourses were kept open and unblocked so that the foul-smelling rubbish and effluvia could run away. Cambridge was probably no worse than any other small town, though the proximity of the river must have made the usual piles of rubbish peculiarly rotten and malodorous, and animals were still brought in at night from the surrounding fields to add to the dung and the stink. It was bad enough in 1351 for the Chancellor and scholars to send the then king a petition asking that the townsmen might be forced to clean up their streets. The King, preparing for a visit in 1388, sent instructions that the pigs and the filth were to be cleared from the streets before his arrival.

An Act was passed in 1388 including at item XIII what was afterwards known as the 'Statute of Cambridge'. It says that 'so much dung and filth of the garbage and intrails...be cast and put in ditches, rivers, and other waters...that the air there is greatly corrupt and infect, and many maladies and other intolerable diseases do daily happen',[34] but the statute seems to have been loosely observed, and carcasses of dead beasts and general filth continued to litter the streets. As the fastidious King Henry VI now wrote to the Abbot of Bury St. Edmunds when he decided not to come to lay the foundation-stone:

> we had disposed us to be there in our own person. Nevertheless, for the aier and ye Pestilence that hath long regned in our said Universitie, we come not there at this time, but send Thiddre our Cousin the Marquess of Suffolk.

His boycott had no effect on the townspeople's dirty habits and an annual proclamation about keeping things under control was read in the town in the mid-fifteenth century.[35]

Henry VI was overthrown in 1460 by Edward IV, and his College shrank in wealth and numbers, leaving its chapel unfinished and its ambitious building plans on hold. The dirt in the streets continued, with 266 townspeople and some senior scholars and college officials (including the President of Michaelhouse, the Master of Buckingham College and the keeper of Trinity Hall) being brought before the town Leet or court in 1502 for offences under the 1388 Act.[36] There was a slow improvement in the later sixteenth century.

Some generous alumni

Benefactions from 'alumni' were already being encouraged. Those who fell in love with Cambridge could be generous and active benefactors to the University and its colleges. John Alcock (1430–1500) was a Cambridge student who became a Doctor of Civil Law in 1459 and eventually Bishop of Ely and therefore automatically Visitor of Cambridge University. He went there often and he seems to have retained an interest in spiritual writings alongside his legal career. He is the author of the highly successful spiritual guide the *Mons perfectionis* ('The hill of perfection'). In February 1488 he preached a sermon in the University Church of Great St Mary's, which lasted more than two hours. In the early 1490s he was to be found residing at Peterhouse for lengthy periods, taking advantage of benefits he felt he was owed in return for his generosity as its patron (he had presented it with several dozen manuscripts). At the end of the 1490s, he acquired a site from the convent of St. Radegund and founded what became Jesus College.

Exchanges and absences

It was not only undergraduates who found they benefitted from the comparative security of a proper college life. The old habits of 'wandering' scholarship persisted, driven in part by financial need. Friars could in any case expect to be moved by their Order from house to house. Frequent exchanges took place between Oxford and Cambridge. At Peterhouse there was even a statute which allowed Fellows of the College to study in Oxford for a period. It was not uncommon to complete part of the requirements for a degree at one university and part at the other.

This seems to have been taken advantage of especially by theologians and lawyers, taking the 'higher degrees' of the two universities. (Medieval higher degrees were still not research degrees but advanced taught courses, in theology, law or medicine.)

These degrees took a good many years to complete and a student in middle age might have professional commitments which meant it was necessary to take time out in the middle of a course and return to complete it later. Clergy with livings might have duties which took them away from the University and some dispensations are recorded to allow them to do so.[37] Career progression still depended more on influence and patronage than on getting a qualification. Bachelors of Arts who were lecturing while working towards graduation as Masters got student tuition fees to help support them and their presence in the University was guaranteed. Some graduates planning to continue their studies taught as schoolmasters to make money and had to be excused from being present at the University by special graces.[38] There was good reason to stay under the protection of the University's umbrella, however. To leave it was to lose the benefit of clergy. It was even possible though unusual to be married while at university.[39]

By contrast, the most powerful in the land could obtain a degree by 'mandate' without having to work for it so they need not attend the university at all.[40] The general looseness of arrangements caused concern in the town and also in the Church, since it was dangerous for those 'whiche warr never brought upp in studye nor lerninge in the said Universitie, ne as Scollers never so accept ne taken before' to be enjoying the privileges of real members of the University although in reality they are merely renting rooms in colleges, It would be unacceptable for them to preach, for example, when they were unlicensed. On the other hand, there were many perfectly respectable college servants and specialist tradesmen such as 'Stacioners', 'Schryveners', 'Parchment-makers', 'Boke-bynders', 'Phisitions', 'Surgeons' and 'Barbers' who had been 'brought up...in the learnynge' of such 'Occupacions', and they should be respected as the servants of the University and should enjoy the appropriate privileges but only as long as they remain in their posts. In cases of dispute, persons claiming to be 'scholers' must obtain a certificate with the Vice-Chancellor's seal on it to show the Major and the Bailiffs. This was not just a matter of claiming privileges. It would also affect the court in which the accused was to be tried, whether the University's court or not. All this was the subject of arbitration and a covenant or agreement was formed in 1503.[41]

* * *

What was it like to study for a degree in medieval Cambridge?

A prospective student who wanted to go to Cambridge in the Middle Ages would not be able to read a prospectus. If he knew anyone who had been to university anywhere in Europe he might know in general outline what he would be learning, for they all followed roughly the same course, though to speak of a 'course' is to beg a question. In the twelfth century there had been no presumption that students would follow a curriculum in the schools from which the universities developed. There was some discussion of the interrelationship of 'parts of philosophy'. Twelfth-century diagrams of 'trees of knowledge' survive, so there was an accepted taxonomy of knowledge.[42] And it was customary for a lecturer to introduce a set book on which he was about to lecture with an *accessus* or introduction, in which he explained not only who the author was and why he had written the book, but also to what branch of study the book belonged.[43]

The statutes of Cambridge contain a list of syllabus requirements, mainly directed towards stipulating the length of time to be spent in each area of study. The academic year was divided into three terms with, from the late Middle Ages, a *terminus autumnalis,* or 'Long Vacation Term', which afforded an opportunity for the students to catch up on missed work or prepare for future work, with some informal lecturing available, but also outside the formal 'requirements' for the degree. Days were appointed for regular lectures, for disputations (*dies legibiles* and *dies disputabiles*) and for cursory and special ('extra-ordinary') lectures. Six to nine in the morning were the regular hours for the ordinary lectures, which were given by the Regent Masters and took the form of commentary on the set texts, citing authorities as appropriate. These were formal occasions for which the dress of both Master and students was prescribed. Here is the origin of the wearing of gowns for lecturing, a practice which died away only late in the twentieth century.

Liberal arts for free men

The 'liberal arts' got their name in Roman times from the fact that they were deemed to be fit subjects for the study of free boys (*liberi*), not slaves. They were subjects which could be expected to produce not skilled craftsmen but cultivated men of the world, equipped to make a contribution to public life as advocates and civil servants, people who would enjoy a little philosophical conversation in their leisure time for the rest of their lives.

The dominant subject in the syllabus in late antiquity was rhetoric, because it was a practical necessity for a man in public life – and the well-born routinely held public office at some time – to be able to make a good speech. The boy prepared for this study by learning Latin and Greek grammar and enough logic to enable him to construct persuasive arguments for use in speeches. It was also useful for him to have a stock of illustrations and examples, which was acquired by reading the poets and good standard authors on history and natural science; and to have a sufficient smattering of philosophy to enable him to handle deeper questions convincingly.

To this 'trivium' or 'three ways' of grammar, logic and rhetoric were added what Boethius in the sixth century called a 'quadrivium' of the four 'mathematical' subjects of arithmetic, geometry, music and astronomy. The academically inclined of the early medieval centuries duly studied these subjects, by means of the available textbooks which had come down in Latin. There was little available in the form of translations from Greek literature, except two of the logical works of Aristotle and a very small amount of Plato.

Grammar: a theory of language

In the Roman world, educated people read and wrote in both Latin and Greek. The creation of translations from one to the other to assist monoglot individuals became a matter of urgency only in the last generations of the Roman Empire. Then, with the breakdown of political unity, its two linguistic halves began to drift apart into mutual incomprehension. Augustine of Hippo (354–430), probably the most influential single figure in the West among the early Christian authors, was poor at Greek and partly as a consequence, his Western readers of the next millennium did not actively seek out classical Greek reading matter, or even the Christian writers in Greek later recognized as 'Fathers' of the Church. Boethius (480–524/5) was sufficiently concerned that his contemporaries were losing touch with the language to plan a translation of the whole corpus of Plato and Aristotle into Latin. His execution at the hands of the political authorities after a period of imprisonment, during which he wrote *The Consolation of Philosophy*, came too soon for him to finish; he had completed only one or two of Aristotle's books on logic; again, the consequences in limiting access to Aristotle in the West for most of the next millennium were huge. Two centuries later, Gregory the Great (c.540–604)possibly did not learn Greek, even though he spent some time in Constantinople.

The medieval university student would not have an opportunity to learn Greek until late in the Middle Ages, with a few notable exceptions such as the Oxford scholar Robert Grosseteste (c.1175–1253), who made unusual efforts to do so. But every student had to learn Latin because, although it was by now no one's native language, that was still the language in which all university studies were conducted.

This universal 'educated use of Latin' created a 'clerical' class with a language shared only with other educated people.

Learned Latinity had the advantage of giving scholars the freedom of Europe, for differences of native language were unimportant where there was a universal 'learned language'. The exception remained the Greek-speaking end of Europe. Although there was a variety of means of achieving a 'higher' education in Byzantium, no counterpart of the Western 'university' existed in the Byzantine Empire. For a thousand years few in the West spoke Greek at an 'educated' level, though trade continued and merchants were well enough able to make themselves understood to one another for the purposes of commerce.

This inescapable requirement to learn Latin dictated the whole approach to the 'arts' syllabus in Cambridge as in the medieval universities because it focused attention not only on the correct use of language, but also on the question what 'language' is and how it 'works'. Grammar meant Latin grammar and it was mastered with the aid of the manuals of Donatus (fl. late fourth century) and Priscian (fl. c.500). These provided an introduction to the concept of the 'parts of speech' (nouns, verbs and the lesser parts such as adverbs and prepositions). Priscian's textbook included discussions which were important in the Middle Ages because they made people think about deeper questions of the nature of language or 'speculative grammar'. Grammatical training for the young boy entering Cambridge would have concentrated mainly on acquiring a vocabulary, learning the grammar of an inflected language, including 'parsing' from authors such as Virgil, who were treated for the purpose merely as exercise material and not as literature, but the subject treated at a philosophical level did not lose its interest for their seniors.

Medieval logic: the 'old', the 'new' and the 'modern'

It is easy to forget that the huge predominance of logic among the subjects which were studied in medieval universities was not a foreseeable or inevitable development. In the mid-twelfth century, Thierry of Chartres had made a collection of the required school texts for the study of the *artes* (with unfinished glossing), which came to be known as the *Heptateuch* because there were seven subjects. This collection reflected the natural primacy of grammar as well as logic in the sheer extent of the texts which represent those subjects. At the end of the Middle Ages, when the literary and the rhetorical became fashionable again, the balance was redressed the other way, and rhetoric became supreme. The first universities put the emphasis on logic partly because it was here that the most interesting cutting-edge work on epistemology and the theory of language was going on, but also because arguing was stimulating and pedagogically useful.

In the *De Inventione* – a textbook used throughout the Middle Ages for lack of anything better, although Cicero had written it when he was just out of school himself – Cicero had distinguished two branches of study for the young orator, which similarly underlined the intimate relationship of rhetoric and logic. There is the finding of 'arguments' (*inventio*) and the process of deploying these '*sedes*', 'topics', paradigms or themes, in sequences of 'argumentation'. The construction of these sequences of *argumentatio* is the business of the logician, and Cicero's fear is that students of rhetoric may become so remorselessly attentive to the technicalities that their skill in argument paradoxically defeats the orator's overriding purpose, which is to persuade and not to convince. In the Middle Ages his fears were realized.

The medieval university logic course began with Aristotle, at first studied principally in his *Categories and De Interpretation,* along with the *Isagoge* of Porphyry and Boethius' commentaries on these basic textbooks. Boethius' ambitious plan to translate the whole of Aristotle and Plato into Latin had been curtailed by his untimely execution. The resulting limited body of material came to be known as the *logica vetus,* the 'old logic'. It was concerned mainly with the definition of terms and the correct formulation of premises and the elementary rules for creating a syllogism by putting two premises or propositions together and drawing a conclusion.

By the thirteenth century all six of Aristotle's logical treatises were being studied in the first universities, the *Prior Analytics,* the *Topics* and the *Sophistici Elenchi* having become available in Latin translations by the mid-twelfth century, and the difficult *Posterior Analytics* soon after that. These were designated the 'new logic' (*logica nova*).

The *logica moderna,* a still further advance on the 'old logic', included topics which are not covered by Aristotle but which came to prominence under the pressure of the interests of later medieval academics and which began to overload the syllabus and make logic very difficult for students. These included, as listed by a sixteenth-century logician, Robert Sanderson (1587–1663), 'supposition, exponibiles, consequences, obligations, insolubilia, syncategorematic terms, sophisms'.[44] Encyclopaedic attempts to embrace the whole syllabus, such as the work of Peter of Spain and Paul of Venice, appeared at the end of the Middle Ages. The arrival of the Greek commentaries on Aristotle changed expectations in the sixteenth century,[45] but Peter of Spain's *Summulae* were still studied in seventeenth century in the universities of Roman Catholic parts of Europe. Cambridge lecturers are not among the notable names in writing textbooks about all this, but they must have been teaching it or students would have voted with their feet.

Probable and necessary arguments

There are two ways of thinking about the 'pursuit of knowledge'. One takes it to be something to be captured ('acquired'), as useful equipment for life and, where appropriate, capable of practical application. The other takes it to be always ahead, dancing teasingly just out of reach, and, when grasped for a moment, likely to turn out not to be what you thought you were looking for at all. These roughly correspond to two sorts of knowledge recognized in ancient logic and throughout the Middle Ages. The first is what can be known for certain and is 'necessarily' true. The second is what is merely 'probable'. We shall meet the desire to discover necessary or demonstrative arguments again, in repeated attempts.

Some things appear to be self-evidently true, such as that two and two make four. Such self-evident truths were identified as 'commonly-held concepts' (*communes animi conceptiones*)[46] by Boethius, and that became the Latin tag normally used in the Middle Ages to describe the self-evident truths from which Euclid's geometry begins. From such truths are derived the conclusions of the 'demonstrative arguments' which seemed so desirable to medieval scholars. A fundamental distinction was drawn in medieval universities between 'probable' and 'necessary' arguments. The difference was that 'necessary' arguments proceeded from such indisputable premises and therefore arrived at conclusions which were not merely valid but guaranteed to be true. 'Probable' arguments also arrived at valid conclusions but the certainty of those conclusions depended on the reliability of the premises or propositions from which they had been derived.

A medieval formal argument in syllogistic form began with the framing of propositions. The conclusion of the syllogism depended for its truth, if not for its validity, on the degree of reliance which could be placed on the propositions or premises. When a proposition consisted of – or relied upon – a quotation from an 'authority', its degree of reliability would depend on the authority in question. A statement by Cicero was less reliable than a statement by Augustine, and Augustine stood lower in this hierarchy of truths than the Bible. In this way the Bible could be used in the process of proving, and Scriptural authority continued to be used for 'proving' into the sixteenth century, whether in formal syllogisms or more informally. Other propositions were themselves the conclusions of arguments, which depended ultimately on their reasonableness.

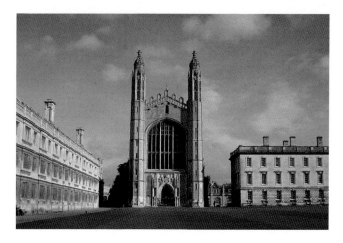

PLATE 1 – A classic view of King's College Chapel, seen from the 'Backs'. The chapel, which took over a century to build and was completed in 1547, is one of the finest examples of late Gothic (Perpendicular) English architecture. Alongside the chapel are the eighteenth century Gibbs Building (named after the architect James Gibbs, who redesigned the front court of King's College) and the Old Court buildings of Clare College. Old Court was built between 1638 and 1715, though there is no record of the architect who designed it. The view as a whole is one of the most famous in England.

PLATE 2 – Here the soaring grace of the medieval ceiling of King's College Chapel is a reminder of the high aspiration its founder had for this College. Few medieval cathedrals can match its architectural glory.

PLATE 3 – Peterhouse is the oldest college in the University of Cambridge. It was founded in 1284 by Hugo de Balsham, Bishop of Ely. Only the dining hall now survives from the thirteenth century, the other college buildings being built later. This is a view of Peterhouse's mostly fifteenth century Old Court.

PLATE 4 - The Senate House is one of the University's principal ceremonial buildings, designed (after some controversy) by James Gibbs and built in 1722–30 in a classical style.

PLATE 5 - Ceremonial officers of the University stand at the entrance to the Senate House during one of the ceremonies held there each year for the formal conduct of University business, the granting of degrees and the regular Discussions of the Senate.

PLATE 6 - Many Cambridge alumni/ae have nostalgic memories of the summer balls they attended as undergraduates. Known as 'May Balls', despite being held in June at the end of the examination period, these are occasions of high glamour and romance, when the colleges which hold them try to outdo the standard set by previous generations.

PLATE 7 - Trinity College, founded by Henry VIII in 1546, was part of the great regeneration of Cambridge under the Tudors and combined the earlier institutions of Michaelhouse and King's Hall. The buildings of Trinity's Great Court date from the sixteenth and seventeenth centuries. The court is famous for its 'Great Court Run', a competition which involves attempting to run round it before the clock has finished striking twelve. The run was immortalized in David Puttnam's Oscar-winning film *Chariots of Fire* (1981), though the scene in question was not actually filmed at Trinity. In 1988 the run was completed for charity by Sebastian Coe and Steve Cram. Coe won, crossing the line in 45.52 seconds as the final chimes of the clock died away.

PLATE 8 - Trinity College's great kitchen is shown here in an eighteenth-century engraving, though the scene would have looked much the same in earlier centuries. Trinity's statutes still require meals to be provided on every day of the year.

PLATE 9 - Sir Francis Bacon (1561–1626) studied at Trinity College as a teenager, with the future Archbishop of Canterbury John Whitgift as his tutor. He became a leading exponent of the move to an 'inductive' method of enquiry, which was the precursor of the modern scientific method.

PLATE 10 - Isaac Newton (1643–1727) was one of Cambridge's early leading scientists, who, by courtesy of Trinity College, enjoyed the freedom to let his research take him wherever his curiosity led.

PLATE 11 - The Wren Library was designed for Trinity College by Sir Christopher Wren, a friend of Isaac Barrow, who was Master of the College at the time. It was finished in 1695. It was intended to make a statement of elegance, presenting a view of the College from the river.

PLATE 12 - Emmanuel College was founded in 1584 by Sir Walter Mildmay on a site formerly occupied by the Dominican Order. Christopher Wren was commissioned to design its later chapel, shown here, and built from 1668 to 1674.

PLATE 13 – Queens' College's 'mathematical' bridge was first built in 1749 and has been rebuilt since. It became the focus of several myths, for example that it was the work of Isaac Newton or that it was originally built without nails or other means of connecting the pieces.

PLATE 14 – One of the most famous of Cambridge's student japes: an Austin 7 van is parked on top of the Senate House roof in June 1958. Youthful exuberance and a sense of humour are here matched with considerable technical ingenuity.

PLATES 15 and 16 – The novelist, essayist and poet John Cowper Powys (1872–1963), author of the massive novels *A Glastonbury Romance, Owen Glendower, Wolf Solent* and *Porius*, among others, was a student at Corpus Christi College. His descriptions of student life at the time demonstrate a strong sense of the distinctive 'Cambridge landscape' and an evocation of place and mood that was used to good effect in his later fiction. Powys, however, disliked Cambridge's 'parrot-like' teaching.

PLATE 17 – Rupert Brooke (1887–1915) was a scholar at King's College just before the First World War, a member of the Cambridge Apostles and one of a group of friends which included members of the Bloomsbury Group. He became one of the First World War poets, described by his fellow-poet Yeats as 'the handsomest young man in England', though he died not in battle, but of an infected mosquito bite at the Greek island of Lemnos on his way to fight at Gallipoli.

PLATE 18 - 'Stands the Church clock at ten to three? And is there honey still for tea?' The immortal closing lines of Rupert Brooke's 'The Old Vicarage, Grantchester' (1912) are commemorated by a pub sign in the village celebrated by the poem.

PLATE 19   Siegfried Sassoon (1886–1967) is today celebrated as one of the most significant poets of the Great War. From 1905 to 1907 he read law and history at Clare College, but never completed his degree. When hostilities broke out in 1914, Sassoon enlisted full of idealism, but after he had witnessed the brutal reality of conflict, and lost close friends in the horrors of the Flanders and Picardy trenches, he became the author of satirical and deeply-felt anti-war writings.

PLATE 20 - Clare College is the second-eldest, after Peterhouse, of the Cambridge colleges which survive today. Founded in 1326 by Richard de Badew, it was originally called University Hall. The buildings of Old Court, shown here, are one of Cambridge's architectural glories, when English Gothic segued into classicism, though they date from a period when Clare had a dispute with neighbouring King's about portions of land between the two colleges.

PLATE 21 – Clare College's bridge, built in 1639–40 by the mason Thomas Grumbold, is the oldest surviving bridge over the river Cam, and is often cited as the most beautiful. Constructed of Ketton stone ashlar, it shows the influence that classicism was having on architecture in England at the time. In the foreground is a punt, a flat-bottomed craft propelled along the river by a pole, that has become emblematic of Cambridge and Oxford (though the competing and contrasting punting techniques of the two universities are jealously defended). Few activities are as pleasurable as languidly punting up or down the river, past the Backs, or to and from the village of Grantchester, on a warm summer afternoon. Nevertheless, Jerome K. Jerome was right when in *Three Men in a Boat* (1889) he wrote: 'Punting is not as easy as it looks... It takes long practice before you can do this with dignity and without getting the water all up your sleeve.'

PLATES 22 and 23 – Oliver Cromwell (1599-1658), Lord Protector of the Commonwealth, attended Cambridge only briefly as a student, but in the course of his ascent to power he was member of Parliament for Cambridge in the Short Parliament of 1640 and the Long Parliament of 1640-9. During and after the Civil War the Roundhead armies, and then the iconoclastic attentions of 'purgers' and 'cleansers' dispatched to transform Cambridge into a Puritan university, had a significant impact on life and worship in the city and colleges. Cromwell himself is forever associated with Sidney Sussex College, where he spent a year as an undergraduate in 1616-17, and where his head was buried in 1960. The plaque pictured here records the burial close to (or within) Sidney's ante-chapel. The plaque is vague on location; and the exact spot is a closely guarded secret for fear of attempts to dig the head up.

PLATE 24 – The Lady Frances, Countess of Sussex, was the benefactor of Sidney Sussex College (in 1596), which was founded after her death on the site of the Franciscan 'house' where Duns Scotus once studied. She was also the aunt of the poet Sir Philip Sidney and a great patron of the arts at court. Her will allowed the money to go to Clare College instead and it was only because of considerable efforts by her executors that Sidney Sussex College began.

PLATE 25 – A view of Sidney Sussex College while its ancient wisteria is in full bloom.

Medieval enthusiasm for the method of argument known as 'demonstrative' proceeded from the recognition that to begin from 'necessary' propositions is to arrive at 'necessary' conclusions. There was a particularly strong motivation to achieve this in the study of theology, for nothing could be more desirable than certainly in that area. But the only subject in which it could be asserted with any confidence that self-evident truths led to inescapable conclusions seemed to be Euclidean geometry. This began from self-evident truths (again *communis animi conceptiones*), statements whose truth all rational persons accept as soon as they hear them. It adds some postulates and some definitions. It then employs formal reasoning to get from these to various conclusions, which can be taken to be so solidly established that they too can be taken to be 'known' and further arguments can be built with these new bricks.

Experiments were made in compiling lists of *regulae* or axioms for theology, for example, by Alan of Lille in the late twelfth century and by Nicholas of Amiens in his *De arte catholicae fidei,* probably in the early thirteenth.[47] Alan tried to create a linear sequence, in which one axiom was derived from another. He found that the further he moved from his starting point that God is a Monad, the less certain subsequent 'axioms' looked. Nicholas was more ambitious and attempted Euclidean demonstrations rather than a line of axioms each derived from the one before. But he too found that he could not 'demonstrate' the whole of Christian doctrine in that way so as to establish it all as incontrovertible 'knowledge'. Again, Cambridge scholars are not to be found in the forefront, but they must at least have been bringing up the rear adequately or the University would have decayed from lack of students.

Three medieval rhetorical arts and university preaching

The rhetorical education which had been central in the late Roman Empire had aimed to equip future citizens with the necessary skills to make a political speech, an occasional flattering speech for a great man (panegyric), and to conduct a case in court, for the heads of households were normally expected to have the forensic competence to act as advocates if one of their household (*familia*) or slaves was accused of an offence or there was a civil dispute to litigate. These needs largely vanished with the end of the Empire and for some centuries the study of rhetoric was in abeyance. In the eleventh century there was a partial revival, with the creation of an 'art of letter writing' (*ars dictaminis*), designed to train the burgeoning civil service of European courts and the papal curia to write business letters. In the twelfth century an 'art of poetry' joined it, and the old rhetorical skills in the deployment of literary devices came back into play. And in the late twelfth and early thirteenth century, an 'art of preaching' (*Ars Praedicandi*) arrived in the new universities, where university sermons began to be delivered, pitched at a level where they were half lectures, half homilies. This practice of preaching official sermons within universities was to lead to a good deal of trouble in Tudor times, as we shall see.

The *quadrivium*

The study of the four 'mathematical' subjects of the *quadrivium*, arithmetic, music, geometry and astronomy was neglected everywhere in medieval Europe in comparison with the study of the trivium. Oxford had some leading mathematicians, particularly Thomas Bradwardine,[48] but Cambridge remained something of a mathematical desert until the seventeenth century, when mathematics began to compete with logic as a main subject for undergraduates. From the early modern study of mathematics was to come the great leap forward which created modern science in Cambridge.

The germ of modern science

In the early thirteenth century, just as the universities were coming into existence, the 'scientific' writings of Aristotle became available at last in Latin translations. After some unsuccessful attempts first to ban the new books altogether at the University of Paris and then, later in the century, to ban the expression of particular opinions, a further cluster of standard set books was added to the syllabus. Cambridge does not seem to have had a similar upset over banning the new books, but it had its own troubles at the time, and it was perhaps too young and new to have Paris's sense that these innovations were too challenging for comfort. European academe settled down to the task of synthesizing these new ideas with the old. It was Aristotle who thus provided foundations in philosophy and natural science. Plato's influence was still mediated mainly through a diffuse 'Platonism', for most of Plato's writings did not become available for general study in the universities of the West until the fifteenth century.

At the end of the fourteenth century, Cambridge students heard lectures on the textbooks of Aristotle's logic throughout the six terms of their first two years and in the third year they had lectures on Aristotle's *Physics* in the first term and the second term and on Aristotle's *On the Soul* or his *Ethics* or one of the scientific books in the summer term. The fourth year took them to Aristotle's *Physics* and *Metaphysics*.[49]

Thus was born the 'arts' course, although it already had embedded within it the core of modern science. Students began with this foundation, often at an age when they would now be in secondary schools, and it was as Bachelors of Arts and then Masters of Arts that they graduated with a 'first degree'. This basic syllabus, its structure and its content, and the methods of instruction that went with it, persisted doggedly beyond the Middle Ages, especially at the level where it set expectations for the most intimate aspects of intellectual understanding of the nature of language and the use of argument and proof. The story of its evolution is the very spine of any account of the way Cambridge developed.

Teaching methods

There is not much evidence of the way teaching was conducted in medieval Cambridge, but we know a good deal about what it would be like for a student from other universities. Throughout the history of universities, the lecture has remained one of the staple methods, and for most of that time it has been a lecture on a 'set book', with study of the book remaining central to the syllabus. The lecturing method was fairly uniform. A short passage, perhaps only a word or a phrase, would be read and expounded, with difficult words explained and the views of 'authorities' adduced.

Even before the emergence of the true 'university', the disputation had developed, initially as a practical method of dealing with questions. Student questions could be a real distraction in lectures. The records of lectures as early as the mid-twelfth century show that it could take a long time to deal with a single question if it happened to raise an issue on which a number of early Christian authors had commented, so that a long series of opinions needed to be reviewed and compared. To set aside a separate period of time to discuss such questions was a means of ensuring that the lecturer stood a chance of covering the whole of the book in the number of lectures available and this was happening in Paris in the middle of the twelfth century, for example, in the teaching of Simon of Tournai.[50]

The disputations quickly developed a pattern. Arguments in favour of a 'yes' answer to the question were set against arguments in favour of a 'no' answer, and the Master would decide (or 'determine') which was the right answer. The students were supposed to learn which points should be raised on the question. This gave rise to the medieval method of examining students at the end of their course of study to show whether they knew enough to deserve a 'degree'. Given a question, they would review the pros and cons and 'determine' the matter before the panel of Masters who were their examiners, and thus demonstrate their own 'mastery'.[51] This system of examination continued in use in Oxford and Cambridge until the nineteenth century.[52] The method of teaching by disputation also lingered long past the Middle Ages. We shall see Gilbert Burnet (1643–1715) put forward proposals for the founding of a new university, to which young men were to come with 'a good Degree of understanding the Latin tongue' and where they were to be put at once to the study of logic and practical disputation. (He proposed to allow no exemptions from serious study for boys of better breeding.)[53]

Taking notes in lectures

Late antiquity developed its own forms of shorthand but no established system. What sort of note-taking was possible for students in medieval Cambridge as they listened to lectures?[54] In the absence of direct evidence we can nevertheless put together a fair picture of the way students tackled this problem. Forms of abbreviation are familiar in medieval manuscripts, enabling words to be compressed for more rapid writing as well as to save space. Professional notaries had skills in shorthand; it has even been suggested that the *ars notaria* was primarily a skill in shorthand rather than the art of legal drafting which is more usually taken to be its meaning. 'The force and effectiveness of this art is that it teaches speed-writing,' says one definition (*artis huius vis et efficacia est velocitatem scribendi docere*).[55] Certainly in the form devised by 'John of Tilbury' at Oxford in the mid-twelfth century, the *ars notaria* apparently involved learning symbols which took the form of a true shorthand in the sense that they were not mere abbreviations of ordinary words.

The idea seems to have been that this would allow a listener to take down notes from a lecture or other dictation or oral delivery, capturing the actual words the master spoke.[56] The need for shorthand continued to affect the way study-records were kept. It is noticeable in the extreme compression of the text in some working academic copies of standard texts in medieval manuscripts. It prompted those running the 'dissenting academies'[57] in the early modern world, to teach students shorthand as a regular part of their course.

There is evidence that lecturers adapted their pace to the different needs of students in different parts of Europe. It was much harder to follow a lecture if you did not have the book in front of you. In Germany and Central Europe, the *pecia* arrangements which enabled booksellers in some parts of Europe to mass-produce copies for student use was not in operation, so lecturers might have to go at dictation-speed to ensure that their listeners were clear what the text being 'read' said and could make sense of the commentary.[58] It was experimentally tested in Paris in 1355 whether it was easier for students to learn if the lecturer spoke at normal reading speed and felt free to ad lib (if a thought struck him or a point needed fuller explanation), so that they could understand and remember; or was it better to go at slow dictation speed (*pronuntiare, legere ad pennam*) so that they could try to write but would be less likely to understand? The conclusion was that the student learned better by listening than by trying to write.[59] Here we must not lose sight of the purpose for which a student needed to make a record of what he heard. He would not be writing essays or answering questions on an examination paper, in which he would need to display what he had learned. But he would be taking part in disputations, both as a means of learning and as a mode of examination. So the essential thing was to grasp key points in relation to specific portions of the text.

A standard method used in the medieval universities came to be known as *reportatio*. As early as the beginning of the twelfth century, Hugh of St. Victor asked one of his students not only to note down what he said (which would be done on wax tablets), but also to polish it and produce a more permanent record with some unity and coherence.[60] This could prove useful to a lecturer who would give a lecture series each year and probably the final version would be approved by the lecturer himself.

We can glimpse how this worked in surviving lecture-notes of the mid-fifteenth century made by a student from Gotland, Olaus Johannis Gutho (d.1516), who studied the Arts at Uppsala, graduating sometime after 1485, before entering the Brigittine monastery at Vadstuna. He left a set of notebooks which preserve in uncommon detail a record of the lectures he attended and the way he studied.[61] Some of the masters whose names he records were Swedish, but these included scholars who had studied in other parts of Europe. Rostock, Leipzig and Greifswald were the three universities in northern Germany most likely to have provided a model on which Uppsala's curriculum could have been based, with Rostock most favoured by Swedish students who ventured abroad.[62] The presumption is that the pattern of study should resemble what was approved elsewhere.

Gutho did what other students had to do. He copied down the textbook, at least where the master spoke *ad pennas,* at a speed which enabled his students to make their own copies, giving them a portion of commentary after each section of the text.[63] This practice seems to have extended to dictating the disputations or at least the determinations, thus radically altering their pedagogic purpose.[64]

A good deal of Gutho's note-taking was on theology, Scriptural commentary, and not on subjects from the *artes*, although there is no reason to suppose he studied theology. This gives an important glimpse of something we know to have happened in Paris. Arts students got interested in theology and would often ask challenging questions which were much too advanced for them to solve but might also turn out to be too difficult for the theologians. The two Faculties of Arts and Theology often wrangled in Paris. There even seems to have been some reference to issues topical today. For example, Gutho took notes from a lecture on the three *fundamenta vel stabilimenta* of the Koran which had it was said presented the final victory of Revelation as a victory over the Muslims.[65] It is entirely probable that the same sort of thing happened in Cambridge.

At Uppsala the first question on Porphyry's *Isagoge*, addressed in the lectures of Petrus Johannis Galle, was what kind of subject logic is. Is it practical or speculative? The lecturer had then given the various standard opinions from the authorities, including Gilbert of Poitiers and Averroes as well as Boethius and the student had duly noted them down.[66] There are 'Questions' and literal commentaries on main textbooks of logic, a Commentary on the popular textbook, Sacrobosco's *Sphere*. Sacrobosco was the Latin name of John of Holywood (c.1195–c.1256), but although he was probably an Englishman he seems to have studied at Paris rather than Cambridge or Oxford.[67] Set books were still almost universally being introduced by an *accessus*. On the *De Anima* of Aristotle, for example, the *accessus* was evidently delivered at a pace which enabled the student to note down the 'five things to be noted before reading the text' (*Antequam accedatur ad textum, quinque sunt prenotanda*), the usefulness, title, intention of the author, the part of philosophy it belongs to and its 'causes',[68] with a little mnemonic: 'I you want to know well first ask the following about a book' (*Si bene vis scire, in libris primo ista require*).[69] The flavour of lectures on the Bible can be caught from a comparison with Greek views in a comment on Revelation 19.[70]

The Faculties and the principle of academic control of academic matters

The medieval practice as it evolved was for the academic community in each university to determine what it should teach. Cambridge was no different, though again we have limited evidence about the way they did it and how they organized their Faculties, of Arts and other subjects. It can be inferred that the University quickly created much the same 'faculty' structures for supervision of teaching as are found elsewhere. The University of Cambridge certainly developed a Faculty of Arts but we do not know when.

Decisions about the syllabus could be left to individual Faculties or approved by the whole community of scholars in a university. The curriculum might then be embodied in a statute and – in some parts of Europe – the approval of the city or prince sought, since in Italy and some other places, the salaries of the lecturers were paid out of local taxes.

So it had to be established as a matter of principle and practice that the content, set books and method of examination were to be regarded as an academic not a political or 'administrative' concern. This autonomy in academic matters was allowed to Cambridge (as it was to Oxford) in the Middle Ages, but it needs to be emphasized how remarkable that was and how hugely important it was going to be for the future. Elsewhere, local politicians and secular authorities did not always understand or wish to respect this. Protecting the distinction between academic and non-academic regulation, and deciding where one ended and the other began, was to be of incalculable importance – and continuing difficulty – far into the future.

As an illustration of the scale of the problems which might arise we make take the crisis which arose in the Arts Faculty in Paris in 1339–40. This was ostensibly over the controversial teaching of William of Ockham, which came to be known as 'Ockhamism'. In September 1339, the Arts Faculty said it had the right to determine the list of books allowed to be lectured on. A Statute was drafted (possibly two):

> We have sworn to observe a certain ordinance which was issued by our predecessors, who were not unreasonably concerned as to the books to be read publicly or privately among us and because we ought not to read certain books not admitted by them or customarily read elsewhere.

and since some have been holding secret meetings to read these banned books, it is decreed by the new statute:

> that henceforth noone shall presume to dogmatize the said doctrine by listening to it or lecturing on it publicly or in private, or by holding small meetings for disputing said doctrine, or by citing it in lecture or in disputations.[71]

Anyone breaching this new rule is to be suspended ('not hold office or degree among us'). The second statute (or Part II of the first), comments that

> bachelors and others present at these disputations dare to argue on their own authority, showing little reverence toward the masters who are disputing, and making such a tumult that the truth of the conclusion being debated cannot be arrived at, so that the said disputations are not in any way fruitful for the listening scholars.[72]

This statute, it is stated, was made by the four Nations comprising the Faculty of Arts and the Rector, according to the time-honoured rule that the Masters determine the curriculum, that is, the set books approved for study in their Faculty. On 12 October 1340, the Faculty of Canon Law passed its own statutes fixing entrance requirements for student lawyers, minimum attendance at lectures, scheduling of lectures on the *Decretales* and *Decretum*.[73] But could even smaller divisions of a university make domestic laws? The English–German nation was anxious to make a statute binding on everyone which will require that no one should be admitted to acts of the Nation unless he first swears to reveal if he knows of any Ockhamist conspiracies or secret meetings.[74] The question of proportionate representation of Nations of students in Faculty organisation arose elsewhere.[75]

What matters were in issue in all this? One was clearly the authority to create a statute, whether it could be done by Faculties, as separate parts of the University in which particular fields of academic expertise were to be found. Another was the need to maintain order, which included expecting students and junior scholars to treat their seniors with respect. Another was the desire to keep a nervous eye on the ideas students were being exposed to and where they might be able to hear them. Here was an early hint of the difficulty of ensuring that a balance was struck between freedom to teach and protection against indoctrination with dangerous ideas, which was to cause problems in many controversies in medieval universities.

In fairness to secular or ecclesiastical outside authorities which might wish to take over and try to enforce outcomes of their own, it must be admitted that academic obscurities could easily make it difficult for outsiders to understand what was at issue in such disputes. The 'presenting' concern may have been that students should not be led into heresy. But the Arts Statute of 29 December 1340 contains some subtle discussion of what 'true' and 'false' mean. The problem is that if one person takes one sense to be true and another another, there can be no real 'disputation' because they are talking about different things.

In Germany, Tübingen had new statutes for the Faculty of Arts in 1477, 1488, 1505, 1536.[76] Tübingen was highly influential not only on Wittenberg but also on Freiberg, whose original statutes of 1463 for the Arts were changed in 1490 the better to match those of Tübingen. The German universities were small and new in the fifteenth century and a little unstable, hence perhaps the frequent revisions of the statutes. They had come into being when German scholars fled Paris and Prague during the late fourteenth and fifteenth centuries. They could not attract students to the higher faculties in the way Paris and Oxford could and tended to depend on French or Italian-trained Masters to teach in these areas.[77] German universities were still making new statutes quite frequently in the sixteenth century, changing arrangements for faculties and also the way the university was run. It was frequently far from clear where the line was to be drawn between academic and political control. At Wittenberg a new Elector would often take the opportunity to issue a new and revised foundation charter which included requirements about academic aspects such as keeping the curriculum up to date and making sure the lecturers conscientiously discharged their duties.[78]

So Cambridge's freedom to run its own academic affairs is noteworthy even at this early stage; we shall see a series of attempts to interfere with it as the centuries went on.

* * *

The Dunce and the dunces: Cambridge as a backwater

John Duns Scotus (c.1265–1308), who gave his name to 'dunces' everywhere, is perhaps the most famous medieval scholar to be associated with Cambridge.[79] He probably came from the Scottish 'Duns' family and became a Franciscan late in the 1270s, though only glimpses of his career can be reconstructed. His years in Cambridge were probably about 1297–1300. He died at the Franciscan house at Cologne in 1308, but during the 1290s and the early 1300s he had, like others of his Order, studied and lectured at various of its houses, in his case at Oxford as well as at Cambridge, with a period in Paris. He made his name as a combative contributor to the debates about the teaching of Averroes, which had reached their height in the previous generation in the 1260s and 1270s in Paris. Much of his surviving work, however, derives from his lectures on Peter Lombard's *Sentences*. The

Franciscan Order gave him prominence as their answer to Aquinas, whom the Dominicans nominated as 'doctor' of their Order in 1314.

Other names of rather modest pretensions to fame appear, such as the logicians William Dallyng and John Felmyngham.[80] Some of Cambridge's scholars are equally associated with Oxford, such as the lawyer John Acton[81] and the theologian Thomas Chobham. Roger Marston, a Franciscan, seems to have come back to England at the end of the thirteenth century from a sojourn at the University of Paris, passing through Cambridge only to go to be lecturer to the Franciscans in Oxford.[82]

Very few records of medical students survive although the earliest medical statutes are from 1270 to 1280, and some colleges include study of medicine in their statutes. Some wrote short research papers in the fifteenth century on the causes of the plague, highly speculative in character, but to try to meet the needs of parish clergy who had to deal with stricken communities, needs which were much more practical.[83] Copies of the example by John of Burgundy survive in Cambridge college and University collections. William Lyndwood author of the *Provinciale seu constitutions Angliae* (1422–30), a digest of constitutions of English synods, had been a Cambridge law student.

So it has to be admitted that Cambridge produced few notable scholars of her own in the Middle Ages. The exciting times for Cambridge, the high drama of the University's influence in national and international affairs through its graduates and teachers, began with the Tudors. This was not for lack of teaching provision adequate to produce promising students or to attract notable teachers. It is just that it never happened to count among its very own scholars any of the notorious of the medieval centuries (such as Oxford's John Wyclif) or any individuals such as Oxford's mathematician Bradwardine, who became the focus of specialist pioneering work and built a high reputation throughout Europe. That does not mean that Cambridge was held in low esteem at the time. These differences are apparent only with hindsight. Yet in comparison with its flood of prominent figures in the sixteenth century, Cambridge has little to show to justify its position as one of England's only two permitted universities in the medieval period.

Being slightly out of touch

Cambridge seems to have been barely touched by the excitements of the Wyclif affair in Oxford at the end of the fourteenth century.[84] This is particularly noteworthy, since Arundel had been bishop of Ely before he became Archbishop of Canterbury, and had had to deal with various matters including a dispute in 1384.[85] The Annals record that in 1384 the Chancellor and the Doctors inspected the books 'intended for use in the University', 'with a view to the detection of heretical opinions, and that such works as were found objectionable in this respect were burnt before the University'.[86] Archbishop Arundel made a Visitation in 1401, mainly concerned with administrative details. But he asked whether any member of the University was suspected of Lollardy[87] or any other heretical wickedness.[88] One scholar, Peter Irford, is recorded as having been accused of heresy and as having recanted in 1413.

'Schools' of thought and their leaders: was there more than one 'way'?

There was always divisive controversy in the late medieval schools, and it is sometimes suggested that it created 'schools' of another sort, 'schools' of opinion, linked perhaps to a famous name, such as Thomas Aquinas (1225/7–74), Duns Scotus (1265/6–1308) or William of Ockham (1288–1347). Statutes and 'graces'[89] in fifteenth-century Oxford and Cambridge suggest that the self-consciously 'Ockhamist' and 'Thomist' division which appears in continental syllabuses did not apply in England, where 'Scotism' dominated with little challenge.[90] But rumour of such division clearly spread and helped to create a persistent mythology. In sermons, John Donne (1572–1631) remarks even in the seventeenth century, 'this hath divided the School into that great opposition which is well known by the name of *Thomists* and *Scotists*',[91] and refers to 'well known families of the School, whom we call, Thomists and Scotists',[92] clearly expecting his listeners to understand the reference.

In one part of Europe something new was stirring at the end of the Middle Ages. In the late medieval German foundations, some universities offered a choice of two *viae* to students, the old 'way' or syllabus, and the new; in some cases a university specialized in one or the other. Cologne (1388) favoured the *via antiqua* and Erfurt (1392) the *via moderna*. Tübingen offered both from its inception in 1477. In some instances a *via* was associated with a particular famous scholar, as in Heidelberg's *Via Marsiliana* (1388) (called after Marsilius of Inghen d. 1396) and at Wittenberg in 1508 three *viae* were offered, the Thomist, the Scotist and the 'Gregorist' (with the *Via Gregorii* named after Gregory of Rimini (d.1358)).[93]

It is extraordinarily difficult to be sure what the terminology used to label such 'alternative' curricula really implied. Alongside syllabuses which could be categorized as 'school of a named individual' and some which lumped such schools together under a particular name (such as 'Ockhamist') which generalized them, there were some which have been variously described as 'terminist' or 'nominalist' on the one hand and 'realist' on the other.[94] Part of the problem was that some of the concerns about the need for reform or for conservatism related to theological opinion and some to the humbler machinery of the way students were taught to think things through, using language and logic in particular ways and on particular assumptions about their relation to metaphysics.

Already by the time of Lorenzo Valla (d.1457) the observer could point in broad terms to opposing factions, the '*antiqui*' and the '*moderni*', moderns disparaging the work of the ancients. Valla, in the preface to the fourth book of his *Elegantiae* suggests that the ancients are like bees producing honey, a real food source, while the moderns are merely like ants who only steal.[95]

Enter the humanists

In every century since the beginning of universities, there has continued to be a wandering *intelligentsia,* travelling in pursuit of knowledge. This liberty has been allowed to academics down the ages, so that a similar *peregrinatio academica* has had scholars appearing in universities all over Europe in the course of their careers well into the modern world; it has allowed exits and entrances, and exchanges with private individuals who were simply pursuing an interest but had the independent means to do so purposefully and the education to set a standard. They could all be the prompters of innovation.

Giovanni Pico della Mirandola (1463–94) is a late medieval example of the 'wandering academic', who could be influential by transmitting 'new' ideas from place to place, and by throwing down a challenge to others to argue with him. After picking up Platonist and other notions elsewhere, he returned to Rome in 1486 and published 900 theses on a wide range of subjects which he promised to maintain against all comers.[96] In his list of scholars with Cambridge connections in the *Annals*, Charles Henry Cooper records how

> Cyprian de Valera (author) 'was born at Seville, and educated at the university in that city, where he studied for six years. Leaving Spain for religion sake he came to this university, and in 1559 or 1560 was admitted to the degree of BA by special grace'. He then incorporated as an MA. 'In 1565 he obtained letters from this university testifying to his godly conversation.[97]

Cambridge had its complement of fifteenth-century humanists who would have engaged sympathetically with these trends, but a modest one. John Gunthorpe was an M.A. by 1452 and he then went to Italy where he studied classical literature in the way becoming newly fashionable. He came back to Cambridge later and studied theology and was warden of King's Hall from 1467 to 1482. A Fellow of King's College who similarly took a Cambridge degree and then went to Italy and came back was John Doket. He learned enough Greek to write a commentary on Plato's *Phaedo*. The most important thing about these examples is that these were individuals who did not start a trend in Cambridge. Their work largely died with them. The surviving library collections do not indicate a strong specialist interest even in embryo. The University Library catalogue of 1473 had Petrarch's *De remediis*. St. Cathareine's College had one of those too, and Peterhouse had another Petrarch text, his letters. King's College did rather better, but that was because part of Duke Humfrey's library had been put in the College's charge after he died in 1447 at Bury St. Edmund's. Even here there were only scraps of a respectable collection, some Bruni, some Poggio, a Latin version of Plato's Republic, a translation of Athanasius.[98]

Cambridge seems, then, to have survived its early ups and downs better than some of its European rivals. It went steadily on through the medieval centuries with no dramatic closures and re-openings, but also with nothing world-shattering to show for its efforts as yet. But that was about to change.

3 CAMBRIDGE AND THE TUDOR REVOLUTION

Margaret Beaufort and John Fisher turn Cambridge's fortunes round

William Wordsworth's journey through Cambridge's centuries is sentimental. He pictures late medieval and Tudor Cambridge as a place of dedicated and self-denying scholarship.

> When all who dwelt within these famous walls
> Led in abstemiousness a studious life;
> When, in forlorn and naked chambers cooped
> And crowded, o'er the ponderous books they hung
> Like caterpillars eating out their way
> In silence, or with keen devouring noise.

His Cambridge scholars, and he includes some of the key names of the Tudor period, such as Melanchthon and Erasmus, were

> ...illustrious men,
> Lovers of truth, by penury constrained.

His version of the Cambridge story is right in bringing in lay students, and students of many social classes and providing the poor ones with financial support:

>   Princes then
> At matins froze, and couched at curfew-time,
> Trained up through piety and zeal to prize
> Spare diet, patient labour, and plain weeds.
> ...When Learning, like a stranger come from far,
> Sounding through Christian lands her trumpet, roused
> Peasant and king; when boys and youths, the growth
> Of ragged villages and crazy huts,
> Forsook their homes, and, errant in the quest
> Of Patron, famous school or friendly nook,
> Where, pensioned, they in shelter might sit down,

> From town to town and through wide scattered realms
> Journeyed with ponderous folios in their hands.

Cambridge's international reputation seemed secure to Wordsworth from the distance of 300 years ('O seat of Arts! renowned throughout the world!'). But his Romanticized Cambridge was already busy fundraising:

> An obolus, a penny give
> To a poor scholar![1]

After its centuries of being a very ordinary academic institution on a European scene full of potential rivals, Cambridge began to come into its own as a leading university in the sixteenth century. This happened with explosive suddenness when it produced graduates notable in Renaissance or Reformation or both. John Fisher (c.1469–1535), graduated in Cambridge in 1488 and became a Fellow of Michaelhouse (an early foundation eventually merged into Trinity College in 1546). Thomas Cranmer, architect of the 'Church of England', and the martyr Nicholas Ridley both took their B.A.s in 1510. The Bible translator Miles Coverdale and Matthew Parker, future Archbishop of Canterbury, were not much behind.

The transformation was achieved by a small number of benevolent and influential hands on Cambridge's tiller. Lady Margaret Beaufort (1443–1509) was of the blood royal (half-blood, therefore at some distance) and controlled great estates. Orphaned in 1444, she was made the ward of William de la Pole, then steward of the royal household. De la Pole found himself under threat of impeachment by the House of Commons and to try to protect himself, he 'married' his son John to Margaret in 1450 while she was still a child. She was rescued from this marriage by the King, who sent for her in 1453 to begin her life at court. She was subsequently buffeted backwards and forwards by the changes of fortune of the houses involved in the Wars of the Roses. She was married again, to Edmund Tudor (c.1430–1456), and widowed in six months, but she was pregnant with the boy who would become Henry Tudor, Henry VII and the founder of the Tudor dynasty – partly as a consequence of her skilful manoeuvring, for she proved to be a wily conspirator in the politics of the day. She won him the throne by diplomacy and by bringing about a marriage to Elizabeth of York which joined the warring houses of Lancaster and York.

The first Parliament of the reign of Henry VII declared her *femme sole*, that is able to dispose of property in her own right even though she was a woman. Henry took advantage of this situation to entrust her with wardships and property which she could thus keep safe for him. She proved as astute and effective an exploiter of property rights as she had been of the political scene in the years when she had been plotting for her son's succession to the throne. She was also proactive in the local government of the regions, for she controlled large areas of England.

She was not all hard politician. Margaret Beaufort was also a patron of learning and the arts. She commissioned one of the first printed books from William Caxton in 1489. She herself was an active translator of pious works, sometimes using a collaborator. William Atkinson, a Fellow of Jesus College, Cambridge, is known to have helped her. Examples are part of the *Imitation of Christ* by Thomas à Kempis, which she had printed for her household to profit from (spiritually that is). She also acted as a patron of church music, again especially for her own household chapel. And she warmed to the idea of giving benefactions to good causes. Erasmus wrote of Margaret Beaufort that 'into that woman, God had infused a mind most unlike a woman's'. He called her a 'holy heroine', for her generosity in creating foundations and establishing Readerships and Professorships.[2]

She became an active patron of the University of Cambridge after John Fisher – who was then a Cambridge Proctor – met her on University business in 1494–5. Margaret Beaufort adopted him as her spiritual director in this last period of her life, in the tradition by now well established in the courts of Europe, by which the great liked to have personal confessors. These were the 'personal trainers' and 'life-coaches' of the time. A confessor could have immense potential influence, and was likely to win ecclesiastical preferment, as happened to Fisher.

This threatened to draw him out of Cambridge and into public life. But he kept up his life in Cambridge, giving lectures and becoming a Doctor of Theology, and, in 1501, Vice-Chancellor. He was also, in 1502, made the first Lady Margaret Professor of Divinity, occupying the new Chair his patroness had created. The King was 'countenancing' Fisher too, making him Bishop of Rochester in 1504. The University made him Chancellor in 1504 and he was steadily reelected until 1514 when he intended to hand over the Chancellorship of Cambridge to the rising star Thomas Wolsey (1470/1–1530), who became both a Cardinal and Chancellor of England in 1515. Wolsey refused and Fisher remained in office until his death.

Fisher proved an effective mover and shaker in the creation of new colleges, too. When she founded Christ's College in 1506, Margaret Beaufort made him its Visitor. Colleges as eleemosynary foundations (charitable foundations providing a form of 'alms') had Visitors who provided a succession after the death of the founder and had the duty (among other things) of ensuring that his wishes for his foundation continued to be respected, by interpreting its domestic legislation if there was a dispute and providing a point of reference and resort when a controversy needed to be resolved. King's College's grand and ambitious buildings stood unfinished after the collapse of its fortunes in the previous century. In his Oration delivered in the presence of Henry VII and Lady Margaret in 1507 in the still uncompleted chapel of King's College, Cambridge, Fisher spoke sufficiently movingly to persuade her son the King to bequeath £5000 so that the chapel could be finished. The resulting magnificence struck William Wordsworth when he was a student:

> TAX not the royal Saint with vain expense,
> With ill-matched aims the Architect who planned –
> Albeit labouring for a scanty band
> Of white robed Scholars only – this immense
> And glorious Work of fine intelligence!
> Give all thou canst; high Heaven rejects the lore
> Of nicely-calculated less or more;
> So deemed the man who fashioned for the sense
> These lofty pillars, spread that branching roof
> Self-poised, and scooped into ten thousand cells,
> Where light and shade repose, where music dwells
> Lingering – and wandering on as loth to die;
> Like thoughts whose very sweetness yieldeth proof
> That they were born for immortality.[3]

Margaret Beaufort's other Cambridge foundation was St. John's College (founded 1511–16), which was Fisher's own special pride and joy.[4] The foundation dated from 1511, when Margaret Beaufort had set about recreating for the purpose the old 'Hospital' of St. John which had been founded about 1200 by the Hospitallers. The early history of St. John's was full of controversy because Margaret Beaufort's endowment had been large and there was eager jostling among her hangers on – including her grandson Henry VIII – to get control of a share. It was not until 1516–17 that the College was able to open for students, and Fisher promulgated its first statutes.[5]

Wordsworth was later a student there and he wrote of its buildings of this period with his most Romantic enthusiasm:

> The Evangelist St. John my patron was:
> Three Gothic courts are his, and in the first

Was my abiding-place, a nook obscure;
Right underneath, the College kitchens made
A humming sound, less tuneable than bees,
But hardly less industrious; with shrill notes
Of sharp command and scolding intermixed.[6]

Fisher proved a competent fund-raiser in a period when there was much afoot by way of new foundations and new benefactions. Because of him, Margaret Beaufort concentrated her charitable activities on Cambridge instead of dividing her interest between Oxford and Cambridge. She recruited Cambridge's graduates into her household and thus assisted them to become influential in their turn.

Fisher encouraged the granting of a royal licence whenever a new lectureship was founded, and Margaret was minded to found several. This creation of salaried 'lectureships' was fostering a transition of immense importance. It undermined the centuries-old practice of requiring recent graduates as Masters to spend a period in lecturing as part of the requirement for the completion of their degrees. This had meant a rapid turnover and a concentration of lecturing in the hands of the young and inexperienced. But the change also weakened the case for keeping power in the University in the hands of the academics, and allowing them to run themselves as a democracy.

The Regent Masters give way to 'paid professionals'

German universities had abandoned the Regent Masters system by the end of the fifteenth century, and the trend of the sixteenth was towards salaried chairs. In Arezzo the city is to be seen budgeting for salaries. From 1530 survives a letter authorizing the doctors of law to make the appointment of a grammar-master (*Grammaticus*), the better to educate the boys of the city, *eo maxime quia ginnasia et ludi litterarii*. In Oxford and Cambridge, the Regent Masters system proved harder to budge. The change was brought about even there by allowing newly graduated Masters to pay a fee in lieu of doing their Regent lecturing and out of the fund thus created a regular lecturing staff could be paid.[7]

At the end of the fifteenth century, Cambridge's Regent Masters took a vote to move to a system of salaried Professorships to provide the lectures students needed. This was a decision partly forced upon them by the decay of the old conscientious performance of the duty of lecturing for a period after graduation, which had formed part of the requirements for a degree. This had been more than 'continuing professional development'. It was a condition of the award of the degree. It emphasized the fact that a degree was not just a 'qualification' but a token of membership. The incentives to pursue an 'academic career' within a university in the Middle Ages included the freedom to participate in running the affairs of the institution in which one taught. Academics remained personally independent insofar as they did not need salaried posts in institutions, or outlets for their work which depended on the existence of an 'academic infrastructure' of institutionalized university life. Personal reputation proved to be portable. It was not necessary to stay in academe throughout one's career. Even in the twelfth century 'higher' education was seen as a route to advancement, perhaps through the civil service to a bishopric, as John of Salisbury (1120–80) found. (He describes in his *Metalogicon* his own dozen years in the schools of Paris in the first half of the twelfth century, lecture-tasting and comparing masters; he evaluates their efforts in retrospect with a sharp critical mind.[8]) The early modern university also allowed for some coming and going. The Oxford and Cambridge models, once the colleges had evolved, assumed a few years' service as a celibate tutor before going off, usually, to a College living.

One year of such duty was exacted, and probably generally performed, at the beginning of the fifteenth century, but by the early sixteenth it had become merely nominal. It was never formally ended, in either Cambridge or Oxford, where much the same change was taking place. In fact in Cambridge the Elizabethan Statutes still required a period of Regency, which was to last not one year but five. Paid lectures appear first in Oxford.[9] (Some of the replacement lectures were offered by colleges rather than by the University.) In 1496 John Fisher was paid to give lectures in Cambridge in the Long Vacation and rather more for lecturing in the Christmas Term.

Professorships and Readerships began to appear, with the names of their benefactors attached to them, as in Margaret Beaufort's time as a great Cambridge patroness.

* * *

The world as Cambridge's oyster

The story of sixteenth-century Cambridge is also the story of circles of personal friendship. *Peregrinatio academica* was now entering a new phase. Scholars visited one another's universities across Europe, were even 'head-hunted' in order to fill the new Professorships with famous names. They were also great letter-writers, in conscious imitation of the Roman models, in which in Roman antiquity, Cicero or Seneca would send drafts of his writings to his friends, ask for comments, share interesting dilemmas about what to say next. The sense of the 'presence' of absent friends is strong in the exchange of letters. John Colet (1466?–1519), Oxford's internationally famous 'visiting renaissance scholar' sought 'a selective cohort of interactive, pious friends'. Erasmus (1466/9–1536), Cambridge's counterpart, sought a 'fraternity really bound together for a Gospel life' with whose members he expected to be able to hold an intelligent conversation. Medieval letter writing, with a few exceptions,[10] has nothing to match this. It had been quite usual in the Middle Ages to leave it to the messenger to deliver the actual message, once the recipient of the letter had been handed some flowery compliments in writing.

The rise of intellectuals as a distinctive class has been put in the sixteenth century.[11] It has been suggested that they were rather alienated.[12] Yet the sixteenth century clearly had a place for intellectuals who felt they belonged to a 'commonwealth of learning', a 'republic of letters', where they do not appear to have felt 'alienated' at all. Politicians respected academics and there was no culture of intellectual anti-élitism in English public life as yet. And the active involvement of Cambridge's academics in the sixteenth-century revolution extended as fully into politics and the Church as it did into 'renaissance' learning. These were no figures in an ivory tower.

At the same time, one of the most important new dimensions of the post-medieval universities was the expectation that they would form not only the mind but the man. Medieval education for the younger child firmly coupled study and discipline, and continued to do so, but this had not traditionally been the way in the universities, which had concerned themselves solely with the students' minds. That is not to say that there were not provisions for maintaining good order but that is a very different thing from designing a syllabus with spiritual and moral formation built into it. 'My intention was to outline a way of life for you, not a course of study,' Erasmus had said in his *Enchiridion* (1503). Erasmus had something in mind not far from the way classical philosophers had understood the intimate relationship of 'progress in understanding' with 'progress in right conduct'. His thinking in tune with Cicero's *De officiis,* with its practical notions of the way to ensure the fulfilment of duties in public life.

In fact some of the Cambridge figures we are about to meet, like John Fisher when Margaret Beaufort tried to carry him off to court, felt a considerable tension between their engagement in public affairs and a desire to continue with academic activities. This too gave them a strong fellow-feeling with the classical and late antique authors they read, some of who said they felt torn in exactly the same way between being in demand at work and longing for time for thought and reflection. Augustine, Bishop of Hippo (354–430), shared Cicero's ambition to retire from public life and discuss philosophical questions with cultivated friends; he actually did so for a time at Cassiciacum on Lake Como shortly after his conversion to Christianity in 386, and the three books he wrote record their conversation. Cassiodorus (c.485–c.585) gave up being a civil servant to found a monastic community and school. Erasmus made plans – which he did not live to realize – to enter with one or two like-minded friends, into a reclusive house inside the walls of a Carthusian monastery, and talk philosophy,[13] as soon as it could be arranged. To many this seemed an ideal life, serious, self-denying, intent upon what really mattered. Academic life seemed to provide a way of living such a life, while affairs of state tugged the successful academics away to public business.

In this new revived consciousness of a way of living last experienced in Europe at the end of the Roman Empire, the 'humanism' which began to stir in the fifteenth century, universities flourished. Under the stimulus of the rediscovering of Greek and its literature from the fifteenth century came a change of 'flavour' in the study of the Latin classics, their elevation from mere practice-texts to enable a boy to learn Latin, to become the subject of 'literary' study in their own right. Scholars suddenly saw them as accounts of real life and real feelings like their own. Antiquity came to life and not merely as the source of authoritative quotations it had been for a thousand years.

Erasmus planned the work which became the *Antibarbari* before he was 20. His 'barbarians' are those who are hostile to the study of the classics.[14] Erasmus wrote and rewrote this work, and his refusal to allow an earlier version to be printed indicates the seriousness with which he took it, and his determination to get it 'right' for its eventual publication in 1519–20. The genre he ultimately chose is that of a Ciceronian[15] philosophical conversation among friends, who happen to meet the Mayor of Bergen, William Conrad, on a recreational country walk. The question they discuss was far from new, but it was novel to treat it almost as a 'novel' in the modern sense. The question was why the study of classical literature is in decline and whether this is attributable to the influence of Christianity. The inclusion of the local Major and of James Batt, secretary to the city of Bergen, enables them to ask whether this has anything to do with current public policy. Batt describes his efforts to bring local educational provision up to scratch after he had been at the University of Paris and understood how unsatisfactory local teaching was.[16]

*   *   *

Cambridge joins the 'Renaissance'

The Dutchman Jan Standonck (1454–1504) was involved in the reform movement in the fifteenth-century French Church, which included an attempt to improve clerical education. Erasmus had been one of his students, though not always an uncritical one. Standonck founded several colleges which insisted on a high sense of vocation in their students, and commitment and strict discipline. These included the Collège de Montaigu, which became part of the University of Paris. Erasmus had had as a pupil at the Collège de Montaigu in Paris about 1498, Richard Whitford, who became a fellow of St. John's College. Whitford was accompanied in his overseas studies in Paris by Lord Mountjoy (Richard Blount) later a patron of Erasmus. Also with the friends was Robert Fisher, a kinsman of John Fisher, for whom Erasmus wrote 'How to write letters' (*De conscribendis epistolis*). The three of them persuaded Erasmus to come to Cambridge, though it took some years to get him to accept and he did not do so until 1511.[17] This, like Cranmer's later 'procurement' of Martin Bucer for a Professorship at the University,[18] was an early example of academic head-hunting.

From 1511 to 1514, Erasmus lived at Queens' College and was a 'presence' in the University. He was given a 'Lady Margaret Readership' in Divinity. 'I taught Greek and Divinity for a great number of months at Cambridge,' he says in a letter. 'Always free, however; I've made up my mind never to depart from this practice'.[19] He admits in another letter, written at the time he was giving these lectures, that, even though the students did not have to pay, the audience for his lectures on Chrysoloras' Grammar is 'small'. 'Perhaps more people will attend when I start Theodore's Grammar',[20] he wrote optimistically. But he was too far ahead of his time. Despite John Fisher's earnest assurance to him that he was 'indispensable',[21] Erasmus was not, in the end, altogether happy with his life in Cambridge, though he had some respect for what he found there. He remarked on the ascetic life and the high religious spirit of the colleges, as he perceived them at the time, in a letter he wrote in 1514: 'In this place are colleges in which there's so much religion and so marked a sobriety in living that you'd despise every form of religious régime in comparison if you saw it.'[22]

135

Possibly the sheer unfamiliarity of the Greek grammarians was what kept the students away. It seems unlikely that the stylish Erasmus was a dull lecturer, though lectures were still in Latin, and his Latin is peculiarly convoluted and opaque.

St. John's College and Trilingualism

There were scholars in both Oxford and Cambridge in the fifteenth century who could have taught Greek, but Erasmus seems to have been one of the first to do so, and to start the fashion. He had the support of Fisher as Chancellor of the University. The Oxford Greek enthusiasts lacked an equivalent 'sponsor', but they had a reputation for keenness and hard work and the Cambridge ones feared Oxford were getting ahead.

Teaching Greek and Hebrew was very much the coming thing in Europe. In 1517 the College of the Three Languages, *Collegium Busleiden*, was founded at the existing (late medieval) University in Louvain, with the financial support and encouragement of a benefactor called Busleiden.[23] Erasmus was heavily involved in the forwarding of this enterprise and his time in Cambridge presumably gave him opportunities to discuss it with academics and patrons of the University. The University of Louvain had begun as a result of a petition by the Duke of Burgundy to the Pope asking him to establish a *studium generale*, though until 1431 there was no faculty of theology at Louvain. Martin V issued a Bull in 1425, conceding to the prince the right to grant privileges to the University. Rectors were elected for three months then later for six, in rotation, by delegates of the faculties, which each took turns. It was well supported by endowments from the family of the Dukes of Burgundy. It benefited from the rise of the Hapsburg dynasty. Louvain, and particularly Busleiden, became in due course a place of refuge for English scholars such as Thomas More, who were uncomfortable with reforming ideas in their own countries.[24] There were other important patrons, such as Adrian Floris, tutor of Charles V, later Cardinal of Utrecht, and finally Pope, taking the name of Adrian VI (1522).

The foundation of St. John's College came to be seen by John Fisher as an opportunity to create a rival in Cambridge. The plan was to create one of the fashionable Colleges of the Three Languages there. There was an intention that nothing but Greek,[25] Hebrew and Latin should be spoken on college premises. This was ambitious with such a novel and untested venture, for there was a good deal to be done to set the thing up satisfactorily, before the courts could ring with Greek and Hebrew conversation. There were quarrels about teaching styles. And Wakefield, one of the proposed lecturers, was obliged to go abroad to improve the standard of his Hebrew before he felt equipped to begin lecturing in 1524.

Fisher himself tried to learn Greek (briefly under Erasmus' tuition). He reached a standard which allowed him to join in debates (though only in Latin) about the Greek terms in Scripture. He tried to learn Hebrew too, contacting the German humanist Johann Reuchlin (1455–1522) through Erasmus. Once Wakefield the Hebrew lecturer had mastered his subject sufficiently to begin work, Fisher took him as a tutor to support his own efforts. These linguistic skills were not only of their time but also as it turned out useful practical skills when it came to assisting in discussions about the theological justification for the King's divorce.

Syllabus change

The problem was that this was not just a matter of adding two important new languages to the 'arts' syllabus, the languages in which the Bible had been written. What was afoot was a complete overhaul of the traditional syllabus, far more radical than the late medieval battle about the 'two ways'. So it is not surprising that there seems to have been resistance from academic conservatives. Erasmus wrote to Colet in September 1511 that he was sometimes having to do battle against 'the Thomists and Scotists'.[26] Colet replied speedily to encourage him with friendly compliments. 'You claim the ability to bring youths to a reasonable command of expression, in both Latin and Greek, in fewer years than the conventional pedagogue requires for giving them baby-talk.' 'How I longed to have you, Erasmus, as a teacher in my school.'[27] Later, in 1517, with some satisfaction, Erasmus called Cambridge a 'changed place'. 'This university now abominates those vain quibbles, which conduce rather to quarrelling than to piety'.[28]

Erasmus conceived the idea of writing the book on the rationale of academic study (*De ratione studii*) in 1511 in correspondence with Colet.[29] Its full title became 'On the method of study and interpretation of texts' (*De ratione studii ac legendi interpretandique auctores*). Erasmus, from whose pen the word 'game' (*ludus*) is rarely far away, approved of the idea that the intellectual formation of the young is assisted by approaching study as a serious game. There should be wit and witticisms and they should learn to handle language confidently enough to play games with it: *per lusum iocumque literarum figuris*. This should, he believes, be coupled with moving to the study of 'modes of speaking' (*ad usum loquendi*) immediately (*statim*) after the children have mastered the elements, as a means of ensuring that they never develop barbarous habits in their Latin or their Greek.[30] The other element in the title refers to teaching students how to read and interpret authors, a change which would also effect a revolution. This book forms a counterpart in subject-matter to the *De Doctrina Christiana* of Augustine, in which Augustine tried to set out ground-rules on much the same fundamentals, how Christians were to 'use' secular authors and the skills of secular rhetoric and how they were to approach the reading and interpretation of the Bible.

'How to give children a rapid and liberal grounding', *De pueris statim ac liberaliter instituendis* appeared in 1529. Why, asks Erasmus, should we consider that age which is appropriate for learning good behaviour to be inappropriate for the study of literature (*ad literas*)?[31] He is convinced that this is the way to form good citizens. *Oportet scholam aut nullam esse aut publicam.*[32] It would be pushing the evidence too far to suggest that his time in Cambridge put these ideas into Erasmus' head, but it evidently helped to crystallize them.

The leaders in radical syllabus change were making their impact throughout Europe, though mainly in Germany. Here Erasmus was of one mind with Melanchthon (1497–1560) who made most of the running. Philip Melanchthon had been intensively home-educated. He was first taught by a private tutor then sent to Pforzheim to live with his grandmother, who was the sister of Reuchlin, who had been pioneering the study of Hebrew. He was taught the Greek and Latin poets by the local rector and influenced by Reuchlin, who took a strong continuing interest in him. At 12 he entered the University of Heidelberg, where humanism had already been partly established by the lectures of Rudolph Agricola (1442/3–85), who had taught there briefly from 1482, and was another student of Hebrew. Melanchthon learned rhetoric with Peter Gunther and astronomy under Conrad Helvetius, a pupil of Caesarius. Meanwhile he eagerly continued his private studies. He gained his B.A. in 1511, but he was too young in 1512 to take his M.A.

He was one of the young enthusiasts who were able to make an individual impact in this period. He moved to Tübingen and continued to study, 'tasting' the old higher degree subjects, particularly law. He got his M.A. in 1514 and began to teach in the University, first Roman poets, then rhetoric. In 1516 he published an edition of Terence and in 1518 a Greek grammar. He dipped into theology, reading the Fathers and the Greek New Testament. Reuchlin successfully recommended him for a Professorship of Greek at the University of Wittenberg in 1518. Wittenberg was still a very young university; he had promulgated its first set of statutes in 1504, basing them on those of Tübingen.[33]

Melanchthon was a passionate educator. He kept a Latin school in his house for a decade, in which he taught boys their grammar in preparation for their university studies. In 1526 he started another experimental school, in Nuremberg, at a slightly more advanced 'pre-university' level. This did not last and Melanchthon was in any case turning his attention to the 'reform' of the conventional university syllabus. His idea was to strengthen the study of the literary classics, as an end in itself and also as a means of beginning a training in rhetoric. There was to be study of Greek and Hebrew. The study of logic, which had bulked enormously large in the late medieval course, was to shrink and be simplified. Melanchthon was also interested in bringing about an alteration in the way Scripture was studied, by considering the text in its original languages.[34] Melanchthon tried these theories about syllabus revision out at Tübingen, and also at Wittenberg – a University at which it was in due course natural to attempt 'reform', since it was 'Luther's' University – at Frankfurt, Leipzig, Rostock and Heidelberg.[35] Newer universities founded at Marburg (1527), Konigsberg (1544) and Jena (1548), also relied on his advice, and his former pupils helped to disseminate his ideas.[36]

One of the characteristics of this new-style syllabus was that learning for students was intended to be fun. The medieval syllabus had provided intense amusement in the conduct of disputations, with students continuing the debate in taverns; there is also evidence that entertainment was to be had from asking the lecturer awkward questions and inviting him to disagree with what other lecturers had said. There were now new kinds of enjoyment on offer. Something of the flavour of Melanchthon's teaching is still to be tasted in his surviving *Declamations*, such as the *Musarum trium ludus* ('The game of the three muses', on the *trivium*).[37] *De Artibus Liberalibus* was given at Tübingen in 1517.[38]

His 'policy statement' 'On the improvement of the studies of youth' (*De corrigendis adolescentiae studiis*), given at Wittenberg on 29 August 1518, begins with a modest disclaimer (itself a recognized topos) of his unworthiness to address this assembly of Masters and Doctors in the presence of the Rector. He wants to discuss the way 'the youth of Germany' are introduced to 'this happy battle of letters', *hoc foelix certamen literarum*.[39] He rehearses the history of schools since the time of Charlemagne.[40] He describes the medieval norms, including mention of the place of the higher degree subjects of medicine and law as well as theology. This *ratio studiorum*, he explains, held sway (*regnavit*) for about three centuries (*annos circiter trecentos*) in *Anglia,* in *Galliis,* in *Germania*. The question now is whether some of these studies are redundant and others might take their place, particularly the study of Greek. What do the students learn now? Too much logic. *Logicum vim omnem ac discrimina sermonis tractat.*[41] How do you avoid their getting bored? *(fastigia studiorum).*[42] The best plan is to get the student to read Greek writings *(iungendae Graecae literae)* as well as Latin in a range of genres, such as works of philosophers, theologians, historians, orators, poets, *ut Philosophos, Theologos, Historicos, Oratores, Poetas lecturus.* The study of natural science is included in the study of Greek. Melanchthon complains that the 'barbarians' demand 'the titles and rights of learned teachers', in which category he himself would prefer to place individuals with cultivated minds and more modern tastes.[43] This address caused a certain furore, as contemporary correspondence shows.

Like Erasmus, Melanchthon strongly favoured the study of rhetoric. This had been the leading area of study in the late antique world, where a young man would have to be an orator in the courts and in politics, even possibly in encomium-writing (the three recognized branches). It will be remembered that in the Middle Ages the study of rhetoric had decayed, partly because there were few available classical textbooks, and partly because no comparably sophisticated political life requiring such skills awaited the educated man. The Middle Ages had invented three new 'arts' of rhetoric, the art of formal letter-writing for the secular and ecclesiastical civil service, the art of poetry and the art of preaching, each involving formalized use of elements of ancient rhetoric. There was also study of 'topics', which in ancient rhetoric had been the skill of collecting ready-made packets of material in the memory, both arguments and illustrations, so that the orator could speak fluently without a script.

In his *Encomium eloquentiae*, 'In praise of eloquence', Melanchthon argues the return to something closer to the ancient uses of rhetoric. Every human society has a need for skills in communication, both public and private: '*Omnis hominum societas, ratio vitae instituendae publice et privatim, conquirendorumque omnium quibus vitam tuemur, denique commercia omnia sermone continentur.*'[44]

The benefits to the trained mind of the study of rhetoric include, in his view, encouraging the students to compare themselves with the best models not only of style but of conduct: *ad eiusmodi scriptorum exempla se comparent.* From good models, the student will learn wisdom in his own dealings.[45] When it comes to the specific areas of rhetorical study, he displays a strong consciousness of 'letters' as 'literary'. The 'high art' approach to writing applies to letters too. He seems, like several of his academic contemporaries, to seek a conscious revival of the Ciceronian letter (as against the formats of the *ars dictaminis*). And he does not confine himself to Latin for letters; sometimes he chooses to write a letter to Reuchlin in German.

Melanchthon designed a set of regulations for the arts faculty at Wittenberg in 1545 which may be regarded as the matured results of this early work, placed in the context of the needs of what was now a Reformation as well as a Renaissance. There were to be ten lecturers, to teach languages and philosophy, with two *inspectores* of the college. Greek texts were specified as well as scientific texts of the ancient world, such as Pliny's *Natural History*, and also moral teaching.[46]

* * *

Erasmus, Luther and a 'Reformation' Cambridge

Less than three years after he left Cambridge, Erasmus published his Greek New Testament, in a dual language text alongside the Latin of the Vulgate. Thomas Bilney, a student at Trinity College, read it soon after it appeared, and it transformed his life. He was known for the austerity of his personal life and his active care for the poor and needy in Cambridge. (He did not approve of ecclesiastical music, though this was apparently a matter of personal taste not of dogma.) He had been ordained in 1519 before he had taken his degree.

What happened to Bilney is reported in the *Book of Martyrs* of John Foxe (1517–87), whose highly coloured version of things became a major influence on the way readers perceived the events of the English Reformation. Bilney had a classic *sortilegium* experience, in which the chance reading of a passage brings about a transforming moment of illumination. 'I chanced upon this sentence of St. Paul' (I Timothy 1, 'It is a true saying and worthy' etc.) and 'This one sentence...did so exhilarate my heart...that even immediately I seemed to myself inwardly to feel a most marvellous comfort and quietness'.[47] This is the classic 'conversion' experience but in Bilney's case, it had the specific effect of making him love the Bible. This was to prove important because the recognition of a new 'feeling' for Scripture was about to bring about in Cambridge a rethinking of the proper sequence of study in theology.

Another Cambridge student, George Stafford, who knew both Greek and Hebrew, used the *Novum Testamentum* and may well have studied under Erasmus, was at Pembroke College. He became

Proctor and University preacher in 1523, and in 1524 Reader in Divinity at Pembroke. Although Bilney lived long enough to be tried for heresy, Stafford – apparently rather a success as a teacher of such novelties – died in 1529 of the plague and did not live beyond the point when Wolsey received ill reports of his orthodoxy. Stafford began to reorder his lectures, beginning not with Peter Lombard's *Sentences* in the way traditional since the thirteenth century, but with the New Testament. This meant not only putting Bible study before systematic theology; it ultimately ousted the study of 'systematic' theology altogether in its medieval form.

The loss of this traditional 'systematic' framework had immense consequences for the controversies of the Reformation period. As Thomas Aquinas had explained in the preface to his thirteenth-century *Summa Theologiae*, the proliferation of questions made theology impossible for students to master. It made sense to begin with fundamentals (What is theology? Is there a God? How do we know? What is God like? What is the world and how was it made? What went wrong? What has God done about it? What will happen in the end?). Peter Lombard's *Sentences* already provided opportunities to consider all these matters in order and the commentaries which record the lecturing upon the *Sentences* decade by decade in every university throughout Europe show clearly how fashionable preoccupations shifted with the debates of the day. But whatever the current arguments were about, the student was unlikely to get lost because the discussion was 'located' in this overall framework. Luther's ideas about 'justification', for example, can be traced to commentary on the relevant portion of the *Sentences*. Once that framework was abandoned – and just as completely new questions began to press themselves – those grappling with currently fashionable topics struggled to position the topics and themselves in an overall framework of doctrine.

Entering the lists against the 'heretics'

The Reformation began in the university world. Martin Luther (1483–1546) taught in the University at Wittenberg from 1512 to the end of his life and it was there that he (or possibly some of his students) posted his 95 theses on the Church door as a challenge to the authorities. 'Theses' were the standard format in which to frame a topic for a disputation. He meant to start an argument, and within a 'University' context. Melanchthon joined Luther as a colleague and ally at Wittenberg (though a more moderate and diplomatic one than Luther himself).

For a considerable time, it cannot have been apparent that the challenging opinions about which news was crossing from the Continent were necessarily erroneous; or that they constituted a threat to orthodoxy; or that, if they did, it was a serious threat. Nevertheless, John Fisher quickly came to fear the 'reformers', and to seek in Cambridge the resources which were going to be needed to counter them. He had to work out a whole 'methodology' – how to argue back, how direct a polemic to attempt, whether to write fiercely or coaxingly; he had to work out the right answer for himself on a number of knotty questions.

He eventually realized that writing against an opinion had a dangerous tendency to disseminate it and make it more attractive. But it was also dangerous to let things go unanswered. A 'reference' literature had to be created from scratch for the use of those keen to ensure that they themselves had not slipped into heresy. Pamphlet warfare followed. Fisher wrote in the 1520s against Martin Luther and Johannes Oecolampadius, publishing the immensely influential *Confutation of the Lutheran Assertion* in 1523 and the *On the Truth of the Body and Blood of Christ in the Eucharist* (1527) against Oecolampadius in 1527. Even King Henry VIII joined in, publishing an *Assertion that there are Seven Sacraments* in 1521 to counter Luther's *The Babylonian Captivity of the Church*.

With royal support Cardinal Wolsey, still Henry VIII's Lord Chancellor, promulgated *Exsurge domine*, a papal Bull against Luther in 1521. When Luther's books were publicly burned in England in 1521, Fisher preached for the occasion. He was particularly worried at signs that reforming ideas might be brewing in Cambridge and he visited it to preach in order to express his concerns seven times in 1521. In 1527 Thomas Arthur, one of the Fellows of St. John's became known as a heretic and Fisher revised the College statutes in 1530 to allow the Master and the Senior Fellows to remove summarily any Fellow even suspected of heresy. This was never actually done.

Shortly afterwards, in 1523, John Fisher and other bishops were pressing Wolsey to make a Visitation of Cambridge to purge the University of heretical opinions. This is an important moment in the history of academic freedom as well as that of Visitations, although Wolsey refused to instigate one on this occasion. Academic freedom was not yet thought of in terms of freedom of speech, but as a matter of institutional autonomy, the right to freedom from interference. The old tradition that episcopal visitation of the universities might be allowable at least where the spiritual welfare of their members was concerned had always met resistance from the universities, but this looked like a new dimension of intrusion upon their independence. Opinions were their trade. It was strongly felt that it was for the universities to control the expression of those opinions.[48]

The 'Heads of Houses' (as the heads of the colleges came to be known) were united in their resistance to the new ideas. Younger men and students were naturally more inclined to take them up. Even those who were later to take the other side can be seen anxiously trying to dissuade their fellows from the new order of study and from embracing the new opinions. Before his own change of position in 1524, Hugh Latimer is recorded as having gone into the schoolroom where students were at their daily exercises in disputation and having 'eloquently' begged them to abandon the 'new-fangled' habit of beginning with the study of the Bible instead of the systematic theology to be found in Peter Lombard's *Sentences*.[49]

It seems that Bilney and perhaps Stafford may have brought about the change in Latimer's attitude, in another moment of dramatic 'conversion'. It was not lost on contemporaries that St. Paul, too, had been fulminating against the Christian faith with notable energy before he stopped resisting and found himself a Christian.[50] The occasion was the examination disputation for the degree of Bachelor of Divinity which Latimer faced in 1524. It was a public occasion; for examinations were public performances. Moreover, Latimer was the chaplain of the University. He was publicly to refute the teaching of Melanchthon, author both of a syllabus reform in the direction of the new Renaissance learning and of Lutheran teachings. Melanchthon's name was well enough known in Cambridge from the lectures William Paget had been giving on his *Rhetoric*. So naturally there was likely to be an audience interested to see how he got on.

Bilney was present at the disputation and he cleverly went to Latimer afterwards to make his confession, as was appropriate since Latimer was the University's chaplain. He confessed his own story of conversion and Latimer's mind was changed.[51]

Cambridge and the sixteenth-century 'war on terror'

The events of the decades which followed, with Cambridge figures moving prominently in and out of the events which were shaking the nation, have aspects which irresistibly recall the talk of a 'war on terror' at the beginning of the twenty-first century. Persons of contrasting religious opinions depicted one another not only as enemies but as dangerous enemies, preachers of hatred and inciters to warfare, enemies of God, of the state, of public order, of all right-thinking people. And there was alarm that the threats were coming from overseas too, when Cambridge was in such active communication with scholars elsewhere.

John Bugenhagen, one of Luther's inner circle, wrote an *Epistola ad Anglos* ('Letter to the English'), which was published in 1525 at Augsburg. Bugenhagen's *Letter to the English* made its appearance in England at a sensitive moment. Thomas More (1478–1535) responded in his 'Letter to Bugenhagen'.[52] He was 'employed' as a tame humanist at Henry's Court but he had had contacts with the Continental 'resistance' to Lutheranism through a meeting with Johann Eck in 1525. Eck had come to England to nerve the resistance there to the invasion of Lutheran ideas. More's follow-up activities were draconian. He was one of a party which tackled the merchants of the Hanseatic League who were based in London in 1525 and insisted that they undertake to destroy any imports of dubious books they became aware of. Under the pressure of a search they all admitted to having encountered Lutheran materials in German although none of them could read Latin.[53] More played the innocent. He pretends that the Letter was left at his house anonymously, that he scarcely knew how to react, that he is no theologian but feels it appropriate to demonstrate that even those who are as ignorant as he can see that a loyal Christian cannot be a Lutheran.[54]

Thomas More's connection with Cambridge as its High Steward was balanced by the fact that he held the same office in Oxford. His sophisticated and restrained handling of himself in the period of personal prominence when he was Speaker of the House of Commons (from 1523), then Chancellor of the Duchy of Lancaster (1525–9) and Chancellor of England from 1529 to 1532 contrasts with some of the more extreme language of others. It provides a striking illustration of the extent to which public life had already tuned itself to the new Renaissance sophistication. When he was elected as Speaker of the House of Commons, he

> pleaded his disabilities as usual [the modesty topos again]; and in his speech brought in a story of Phormio, the philosopher, who desired Hannibal to come to his lectures, which when he consented to and came, Phormio began to read *De Re militari*, of chivalry; that as soon as Hannibal heard this, he called the philosopher an arrogant fool, to presume to teach him, who was already master of chivalry and all the arts of war.

So he begged the King to choose someone more suitable for the post, to which 'the Cardinal, as Chancellor, replied that the King 'was well acquainted with his wit, learning and discretion', so he considered the Commons had made the right choice.[55]

John Foxe suggests that by the 1520s a considerable group of Lutheran 'followers' was meeting regularly in Cambridge at the 'White Horse Tavern'. It has been said that Lutheranism surfaced in England in a sermon delivered by Robert Barnes at Cambridge. Robert Barnes was at that time still an Augustinian Friar in Cambridge. He preached on Luther's 'postil' (gloss or comment) on the Gospel for the day and Hugh Latimer is said to have preached a 'Lutheran' sermon of his own on the same day.[56]

When this is set against records of the Convocation of Canterbury, the 'parliament' of the clergy of the province, it is clear that there was alarm in official Church circles about what was going on in universities. The first items in the early sixteenth century concern routine familiar questions about protecting 'privileges', that is exemptions of the universities from paying subsidies. But in the Convocation of 1529–36 *(De qualitate ordinandorum)*, among the categories of ordinand who are acceptable are listed those students of Oxford and Cambridge who have the sealed letters of the Commissary or Vice-Chancellor as testimony to their acceptability as safe and satisfactory prospective clergy.[57] Meanwhile, Convocation supported the idea that an inquisition should be conducted into the 'heretical wickedness' and the 'mode of study' of the universities: *De inquisitione habenda tam super haeretica pravitate quam de modo studendi in universitatibus.*

> It is not in dispute that those universities of Oxford and Cambridge are springs, from which the rivers of all knowledge flow, and if they are corrupted, muddied with errors and the muckiness of heresy, how greatly is it to be feared what will flow from those springs to infect the whole kingdom with heresy.[58]

To try to deal with this problem, the Convocation decreed that Oxford should be under the Bishop of Lincoln and Cambridge under the Bishop of Ely's jurisdiction and they should inspect them for heresy. Arundel's visitation rules are to apply.

Towards protestant nationhood: The king's divorce

But the national attitude was about the change. Cambridge's academics played an active part in the process by which England passed through the Reformation and transformed its public life, not only while reforming ideas were being resisted but also when everything turned upside down and were being officially encouraged. This involvement was very noticeable in the course of the turmoil which led both to the King's divorce from his first wife Catherine of Aragon and to his setting himself up as the head of the Church in England. Here was Reformation as a political reality.

John Fisher was consulted early on when Henry decided he wanted to divorce Catherine in the hope that a new marriage would bring him a male heir. Fisher was confident the Pope would be able to settle the matter. He spent a considerable amount of time researching and writing, on the fine points of the legal and theological argument about the extent of the Pope's authority in the matter, seeking to balance the arguments for and against in the manner in which scholastic disputation had trained him to approach any *quaestio*. But this was not merely an abstract question which could be satisfactorily 'determined' by a senior academic, and in any case, the scholastic tradition was that there were usually two sides to a question.

The King was not pleased by Fisher's conservative and balanced method of approach and in 1527 he enlisted Wakefield, the lecturer in Hebrew from St. John's, to make a case to meet his own wishes. Fisher punished Wakefield for his defection by replacing him at St. John's with Ralph Baynes, who prudently remained loyal to Fisher in the ensuing and increasingly acrimonious arguments. The debate continued for two years, with both Fisher and Wakefield assiduously searching the Scriptures for a clinching passage.

In the summer of 1529 a tribunal was held at Blackfriars in London to decide whether the King's marriage was valid. It was impossible for it to arrive at a binding decision once the Queen had appealed to Rome asking the Pope to rule that the tribunal had no jurisdiction. Cardinal Campeggi had in fact worked with Cardinal Wolsey to set up the Blackfriars hearing, but he duly removed the case to Rome for consideration. Fisher was now irrevocably committed to supporting Catharine's side, and continued so for the six years of wrangling which followed. Henry VIII began to put pressure on the English Church, extending the powers of the secular authorities to see how far he could go. Fisher tried to protest at what seemed to him a national apostasy, but the King had his way and Parliament made the necessary legislative changes. Fisher and the bishops who had supported him were imprisoned (though not for long).

Of the other 'players' in this process, Matthew Parker, later to be Archbishop of Canterbury, became a student at Corpus Christi College in 1522 and was a Fellow by 1527. Thomas Wolsey was eager to have him as well as Thomas Cranmer for his own new college of Christ Church, which he was founding in Oxford. Both refused to move. Parker's loyalty was not only to Cambridge but to the burgeoning 'reforming' movement there. For in contrast with Fisher, Parker had been drawn into the reforming party in Cambridge and he stood so starkly on the opposite side that he became chaplain to Anne Boleyn once she replaced Catherine of Aragon as Queen, and in 1537, Chaplain to the King. He became Cambridge's Chancellor in 1540, when Cromwell was executed.

Thomas Cromwell (c.1485–1540) was by contrast not a 'university' man, though he came to have strong links with Cambridge. He spent his youth travelling the Continent and in trade. He moved into the law by providing business and sometimes diplomatic legal services and also, as his reputation grew, assistance in ecclesiastical cases, including appeals to the papal curia. By the 1520s he was known and respected as a lawyer. He became a Member of Parliament in 1523. Cromwell was not without intellectual interests or Cambridge connections, however. He was a friend of Miles Coverdale, the Bible translator, then still an Augustinian friar in Cambridge, who wrote to him before 1527 to ask him for books to assist him in his own studies.[59] Wolsey commissioned Cromwell to deal with the legal and particularly the conveyancing work inseparable from his own plan to build the immense and grand new Cardinal College in Oxford (which became Christ Church in 1546). Cromwell, in company with other officials of the time, was not above pocketing revenues. He rose socially and, despite his own links with Oxford, he sent his son Gregory to Pembroke College, Cambridge.

Thomas Cranmer rides out the changes

The remaining key Cambridge figure in these events was Thomas Cranmer (1489–1556).[60] He went to Jesus College, Cambridge, in 1503, another college which had benefited from the patronage of Lady Margaret Beaufort. He was to remain in Cambridge until 1529.[61] He took an unusually long time, 11 years, to complete his first degree. There are hints that he was an over-conscientious student of the more recondite corners of scholasticism. His early anonymous biographer provides a famous description of Cranmer as 'nosseled [trained] in the grossest kynd of sophistry, logike, philosophy morall and naturall (not in the text of the old philosophers, but chefely in the darke ridels and quidites of Duns and other subtile questionestes).'[62]

His lack of early reformist tendencies can be seen in the notes he made in a copy of John Fisher's *Assertionis Lutheranae confutatio*, the editions published in Antwerp in 1523. He was shocked to read Luther's criticisms of the Pope. There were already hints that he thought the best way to resolve the growing controversy was by holding a General Council of the Church.[63]

Cranmer became a Fellow of Jesus until, sometime before 1519, he married. That lost him his Fellowship, for it had to be given up on marriage. It seemed likely that a non-clerical career now lay before him. He compromised by becoming a 'reader' for the house of Benedictines which was to become Magdalene College, refounded in 1542. But his wife, Joan, soon died in childbirth. Cranmer was then able to rethink his career and Jesus College generously took him back into the Fellowship. This was timely, for Luther was becoming controversial in Germany and Cranmer began to interest himself in the new theology. He applied himself to the study of the Bible. He equipped himself so satisfactorily from the College's point of view that by the late 1520s it appointed him to a college lectureship in Greek and Hebrew.

The custom of looking in the universities for likely academics who could be used in the service of the Government was now well-established. Cranmer seems to have been head-hunted by Wolsey, for he appears on a diplomatic mission to Spain in 1527. He is glimpsed carrying a business letter for Wolsey which had been written by Thomas Cromwell as his agent. He was beginning to be drawn into the circles of central Government. About this time he also began to support the King's wish for an annulment of his marriage.

In the summer of 1529, he stayed with the Cressy family in Essex, probably because he did not want to linger in Cambridge, where there was once more reported to be an outbreak of the plague. He was tutor to their two sons at the time. There he met Stephen Gardiner (1497–1555), another of the Cambridge students who had encountered Erasmus in Paris, in his case in 1511, and Edward Foxe, Provost of King's College, who were staying there too. They were both in the service of Thomas Wolsey and they were able to give him an up-to-date account of the progress of the divorce. Cranmer suggested that a cheaper and possibly more effective way to go about it was not to hire lawyers but to seek the views of Europe's leading theologians. He himself was of course potentially one of these and Thomas More remembered Cranmer being sent to him in October to give an opinion, not long after he was elected Speaker of the House of Commons in 1523.

Cranmer was now put under pressure by the King to assemble arguments in favour of the annulment of his marriage, and to smooth material provided by others so that it read well and sounded convincing. Gardiner and Foxe claimed to have used his work in 1530, in their attempt to persuade Cambridge to provide an official opinion on the King's side. In April 1531 the *Gravissimae…academiarum censurae* was published in November 1531, in an English version, asserting that it contained the opinions of the universities of France and Italy, 'The determinations of the most famous and most excellent universities of Italy and France, that it is unlawful for a man to marry his brother's wife; that the pope hath no power to dispense therewith.' Cranmer's personal opinions and his hired work seem to have coincided, for he was beginning to question papal authority for himself.

Cranmer's links with the Continental reformers and the university world of mainland Europe continued even after he had left Cambridge for the King's service. He exchanged letters with Bullinger and Martin Bucer. 'Academic exchanges' were arranged with Zurich. We shall hear more of those.

In 1531 Henry was seeking recognition as supreme head of the Church of England. This was in accordance with the developing Lutheran argument, articulated in 1530 in the Augsburg Confession, that although a monarchical Papacy was unacceptable it was in line with the practice of the early Church of allowing a Christian monarch to preside, at least in non-sacramental matters. Had not Constantine the first Christian Emperor summoned the Council of Nicaea in 325, the Council which produced the Nicene Creed?

Fisher objected, though, inveterate 'fixer' as he was, he offered possible compromise wording. Drafts of his continuing attempts to object survive. However, by 1532 Fisher was becoming aged and ill and his energies were diminishing – though he had his supporters among the clergy, including Nicholas Ridley (d.1555). In Cambridge the Master of Christ's College, John Watson, also stood up for him. Supporters of the King tried to have him poisoned, but it was Fisher's custom to give his food to the poor and needy and it was two of those who died.

In 1533 Thomas Cranmer was made Archbishop of Canterbury and obliged to take a direct part in the legislative changes which fixed the breach with Rome as a reality for England, including new powers for himself as Archbishop. (The Act of Dispensations allowed for Cranmer to issue dispensations instead of the Pope). In 1533 Cranmer published the decree which granted the King his divorce. Fisher tried to speak 'against' once more but he was arrested and the draconian Stephen Gardiner, now Bishop of Winchester, was put in charge of him. Cranmer would not take the required oath recognizing the remarriage and in April 1534 he was put in the Tower of London. Later in the year he was deprived of his ecclesiastical offices. In 1535 Henry became 'Supreme Head of the Church of England' and Fisher refused to countenance that either. Fisher was tried and sentenced and his head was cut off on Tower Hill in 1535, to be displayed on London Bridge for the public to see as a warning to others. His career as a Cambridge academic who entered public life without suppressing his conscience, illustrates the dangers that might lead to in Tudor time. Ironically, his favourite college, St. John's, became in due course a hotbed of puritan opinions.

* * *

The Cambridge translators

The great early sixteenth-century translators of the Bible into English were Cambridge men, for one of the natural consequences of the new popular enthusiasm for Bible reading was a reawakening of the calls for English translations which had produced a first 'English' Bible shortly after the death of John Wyclif. For Protestants of the sixteenth century, the Bible was the Word of God, sole and sufficient authority for the Christian. No gloss or commentary could add to it in any way. As Zwingli put it in the fifth of his 67 'Conclusions', 'All who consider other teachings equal to or higher than the Gospel err, and do not know what the Gospel is'.

The initiators of sixteenth-century English translation were Miles Coverdale (1488–1569) and William Tyndale (1494–1536). The first copies of William Tyndale's translation of the New Testament, prepared abroad, were brought secretly into England in unbound sheets in the 1520s. There was good reason to be afraid of censorship. There was a new book burning in 1526, which included some of this smuggled material.[64]

Tyndale's Preface to the New Testament (1526) acknowledges that Scripture can be hard to understand. But before the reader grappled with what it said, first it needed to be established which is the actual text. Since the fifth century everyone in the West had used the Vulgate Latin version made by Jerome, but now there were Greek and Hebrew versions to contend with too. Tyndale's Preface reflects his realization of the complexity of this task:

> I have looked over again ... with all diligence, and compared it unto the Greek, and have weeded out of it many faults ... If ought seem changed, or not altogether agreeing with the Greek, let the finder of the fault consider the Hebrew phrase or manner of speech left in the Greek words.

He was distressed to learn that George Joye (1495–1553), who had graduated from Christ's College in about 1514, was similarly engaged in making corrections, though he says that he restrained himself from entering into a dispute with him as to which of them should do it

151

or whether they might not collaborate. Joye was a serious rival. He had 'form' as a controversial reformer. When Cambridge University buildings were searched for seditious literature in 1526, Joye was found to have a copy of some of Chrysostom's sermons on Genesis and other undesirable texts. In 1527 the Prior of Newnham Priory denounced him to the Bishop of Lincoln as a heretic and he was taken off to be examined by Cardinal Wolsey, with Thomas Bilney and another 'heretic, Thomas Arthur. When he saw the manner in which they were interrogated, he decided to leave the country.

Then someone brought Tyndale a copy of Joye's work:

> and showed me so many places, in such wise altered that I was astonied and wondered not a little what fury had driven him to make such a change, and call it a diligent correction ... if that change ... be a diligent correction, then must my translation be faulty in those places, and St. Jerome's.

Once settled, the text needs clarification. The glosses and commentaries of the existing academic and ecclesiastical tradition are dangerous and likely to mislead; my 'clarification' may be your 'deceitful gloss', Tyndale seems to warn:

> I thought it my duty (most dear reader) to warn thee before, and to show thee the right way in, and to give thee the true key to open [the Scripture] withal, and to arm thee against false prophets and malicious hypocrites, whose perpetual study is to leaven the Scripture with glosses.

If private individuals are to be set free to read the Bible for themselves – as was the purpose of providing vernacular translations such as Tyndale's own – problems are going to arise about the freedom this allows readers to come to any conclusions they wish about the meaning of Scripture:

> if it were lawful ... to every man to play boo peep with the translations that are before him, and to put out the words of the text at his pleasure, and to put in everywhere his meaning or what he thought the meaning were; that were the next way to stablish all heresies and to destroy the ground wherewith we should improve them.

This was a well-trodden area of dispute. Thomas More was suspicious of allowing translations at all, because it could so easily result in the choice of the wrong word and mislead the unwary reader who had insufficient theological education to keep out of error. The typical Protestant way of dealing with this difficulty was to postulate that the Holy Spirit could be trusted to guide the faithful soul in reading the Bible.

The general thrust of the century was towards making the Bible accessible to ordinary readers and trusting that a reasonable person would be able to make sense of it (and the *right* sense of it). Tyndale's Preface to the Pentateuch of 1530 comments:

I had perceived by experience how that it was impossible to establish the laypeople in any truth, except the Scripture were plainly laid before their eyes in their mother tongue, that they might see the process, order and meaning of the text.

Miles Coverdale had shown himself to be sympathetic to the reformers as a Cambridge student. He acted for the defence in the trial of Robert Barnes in 1526. Thomas Cromwell, the King's aggressive right-hand man, became his 'protector' in the dangerous and controversial years which followed, though he found it prudent to live mostly abroad. In the years 1528–35 he spent most of his time on the Continent.

By 1535 he was ready to publish the first complete English Bible of the century. He was neither a Greek nor a Hebrew scholar so he relied on existing sources, including William Tyndale's New Testament in English which was first published in Cologne. Coverdale wrote to Thomas Cromwell from Paris in 1538, jointly with Richard Grafton, to tell him that they had 'entered into your work of the Bible. They are sending 'two ensamples'. There are to be two special copies on parchment, one for the King and one for Cromwell himself, and the rest will be on paper.

We follow not only the standing text of the Hebrew, with the interpretation of the Chaldee and the Greek; but we set also in a private table the diversity of readings of all texts, with such annotations in another table, as shall doubtless elucidate and clear the same, as well without any singularity of opinions, as all checkings and reproofs.[65]

In 1539 Miles Coverdale was invited to publish the Great Bible, a project dear to the King though he left Cranmer to organize it. It was put in all English churches in 1540. After Cromwell's execution in 1540 he had to return to exile. But he continued to work. Coverdale's *Abridgement of the Enchiridion of Erasmus* was published in 1545.[66]

* * *

Visitations: the bid for state control of Cambridge

Wolsey fell from royal favour and from power in 1530, because the King was angry that he had not been able to procure him a divorce. Thomas Cromwell was fearful for his own future, for he had no official status; a speedy move to get himself elected M.P. for Taunton protected him. By active 'networking' he secured in 1535 the King's continuing favour and a new task, 'visiting' Oxford and Cambridge.

Few institutions in the nation were so important for a Government to bring on board as the universities. So the Royal Visitations of Oxford and Cambridge in 1535 should be seen as running alongside Henry VIII's bid for independence of the authority of the Church of Rome. This 'Visitation' had a dual purpose: ensuring subscription to royal supremacy over the Church and also listing the endowments of the colleges so that the State would have a more accurate picture of their resources for its own ends. The King was unlikely successfully to establish his 'royal supremacy' over the Church if he could not also dominate the universities where the more able and influential clergy would continue to study. Oxford and Cambridge were already immensely powerful in their influence on public life. Their colleges were also temptingly wealthy.

Thomas Cromwell had even more ambitious ideas, which intruded upon the academic activities of the universities. Lutheran concern to transfer oversight of the Church into the hands of a secular 'Magistrate' was mirrored in the German attitude to the way universities should be run and it was to spill over into Tudor policy about control of Oxford and Cambridge.[67] So Cromwell wanted to interfere with the syllabus and methods of instruction. He did not go to Cambridge himself. Thomas Leigh of King's College was appointed to do the Visiting. The University received Injunctions, in two sets. The first set of Injunctions required the colleges to institute daily public lectures in Greek and Latin

1. that allegiance under the common seal of the University to the statutes regarding royal succession and supremacy be sworn by all.

2. that in all of the colleges there should be founded at their own expense two daily public lectures, one in Greek and the other in Latin.

They prohibited the study of the *Sentences* of Peter Lombard and required direct study of Bible instead, as at Oxford.

3. that no lectures be given … on the *Sentences* or any doctor who commented on them but rather all theology lectures should be on the Bible …

He set out in detail the content of the syllabus for the arts course of the future:

7. that instruction in the subjects of the faculty of arts should be in Aristotle, Rudolphus Agricola, Philip Melanchthon,

Trapezuntius, etc, and not the frivolous questions and obscure glosses of Scotus, Burley, Anthonius Trombetta, Bricot, Bruliferius, etc.[68]

There had been some changes in this direction already. A Cambridge statute of 1488 said that during the first two years there had to be lectures in 'humane' letters (including the Roman playwright Terence, who was hardly likely to be read primarily for edifying content). There had been a change of culture and expectation under the influence of Erasmus and others. But this was something quite new, attempted state control of the design of the syllabus.

Further injunctions were added. These were a mixture of the academic and the financial. They included strictures against the selling of Fellowships in the colleges, and a requirement that elections be made on merit. There was also a demand that colleges should yield up all their 'papistical muniments' and present inventories to Cromwell 'to await his good pleasure'. All these injunctions were to be read out in public monthly.

Regius Professorships

In the 1540s a series of Regius Professorships was endowed by the Crown, even-handedly in Oxford and in Cambridge alike, in Divinity, Civil Law, Physic, Hebrew and Greek. These marked a significant new departure. The originator of this munificent scheme was Thomas Cromwell and he saw to it that his own nominees held these desirable new positions first.[69] Such provision did not necessarily ensure that the subjects concerned had appropriately qualified expert Professors, especially as the number and range of Professorships grew in the following centuries. The new Professorships we shall meet in the seventeenth and eighteenth centuries were in any case often in subjects which did not feature at the time on the curriculum for undergraduates reading for degrees. With the departure from Regent Masters came a loss of formal contact between the ordinary student and the most highly respected famous teachers in Cambridge.

An era of change: fresh thinking about the purpose of a university

These were substantial shakings up of comfortable old Cambridge certainties. Similar major rethinking about the purposes a university could serve in the modern world was going on elsewhere in Europe. In the mid-1530s Erasmus expressed a wish in his will that a study-foundation should be established. It was launched as the Erasmusstiftung in 1538 in Basle. This had welfare as well as an educational objectives; it set out to help the aged in need, pilgrims, young men who wanted to learn a trade, even indigent young women.[70] Erasmus thus either intended to create a hybrid of existing types of provision or envisaged something quite new, involving a novel method of 'widening access'.[71]

Erasmus could see in the 'three languages' *Collegium* of Louvain, created in 1517 with the aid of a bequest from one of his friends and with the purpose of providing trilingual teaching, a useful earlier experiment in doing good through such a higher education bequest, coupled in his case with the growing aim of also doing general social good. The law Professor Bonifacius Amerbach, who carried out the wishes expressed in Erasmus' will, arranged for the foundation to award five scholarships a year to university students, conditional upon their working hard and upon their good behaviour.[72] One of Erasmus' principles was that grants should not be limited to local students. It has been calculated that in the period 1538–1600, about 20 per cent went to Germans, 7 per cent to Swiss, 4 or 5 per cent to Italians and French, with about 2 per cent to the Low Countries and 1 per cent to Bohemia.[73] The same spirit of internationalism in the provision of financial support for students seems to have affected other local grant-giving bodies, such as the Academy which was funded by the state; on the other hand, the Academy of Basle may have recognized its need of new blood from across Europe if it was to raise its academic standing. Academic exiles (often for religious reasons) feature in the lists.[74] These experimental variations explored by Erasmus are of interest because they tested the 'boundaries' of the idea of a university in a period when it was meeting its first general challenge from the secular authorities on a more than local scale. The persistence of Europe's universities as institutions through the often threatening changes brought about by the Reformation is striking evidence of their powers of endurance.

The King chooses a Vice-Chancellor

There were opportunities for exchange of ideas on such matters between those with Cambridge links, but projects other than reforming Cambridge seemed more urgent. For instance, a 'Lutheran party' came to England in 1538 and there were hopes of a rapprochement between the Lutherans and the English reformers, though Cranmer was under too much pressure to give the exercise the time and attention it needed so little was achieved. He did, however, begin to work on the reform of the liturgy in connection with this attempt, drawing on both Lutheran and Roman Catholic models. And Cranmer had his enemies at the universities. Oxford academics and Canterbury cathedral canons united in an unsuccessful plot (the 'prebendaries' plot) in 1543.

It is in this context of destabilizing pressures and tempting comparisons with radical plans on the Continent that we need to set the events which affected Cambridge in the last years of the reign of Henry VIII. In 1544, Matthew Parker became Master of Corpus Christi College and in 1545, he was elected Vice-Chancellor, at the King's wish. The King's interference was subtle but persuasive. He wrote to the Fellows of Corpus Christi College, 'within our University of Cambridge'

> to commend unto you our well-beloved chaplain, doctor Parker, a man as well for his approved learning, wisdom, and honesty, as for his singular grace and industry in bringing up youth in virtue and learning, so apt for the exercise of the said room, as it is thought very hard to find the like for all respects and purposes.

Within two months, early in 1545, Parker received a letter 'certifying...that it hath pleased the University to choose you unto the office of the Vice-Chancellor, and Mr. proctors be very desirous to have you at home for to be admitted. Doctor Smith gave over his office on Saturday at iv. of the clock and you were chosen on Sunday at iii. of the clock'.[75] It was a real election, with three other candidates, and Parker got 79 votes with less than 10 for each of the other three candidates, a total of 98 voting.

Parker was thrown at once into the disputatiousness of the University world. The students of Christ's College had performed *Pammachius*, a mocking and disrespectful play, and the ecclesiastical authorities were not amused. Bishop Gardiner of Winchester (1497–1555), who was Chancellor of the University from 1540, wrote to demand that the Vice-Chancellor should investigate.[76] The affair threatened to escalate to the point where it could have provided a further justification for government interference in the University's conduct of its affairs.

The test Parker tried to set for 'the doctors and presidents of all the Colleges of the University' was whether anyone had been offended. 'The answer of them all, after their examination at our next meeting,' he reported, 'was, that none of their companies declared unto them that they were offended with any thing, that now they remember was then spoken'. There were of course some absentees, and on further inquiry Parker had found two 'that were offended' one of whom was a Mr. Scot, who had himself caused offence in the University by making submissions to Gardiner.[77]

Gardiner was not prepared to let it go and wrote back to say he had inspected the copy of the play which had been used and found much in it to offend, and that he believed that those who said they were not offended were offending further in 'denying what is true'.[78] He had his own 'agenda', for he asserted that 'where open faults be thus neglected and pretermitted' here is 'small hope of conservation of good order'. 'I hear many things to be very far out of order, both openly in the University and severally in the Colleges' (including the mispronunciation 'of certain Greek letters agreed unto by the authority of the whole University').[79]

Only a few days later, on 12 May, the Lords of the Council were writing to Parker, insisting that he should call the parties before him and admonish them and make sure that in future

> no such matter either in play or earnest be moved or meddled with as should offend the laws and quiet of this realm, so as you, that there [i.e. Cambridge] be assembled and under the King's majesty's special protection be maintained to live quietly for the increase of virtue and learning.

If the 'youth' misbehave such 'misorder' must be reformed.[80] So Cambridge was exposed once more to direct state interference.

In 1545 Henry VIII, still greedy for Cambridge's wealth, threatened to seize endowments.[81] An Act for the Dissolution of Colleges[82] empowered the King to enter into all Colleges and have all their possessions vested in him.[83] The King wrote to Cambridge's Vice-Chancellor to say that Parliament had authorized him to reform the colleges. 'Myndinge...encrease of good learninge of the commonwealthe of this our realme,' he was sending his Commissioners to make a list of all possessions of the colleges. Cambridge wrote to the current Queen (now Katherine Parr) to ask her to speak to the King on its behalf.

Henry VIII appointed the two special bodies of commissioners to examine the foundations, statutes and ordinances of the universities. They were also to take note of the state of the colleges: 'to inquire how they were observed, and what were the values and nature of all true possessions of the colleges, hospitals, chantries, and free chapels within each university?'[84]

The Royal Visitation which followed in 1546 was, thanks to adroit moves by Parker, turned into a survey which was to be conducted by himself and John Redman, Master of Trinity College, and William May, Master of Queens'. The King's commission was that they were with 'full power and authority' to call before them 'the masters and heads of every of the Colleges and other houses endowed with any manner of possessions within that our University of Cambridge', peruse their 'Foundations, Statutes and Ordinances', creating a veritable 'Domesday Book' of information for the King. This became an internal review of the lands and benefices. When they took their list on a fair sheet of vellum to the King at Hampton Court, the shrewd monarch commented that never had he seen 'so many persons so honestly maynteyned in lyving bi so little land and rent',[85] and enquired how it was that the Colleges annually spent more than appeared to be their income. But, with good humour, he said he 'would force [the University] no further'.[86]

A conscious bid was once more being made here by a monarchy imitating European models (and especially the Lutheran example), to assert 'princely control' over the self-governing communities of Masters which made up Oxford and Cambridge, and the self-governing independent charitable foundations of their colleges. Colleges and University taken together were rightly perceived to be wealthy, and Henry VIII had only recently been engaged in the dissolution of the monasteries (1538) and the seizure of the assets of a number of bodies which could be argued to be analogous with the colleges or even the universities. The question what was to become of the Oxford and Cambridge colleges which had been supported by now dissolved monasteries had not yet been addressed. Papal permission to dissolve monasteries had included a requirement that the proceeds should be used to fund establishments for education.

* * *

Edward VI and Cambridge

Edward VI succeeded to the throne in 1547 at the age of nine and the kingdom was consequently in the hands of his 'advisers'. Henry VIII's will had attempted to provide for a 'minority' until Edward was 18, but there were predictable attempts to manipulate the list of those who would exercise power as a 'Council' during this period. For example, Stephen Gardiner was kept from direct contact with the young King towards the end. Edward Seymour, Earl of Hertford and Duke of Somerset, became the Lord Protector, although Henry's will had not envisaged such an office, preferring an arrangement of shared power with its built-in checks and balances. Somerset was autocratic from the first and exercised personal monarchical powers nominally on behalf of the young King, buying off those who might challenge him. The ensuing power struggles, which in due course replaced Somerset with Northumberland, ensured that the attention of Government was not primarily focused on the universities.

The same was not true for the Church's authorities. Thomas Cranmer remained Archbishop of Canterbury and set the tone for religious affairs, the aspect of national Government which most directly affected the universities. Cranmer set about institutionalizing protestantism in the Church in England, and he included in his brief a desire to continue Henry's policy of taking over control of Church property, by dissolving chantries. He was soon organizing commissions to spread out across the kingdom.

Cranmer also supervised the religious education of the child King. The young Edward wrote a treatise on the Pope as Antichrist when he was 11, so the direction in which he was being influenced is clear. He was encouraged to take an active interest in the theological controversies of the day and seems to have turned into a pious prig with puritan leanings.

Edward VI's adult mentors had their agendas for the universities and made their own bid for control by helpfully framing new statutes:

> It has seemed fit to us to give [the Visitors of the University] some laws, collected in this volume, which we have framed specially for your good, that they may deliver them to you, in order that, your statutes being antiquated, semi-barbarous, and obscure, and for the most part unintelligible on account of their age, you may henceforth obey royal law framed under our auspices.[87]

Oxford's then Vice-Chancellor (1547–52) and Dean of Christ Church, Richard Cox, was anxious what this would mean for the colleges, however, and wrote urgent letters. The King promised the 'Heads of House' that they should keep their houses and lands, but soon after he made this promise he died. The first Parliament of Edward VII, in November 1547, passed a new Chantries Act, with the preamble that the intention was to give the King, 'the power of converting the foundations which came under the Act 'to good and godly uses as in erecting of Grammar Schools, the further augmenting of the Universities', and better provision for the poor and needy, leaving some over for the Exchequer.[88]

An Act was passed in 1550 'for the abolishing and putting away of divers books and images'. The books were principally those which did not form part of the new liturgical apparatus (such as 'Antiphoners', 'Missals', 'Processionals'); the images envisaged were those which people were keeping at home (together with some of the books now objected to), having taken them out of churches into 'their custody'. These were to be handed over to the local authorities who were, within 40 days, to burn, deface or destroy them. Only figures on tombstones were to be left alone, since it was feared that harmless figures of a 'king, prince, nobleman or other dead person' might be mistaken for that of a saint and damaged. This was not directly aimed at the universities and their colleges, but its requirements caught them in its net.

By 1551, a precocious young Edward was entering with determination into his role as Supreme Head of the Church. Cranmer wanted Continental participation in and approval of England's reforming activities, and he turned accordingly to Bullinger, Calvin and Melanchthon when he wished to propose that there should be a 'protestant' general council to rival the great Council of Trent which began to meet in 1545 (and was to continue until 1563 in a series of sessions). The Council was planned by the Roman Catholic Church as a Council at which the whole Church would route the reformers once and for all.

It had reached its twelfth to sixteenth sessions in 1551–2 when Cranmer wrote his letters to these leaders of the Continental Reformation. To Henry Bullinger he wrote in 1552 – in Latin as the common language of clerical scholarship – deploring the fact that 'our enemies' (*adversarii nostri*) are 'having their councils to confirm their errors' (*habent sua concilia ad errors confirmandos*) and suggesting that 'in England or somewhere else, a synod of the most learned and the greatest men should be convoked, in which there might be discussion of the purity of Church doctrine and especially an agreement on the sacramental controversy'. To call together 'the most learned' (*doctissimi*) was going to involve resort to the universities. He explains that he has also written in the same terms to Calvin and Melanchthon.[89] To Calvin he wrote more briefly, to challenge him. When our enemies are meeting at Trent, 'can we neglect to call together a holy synod to refute errors, and purify and disseminate dogmas'?[90] He wanted to bring together 'educated and pious men, outstanding in learning and judgement.[91] He had in mind the creation of a list of *sententiae* by way of 'decrees' of this meeting.[92] Melanchthon's letter is similar, emphasizing especially the need for a resolution of the Eucharistic controversy.[93] Letter VII to Joachim Vadianus is also preoccupied with that point.[94]

Head-hunting famous Professors for Cambridge

During these years some government expenditure seems to have been made on an effort to settle Philip Melanchthon in Cambridge

University,[95] where it was thought he could have been a great help. But the real coup was the capture of Martin Bucer (1491–1551). Bucer began as a Dominican friar and studied at Heidelberg. He became involved with the continental reforms, publishing a *Confessio Tetrapolitana* in 1530. He was invited – though he had some strong objections – to be one of the signatories to the Augsburg Interim of 1548, an imperial decree of the Holy Roman Emperor Charles V, in what turned out to be an abortive attempt at a compromise between reformers and Roman Catholics,

Thomas Cranmer invited him to England, where in 1549 he was made Regius Professor of Divinity at Cambridge. Thanks to his introduction into the scene of the English Reformation in this way by an Archbishop of Canterbury who had never ceased to keep up with his academic interests, and well understood the potential value of skilled help of that kind, he was 'consulted' by the King and the Protector Somerset in the reign of Edward VI about the revisions which were being made to the Book of Common Prayer. He wrote his *De Regno Christi* 'for' the King. In summer 1550 he published 'A defence of the true and Catholic doctrine of the sacrament of the body and blood of our saviour Christ'.[96] He lived only until 1551 and died before his projected ten-volume theological study had got beyond its first book. But Cranmer's invitations had been more extensive. The Hebrew scholar Paul Fagius had accompanied Bucer to Cambridge and it was Cranmer's plan to create a 'team' to draft a new Latin version of the Bible with a commentary, to replace the Vulgate with all its now acknowledged errors, as a standard text for international academic use. Scraps of this survive in the library at Corpus Christi College.

A new liturgy contains a reformed theology

Among Cranmer's most lasting achievements was the new Prayer Book. This was an attempt to replace the Roman liturgy with a form of service for the English Church whose vocabulary would be carefully selected to ensure a 'reformed' theology was embedded within it. Movements and gestures were also covered. The elevation of the bread and wine after they had been consecrated in the Eucharist was stopped, offending the conservatives. Other points retained offended those on the other wing of the Church in England, who thought they represented a continuation of 'popish practices'.

The Prayer Book was put out for use in March 1549 and it became compulsory to use it from June of that year. Much of the work which had gone into it was Cranmer's own, and it embodied the fruits of research into the liturgies of earlier centuries which he had been able to carry out with the aid of his own extensive library. He had done his best to build solid and defensible foundations. But conservative senior clergy, such as Stephen Gardiner and Edmund Bonner, remained hostile. Both bishops found themselves deprived of their sees and put in the Tower.

The Prayer Book was followed by the Ordinal of 1550. Here, too, controversy resulted. John Hooper, named as the next Bishop of Gloucester in 1550, was not consecrated until 1551. The delay was because he objected to some details of the liturgy of the new Ordinal (swearing by the saints and the use of Romish vestments). Ridley and Cranmer persuaded the Privy Council that Hooper was a danger to the State and he was imprisoned until he agreed to stop his protests. The Prayer Book of 1549 was revised – under Cranmer's supervision and with advice from Peter Martyr and Bucer – in time for the passing of the Act of Uniformity in April 1552. There were to be further revisions in 1559 and 1662, but the essence of this second version remained and with it the stylistic standard set for English by Cranmer himself.

* * *

Queen Mary and the martyrs

Mary's reign followed upon the death of her young brother in 1553, leaving her as his elder daughter the next surviving child of Henry VIII with a claim to the succession. It took some adroit movement and gathering of supporters across East Anglia to achieve the crown. The greatest threat came from the Duke of Northumberland, John Dudley, who wanted to claim the throne for Lady Jane Grey, who was married to his son. Mary had him executed, as the only safe course of action. As the daughter of Catherine of Aragon and a lifelong Roman Catholic, she immediately set about undoing the English Reformation.

Cambridge was frightened at the news of Northumberland's arrest and some of its senior members held an urgent meeting where it was ordered that

> Dr. Mouse and Dr. Hatcher should repair to Dr. Sands' lodging and fetch away the statute book of the University, the Keyes, and such other things that were in his keeping, and so they did, for Dr. Mouse, being an earnest protestant the day before, was now become a papist and his great enemy.[97]

The Vice-Chancellor tried to argue his corner at a Congregation but his enemies dragged his chair from under him. He pulled a dagger and was only prevented from killing some of his attackers by Dr. Bill and Dr. Blith who urged him 'to hold his hands and be quiet and bear that great offered wrong'. So the academics made him give up his office. Cambridge's academics prudently turned Roman Catholic and sent a letter to the new Queen at once congratulating her and making it clear that the tenor of their former Vice-Chancellor's sermons had nothing to do with them.[98]

She too thought it wise to 'Visit' the universities, to ensure that her revocation of everything which had been changed since her father's death had been taken seriously. Her letter of instruction argued that the changes had been the work of a few misguided individuals and had overturned the right order of centuries, with no proper authority.[99] In 1555 it was agreed by Grace that all graduates must subscribe to certain articles, including acceptance that there are seven sacraments. The Visitors loomed at the end of 1556 and arrived in January 1557, for although they had searched the record anxiously, the academics could not find authority in their records to claim 'they be exempt from this visitacioun'.[100] A Grace was passed to allow the muniments to be taken 'owte of the universitie hutche' (presumably the Chest).[101] From college to college went the Visitors, chosen by the fearsome Cardinal Pole, demanding to hear and receive condemnations of Bucer and others. A climax came when the bodies of offending protestant academics were exhumed, stood on end in their coffins in the markctplace and burnt along with their books. The town was full of country people – it was market day – and reactions were mixed. Some 'detested and abhorred the extreme crueltye of the Commissioners towards the rotten carcasses'; some 'laughed at theyr folly' in burning dead bodies who could do no further harm.[102]

Having a good argument

If we look at this horror-story from the point of view of the working life of the universities, we have to locate it in a surprising place. The process of 'trial by disputation' leading to execution of the loser which was to follow, sits in the area of Cambridge's 'use' of logic in its regular teaching and examining.

The old mainstream logic was changing, being deliberately 'dumbed down' in the face of mounting complaints that the syllabus was too difficult and stuffed too full. But logic could not be dropped altogether, not only because it had always been one of the three subjects of the trivium, along with grammar and rhetoric, but because lawyers needed it as a skill, if they were to be able to argue effectively.

The young Peter Ramus (1515–72) published the *Aristotelicae Animadversiones* (1543), seeking to dismiss not only the work of the scholastic logicians, but that of Aristotle himself. His *Dialecticae partitiones* (also 1543) proposed a new way forward, and further volumes of further *Aristotelicae Animadversiones* continued to appear over subsequent years. In 1562 Ramus became a protestant and was killed at the massacre of St. Bartholomew in 1572, which made him something of a hero in the eyes of protestant scholars throughout Europe, regardless of the merits of his 'alternative logic', which many began to doubt. Among the new-style Latin textbooks of the sixteenth century were John Seton, *Dialectica* (1545), sometimes said to mark the beginning of a humanist approach in Oxford. John Argall, *Ad artem dialecticam introductio* (1605), was expressly designed for beginners. (The use of Latin for the purpose was no bar, for that was the language in which young men were expected to learn logic in their undergraduate years.)

Manuals in the vernacular mark a significant departure. The earliest handbooks on logic for 'practitioners', people who were going to need to argue for a living, appeared in English in the sixteenth century, including the Cambridge Thomas Wilson's *The Rule of reason* (1551); the Oxford Ralph Lever's *The Arte of Reason, rightly termed Witcraft* (1573) and the Cambridge Abraham Fraunce's, *The Lawiers Logike* (1588), an attempt at applying Ramist logic to the needs of lawyers.[103] Fraunce, a graduate of St. John's College, Cambridge, and a protégé of Sir Philip Sidney, explains in his prefatory letter to the reader that he had made the experiment of applying logic to law when he went to Grays Inn to study and change his 'profession'; he was confident that nothing need be lost with the removal of the old fierce technical requirements. He gives a speech to 'a raging and fiery faced Aristotelian', who complains that now 'Antiquity is nothing but Dunsicality [after Duns Scotus, who gave his name to the "dunce" and remains one of the few major names to be associated with medieval Cambridge], and our forefathers inventions unprofitable trumpery'. Any beginner, or 'newfangled, youngheaded' boy now talks of method. It does not follow, urges Fraunce, that because 'the wordes and tearmes of logike bee not named, therefore the force and operation of logike is not there used and apparent'. We can speak grammatically without identifying each part of speech aloud. So it is with logic.[104]

Apart from those who intended to specialize in law, all students needed to learn logic because 'disputation' was one of the teaching methods still in use, and a lively one which could draw a crowd. They also still took their examinations by disputation, and continued to do so in Cambridge until the nineteenth century. The continuation of disputation as a pedagogical method, and also as a method for conducting examinations, undoubtedly did a good deal to keep the study of logic alive. A variety of disputations was held at Wittenberg long after Melanchthon had brought about changes to the syllabus and introduced a much more 'humanist' approach. Disputations from 1539 to 1544 survive, including examinations ('promotions disputations') and others which were simply teaching and practice exercises.[105] Adversarial disputations remained the backbone of university study and examination in England into the nineteenth century.

Disputation also remained the natural way to conduct a trial for heresy, or to determine whether an opinion might be heretical. The set-piece debates of the Reformation period, such as those in which Luther and Eck engaged in combat, and the public 'heresy trials' in which Luther and others were brought before the authorities to defend their opinions, were essentially traditional disputations, with 'theses' to be defended and attacked until a determination was reached. The same underlying structure shaped the Augsburg Confession which Melancthon composed for the Reichstag of Augsburg (1530). The point to be 'proved' was that the reformers were still truly members of the Church, so Melanchthon adduced texts in support which the ecclesiastical authorities would respect. The Leipzig Interim (an attempt to rescue the Augsburg Interim) was another occasion when, in April 1548, a 'conference' was held which was really a disputation, to discuss what matters ought to be considered Church-dividing and which were 'indifferent' (*adiaphora*) and could safely be left to the individual opinion or practice of the faithful. Matthias Flacius Illyricus was among those who took the opposing side on this occasion.

Cranmer took part in a disputation at Oxford with Ridley and Latimer in 1549, when the three were taken from their imprisonment in the Tower to Oxford, where they were to dispute with doctors of both universities, in 'scarlet robes' (which the Cambridge men had mostly brought with them though two of them 'borrowed of the Oxford men').[106] There was a plan to hold a similar debate in Cambridge, which is referred to in a letter of Ridley to Bradford.[107] Three disputations were held at Cambridge, on 20 June 1549, on the sacrament, with a Determination by Nicholas Ridley. He begins: 'There hath been an ancient custom amongst you, that after disputations had in your common schools, there should be some determination made of the matters so disputed and debated, especially touching Christian religion.'[108]

However, his methodology is more 'modern'. 'It hath seemed good unto these worshipful assistants joined with me in commission from the King's majesty, that I should perform the same at this time; I will by your favourable patience declare, both what I do think and believe myself, and what also others ought to think of the same'.[109] In the body of his determination he relies first and foremost on Scripture and then on 'the most certain testimonies of the ancient catholic Fathers'.

Mary tried to arrange a disputation in Cambridge like the one in Oxford, in which Protestants and Catholics would be pitted against one another. But the prisoners being held in London whom she intended to bring to Cambridge for the purpose, declined to oblige. A letter signed by Robert Ferrar, who had been Bishop of St. David's, John Hooper, the former Bishop of Gloucester, Miles Coverdale and others, including John Philpot, John Bradford and John Rogers, said they would not join in a disputation except before the Queen in Council or Parliament.[110]

From disputation to polemic

There was a certain gavotte-like character to a disputation. Fierce it may have been but the Master who presided kept order and his decision was 'final'. Polemic was an offspring of disputation, but far less polite. It was war. That is obvious from the titles. For instance, in 1534 Erasmus published his 'Against the most calumnious letter of Martin Luther' (*Adversus calumniosissimam epistolam martini lutheri*).[111] In similar hot blood, John Hooper replied to Stephen Gardiner's book 'A detection of the devil's sophistrie', which had reached him in Zurich in April 1547.[112] Gardiner wrote, 'An explication and assertion of the true catholic faith touching the most blessed sacrament of the altar. Against it Cranmer wrote 'An answer to a crafty and sophistical cavillation devised by Stephen Gardiner',[113] in which he says he looks in vain for two things, 'the one is truth with simplicity' and the other 'that ... you ... had so much learning as you think you have, or else that you thought of yourself no more than you have in deed.[114] He addressed head on the embarrassing difficulty that Lutherans and others, including Bucer, had held positions, at least for a time, which lay somewhere between the controversial doctrine of transubstantiation and its total rejection:

> M. Luther, Bucer, Jonas, Melancthon, and Oepinus ... in this and many other things have in times past, and yet peradventure some do (the veil of old darkness not clearly in every point removed from their eyes), agree with the papists in part of this matter, yet they agree not in the whole.[115]

Examples could be multiplied.

The martyrs who lost the argument

This was a time of martyrdoms in both Oxford and Cambridge, where principled academics would not accept the volte-face of theological opinion required of them. Mary and her advisers saw no reason, moral or political, not to take the directest possible route to bring England back to what she believed was the true Church. If influential people would not come back voluntarily, they must die. It was in Oxford not Cambridge that Cranmer, Latimer and Ridley were burnt at the stake for their Protestant views in one of the most violent episodes of the bloody Tudor age and that story must wait for the companion volume to this one.

Cambridge had its martyrs too. John Bradford, Fellow of Pembroke Hall, was martyred in 1555. His 'Farewell to the University and Town of Cambridge', was written to all in the university and town alike: 'Thou, my mother, the university, hast not only had the truth of God's word plainly manifested unto thee by reading, disputing, and preaching, publicly and privately, but now...thou hast my life and blood as a seal.'

He reproaches both his mother the university and his 'sister' the town for returning to 'Romish' allegiances after having accepted reformation:

> Let the exile of Lever, Pilkington, Grindal, Haddon, Horne, Scory, Ponet,&c., something awake thee. Let the imprisonment of thy dear sons, Cranmer, Ridley and Latimer, move thee. Consider the martyrdom of thy chickens, Rogers, Saunders, Taylor; and now case not away the poor admonition of me going to be burned also...O Perne, repent; O Thomson, repent: O ye doctors, bachelors and masters, repent; O mayor, alderman and town-dwellers, repent, repent, repent, that ye may escape the near vengeance of the Lord.[116]

*   *   *

Queen Elizabeth, Cambridge and protestant nationhood

> And that gentle Bard,
> Chosen by the Muses for their Page of State –
> Sweet Spenser, moving through his clouded heaven
> With the moon's beauty and the moon's soft pace,
> I called him Brother, Englishman, and Friend!
> Wordsworth, *The Prelude*, III, 279–82

Edmund Spenser (1552–99) entered Pembroke College Cambridge as a sizar but he spent his early adult life in Ireland. The 'sizar' system seems to have begun in the late sixteenth century and was a feature of Cambridge and Trinity College, Dublin. It saved on the cost of servants. It enabled able boys who did not come from families which would or could support them through university to work their way through their studies by acting as servants to other students or within the college. *Spenser's Faerie Queen* has been described as an 'allegory of Protestant nationhood'.[117] He brought it to court, accompanied by Sir Walter Raleigh, to present it to the Queen. But he foolishly offended the Queen's secretary (and Cambridge's Chancellor from 1559 to 1598) Lord Burghley and never got the reward he believed he deserved for his loyal and patriotic composition.

Spenser had hit on an important feature of the late Tudor realm. There was a great deal of dust to be settled after the vicissitudes of previous reigns and if England was truly to be 'protestant' for the future, with a head of the Church who was also head of state, it also had to establish its identity as a nation, for the two 'headships' were going to be bound together as never before.

That does not mean that the priorities of good government looked the same then as now, though some of the exigencies of politics turned out to be the same. Sir Francis Walsingham, when Elizabeth I's Secretary of State, ran a secret service in which he may have employed at least one Cambridge spy, the playwright Christopher Marlowe.[118] Propriety in public life of the modern sort was not yet thought of. A letter from John Palmer to Lord Burghley in 1590 lists acts of patronage and favour with no sense of a need to feel shame about such practices:

> How many wies, from tyme to tyme, I have bene bound unto your honour, is well knowne to many beside my self, namely, that I was first preferred to the rome of a fellowship in our colledge of St. Johns by your lordshippes letters, and after, in the divertinge of my studies from civill law to dvinitie, supported againe by dispensation; and not long since it pleased you lordship to wright your letters in my behalf for the place of the orator in our University.[119]

Strength and decisiveness involved ruthlessness. Those who offended a monarch or a monarch's favourites could still expect to lose their heads, or at least their positions and anticipated rewards, as Spenser found.

Elizabeth's 'Cambridge' education

Elizabeth's tutor when she was a girl had been Roger Ascham (1515–68). He was a student at St. John's College, Cambridge, from about 1530 and he learned Greek there before taking his M.A. in 1537 and becoming a Fellow of St. John's. He remained in Cambridge to teach, apparently with considerable success. John Astley wrote to Ascham when he was tutor to the young Queen Elizabeth I, a letter, recollecting 'our friendly fellowship together...our pleasant studies in reading together Aristotle's Rhetoric, Cicero and Livy.'[120] His pupil William Grindal became tutor to the princess and when he died in 1544, Ascham replaced him. Elizabeth was then 11 years old.

Something of Ascham's style of instruction – adapted for the very young – can be reconstructed from his book *The Scholemaster*. He was anxious to produce a pupil quite unlike the ones he had observed as a boy:

> I remember, whan I was yong, in the North, they went to the Grammer schole, litle children: they came from thence great lubbers: always learning, and litle profiting: learning without booke, euery thing, vnder-standyng within the booke, litle or nothing.

Young Elizabeth was no 'lubber'. Ascham's method of teaching was gentle but extremely 'academic'. He did not see her sex as a reason for not stretching her intellectually. He suggests that every few days the schoolmaster should select a piece of Cicero with which his student will not be familiar, 'some Epistle ad Atticum, some notable common place out of his Orations, or some other part of Tullie [Cicero], by your discretion, which your scholer may not know where to finde', translate it 'into plaine naturall English' and give it to the pupil 'to translate into Latin againe: allowyng him (or her) good space and tyme to do it, both with diligent heede, and good aduisement'. He describes the purpose of this exercise in some detail: 'Here his witte shalbe new set on worke: his iudgement, for right choice, trewlie tried: his memorie, for sure reteyning, better exercised, than by learning, any thing without the booke: & here.'

He is confident that it will be apparent both to tutor and to pupil what has been learned:

> Whan he bringeth it translated vnto you, bring you forth the place of Tullie: lay them together: compare the one with the other: commend his good choice, & right placing of wordes: Shew his faultes iently, but blame them not ouer sharply: for,

of such missings, ientlie admonished of, proceedeth glad & good heed taking: of good heed taking, springeth chiefly knowledge, which after, groweth to perfitnesse.

His experience is that in this way a real fluency in Latin is to be acquired, and speedily. And it is a process the student will also enjoy, for thus 'the scholer is alwayes laboring with pleasure, and euer going right on forward with profit'.[121] This is not of course 'the Cambridge way' as such, but it was an approach bred in Ascham in Cambridge, not in his own earlier schooldays. He made an intelligent young girl literate, cultured and witty.

He must also have given her an informed capacity to understand at least some of the issues which were engaging Cambridge's academics. Queen Elizabeth of England had a thesis debated before her in 1564 when she made a state visit to Cambridge. The thesis concerned the question of the authority of Scripture: that 'the authority of Scripture is greater than the authority of the Church'.[122]

Ascham reached out from beyond the grave with a reminder. A serious-minded sixteenth-century approach to forming the student to fit him (or rarely her) for life's duties, extended to princes too. Robert Ascham's *The Scholemaster*, published posthumously in 1570, and dedicated to his old pupil Queen Elizabeth, reminded her that it is a Prince's duty to lead 'scholars and learners' and the Prince ought therefore to attend to his own education so as to be effective in his office and an example to his or her people.

The Visitation of 1559

Once she was Queen, Elizabeth – prompted by her advisors – lost little time in instigating a Visitation of the universities, as part of the general review of institutions with ecclesiastical connections which took place in what has come to be known as the Elizabeth Settlement. There was a good deal of uncertainty in the air for individuals as well as for the monarch. The reformer Thomas Sampson (c.1517–89), a graduate of Pembroke College, Cambridge, had been in exile during Mary's reign and did not feel it safe to return to England until 1560 (he became Dean of Christ Church). In 1558 he wrote to Peter Martyr to ask 'how ought we to act with respect to allowing or disallowing the title of "after Christ supreme head of the Church of England" &c? All scripture seems to assign the title of head of the church to Christ alone.' His worry was that the Queen might 'invite' him to some ecclesiastical office. Can I accept such appointment with a safe conscience, he asks?[123]

171

The Visitation of Cambridge was led personally by William Cecil, the future Lord Burghley, with a team of seven which included Matthew Parker, and with instructions closely similar to those which had been given to the Commissioners of 1549. It was foreseen that there would be adroit footwork by colleges which feared that their complement of Fellows would not appear to the Visitors to be balanced as it should.[124] There were attempted timely resignations by Masters of Colleges who thought they might be ejected. The Master of St. Catherine's, Edmund Cosyn, a Roman Catholic, removed himself from his office and also from the Vice-Chancellorship and, unable perhaps to bear to take himself out of Cambridge altogether, went to live in retirement at Caius. William Taylor, Master of Christ's from 1556 to 1559, left in such a hurry that his room was found in a jumble with clothes and papers and even the rushes which covered the floor all mixed up.[125] Of those Heads of House who sat it out and waited for the arrival of the Commissioners, some were indeed removed and replaced.

The Fellows who remained were not always content with the changes which had taken place. A notable case is that of Gonville Hall, founded in 1348, but financially struggling by the mid-sixteenth century. John Caius (1510–73) gave his name to what became 'Gonville and Caius', and a College, upon entering the Mastership in 1558. He was a funder as well as Master, and although he had been a student at Gonville Hall he had graduated in 1533 and spent his subsequent career largely abroad. He arrived now as an outsider, coming from medical practice in London. He proved high-handed, expelling Fellows who displeased him and giving rise to a good deal of dispute. He himself displeased those Fellows who leaned towards puritan views, since he kept a crucifix and various images in his room. Colleges were obliged to make adjustments as they took their modern form, teaching students as well as providing somewhere to live, expanding, and having to decide how to run themselves, whether 'collegially' and democratically or by monarchical government by a Master.

Cecil, created Lord Burghley by Elizabeth in 1571, became Chancellor of this potentially troublesome University in 1559 and remained in the office until he died in 1598. He found it a rough ride from the beginning. As early as 1562 he sent in his resignation. He was not 'mete for the office' he said, 'havng no lerninge to judge of men learned'. Nor, he regretted, did he have time to 'here the causes', the frequent disputes which came before him. Controversies ('factions and contentions') are numerous 'and are likely to encrease. The redresse whereof cannot come from me as yt ought to do from a Chauncelor; because I can neither skill to judge of the controversies ... nor can come thether to subdue the same with my presence & with the authoritye of the office.' He puts this down to the failings of the 'hedds of houses', who are not keeping control of the Regents.[126] The University begged him to stay on and he consented.

Questions, complaints, disputes and squabbles continued to multiply. Some of those who ventured to trouble him proved to be temporizers. John Whitgift (c.1530–1604) got his early education from his uncle, who was an abbot; he went first to Queens' College, Cambridge, but then moved to Pembroke College, where the Master, Nicholas Ridley, was of a sympathetically reforming persuasion. He matriculated there in 1550. He became a Fellow of Peterhouse in 1555. He had remained rather quiet in Cambridge during Mary's reign, but came to prominence with the succession of Elizabeth. He wrote, with others, to ask William Cecil to lift the order that surplices must be worn in chapels in the colleges. His main reason seems to have been that he feared that for the University to take too extreme a position on this point would lead to some of the brightest of the young going elsewhere for conscience' sake. When the call was refused he regrouped and found himself able to support the authorities and the surplices. He was rewarded. His salary was increased as Lady Margaret Professor in 1566 and in 1567 he was made Regius Professor of Divinity, and in rapid succession Master of Pembroke College and then Master of Trinity.

The Elizabethan Settlement and the 'commonplaces'

Elizabeth was also anxious to 'settle' the Church's affairs as rapidly and decisively as possible after the chopping and changing of her siblings' reigns. Cranmer's work on the Prayer Book and the homilies provided a solid foundation. The other text a protestant Church was likely to need was a set of 'articles'. Lutherans had some. Several unsuccessful attempts had been made during the Tudor reigns to draw up a list (10 articles in 1536, 6 articles in 1539, 42 articles in 1552). In 1563 the Thirty-Nine Articles were approved by Convocation, under Matthew Parker who was now Archbishop of Canterbury. It is not always realized what these were and how much they owe in form and concept to the logic teaching and disputation-methods of the universities.

The Thirty-Nine Articles of the Church of England are really 'commonplaces'. Such 'articles' of faith were commonly used in confessional documents of the sixteenth century, as in the Lutheran Augsburg Confession (which was strongly imprinted with Melanchthon's ideas). Sixteenth-century debaters loved 'commonplaces', short pithy statements which strike the reader at once as self-evident truths. Cambridge's combatants were no exception. 'Commonplace' is the English translation of *locus communis*, and *locus* is the Latin counterpart of the Greek *topos* ('place'). So this was really a form of 'topics'. Sixteenth-century authors used other terms for this sort of statement. It might be called an *axioma* or a *conclusio* or a *thesis* or an *articulus* or a *quaestio*. It became a favourite academic activity to find and list them, and a cat's cradle of interconnected *axiomata* was created by the very process of adversarial disputation, as *conclusiones* became *quaestiones* for the purposes of having a debate about them, and the opinions of rival masters were cited alongside the old 'authorities' *(auctoritates)*.

When Luther (or his students) posted his 95 Theses on a door at Wittenberg they were intended to throw down this sort of challenge. Philip Melanchthon published a first version of his 'Commonplaces on theological matters' *(Loci Communes rerum theologicarum)* in 1521 and the final version in 1555. Melanchthon begins (1555 version) with this first 'commonplace': 'In earnest invocation of God it is necessary to consider what one wants to address, what God is, how he is known, where and how he has revealed himself, and both if and why he hears our pleas and cries.'[127]

It may not be easy for a modern reader to see why this sort of thing should have been so popular, but it was; eighteen Latin editions and several German translations were published within a few years. The excitement perhaps lay in the air of controversy and the perception that what was happening was a battle for the souls of the faithful between reformers and conservatives. Martin Chemnitz (1522–86) published his own *loci communes,* including some prefatory epigrams and an oration on the study of the Fathers, and with an approving discussion of Melanchthon's work. He explains why this is such a good method of resolving differences. It sets out points of doctrine so that they are pithy and clear and their interrelationship ('ordering') is apparent *(breviter, ordine, proprie, et perspicue explicata)*. He believes the *locus* was in use even *(etiam)* before the time of Peter the Lombard.[128] The Roman Catholic side used commonplaces too. Richard Smith (1500–63), by contrast, was against Melanchthon in his *Refutatio locorum communium theologicorum Philippi Melanchtonis* (1563).

'Articles' were a favoured genre in academe. 'Articles by the theological faculty of Paris. The dean and faculty of theology of Paris to all the faithful in Christ', prompted John Calvin (1509–64) to publish an 'Antidote' to each. He uses heavy irony. 'It has seemed proper to set down briefly, in the following order, what, in reference to the Articles generally controverted, Doctors and Preachers ought to teach, and the rest of the faithful, with the whole Church, believe', if this is to be taken as reliable, settled, not to be questioned, because it is a corporate decision of the Masters of the University of Paris: 'This being a magisterial definition, it is to be observed, that proofs are not added, because to do so were to derogate from the ancient privileges of the School of Paris.'

And, it is teasingly added, such a joint decision ought to have more force than the view of a single individual:

> since in the school of Pythagoras the authority of one man prevailed to such a degree that his ipse dixit sufficed for proof, how much more ought that which so many of our masters have together, and with one voice pronounced, to suffice?[129]

The dangers of unregulated preaching again: the Thomas Cartwright affair

Others, however, caused lasting problems and risked damaging Cambridge's reputation, positively courting state interference. The most blatant example of this is the handling of the Thomas Cartwright affair which threw into unwelcome prominence claims of 'abuse' of the freedom to preach in College chapels. Cartwright was not the first to create a problem about college preaching in Cambridge. Part of the 'war on terrorism' flavour of the state's response to reformation debates was panic about the danger that preachers would not only lead the faithful astray but also cause disorder and rebellion in the kingdom. As in more recent times, this panic led to 'panic measures' repressing civil liberties. Academic freedom was not yet a developed concept and certainly not thought of as fundamental. The universities continued to see themselves as producing clerics in the dual sense of future clerks and civil servants, and future clergy, with the emphasis on the expectation that for many students, ordination would follow. This was the century and this the period of transition when a new relationship between state and Church was going to consolidate a new attitude to the duties of the universities in this respect. Universities could reasonably be expected to behave responsibly as good citizens under the Government.

Archbishop Parker had written to Burghley on 9 April 1565 about the problem of unlicensed preaching in the University, sending 'some part of my University notes concerning preaching'. 'Your honour had need look into it, it will else grow to much inconvenience', he warns. He declares that he will 'receive' no preacher claiming to come with a licence from Cambridge unless the Chancellor's name is 'prefixed'.

He raises the problem of a variety of practice. 'In my opinion, it were well done that they had a form prescribed' for their 'licences, and so expressed in the proctors' books, and by a grace established, with the annulling of all licences passed before.'[130]

So the Thomas Cartwright affair was one of a number of cases where puritan preachers caused offence by stirring up anti-episcopal feeling in their sermons. The potential for disruption proved so great that Cranmer's provision of a series of official homilies designed to ensure that even where clergy were not 'safe' or equipped to preach in their own words, the people could be taught and exhorted without being 'misled' began to seem wise. It is probable that he wrote some of them himself.

Cambridge responds to the Cartwright problem

Thomas Cartwright (1535–1603) entered Clare Hall as an early 'sizar' in 1547. During Mary's reign he went off to qualify as a lawyer. He returned to Cambridge when he felt it was safe on Elizabeth's accession. He became a Fellow of St. John's and then of Trinity. In 1564 he came to some prominence in a disputation which took place during a Royal visit. By 1567 he had been chosen as University Preacher with the Lady Margaret Professorship following in 1569.

As a preacher he attracted huge crowds, so that it was said the windows of Great St. Mary's Church almost had to be taken out to accommodate them. He was exciting because he was calling for the abandonment of an episcopal system and the adoption of a presbyterian form of Church-government, as being more 'scriptural'. This was one of the significant lingering divisions after the Elizabethan Settlement. The Chancellor received numerous representations from both sides during the summer and he sought to find a way to resolution of matters by arranging for a 'Conference' to be held in the Michaelmas Term. 'Conferences' were indeed held with Cartwright but they proved inconclusive. and Whitgift summoned him in December to appear before the Vice-Chancellor's consistory court. There, Cartwright was shown a list of articles which it was claimed represented his opinions as preached in sermons and stated in his writings. He was ordered to recant. He refused. Whitgift joined forces with other heads of college to take away Cartwright's Professorship and in 1571 he used his personal authority as Master of Trinity to deprive him of his Fellowship there too.

Cartwright left. He went to Geneva and while he was there he visited Theodore Beza. Beza (1519–1605) was a French protestant who had been a close ally of Calvin, and he had friendly relations with the University which do not appear to have been damaged by this encounter. He had published an annotated Greek New Testament in 1565, basing his work on manuscripts of considerable importance, one of which he eventually presented to the University. The University thanked Beza in June, 1582, for his gift of three books for the Library.[131]

Curbing freedom of speech

One of the consequences of this episode was the increased repression of freedom of speech in Cambridge. It should, however, be kept in perspective amongst the endless squabbles and disputes in the University, many of which had nothing to do with religion or if they did, also involved a number of other alleged misbehaviours. The playwright Thomas Legge (1535–1607) seems to have been delated to the Queen by Fellows of Caius College, of which he became Master in 1573, probably for popery. He was sent to prison for 'contempt' of royal letters sent to him following this up. He was also accused of 'having misappropriated the college revenues and misgoverned the society'. Cooper quotes one of the articles against him, namely that 'whereas the statute permittethe not small birdes to be kept in the colledge, for troubling the studentes, the master hath used continuall and expressive loud singinge and noyse of organs, to the great disturbance of our studdyes.' He adds, 'The visitors were called in, and the matter was in agitation a considerable time'.[132]

In 1572 John Field and Thomas Wilcox published *An Admonition to the Parliament*, which Cartwright publicly approved of. This was prompted by the widening gulf between puritans and the bishops in the new Elizabethan Church Settlement and a contretemps about puritan calls to ban by law what were alleged to be 'popish abuses' in the Prayer Book. In return the bishops demanded that some of the known radicals among the clergy should subscribe, and be seen to subscribe, to the Thirty-Nine Articles, which had just been given the force of law. The *Admonition* set out the case for abolishing bishops and setting up a presbyterian Church order, and it returned to the subject of the alleged 'popish abuses', criticizing the bishops of the day in the process. A Bill on 'rites and ceremonies' was 'confiscated' and Elizabeth ordered that these inflammatory matters should not be discussed by Parliament until both the House of Bishops and the lower House of Convocation had approved a position. Whitgift was president of the house of clergy at the time. The *Admonition* and its proposers were, however, such extremists that they offended a number of their own 'party'.

Whitgift made a further attack on Cartwright's and the *Admonition*'s position in the form of an 'Answer', to which Cartwright wrote a 'Reply' and Whitgift a 'Defence to the Answer', in a 'pamphlet war' which contains the personal attacks typical of the genre:

> Touching his manner of writing I shall not need to say much; for any man of judgement that readeth his book may easily perceive, with what haughtiness of mind, what contempt and disdain of others, in what slanderous and opprobrious manner it is written. (Whitgift in 1574).[133]

Cartwright's arguments are fierce but also academic and technical, strongly stamped with the skills learned in the University. His aim, again and again, is to expose a fallacy in Whitgift's argument.

Whitgift preached before the Queen at New Year in Greenwich, setting out the case for an episcopal order. He also has a good deal to say against scholasticism, 'the vain curiosity of the schoolmen, who have pestered their volumes and troubled the Church partly with wicked and impious questions – with vain and frivolous questions'.[134] He did his own career no harm. Whitgift was made Archbishop of Canterbury in 1583, in succession to Edmund Grindal, and he was to occupy the position until 1604. Grindal had been unwise enough to disagree with the Queen and had been placed under house arrest.

Thus it began to seem to the Queen and her Government that it might be wise to ban books which were rousing a threat to episcopal government of the Church. These were crucial years in the settling down of the 'Settlement', and Whitgift's part in events was decisive.

New statutes for a new-style Cambridge

A second consequence of the Cartwright affair was the attempt to alter the balance of power from a democratic to a top-down style of governance in the University. John Whitgift argued that the Cartwright business had demonstrated the need for a new set of statutes for Cambridge. The statutes of Oxford and Cambridge had hitherto been of their own making, but the universities themselves wanted them to have the strongest possible authority; and the state wanted to ratify and if possible to issue them, for that would ensure that it would have control of them. This wish on the part of external authorities had become particularly noticeable during the Tudor period, following the intrusive royal visitations of Henry VIII. Edward VI had made his bid for direct control by new royal statutes, on the grounds that the existing ones were 'antiquated, semi-barbarous, and obscure' and it would be better for the University to 'obey royal laws'.[135] Queen Mary had replaced the Edwardian statutes with her own, framed and promulgated by Cardinal Pole, and thus having about them a whiff of an equally strong *papal* desire for control.

Elizabeth's reign saw the passing of the Act of 1570 'for the Incorporation of the Universities' – whose main effect was to clarify their legal rights and ensure the continuity of their liberties and control of their possessions' – and the creation of the ultimately decisive 'Elizabethan' Statutes. They were the work of Whitgift with three others, Andrew Perne of Peterhouse, John Caius and John Mey, Master of St. Catherine's, they were approved by the Chancellor and then issued by the Queen.

These statutes were intended to have the effect of adjusting a perceived imbalance between the powers of the Regents, the ancient democratic arrangements under which the academic community ran its own affairs, and a more top-down style of leadership in which powers in the University which did not exist in its earliest medieval governance might dominate. These were to be the Heads of House, the Masters of the Colleges, whose position and role in the University had changed radically during the last century. The Colleges were no longer just residences and clubs for their 'Fellows'. They had now taken upon themselves a significant teaching function and they admitted undergraduates, so they were rapidly developing into the entities familiar in the modern world.

The Masters objected that their democratic liberties were being interfered with. Instead of electing their own Vice-Chancellor they were merely to say which they preferred out of two nominated by the Heads of House. In 1572 a long list of signatories sought 'reformation of certain matters amisse in the newe statutes of the said Universitie'.[136] The Heads of House rejoined, objecting to the 'stirring upp of the myndes of the regents and non-regents to the contempt of the statutes' thinking to 'prevayle' by 'the number of hands procured' rather than 'with the waight of good reasons and matter'.[137] Three bishops held a hearing in May 1572, Canterbury, York and Ely, 'the masters and regents playntife' on one side, and 'the masters and heades' on the other,[138] with the complainants arguing under various heads that the effect of the changes to the statutes was to take power and control out of their hands. The 'Heads' responded that the new way was tidier and more likely to avoid controversies and 'fruvilouse appellations'.[139] Burghley commented shrewdly that everyone seemed to be looking for reasons to quarrel ('occasion of varyance').[140]

It was not only the University as a whole which was thus stirred up by these developments. There was also bad feeling among the colleges. One of the bones of contention was the allegation that some colleges were capturing all the lectureships for themselves. Burghley suggested a practical solution, that if the heads of particular colleges are absent, 'the vice-provost, vice-masters, vice-presidents, or others occupying the places of the said masters and heads of such colleges' should look instead 'to the intent that there may be a generall and full assembly, and due form observed, for the preservation of the severall interests of every college in the lectures and offices aforesaid'.[141]

The situation gained a sharper tension from the fact that this was also a period of active controversy in which strengths and weaknesses of authority became entangled with impassioned disagreements arising as the Elizabethan 'Settlement' also had to try to settle the dust-storms raised in the skirmishes of puritans with those who favoured a good old-fashioned episcopacy, on such subjects as the wearing of surplices in college chapels. Mr. Charke, Fellow of Peterhouse, was expelled for preaching that there should be no hierarchy in ministry and bishops, archbishops and Pope were an introduction of Satan. Charke wrote to Burghley and seems to have got some support, at which the Heads of House wrote to protest. Charke was not the only preacher in trouble. Nicholas Browne found himself in a similar position after he had preached two sermons on ministry in Trinity College Chapel, just before and soon after Christmas in 1572–3. His theme had been the need for 'new calling' and ordination for those ordained in the Roman Catholic Church, but he retracted, claiming that he did not mean to impugn the 'manor and forme of making and ordering of ministers and deacons in the Church of England now established' ('I never ment so').[142]

The Vice-Chancellor, Thomas Byng, wrote to the Chancellor in 1572, to describe the procedure which had been followed. Mr. Charke had been summoned to answer the charge that his teaching was 'repugnant to the government in this churche of England established', before the Vice-Chancellor and the rest of the Heads of House. He 'did earnestly stand to the defence' of what he had said. He was shown 'what danger would ensue if he so persisted'. He was given time (until Ash Wednesday next) to talk to theological experts and to alter his views. He was also given permission to 'depart' in the meantime if he chose. Under the statutes, if he chooses not 'to revoke his opinion' he must be 'expelled thuniversities'. At the same time, and in the same letter, Byng writes that offences at the other extreme are also occurring. By 'a greate oversight' Caius has 'long kept superstitious monumentes in his college', when the Heads of House had agreed 'to burne the bookes and such other things as serve most for idolatrous abuses, and to cause the rest to be defacid'.[143]

The authorities (surprisingly since they were mostly Cambridge men themselves) declared themselves bewildered by the effrontery of some of those involved. Parker, Archbishop of Canterbury, wrote to Lord Burghley as Chancellor in 1573, regretting that Thomas Aldrich, 'for whom I laboured so much to have him preferred', now 'hath stowt hart against me' and is seeking to get a royal dispensation to enable him to continue as Master of Benet College (Corpus Christi) 'without his degre', 'in despising of the degrees of thuniversite, and a grete mayneyner of Mr. Cartwright'. He had a duty in this office to take the degree of Doctor of Divinity within three years and he was also accused of various corrupt dealings disadvantageous to the College, which he had entered into so as to stand well with the local gentry. Significantly, the Archbishop has tried to get him to 'consider of his duetye to the realme, etc.' but 'al in vayne'.[144] The ecclesiastical commissioners sent for him and the Heads of House wrote to the Chancellor to say that this was a matter they preferred to deal with internally and they rejected external interference.[145] Aldrich himself wrote to the Chancellor with some Fellows of his college as co-signatories, describing the Chancellor as *quasi communis nostri capitis imperium,* and asking him to adjudicate.[146] The Chancellor entrusted the task to the Heads of House, who were inclined to the view that the College's statute should be obeyed but who referred the matter onward to the Archbishop for his determination.

It should not be forgotten that the problems about filth in the streets and the recurrence of plague had not gone away. The Vice-Chancellor, Andrew Perne, wrote to Burghley the Chancellor in November 1574 to tell him about the new spate of deaths and to suggest that the cause was perhaps not unclean habits and bad air but human sinfulness, the 'principall cause of this and all other plagues sent by Allmightie God', or perhaps more particularly, a 'secondarie cause' which God has used as a means to bring the plague, the arrival at Midsomer fair of a visitor from London who died of the plague at Barnwell and whose 'apparell' spread the disease.[147]

The disputes at Caius reached a high point in 1582, and show in a poor light the tendency for extreme behaviour to be matched only by the triviality of some of the points of disagreement, with consequent setting of a bad example to the young. The spirit of the thing is nicely evoked in surviving descriptions: 'Mr. Rabbet...hath bene excepted against...as threatened often by Mr. Booth to be thrust out of the colledge by the eares...the sayde Booth...taking the deane by the bosome...with menacinges and revilinges before all the scholers.'[148]

In July 1582 a letter was written by Christopher Hatton to Burghley the Chancellor claiming that some of the Fellows of Caius have not accepted the election of a Proctor though it has been done in the proper way according to the statutes, and 'either for ill will or other private regard, doe oppose themselves against it'.[149] For their part, the Fellows wrote to complain that they are 'dayly molested', especially by Mr. Booth, 'their common instrument, who to our faces openly doth deride us, and some by name shamefully revileth'.[150] He is the ringleader of 'the inferiour schollers'. The visitors of the college write about what they have done to restore order.[151]

Peace was not unheard of. It is recorded that at Christ's College: 'We whose names are subscribed doe forgeve and forget all injuries past whatsovere, and doe promise to deale Christianly and friendly hereafter, one with another, in wordes and actions.'[152]

Finding a middle way

At the end of Elizabeth's reign, 'Papistry' was as much a cause of offence in Cambridge as Puritanism, for both were deemed to constitute a threat to good order in the State as well as within the University; in both cases they raised extremely awkward questions about the way they should be dealt with, whether internally by the University or externally by the state authorities. The range of topics widened, with the Eucharist and the question of 'assurance' (the Calvinist conviction that those who are saved know who they are), prompting disputes alongside the core issue of the right form of Church government. At Caius in 1581 the Master, Thomas Legge, was accused of Popish sympathies. The Fellows made a list of 'articles', accusing him of having 'open papistes' as pupils, who had dubious books in their rooms with his knowledge, of trying to expel those who did not share his sympathies, or deny them their well-earned degrees, without the consent of the Fellows.[153] There is frequently, as here, to be glimpsed in this list of accusations the familiar squabblesomeness of contemporary Cambridge life. The Fellows added a list of accusations that the College had suffered in its wealth too under this Master. Depositions were made by witnesses.[154]

William Whitaker (1547–1626) was Regius Professor of Divinity from 1580. He was elected Master of St. John's College in 1587, under pressure from Archbishop Whitgift and the Chancellor (still Burghley). Some of the Fellows objected to his extreme Calvinism, among them

Edward Digby, who was something of a Platonist and of much more liberal inclination. Whitaker sought to condemn him for breaches of the College Statutes. In his view the price of stability in the Church was eternal vigilance, and there was nowhere better to mount the watch than Cambridge itself. In 1588 he was writing to Burghley, still manfully continuing as Chancellor, to say:

> I this day enter upon a new undertaking, often demanded by many and not unworthy of our university, the attempt to go through those controversies ... which are agitated between the Roman popish synagoge and our churches reformed according to the word of God.

There follows his 'Preface to the controversies delivered to the Audience at Cambridge'.[155] Whitaker explains that he is anxious to counter arguments which are circulating on the Continent, especially in the writings of Bellarmine; these have not been not published (which would allow everyone to see what was being said) but are, much more dangerously, circulating in handwritten copies. 'Many copies of these lectures fly about everywhere.' He plans by producing 'a complete body of controversies' which can be put 'into men's hands', to set out the opposing view.[156] He proceeds by dividing up the controversy into particular questions, beginning with questions about the use of Scripture.[157]

In 1590 Whitaker was again writing anxiously to the Chancellor Lord Burghley, begging that there should be no Visitation. He recognized that there was a great deal needing 'reform', 'but cause there is to feare, that this visitation would rather serve to root out such as speake against disorders, then to remove the disorders themselves'.[158] He was soon to find himself the subject of accusations, and he begged the Chancellor to let him 'have that writing that was exhibited against me', so that he could answer the accusations.[159] The Vice-Chancellor wrote to Burghley, too, reporting plotting and scheming everywhere in the University ('these hurtes and incumbrances do principallie rise from Mr. Johnsons complottinge with his associates').[160]

At the end of April 1595 a sermon was preached in the University church by William Barrett, Fellow of Caius. He denied the fundamental Calvinist teaching that those who are saved have assurance of their salvation. He said that it mattered what sinners did. These were challenges to positions known to be held by Whitaker and his allies, so this was a direct challenge to authority in the University as well as to doctrine. The Heads of House made him recant and a petition was got up by several dozen academics who wanted him punished.

Barrett appealed to Whitgift but his enemies answered that he was a papist. Whitgift interestingly objected to all this on the grounds that as Archbishop he must uphold the Thirty-Nine Articles. The Heads of House and all the rest of the Cambridge disputants alike had failed to accept his and their authority. The Heads of House appealed to Burghley. A form of peace was achieved by the Archbishop of York, but there was unfinished business both about matters of doctrine and about matters of authority.

Town and gown problems were not a thing of the past, either. There was a dispute with Lord North, 1597, after he complained that he had been set upon by 30 or 40 armed scholars in the street near St. John's demanding that he hand over Parris, one of his employees who was said to have stabbed a scholar. The University protested its innocence. 'Wee deny that his lordships lyfe was by any scholer indaungered...Wee deny than any ambuskados were laied.'[161]

So by the end of the sixteenth century, the scene was set for the modern style of Cambridge politics. There was a metaphor in the way College gardens were being set out for the personal pleasure of heads of colleges, and also for their Fellows. In 1532, Queens' College's President was provided with his own special fruit trees:

> That whereas the president of this College hath before this tyme no garden appointed severally for himself, nether for frute, nor to walk in...Now...the said president shall have, enjoy and take from hensforth the Garden or Orchard over against the College brode gaates with all the frutes growing within the same to his own propir use

though he lost the right to eat the fruit from the general college orchard.[162] At Queens' in 1575:

> Item, to Robert Geordenor carpenter and vij of his men for xj dayes woorke setting up the frame of the vine in the fellowes garden, xxviijs vjd. Item, toThomas Thatcher and his man for iij dayes woorke in framing the stones to sett the vyne's frame on and making holes in the wall for the same, vs.iiijd. Item, payed for 3500 privie and one thousand of hunnysucles for the iland and other places of the colledge, ixs xd.[163]

4 SEVENTEENTH- AND EIGHTEENTH-CENTURY CAMBRIDGE: PURITANS AND SCIENTISTS

James I and Cambridge

James I succeeded Elizabeth in March 1603. The new King regarded the universities as serious 'players' in the affairs of his kingdom, 'nurseries and fountaines of our Church & common wealth'.[1] So their representatives were going to be encouraged to be involved in significant events, and after the active participation of the previous century they would hardly be likely to expect anything else. The University authorities took a strong grasp of the reins. A letter from the Chancellor, now the Earl of Salisbury, to the Vice-Chancellor and Heads of House, on 15 December 1604 was firm:

> How necessarye it is, that a good conformitye be had and observed in all the Members of the Universitye, with the avoydinge both of distraction in opinion, and diversitye in practice (especially in matter appertayninge to Religion) there is no man of any upright Judgment, but will acknowledge.[2]

In 1604, the Chancellor's general right to Visit and search was confirmed by the new King.[3]

In 1604, a Conference was held at Hampton Court. This was partly at the instigation of puritan leaders, who had been pressing for it from 1603, with a Millenary Petition which claimed to have a thousand signatures. Whitgift and a bevy of bishops were to face the puritan representatives led by John Reynolds (or Rainalds) of Oxford. The matters under discussion were mainly fine-tuning of the norms and an attempt to reset the standards on points where puritans thought the Church of England was too 'popish' in its practices. There was no serious attempt here to overturn episcopal government in favour of presbyterianism. Richard Bancroft (1544–1610) had studied at Christ's College and later at Jesus College, Cambridge. He soon became chaplain to the Bishop of Ely and settled in Cambridgeshire, acting as preacher to the University. By 1584 he was based in London, where he began to make his name as an enemy of the puritans and in this direction he influenced the new King. His ultimate loyalty was perhaps to Oxford, whose Chancellor he became in 1608. He was in the party which was arguing against the puritans at Hampton Court, and became Archbishop of Canterbury from 1604 in succession to John Whitgift.

An Authorized Version of the Bible was put in hand in 1604, and published in 1611. This was in part a fruit of the Hampton Court Conference, with the King giving instructions that the translation's choice of renderings should reflect the ecclesiology of the Church of England. It was a joint effort, with six 'companies' or committees set up to supervise sections of the Bible, two for Westminster, two for Oxford and two for Cambridge. One Cambridge group, including the University's leading Hebraists and consisting of Edward Lively, John Richardson, Lawrence Chaderton, Francis Dillingham, Roger Andrewes, Thomas Harrison, Robert Spaulding, Andrew Bing, translated from 1 Chronicles to the Song of Solomon. The second Cambridge group, which translated the Apocrypha, included John Duport, William Branthwaite, Jeremiah Radcliffe, Samuel Ward, Andrew Downes, John Bois, John Ward, Leonard Hutten, Thomas Bilson and Richard Bancroft himself.

These were uncomfortable times for Cambridge in its relations with secular authorities, both local and national. When Parliament met in 1614, Francis Bacon (1561–1626), who had been at Trinity College Cambridge from 1573 to 1576, was elected as Member of Parliament for St. Albans and Ipswich as well as Cambridge University, though he sat as M.P. for Cambridge. There were complaints that he should not be allowed to be in the Commons while Attorney-General. The question had not arisen before so it was allowed in his case but a ruling established that it must not happen in future.

His links with Cambridge remained finely balanced. Correspondence of the University of Cambridge with Francis Bacon survives from the period when the town was petitioning to be made a city. The University had its concerns about the town's proposal. It entreats that 'the University and our selfes may be freed from that danger which by them is intended to us':

> When they were at their lowest and in their meanest fortunes they ever shewed them selfes unkinde neighbours to us...and therefore wee cannot expect peace amonest them when their thoughts and wills shallbe winged and strengthned by that power and authority which the very bare title of a citty will gieve unto them.[4]

The University wrote to Bacon calling herself his 'mother'. Bacon wrote to Cambridge in 1617 as his 'deere and reverend mother' and signing himself 'your most lovinge and assured friend and sonne.'[5]

Moreover, the King's willingness to take the universities seriously worked both ways. It tempted him to further 'Visitation' and intrusion into Cambridge's affairs. In 1616, with the agreement of the Registrary, James Tabor, were implemented:

> His majesties directions to the Vice-Chancellor and heads of houses in the University of Cambridge, given by himself to Dr. Hilles, Vice-Chancellor [and others]...First, his majesty signifieth his pleasure that he would have all that take any degree in schools to subscribe to the three articles. Secondly, that no preacher be allowed to preach in the town but such as are every way conformable both by subscription and every other way. Thirdly, that all students do resort to the sermons at St. Marys, and be restrained from going to any other church in the time of St. Marys sermons'...Eighthly, that young students in divinity be directed to study such books as be most agreeable in doctrine and discipline to the church of England, and excited to besto their time in the fathers and councels, scholemen, histories, and controversies, and not to insist too long upon compendiums and abbreviators...Ninthly, that no man either in the pulpit or in schools be suffered to maintain dogmatically any point of doctrine that is not allowed by the Church of England.[6]

Further 'royal orders' go into more detail still. The King says,

> We do require and command, that upon the discovery to the Chancellor or Vice-Chancellor...of any fanciful conceit, savouring of Judaism, popish superstition, or Puritanism, disagreeing from the laudable and approved customs of our church of England, that the same be in due time speedily checked and reformed,

and he commands,

> that a copy of these our directions be delivered to the master of every college, requiring that he deliver the same, or a copy thereof, to the special visitor of the said college...and howsoever we deliver this adminition in generally terms, our will is not that the same be understood as an aspersion upon the whole University for inconformity, but rather as an encouragement to these colleges and governors that,

according to duty, keep order, and as an injunction for speedy reformation in such as are culpable.[7]

There were good reasons for the continuing nervousness of the secular authorities about the behaviour of the University. Sedition was apparently brewing. Ralph Brownrigg (1592–1659), went to Pembroke College, Cambridge, as a scholar in 1606. He became a Fellow immediately on graduation. In 1617 he was heard to wonder in a private discussion in his rooms in college 'Whether a King breaking fundamental laws may be opposed'. He did this 'being then in his chamber, to Mr. Owen of Clare Hall, 23 January last past', two others being present. This David Owen, who was a strong believer in the Divine Right of Kings, reported him for having raised 'seditious and treacherous questions'.[8] The Vice-Chancellor dealt with this matter with common sense and moderation and got him to 'submit'; the King accepted that since the Vice-Chancellor considered 'his punishment to have been convenient and somewhat proportionable to his offence, his majesty is graciously pleased to forgive all, and receive him into his favour.'

The Chancellor of the University wrote to Heads of House in 1618:

> I am heartily sorry that I am eforced to write to you as the necessity of these enormous times requires, which have begot such a height of disorder, that his royal majesty and state is therewith much troubled, as you may see by his princely letters … You have good laws and constitutions, and excellent orders, and power enough. Nothing is wanting but care and courage to give life unto the laws which have so long slept, that they seem, and indeed are, no better than half dead.[9]

It is evident that great matters were engaged here, both at a theoretical level (what is the relation of order to treason and religious conformity?) and at a practical level (was freedom of speech and opinion to be allowed in the University?). It is also clear that the King felt insecure, to a degree which was to prove to be fully justified in the light of the events of the following decades.

* * *

Hybrid vigour

Cambridge's educational challenge was now to make sense of a world in which a student could, while subscribing to the Thirty-Nine Articles, engage with the challenges of experimental science. In all the rich and complex debates about science and religion which engaged the leaders of seventeenth-century thought, the two areas of endeavour were never fully separated in the minds of scholars. In the seventeenth and eighteenth centuries, Cambridge, like Oxford, was still educating a high proportion of its students for ordination in the Church of England; and it was normally a requirement that those who became Fellows of colleges should themselves be ordained.

This began to create a tension with another trend, which was to revolutionize the social framework of academe. Some of Cambridge's early modern graduates were individuals of private means and good-to-middling birth who were sent to spend time at Cambridge, and if possible to get degrees, as a means of 'finishing' their education, after which they might go on to play an active part in public life or retire to run the family estates and engage in intellectually challenging correspondence. Thus Cambridge – and Oxford – began to produce the educated 'gentleman'. Others were self-made men like many of the parvenu Tudor heroes and anti-heroes of the last chapter, who depended on patronage or the availability of sizarships to get them started but could then look to considerable upward social mobility.

Applied science and 'useful' studies

> 'A Vulgar Mechanik can practise what he has been taught or seen done, but if he is in an error he knows not how to find it out and correct it, and if you put him out of his road, he is at a stand; Whereas he that is able to reason nimbly and judiciously about figure, force and motion, is never at rest till he gets over every rub.'
>
> Isaac Newton to Nathaniel Hawes, 25 May 1694.[10]

Among the proto-scientists of the day were those (particularly among the 'dissenters' who could not got to Oxford or Cambridge because they would not subscribe to the Thirty-Nine Articles of the Church of England) who wanted to see science taught as an applied discipline.[11] Gerrard Winstanley (1609–1676), himself not a university man but a former apprentice with ideas and a strong social conscience, wrote a treatise arguing for practical study (of scientific and commercial subjects) through living experience, in which he enters into disagreement with a 'zealous but ignorant professor', who is suspicious that 'this is a low and carnal ministry indeed, this leads men to know nothing but the knowledge of the earth and the secrets of nature'. 'God manifests himself in actual knowledge, not in imagination,' replies Winstanley:

> But when a studying imagination comes into man, which is the devil, for it is the cause of all evils and sorrows in the

world: that is he who puts out the eyes of men's knowledge, and tells him he must believe what others have writ or spoke, and must not trust to his own experience … examine yourself, and look likewise into the ways of all professors, and you shall find that the enjoyment of the earth below, which you call a low and carnal knowledge, is that which you and all professors … strive and seek after.[12]

Not 'two cultures' but a single body of knowledge

C.P. Snow (1905–1980), who was a Fellow of Christ's College from 1930, made the famous assertion, that there are 'two cultures', in his Rede Lecture of 1959. The notion that the arts and the sciences were two distinct worlds of thought would have made little sense in the seventeenth and eighteenth centuries.[13] In early modern Europe, the task intellectuals faced was to create a working relationship between the study of Christian theology and the study of the natural world. The assumption of the time was that these broad areas formed a single body of knowledge, in which light might be thrown on a given question from various angles. 'There is such a connection of things, and dependence of notions, that one part of learning doth confer light to another',[14] as Isaac Barrow (1630–1677), one of Isaac Newton's teachers and himself formerly a student at Trinity College, Cambridge, was to put it.

Isaac Barrow used a travelling Fellowship from Trinity College in 1655 to go to Paris and then Florence; he then went on by ship to the Middle East, stayed in Smyrna for some months and moved on to Constantinople. He was an excellent linguist but he does not seem to have taken the opportunity to learn Arabic on this trip. When he returned to Cambridge (via Venice) in 1659 he had transformed himself, despite his youth, into a likely candidate for one Cambridge Chair after another, the Regius Professorship of Greek (1662), then the Chair of Geometry, then the first Lucasian Professorship of Mathematics in 1663. So, like other scholars of the sixteenth, seventeenth and eighteenth centuries, Barrow felt fully competent to write on philosophical, literary and scientific subjects as though they formed a continuum. For despite the occasional protest that some things required 'professional' knowledge, few thinkers felt constrained from discussing any branch of knowledge they chose.

The result was a period of 'hybrid vigour', of startling innovativeness and intellectual adventure and a sense of freedom to mount challenges to old certainties. This was particularly noticeable among the university-educated 'gentlemen' of good family whose names appear again and again in this chapter. But it was also a product of the spirit in which the 'dissenting academies' set about educating the students who came their way as a consequence of the banning of all but practising members of the Church of England from the two English universities. England was unique in Europe in the complex Protestantism which was now emerging from the century of combative adjustments in which Cambridge had played so prominent a part.

* * *

The Cambridge Platonists and the redrawing of the boundaries of theology

> No models of past times, however perfect, can have the same vivid effect on the youthful mind as the productions of contemporary genius... The great works of past ages seem to a young man things of another race... But the writings of a contemporary, perhaps not many years older than himself, surrounded by the same circumstances and disciplined by the same manners, possess a reality for him and inspire an actual friendship as of a man for a man.[15]
>
> Samuel Taylor Coleridge, *Biographia Literaria*, Chapter 1

The intellectual experience of the seventeenth and eighteenth centuries was, perhaps for the first time, to give students and academics a conscious sense of living among thinkers in their own times – including those in Cambridge itself – who might be of an importance comparable with the authoritative names of the past.

Henry More (1614–87) went to Christ's College, Cambridge, in 1631. It was a family preference. His uncle was a Fellow there and three of his brothers became students at the same college. He did not take his B.A. until 1636, taking a leisurely view of the urgency of completing his degree, apparently because he was busy reading widely in areas which interested him. In 1641 he was elected to replace his tutor Robert Gell as a Fellow of the College. An uncle ensured he had a living once he was ordained but he stayed in Cambridge all his life, writing on philosophy and theology.

More had been brought up in a strict Calvinism, against which he later reacted. He says in an autobiographical note that he had been shocked when he first understood the implications of the Calvinist doctrine of predestination. The Solemn League and Covenant, approved unanimously by the Westminster Assembly in 1643, involved an oath to resist unscriptural 'innovations' which were also declared to be unlawful – that is, contrary to Acts of Parliament – and likely to bring back tyranny and the dominance of the Papacy. Yet when the Earl of Manchester put pressure on Cambridge's academics to accept the Solemn League and Covenant on pain of being forced to leave the University, he seems to have capitulated; like the *traditores* ('handers over') of the early Church, he was willing to be a 'traitor' to save his skin, though no handing over of the Scriptures was of course required.

In his work, More combined both 'Platonic' and what came to be known as 'latitudinarian' interests; and it is perhaps partly through his many writings that the two became associated in the 'movement' known as 'Cambridge Platonism'. Platonism in the late antique world had had a tendency to become infected with mysticism, particularly in the Greek-speaking parts of the dying Roman Empire in the early Christian period. Reading Greek patristic authors was still something of a novelty for Western theologians in the early seventeenth century, and sometimes they liked to drop quotations into their remarks to show off their knowledge. Henry More, for example, quotes Clement of Alexandria's 'Miscellanies' (*Stromateis*) and says vaguely 'as Plotinus somewhere speaks', in his introduction to a group of collected works published in 1662.[16] More's own first self-consciously Platonic writings were philosophical poems, beginning with the *Psychodia Platonica*, published in 1642. These were modernist in their thrust, attempts to incorporate Galileo and Copernicus and Descartes into an essentially 'Platonic' system of knowledge.

René Descartes (1596–1650) was himself a novelty among the authorities assiduously read in Cambridge by ambitious young intellectuals; he provides an example of the way in which some but not all authors of the day found their way to respectability and to influence. (It is an interesting question how particular new books came to 'count' as shapers of future directions of study.) Descartes made efforts to establish his own reputation with academe. His *Meditations* begins with an address to the Professors of the Sorbonne, seeking their patronage, since (he suggests) their reputation on philosophy and theology stands high. He became something of a fashion among the dons who were writing within the 'Cambridge Platonist' group. Such processes of lionization could only be assisted by contact with a living writer. Through Samuel Hartlib, always an enthusiastic 'networker' and broker of new connections, Henry More entered into personal correspondence with Descartes in 1648.

It is possible to see in this correspondence the way a complex of concerns was in process of being sorted out in this key period of intellectual reconfiguration, and also how inseparable the religious and theological questions were from the scientific and philosophical. How did 'spirit' differ from 'matter'? Of what kind were the 'forces' which operated in the physical world and the 'laws' of nature? Henry More discusses what he had wanted to achieve in the preface to a collection of his earlier writings published in 1662. 'My interweaving of Platonism and Cartesianism so frequently' is, he explains, intended to provide 'invincible bulwarks against the most cunning and most mischievous efforts of Atheism.'[17] More favoured explanations of forces in the natural world which included the spiritual. That set him against Hobbes, whom he considered too materialistic.

Descartes proved very 'accessible'. He wrote letters to More in response to More's enquiries and suggestions:

> Sensory nerves so fine that they could be moved by the smallest particles of matter are no more intelligible to me than a faculty enabling our mind to sense or perceive other minds directly... For my part, in God and angels and in our mind I understand there to be no extension of substance but only extension of power. An angel can exercise power now on a greater and now on a lesser part of corporeal substance; but if there were no bodies, I could not conceive of any space with which an angel or God would be co-extensive.[18]

Descartes argued that as conscious minds, we have no direct experience of what it is for bodies to act on bodies:[19]

> motion is not a substance but a mode... what is appropriate to shape is not appropriate to motion; and neither of these is what is appropriate to an extended thing. Remember that nothing has no properties, and that what is commonly called empty space is nothing but a real body deprived of its accidents.[20]

His reasoning was that this places the human observer (and therefore the scientist) at a distance from the physical world of which he is attempting to make sense:

> The human mind separated from the body does not have sense-perception strictly so-called; but it is not clear by natural reason alone whether angels are created like minds distinct from bodies, or like minds united to bodies... I agree that we should not think of God except as being what all good people would wish there to be if he did not exist.[21]

More carried on thinking and writing and proposing innovatory solutions to these key questions of the location and nature of the boundary between the material and the spiritual world and of any forces transmitting effects from one to the other. His *The Immortality of the Soul* appeared in 1659 and his *Enchiridion metaphysicum* in 1671. He was ambitious to demonstrate by reasoning that substances which were incorporeal could and did exist, and in this work he adumbrated something like the Platonic *anima mundi*, a spiritual force or power which operates and animates the natural world. This Spirit of Nature he called the *Principium Hylarchicum*. He was beginning to move away from Descartes as he developed these ideas, adopting – as he believed – some of the thinking in Robert Boyle's *New Experiments Physico-Mechanical*. Boyle did not consider that he had been understood. He wrote a riposte[22] and there was further criticism in Matthew Hale's *Difficiles nugae* of 1675.

Areas on the fringes of these central questions repeatedly attracted seventeenth-century thinkers. Like Isaac Newton, a later Cambridge figure, More was one of those who dabbled in alchemy, writing as 'Alazonomastix Philalethes' against 'Eugenius Philalethes' (Thomas Vaughan, 1622–66)[23] in a controversy of 1650–51. Behind the attraction of alchemy lay the 'Hermetic' tradition, a late-antique Egyptian hotchpotch of beliefs, made precariously respectable by Augustine of Hippo's discussion of it; an interest in prophecy (Apocalypse and Daniel) and all the apparatus of soothsaying and fortune-telling which went with it in the ancient world; cabbalistica. (More mentions that he had discussed the book of Revelation with Isaac Newton in 1680.)

Even the most sober intellectual thought that secrets were to be discovered, that hidden truths might lie within texts. And while it remained undetermined where science ended and religion began, so that for example chemistry and alchemy overlapped a good deal, grey areas stretched temptingly in several directions. More's *Conjectura cabbalistica* (1655) was dedicated to his fellow 'Cambridge Platonist' Ralph Cudworth. Excavating the text of Genesis, he believed he had glimpsed hidden clues left there by its divine author. Even the question on the ways in which God spoke through the human authors of the Bible formed the subject of a book, More's *Enthusiasmus triumphatus* of 1656. Works intended to have a popular appeal included *Enchiridion ethicum* (1667), and *Divine Dialogues* (1668), whose dialogue form was considered an attraction. The topics were grand, perennial issues of philosophy and theology. The subject of the immortality of the soul took More into controversy with thinkers outside the academic world, such as Richard Baxter in 1681–2.

Despite this – to modern eyes highly mixed – body of writings, in 1664 Henry More was elected a Fellow of the newly created Royal Society.

Societies for conducting experiments and discussing scientific questions

Societies were now springing up locally and nationally, independently of the universities but including in their membership a good many interested academics. It was not all serious science. Mere curiosity and the love of a show and a wonder were great incentives to take an active interest. John Evelyn noted in his Diary for 13 July 1654 a visit to 'Waddum' (Wadham College, Oxford) in which Wilkins had shown him his transparent apiaries and a great many curiosities: 'a variety of Shadows, Dyals, Perspectives…and many other artificial, mathematical, Magical curiosities'.[24]

Sir Robert Moray (b.1608/9 so about 50 at the time) stands out as the driving force in the founding and the early development of the Royal Society, which was prominent among these societies from the first. It is unclear how much formal higher education he had. He may have studied in France but he was a soldier by profession. He was one of the early Freemasons. He was a Royalist in the Civil War. He was attracted to a Christian stoicism and practised the control of feeling and its expression. His own special scientific interests were in magnetism, tides, horology and chemistry.[25] In a letter to the Earl of Kincardine of 31 December/10 January 1658, he comments on his own strong consciousness of the ill-focused character of the new experimental and practical scientific work: 'All my physicall skill, I mean in the medicall sphere, is nothing else but the effect of loose ratiocinations built upon no great stock of knowledge of natural things, and managed with a pretty baugh [weak] logick.'[26]

A decisive meeting of 12 was held at Gresham College in London on 28 November 1660, the culmination of earlier meetings over a decade or more held in Oxford as well as London, and the Royal Society was born. The Royal Society and other bodies and institutions like it were attempting something which was not being done by universities as 'institutions'. Part of the problem was that they did not have the experimental equipment, and experiments were the coming thing. John Evelyn's *Diary* for 25 April 1661 describes watching the experiments conducted at meetings of the Royal Society:

> I went to the Society, where were divers experiments with Mr. Boyle's pneumatic engine. We put in a snake, but could make it only extremely sick by exhausting the air, and could not kill it; but a chick died of convulsions in a short space.

He went again:

> July 17, 1661, I went to London. At our assembly, we put a
> viper and a slow worm, or aspic, to bite a mouse, but could
> not irritate them to fasten at all. Mr. Boyle brought two polished
> marbles of three inch diameter which, when first well rubbed
> and then treated with a drop of olive oil which was afterwards
> clean wiped off, and when clapped together, stuck close – even
> so close that the nether stone, having a hook inserted, and the
> upper a ring, took up forty-two pound weight by the power of
> contiguity before they separated. The oil was added to fill up
> any possible porosity in the polished marble. The 19th, we tried
> our diving bell, or engine, in the Water Dock at Deptford, in
> which our curator continued half an hour under water.

These are descriptions of enquiries more ambitious than just trying
things to see what would happen. The experimenters were searching
for natural laws (such as might govern the effects of 'contiguity'), and
for the properties of living things (a snake seems to need less air than a
chicken). Underlying the relatively simple question whether it was better
to try things out or to arrive at conclusions by thought was the need to
revisit profound epistemological and metaphysical presumptions.

More Cambridge Platonists

The Cambridge college which had the most numerous cluster of
'Cambridge Platonists' was Emmanuel. Emmanuel College had been
founded in 1584 on the Dominican site, by Sir Walter Mildmay,
himself of strong puritan sympathies, and a supporter of individual
puritans in trouble on the Continent and in England, although he
upheld the Elizabethan Settlement. He wanted his college to ensure
that the training of ordinands would provide a satisfactory foundation
of the right kind of theological study. John Smith (1618–52) was
admitted as a pensioner at Emmanuel College in 1636; his tutor was
to be Benjamin Whichcote (1609–83). Whichcote looms large as a
putative influence on the group known as Cambridge Platonists,
though he was not a great publisher of writings in his lifetime.

Smith was to die young, but not before he had written a number
of pieces on the topics of the moment, which were collected and
published by his friend John Worthington in 1660 under the title *Select
Discourses*. Like others in the 'group', he held views not far from those
of the Quietists, emphasizing the importance of the practice of Christian
living. For these Cambridge Platonists shared with the early Christian
'philosophers' an assumption that philosophy was a way of life for a

reasonable and moderate man or woman, as well as a way of viewing the world. They also took spirituality seriously and tended to consider it more important than holding the finer details of doctrinal opinion.

Another 'Cambridge Platonist' who died early was Nathaniel Culverwell, but not before he had more or less ready for publication (his young brother completed it), a book derived from the exercises students were required to perform as part of their degree work, *An Elegant and Learned Discourse of the Light of Nature* (1652).

A third member of this group was Ralph Cudworth (1617–88), who went as a pensioner to Emmanuel College, Cambridge, where his father had been a Fellow. Ralph matriculated in 1632. Benjamin Whichcote, who became a Fellow in 1633 and a tutor in 1634, seems to have been a strong influence on Cudworth. Cudworth graduated in 1635 and became a Fellow himself the year after. He was a notably successful tutor, with 28 pupils at one time. Like More, Cudworth helped to introduce the study of Descartes into Cambridge.

Cudworth was considered by the Parliamentary Visitors a 'safe' replacement for Thomas Paske who was ejected from the Mastership of Clare College in 1645. In the same year he became Regius Professor of Hebrew, contentedly burying himself thereafter in 'Jewish antiquities' and giving regular lectures on the Temple in Jerusalem. In 1647, Parliament heard one of his sermons, distinctly Quietist in tone, and arguing that simple goodness of life is all that is required, not a deep knowledge of the finer points of doctrinal debate.

* * *

Cambridge adjusts the relationship between God and nature

In 1678 Cudworth published *The True Intellectual System of the Universe, wherein All the Reason and Philosophy of Atheism Is Confuted, and Its Impossibility Demonstrated*, attacking Hobbes's alleged 'materialism'. He wanted to strike a position between regarding the created universe as a mere mechanism and imputing to God so direct a hands-on way of running it that everything required divine intervention. He suggests that 'plastic nature' acts according to the laws of the 'Regular and Orderly Motion of Matter' God has imposed on it, though God can interfere if he chooses. We are moving here into intellectual and theological territory which was going to open the way for Deism.

The preface to the French edition of Descartes' *Principles* compares philosophy to a 'tree', whose roots are metaphysics, with physics as the trunk and all the other sciences emerging from the trunk as the branches of the tree. There are three main 'branches', says Descartes, medicine, mechanics and morals. 'By "morals" I understand the highest and most perfect moral system, which presupposes a complete knowledge of the other sciences and it the ultimate level of wisdom.'[27] Cambridge scholars too were wrestling with these fundamental abstract questions about what the fundamentals actually were. John Aubrey, who was secretary to George Villiers the Duke of Buckingham when he was Cambridge's Chancellor, remarks in his *Brief Lives* on exactly this question of the level of abstraction at which it was necessary to begin:

> If the Intellect be so cleare and Infallible as the Philosophers would have it, why do's it perpetually submit to the Judgement, and Arbitration of Sense? As in the Mathematiques the Principles thereof are Intellectuall and Abstract, and yet they can produce no conclusions that can pass for certaine and True until they have past the test of Sense.[28]

The first task was to work out what a 'law of nature' is and make a list of such laws and their operation; here Cambridge scholars were prominent. The problem as it presented itself in the early modern period began with the rethinking of the nature and position of the boundary between physics and metaphysics, natural and supernatural. 'Physics' as used in the seventeenth century referred to the study of 'nature' at large (Greek *physica*), not to the specialist area to which it is now usually taken to refer.

Henry More had some correspondence with Descartes in which the two discussed this great intellectual problem of the age. In one direction this was forcing hard thinking about matters which remain among the fundamental questions of modern physics. Descartes wrote to More:[29]

> motion is not a substance but a mode ... what is appropriate to shape is not appropriate to motion; and neither of these is what is appropriate to an extended thing. Remember that nothing has no properties, and that what is commonly called empty space is nothing but a real body deprived of its accidents.[30]

What if any was the different between a law by which nature operates and a spiritual force? Thinkers were discovering that this discussion was making them view in a new light the nature of God himself. Descartes to More again:

> The human mind separated from the body does not have sense-perception strictly so-called; but it is not clear by natural reason alone whether angels are created like minds distinct

from bodies, or like minds united to bodies...I agree that we should not think of God except as being what all good people would wish there to be if he did not exist.[31]

Natural and revealed

It was a medieval commonplace that though we 'know' some things because they seem to stand to reason, others we learn because God 'reveals' them to us. Seventeenth-century Cambridge scholars now joined in the contemporary debate about the means of studying the world available to those who wanted to resolve these difficult problems about the nature of the laws which make it spin.

The Bible is manifestly deficient as a scientific and also perhaps as a philosophical and ethical textbook, at least in the sense that it does not contain *expressis verbis* all the answers needed. Does that undermine its claims to be the Word of the God who created the natural world? The followers of Copernicus (1473–1543) had argued that it had never been God's intention as he dictated Scripture to include instruction in science. Galileo (1564–1642) agreed. The Council of Trent's Session IV was cited in support by those conservatives who were hostile to this position.[32] The Jesuit Giovanni Battista Riccioli tried to distinguish the question whether the Bible contains teaching on physics and astronomy from the question whether those remarks on the subject which the Scriptures do contain are really about the faith and not about science.

This became newly important in the seventeenth century as those who taught in universities and independent enquirers alike sought to reposition the 'evidence' of the Bible among other kinds of 'evidence'. Isaac Newton's (1643–1727) *Mathematical Principles of Natural Philosophy* (1687) shows a remote God ordering the cosmos, not a daily intervener in the details of life, but the Christian tradition generally had preferred the 'hands-on God' who took a close and continuing interest in his creation and had 'written' in Scripture about those matters which could not be known purely by the exercise of reason. At the same time, the created world was itself an act of revelation, arguably a proof that it had a creator, and a pointer to the kind of creator he was. These distinctions are still in play in the seventeenth century.

* * *

Isaac Newton: a Cambridge character in close-up

> Near me hung Trinity's loquacious clock,
> Who never let the quarters, night or day,

Slip by him unproclaimed, and told the hours
Twice over with a male and female voice.
Her pealing organ was my neighbour too;
And from my pillow, looking forth by light
Of moon or favouring stars, I could behold
The antechapel where the statue stood
Of Newton with his prism and silent face,
The marble index of a mind for ever
Voyaging through strange seas of Thought, alone.
William Wordsworth, *The Prelude*, III, 53–63.

'Certain questions': Isaac Newton (1642–1727) works it out

Isaac Newton's father does not seem to have been able to sign his name. Newton was fortunate to be able to begin his education even in local day schools. He was then sent to the free grammar school in Grantham, which meant he had to live in lodgings. Then his mother had made an unsuccessful attempt to bring him home to run the family estate. Nevertheless, he was able to go to Cambridge in June 1661, thanks to the provision of a sizarship. In fact, he entered Trinity College as a sub-sizar. That meant that he paid for his keep by acting as a servant to Fellows and richer students. (The distinction between the classes of student was marked by separate dining arrangements.) In Newton's case this may have involved an 'arrangement' with Humphrey Babington, who was one of the Fellows but a man of absentee habits and therefore in need of a 'representative' to keep an eye on his college affairs for him and alert him if he needed to return.

This was a period of self-education and intellectual self-reliance for Cambridge students. In some cases, this was because of the likes of Babington, who did not connect their academic positions with any particular duties towards students. But in possibly the vast majority of cases, the reality was quite different. Tutors were assiduous but they saw their task as principally one of directing the student's private reading. Newton was free, as other students were, to follow a course of reading of his own choice. His tutor would make suggestions but the syllabus was nominal and an enterprising undergraduate could develop his own interests. Pragmatic advice was to be had, advising the student how to conduct his inner intellectual life and manage his energies and interests, but ultimately the responsibility was his own. Daniel Waterland published 'Advice to a young student' in 1730, but originally devised it three decades earlier to meet the needs of the students to whom he was tutor at Magdalene College, Cambridge.

He takes it that the task of the tutor is to guide and encourage what is essentially the independent effort of the young man to educate himself by reading.

This remarkable freedom could even apply to the student studying for a profession. Isaac Barrow did not have to pursue a higher degree in medicine when he considered entering the medical profession. He merely had to read. And the reading included looking into contemporary fashions in natural science, specifically in chemistry and botany, astronomy and mathematics, as well as anatomy. 'Design your own Accomplishment, and therewith the truest Pleasure'[33] urged a commentator in the 1770s. These were also to be the sentiments of Joseph Priestley (1733–1804), in his prefatory remarks to his students at the beginning of a set of science lectures in the 1790s.[34]

Newton's tutor at Trinity was Benjamin Pulleyn. He offered a conventional curriculum of reading based on Aristotle. Newton soon ceased to pursue this at all systematically and took up more modern and fashionable authors instead.[35] He got away with it. There was an exception to this rule of permitting independent reading, which was that a student who wanted eventually to hold a Fellowship at Trinity College after graduation would first have to be elected to a scholarship, which would mean that he would have to have the approval of a tutor. These competitions were not held annually and it is of interest that Newton was elected in 1664, despite his failure to apply himself to the usual course of reading.

The notebooks he kept while he was at Cambridge and afterwards show that Newton taught himself by reading to a plan. He learnt Bible-reading according to a scheme which survives in his notebook preserved as King's College, Cambridge, Keynes MS 2. He also read widely in the Fathers and became interested in the doctrinal controversies of the early Church, especially the ones concerning the Trinity. He took against Athanasius and came to the view that the orthodox doctrine of the Trinity was unsatisfactory.

Keeping a notebook of one's reading was a practice common in other centuries and it could include, as it did in Newton's case, jottings of thoughts and insights and plans. On one page in the middle he wrote a heading: 'Questiones quaedam philosophcae' *[sic]*, with 45 headings under it.[36] The entries under these heading show that he was reading the fashionable and controversial Descartes, Walter Charleton's English digest of Pierre Gassendi the 'atomist', from Galileo's *Dialogue*, and from the writings of Robert Boyle, Thomas Hobbes, Kenelm Digby, Joseph Glanville and Henry More.

The frame of reference of academic knowledge was in process of being disassembled and reconstructed so Newton had considerable freedom to think radically. And the problems he was interested in could be addressed by the solitary student with a combination of thought and relatively simple experiments which did not need vast resources of equipment. Newton was doubly fortunate that these requirements were at a crucial stage of development in his own day. It was the style of the times that, even if he was by nature an isolated thinker, he was able to be drawn into the exchanges of the day and have his contributions taken seriously.

By now the Cambridge tradition differed from that at Oxford in its emphasis on the study of mathematics, and this was Newton's point of entry to all these matters, though it seems he largely taught himself even this conventional part of the syllabus. His niece's husband, John Conduitt, wrote that

> He bought Descartes's Geometry & read it by himself...when he was got over 2 or 3 pages he could understand no farther than he began again & got 3 or 4 pages farther till he came to another difficult place, than he began again & advanced farther & continued so doing till he made himself Master of the whole without having the least light or instruction from any body.[37]

Newton identified from his reading a series of puzzling fundamental questions. What are colour, motion, gravity? From the beginning of his student life he was trying to resolve them:

> In the beginning of the year 1665 I found the Method of approximating series...The same year in May I found the method of Tangents of Gregory & Slusius, & in November had the direct method of fluxions & the next year in January had the Theory of Colours & in May following I had entrance into ye inverse method of fluxions.
>
> the same year I began to think of gravity extending to ye orb of the Moon & (having found out how to estimate the force with wch [a] globe revolving within a sphere presses the surface of the sphere) from Keplers rule of the periodical times of the Planets being in sesquialterate proportion of their distances from the center of their Orbs, I deduced that the forces wch keep the Planets in their Orbs must [be] reciprocally as the squares of their distances from the centers about wch they revolve: & thereby compared the force requisite to keep the Moon in her Orb with the force of gravity at the surface of the earth, & found them answer pretty nearly. All this was

in the two plague years of 1665–1666. For in those days I was in the prime of my age for invention & minded Mathematicks & Philosophy more than at any time since.[38]

A feature of his method of work (as Conduitt notes) was that he would seize on a topic and work at it intently until he had resolved the question which had struck him as far as he could at that time. The solution would be recorded, as happened in a paper he produced in November 1665. Then he would perhaps drop the subject altogether or pause and move on to something else. He was also exploring 'method' as a topic in itself. A paper of 1666 was entitled 'To Resolve Problems by Motion these Following Propositions are Sufficient' (*Mathematical Papers*, 1.400–48). Here we see him picking up quite naturally the academic tradition of the 'necessary argument', using 'propositions' which belong in the same family as the *propositiones*, *articuli* and *loci communes* of earlier centuries.

So what *is* colour? Descartes and Gassendi and their respective followers both tended to see colour as a unified phenomenon. Newton wondered whether there might be different patterns of refraction of different coloured lights. He designed a way of testing this. He coloured a thread blue at one and red at the other and looked at it through a prism. The thread appeared to be broken. Experiments which had been suggested by Descartes' success in focusing parallel rays involved the creation of special equipment in the form of lenses with particular cross-sections in the form of an ellipse or a hyperbole. Newton set about making such lenses in order to see whether he could show by this method that different coloured lights would behave differently, and thus demonstrate that coloured light was not homogeneous. Another device was to use a prism to thrown a beam of light a sufficient distance to reveal if there was a spread of the refraction depending on the colours used. He was careful to try to 'control' his experiments so as to eliminate factors which could have distorted the results. Newton wrote 'Of colours' about 1666 in another notebook he kept as a student.

Two of the 'Quaestiones quaedam', the 'certain questions', are concerned with motion. The starting point for the theory of motion embraced by Gassendi and the atomists was that motion has its origin in the 'body' which moves. And when one body strikes another there is an 'impact'. How are we to understand what has happened? Newton was asking himself about this too.[39] He began with Descartes, who had written on the subject in his *Principles of Philosophy*. Descartes thought that the atoms which make up a body continue as they are (at rest or in motion) until another body interferes. Newton began to think about this in a quite different way, postulating a 'force' imparting motion to bodies in a manner which could be described mathematically. When two bodies impact upon one another each imparts an equal and opposite force to the other.

Motion in circles presented different problems. It was known that centrifugal forces acted when things spun round. But that raised questions about the behaviour of heavenly bodies. Galileo's revised universe had been met with the objection that if the earth really did revolve on its axis, everything on it would fly off into the space around it. So something must be holding everything down on the earth. Newton did the sums more accurately than Galileo had been able to do. He found that the earth's gravity is roughly 150 times the centrifugal force, holding things in place quite satisfactorily. He tested the implications for other planets, to try to establish why whole planets did not fly away if they were really going round the sun. Here he used Kepler's third law and found that the centrifugal force of the planets varies inversely as the square of their distance from the sun. This did not yet include the notion that gravity might be a universal force of attraction between heavenly bodies.

Another interlude of Plague

In 1665 Newton took his degree, but it was soon urgent to leave Cambridge for a time because 1665 and 1666 were years when the plague struck in Cambridge and the University was closed down for a time, so Newton had to retreat to his home at Woolsthorpe in Lincolnshire, where stood the tree from which the apple fell and prompted him to think of the law of gravity. At least so he told the story himself in old age. The plague was by now a seventeenth-century pandemic, probably a bacterial infection carried by the rats which ran boldly about everywhere and probably (not certainly) the same old Cambridge plague of earlier centuries. It spread with terrifying speed and killed in thousands those who succumbed to it with the characteristic 'bubos' or swellings of the lymph glands which came up in hours after the first flu-like symptoms appeared. There had been an outbreak in 1630, apparently caused by a soldier who had died of it. Then as in Newton's time, the colleges decided to 'breake up' and close their kitchens. At Trinity, we read that everyone was instructed to fend for himself and not to expect to reenter the College 'till it please God to lessen or remove the great danger in which we live'.[40]

Nine hundred and twenty persons were recorded as having died in Cambridge in the period when Newton prudently went somewhere else. Bills of Mortality were drawn up every week or two during this year and they record ('God be praised') that no one died in the colleges for the good reason that the colleges encouraged their members to leave the city. 'Pest-houses' were erected on Midsomer Common. One needed to get a certificate from the Vice-Chancellor and the Mayor before one could leave, to prevent the plague being carried to other places.[41]

An academic career begins

In 1667 Newton was back in Cambridge and seeking election to a Fellowship. His success in getting one set him up for life. It gave him the chance to remain at Trinity indefinitely with an annual income, and free accommodation in the College. He was allowed to act as a tutor if he wished, and he did so for three students in the many years he spent as a Fellow. But he was to have few formal duties for the next 28 years.

Professorships in Cambridge were still few, but one of the eight then in existence was the new Lucasian Professorship. Isaac Barrow, who had corresponded with Newton, was sufficiently impressed by the young man to support the appointment of Newton as his successor. Newton's duties as Lucasian Professor were not particularly onerous. The first scientific Professors in Cambridge were freed for what would now be called 'research', the independent exploration of intellectual interests, writing and publishing. In effect Newton became one of the first of Cambridge's 'research academics' in the modern sciences. Newton was supposed to give one lecture a week during the terms of the academic year, and he seems to have done so until the mid-1680s when he began to behave as other Professors commonly did, and treat the post as a sinecure.

The first course of lectures Newton gave were his *'Lectiones opticae'* ('Optical lectures'), in which he tried out much of the subject matter of the first part of what became his book on *Opticks*. He was also being 'noticed' by the Royal Society, which was impressed by his invention of the first reflecting telescope and elected Newton as one of its Fellows in 1672. Flattered, Newton sent the Society an account of his theories about colour. The Society published it in its *Philosophical Transactions*.[42] The piece is an experiment in genre. It is a cross between laboratory notebook and a research publication. It is written in the first person and describes Newton's thoughts and his actions in the course of testing his hypotheses, with his further thoughts as the work proceeded and he began to move to further tests.

Newton was now going to discover how harsh 'review' by his 'peers' could be. He had hitherto worked in relative isolation, avoiding

much interaction with fellow scientists, but now he discovered the
fierce competitiveness and acrimony they could show and also that
science now had a world stage. Robert Hooke (1635–1703) of the
Royal Society held his own expert views on optics and he vocally
disagreed with Newton. Newton held back his indignation for some
months and then sent him a lengthy and insulting letter.[43] Huygens
also disagreed with him.

Newton curled up in discomfort. He withdrew from the Royal
Society. But he was also to learn how tides in academic favour can
turn. By 1675, the climate had changed and he found that he was being
lionized, and that Hooke was defending him against further criticism.
This time the controversy was caused by Newton's experiment with
the prism which had been robustly criticized by Linus, an English
Jesuit in Liège. The Royal Society closed ranks in support of Newton.

Newton got to know Robert Boyle too, and corresponded with
him with a new boldness and confidence and willingness to discuss
his difficulties. In 1678/9 he was still struggling to articulate the idea
of 'ether':

> The truth is my notions about things of this kind are so
> indigested yt I am not well satifyed myself in them, and what I
> am not satisfied in I can scarce esteem fit to be communicated
> to others, expecially in natural Philosophy where there is no
> end of fancying.

His hypothesis required him to look on this ether as perfusing all nature
in such a way that bodies are to be seen as 'not to be terminated in a
mathematical superficies but to grow gradually into one another', the
ether filling the spaces between the particles which make up bodies, and
capable of being 'rarer' or 'denser'. It is on this view of what we might
now call the atomic and sub-atomic structure of things that he tries to
construct an explanation of what happens when bodies collide.[44]

'An hypothesis explaining the properties of light' was 'read' to the
Royal Society at this time, ambitiously trying to explain nature as a
system at large on the basis of the notion of a universal ether. Here we
can see how precarious still was the positioning of the line between
physics and metaphysics, natural and supernatural. The problem of
establishing the difference between chemistry and alchemy is a case
in point. He had been interested in both subjects as an undergraduate
and in the late 1660s he bought the expensive *Theatrum chemicum*
of 1602, so as to equip himself with a comprehensive collection of
alchemical treatises. He saw this as an experimental science, as did
many contemporaries. But he was also feeling for principles and laws

without making a clear distinction between those which were subject to measurement and testing and those which more closely resembled concepts. For example, he described the 'principles of vegetable actions' as 'the seeds or seminall virtues of things those are her only agents, her fire, her soule, her life'.[45]

Something of the difficulty of clearing the mind about the difference between science and pseudo-science, science and metaphysics, can be seen from a letter Newton wrote to Oldenburg of the Royal Society on 7 December 1675, suggesting that we have sensations of light of different colours because

> the agitated parts of bodies according to their severall sizes, figure and motions, doe excite Vibrations in the Aether of various depths or bignesses, which being promiscuously propagated through that medium to our Eyes, effect in us a Sensation of Light of a white colour, but if by any meanes those of unequal bignesses be separated from one another, the largest beget a sensation of a Red color, the least or shortest of a deep Violet, and the intermediate ones, of intermediate colours.

This he sees as analogous with the way 'severall tones in sound' are produced by 'Vibrations in the Air of various bignesses'. But a few paragraphs later, he is trying to describe the 'Aether', which he postulates is 'much of the same constitution with air, but far rarer, subtiler and more strongly Elastic'; and not 'one uniforme matter, but compounded partly of the main flegmatic body of aether partly of other various aethereall Spirits'.[46] Newton has not left the humours behind in his thinking and the 'Spirits' hover in conception between the physical ('vapours') and the metaphysical. They are 'wrought into various formes, at first by the intermediate hand of the Creator and ever since by the power of Nature, wch … became a complete Imitator of the copies sett her by the Protoplast', so 'Thus perhaps may all things be originated from aether'. Here is an admixture of Platonism.[47]

Newton was not the only early modern scientist who was prepared to work in this grey area. Hooke stood up at the end of the reading of the paper Newton had sent to the Royal Society, to claim that Newton had taken his ideas from his own *Micrographia*. When Newton was told that this had happened he was angry and old hostilities had to be calmed again. Other sources of disturbance were the campaignings of Anthony Lucas, the pupil of Linus, which Newton found upsetting and time-consuming:

> I will not run into any other dispute till I see a full end of what relates to Mr. Linus.[48]

He tried to withdraw from contact with his peers once more, though there was some contact with Gottfried Wilhelm Leibniz in 1676 about problems in calculus, which he made as so often through Oldenberg.[49]

The continuing viability of the use of Latin meant that there were in effect no language barriers separating scholars across Europe who found themselves working in the same area. Some of the surviving correspondence is in Latin (though was relayed to Newton in French).

Newton and theological matters

Newton avoided complying with the usual requirement that Fellows of Colleges should be ordained as Church of England clergy. That does not mean that he was not as interested in the contemporary theological debates as anyone else. Once he had formed doubts about the doctrine of the Trinity, he read what he could of the debates of the early fourth century when the doctrine had taken its final 'credal' shape in the Nicene Creed. A manuscript of 'Paradoxical questions concerning the morals & actions of Athanasius & his followers' survives (King's Cam., Keynes MS 10), in which he accuses Athanasius of faults of every kind. His frank scepticism on this central plank of Christian doctrine nearly cost him his comfortable position in Cambridge life.

He also took an interest in the contemporary arguments about prophecy and miracles. It was being asked whether the descriptions of these things in the Bible could be taken literally by educated modern people. If then, why not now? Some were claiming that there had been an age when such things really did happen, and the descriptions in Scripture were no less than the truth. But now these phenomena had ceased. To Newton's mind, such questions were inseparable from the fundamental issues he was engaged with as a scientist, for a miracle appears to be a departure from the operation of natural laws, and a fulfilled prophecy seems to argue some form of determinism. He became engrossed in the book of Daniel and the Book of Revelation.

Newton's definitive *Principia mathematica* was not to be completed until 1687. But already in 1679 Hooke, who became secretary of the Royal Society on the death of Henry Oldenburg, was making pleas to Newton to resume his relationship with the Society. Hooke was working on the puzzle of the attraction planetary bodies appear to have for one another; he asked Newton for his views. Centrifugal force, easily demonstrated, seemed to pull the opposite way. So what was keeping the circling planets from flying apart? Newton did not respond with enthusiasm to this overture. He said he was busy. But in due course Newton suggested the term 'centripetal force' for this counter-force and began to think about the problem himself. This line of enquiry was eventually to lead to the concept of a universal gravity.

In 1680 two comets appeared, one of them of great magnitude. Newton observed it. He wrote letters about it to fellow scientists, still through his preferred method of using an intermediary so that he did not actually have to write to them himself. This time he chose John Flamsteed (1646–1719), who had been given a Master's degree by Cambridge in 1674 on the merits of his work, although he had not studied there for the required period. He was now the Astronomer Royal, and observing these comets himself. Edmund Halley (1656–1742), like Robert Hooke, an Oxford not a Cambridge man visited Newton in 1684. In conversation Newton declared that he had already solved the problem which Christopher Wren and Hooke and others had said they could not solve, but whose solution was essential to the understanding of the behaviour of the comets. He asked Halley for data about the movements of Jupiter and Saturn and their satellites and began a period of several years of intensive work.

He sent Halley his *De motu* ('Concerning motion'), in which a theory of orbital dynamics matured to the stage when it needed only to be recast slightly for the *Principia*. In early 1685 he articulated three laws of motion. And he arrived at the concept of universal gravitation.

In 1686 he sent the completed manuscript of Book One of his *Principia Mathematica* to the Royal Society. Hooke accused him of plagiarism. Halley was paying for publication, for the Royal Society was extremely short of funds and could not afford to publish it. So when Newton angrily threatened to withhold the vital third book, and he did not reveal its contents until Halley was in progress with the publication of Book Two and could scarcely now stop. What Newton had done was to consider the options currently in place (such as vortices, the effect of a dense medium), and substitute his idea that there might be an attraction which worked through space. At first glance, this seems as absurd as some of the other notions being tried out in the course of the century.

The *Principia* made the still slightly reclusive Newton famous. John Locke (1632–1704) wanted to know him, and William Whiston (1667–1752), who was to succeed him as Lucasian Professor. Richard Bentley, of whom we shall hear more later, had been chosen to give the first series of Boyle Lectures on religion and he applied to Newton for comments on his drafts as he prepared them for publication. Fame seems to have given Newton confidence to come out into the open and support Cambridge in its resistance to the attempt by the King to impose a Benedictine Monk, Alban Francis, on the University and force it to give him a degree although he was a Roman Catholic. He went with seven others to be examined before the notorious Judge Jeffreys.

But as it turned out this was also the peak of Newton's creative work. He had a breakdown in 1693. He found he could not solve the problem of the moon. In 1696 he left Cambridge to work in London on the new coinage, in a Royal Mint appointment which had been intended as a siecure but which he took seriously. Here were simple practical problems requiring the putting of things into order. He could do that with satisfaction. Once Hooke was out of the way after his death in 1703 Newton was able to return to some participation in the affairs of the Royal Society. He was elected President. He was invited to stand for election as M.P. for Cambridge in 1705, though he did not succeed. He was, however, knighted.

* * *

Cambridge 'networking' on the international scene

One of the most well-known of the independent scholarly circles which intersected with the academic world of seventeenth-century Cambridge is the 'Hartlib circle'. Samuel Hartlib (c.1600–60) was born in Prussia, where he was educated at a Gymnasium in and possibly at the University of Königsberg, before studying briefly at Emmanuel College, Cambridge, in 1625–6, though he did not matriculate or work towards a degree there. John Preston (1587–1628), then Master of Emmanuel, and something of a networker in court circles, seems to have made him welcome in this somewhat anomalous capacity of college guest.[50]

Samuel Hartlib became a flypaper for the ideas of those who were radically rethinking education, its methods and its purposes in the first half of the seventeenth century in England. He drew round him by meeting and correspondence an international circle which had a common interest in the educational implications of the great contemporary task of making sense of the new world of knowledge and reconfiguring it so as to give a satisfactory account of it to a new generation. This was far from being an exclusively Cambridge circle, but it had its share of Cambridge members. The circle included John Durie or Dury, a friend with whom Hartlib framed a plan of starting a model community, an ecumenical though protestant utopia, on a Baltic island they planned to call Antilia. Durie travelled Europe in search of a way forward with this plan and sent back news of inventions and scientific 'discoveries'. Hartlib had become interested in the reform of methods of study, partly, like so many others, under the influence of Francis Bacon. Refugees from Europe sought shelter with Hartlib, who was something of a refugee himself, from the wars in his native country.

Others failed to arrive in person, but 'joined in' from a distance. In the early 1630s Hartlib began a correspondence with the Czech Jan Amos Komenský (Comenius) and sent him Francis Bacon's writings. Attempts were made to raise funds to bring Comenius to London. He did not come at the time but a copy of his *Conatuum Comenianorum præludia* did; this Hartlib published without his permission,[51] a decision regrettable but helpful to the dissemination of contemporary writings and ideas. Comenius eventually arrived in London in 1641 and stayed with Hartlib for nine months.

The 'Hartlib Circle' was engaged in a form of 'social' intellectual activity. The 'English' or British members of the circle included John Pell (1611–85), John Hall (c.1627–56) – an undergraduate at St. John's College, Cambridge, later a lawyer and an energetic communicator within the circle – John Milton and others. Several of these were busy considering (among their other interests) the purpose of education.[52] The members of this circle tended to see things in terms of a combination of intellectual and moral improvement of society. They were more or less agreed that pursuit of knowledge involves life-long learning. It is also, they took it for granted, the road to salvation. Everyone in the community should be involved. Education should fit one for vocational and practical life. Natural philosophy is important because it helps one understand God's purposes for the universe.

*   *   *

Puritan rigour, Civil War and Restoration

Oliver Cromwell as a Cambridge man

Oliver Cromwell (1599–1658) was briefly a student at Sidney Sussex College, Cambridge, from 1616 to 1617, when his father died and he had to leave. Little is known about his early life except that his family lived in East Anglia and seems to have been involved, as he was, in a 'puritan' movement particularly strong in the region. He is recorded as having supported the need for 'lectureships' (for peripatetic preachers), as a means of ensuring that the 'enemies of God' were resisted.[53] Other indications of the 1630s suggest that he was already an extremist, and a well-connected one.

In 1640 Cromwell became Member of Parliament for Cambridge. This was remarkable given his lack of campaigning funds and the fact that this was usually a safe seat for the preferred candidate of powerful 'local interests'. He must have had influential backers with their own agenda. Cromwell made himself prominent in the Long Parliament as a busy committee man, including helping to draft the Bill for the suspension of the episcopal 'government' of the Church of England. His utter conviction that he was defending the truth and doing God's will made him formidable, but he was also looked at askance as an uncomfortable ally and he was not always allowed to enter the mainstream of what was happening as King and Parliament squared up for battle.

On 25 July 1642, the King wrote to the Vice-Chancellor of Cambridge to ask for the loan of plate from the colleges to fund royal military action if it should prove necessary. The House of Commons sent Cromwell to stop them providing it; he took a couple of hundred armed men with him and created roadblocks. He also succeeded in getting into the castle on Castle Hill and seizing the arms which were kept inside it. On 22 August 1642, the King raised his standard at Nottingham and the country was at 'civil' war.

Cromwell continued to take a characteristically aggressive approach. He raised a company of cavalry, creating as officers two of his relatives, and took these men on searches of the houses of those in the area suspected of being supporters of the King. He was asked to join this force to the army the Earl of Essex had raised to fight for the parliamentary cause and he arrived in time for them to take a small part in the battle at Edgehill (23 October 1642). The same united force held off the King's attempt to get into London at Turnham Green on 13 November. This drove the King back to Reading and then further to Oxford. Thus it was that the two sides in the war established their bases at Oxford and in the Cambridge area, respectively. Of the two universities, Oxford became the 'Royalist' stronghold and Cambridge the 'Puritan' one, but this was a far from straightforward division, for individual academics changed places and reappeared in the other university. There was already a 'triangle' formed by London, Oxford and Cambridge, and former students and continuing scholars moved round it quite readily or corresponded as though the distance were nothing. Abraham Cowley (1618–67), invited to Cambridge, wrote:

> ...I would meet
> Thee there, but plummets hang upon my feet.

As good friends, he argues, they will not be separated by a mere 'forty miles',

> Though envious Fortune larger hindrance brings,
> Wee'l easely see each other, Love hath wings.[54]

The 'Parliament' party of rabid puritans had had a mixed agenda of interrelated objectives when the events which were to lead to war began to unfold. It sought to unite a revived Parliamentary democracy with getting rid of bishops. The revolutionaries linked improved Church government (of a presbyterian sort) with the call for a puritan discipline of life and all that went with it in the conduct of the population. The concern to bring Cambridge into the 'fold' by reforming it arose in large part from the consciousness that so many were trained for ordination there that it was important that they were trained in the right theological views.[55]

The Westminster Assembly of Calvinist theologians and senior ministers of religion was a creation of Parliament in 1643 (after a period of wrangling), and remained subject to Parliament as to what it was to discuss and the authority of any resulting recommendations. Its members were eager to destroy or at least radically to modify episcopacy both as a form of Church government and as a secular power in the land. The Solemn League and Covenant won the strong support of Scotland, where episcopacy had already more or less lost to presbyterianism. But there were reservations among its English supporters that it envisaged allowing only a 'presbyterian' form of Church government and would therefore deny the freedom many dissenters in England sought to form 'congregational' churches instead. Lessons were learned the hard way by idealistic individuals who believed their proposed revolution could do nothing but good, as they saw their 'movement' descend into bitter in-fighting. The Earl of Manchester, chief 'purger' of dons with the wrong opinions, wrote a letter to the House of Lords, 4 November 1644, in which he expresses fears for member of his own class of the nobility – a concern that he may have been deceived in Cromwell, of whom he had thought well, since he now believes he is eager to expunge the nobility from England.[56]

The puritans evinced a style of life which was not to everyone's taste. Abraham Cowley probably wrote 'The Puritans Lecture' in

Cambridge after 1642. (A Fellow of Trinity College, Cambridge, from 1637, he was among those ejected in 1643, and went to Oxford.) The poem expresses intense dislike of the typical puritan style of pulpit rhetoric:

> He whines now, whispers strait, and next does roare,
> Now drawles his long words, and then leaps them o'er.[57]

To this is added a wry comment on the immense length of the puritan sermons:

> 'Twas the most teadious Soule. The dullest he
> That ever came to Doctrines twenty-three,
> And nineteene uses. How he drawes his Humme
> And quarters Haw, talkes Poppy and Opium!
> No feaver a mans eyes could open keepe.[58]

But the congregation is moved; the women weep and 'sob aloud', and the preacher easily excites them to support contradictory notions, 'with wrested Scripture'.[59]

Preachers on the 'other side' had their critics too. A mocking account of royalist preaching is to be found in *The Arraignment of Persecution* (1645). 'In the Pulpit, thumping it devoutly,' the preacher rails against Anabaptists and Brownists and others, and he skips from pulpit to pulpit, from University to University, from 'Colledge to Colledge', and then from Parsonage to Parsonage. He is caught and arraigned before a 'jury of life and death' including 'Gospel', State-Policy', 'National loyalty', Liberty of Subject', 'Innocent-blood', Good-Samaritane', Trueth-and-peace'.[60]

Purges and cleansings in Cambridge

The tensions in the nation linking political with religious disquiets could not but affect two universities which were so heavily concerned in the teaching of students who were preparing for ordination and also provided the majority of those who were, in adult life, going to be running the country, one way or another.

For an outside authority to try to tell the independent colleges who they might have as heads and Fellows, and the two universities who might study and teach in them, was not unprecedented. It was reminiscent of the Tudor intrusions. But that did not make it less offensive to the independently-minded University. If the Commonwealth authorities had been more efficient about it and more persistent, the consequences for the long-term freedom of Oxford and Cambridge from state control might have been very considerable. As it was, they made no more than brief sallies. Twice, in 1643–4 and in

1649–51, purges of those thought to have royalist sympathies drove dons and students from Cambridge to Oxford. The test was a don's willingness to sign the Solemn League and Covenant.

It is an irony that after the centuries of efforts to clean up the filthy streets of Cambridge, concern should now shift to moral turpitude. This new kind of cleansing process was conducted by Edward Montagu (1602–71), who became Earl of Manchester on his father's death in 1642. He had been a student at Sidney Sussex College from 1618 (just after Cromwell had had to leave it). He was unusual among the higher aristocracy in staying loyal to the Parliament side when opposition to the King began to crystallize, though he had earlier associated with a group of peers critical of the behaviour of the monarchy and he voted against the King on questions of supply in 1640, during the Short Parliament. He was one of six the King impeached for high treason in January 1642, though the King did not pursue the matter. Once it came to war, he proved an energetic and effective commander of Parliamentary troops. He came to know Cromwell well and they seem to have worked harmoniously in both military and constitutional matters until 1644. In an ordinance of January 1644, Manchester was given authority in Cambridge and authorized to conduct a purge of the University and bring it under supervision. He took up residence in Cambridge and appointed like-minded 'commissioners' to work with him.[61]

What was the mindset of the puritans with reference to the universities? Politicians had rightly seen them as seats of power and potentially useful sources of wealth in the sixteenth century, when Henry VIII had been minded to dissolve the colleges like the monasteries. Royal visitations had arrived, seeking to intrude on the autonomy of the universities and that of the colleges and to insist on radical changes to the syllabus. The wealth was still tempting. The King tried to borrow the colleges' plate to fund the Civil War, but there was little serious attempt in the seventeenth century to bring about state-driven change to the syllabus or the academic activities.[62]

'In 1643, Cromwell took possession of Cambridge for the Parliament; and the Earl of Manchester being sent down to visit the university, expelled a great number of the most eminent loyalists'.[63] The Parliamentary Visitation of Cambridge which took place from 1644 to 1645[64] began with a clear-out of dubious dons, and Manchester followed it up by nominating a committee of 11, to whom he subsequently added 27 more, who were to 'regulate' the University. 'On the 15th of March [1644], the Earl of Manchester appointed ... Commissioners for putting in execution the ordinance for regulating the University'.[65] New Heads of House were appointed by Manchester and his commissioners to fill the vacancies created by the removal of the ten ejected. Reforms proposed included seeking to ensure that absentee dons were not allowed to draw the incomes of their college offices.[66] However, there were other urgent matters to attend to in wartime and little was carried through.

Puritan vandalism

Manchester appointed William Dowsing to remove and destroy the local examples of 'superstitious images'. Neither process was conducted with entire integrity. Trinity Hall, full of lawyers, was not troubled by the purgers and neither was Sidney Sussex, which was Cromwell's own college. Both Manchester and Dowsing were very soon to see that they had made a mistake, but not before the damage had been done.[67] We know something from the royalist tract the *Querela Cantabrigiensis,* of how Cambridge contemporaries felt about the vandalism for which Dowsing was to be responsible:

> John Dowsing...by vertue of a pretended Commission goes about the country like a Bedlam, breaking glosse windowes, having battered and beaten downe all our painted glasse...defaced and digged up the floors of our Chappels, many of which had lien so for two or three hundred yeares together, not regarding the dust of our founders and predecessors, who likely were buried there.[68]

William Dowsing (bap.1596, d.1668) was a farmer, possibly with a grammar school education but not a graduate. He was bookish enough to collect a library of religious literature and he was able to read Latin and Greek. His taste was for dissident writings and his copies are annotated and cross-referenced, so he read them intently. Despite living a quiet life without seeking public office, Dowsing may have come to the attention of those leading the Parliamentary armies because he had written a letter to the 'preacher' at Dedham in 1643, calling for something to be done about blasphemous images in the area. He was useful in organizing supplies for the army while it was besieging King's Lynn and on other expeditions. It was at Manchester's instigation that he was sent to destroy the images not only in the University but also in churches throughout Cambridgeshire, and possibly further afield, to help him with which he appointed eight deputies. His appointment was unusual. Elsewhere this work of 'cleansing' tended to be given to the local churchwardens, as was required by Parliament's ordinances in 1643 and 1644, or took the form of looting and destruction by armies running out of control. Pembroke College argued him down, the Fellows disputing his interpretation of Scripture, but for the most part, he got his way in ordering the destruction to be carried out.

Dowsing's own conscientiously kept 'journal' records the destruction:

> We went to Peter-house 1643, Decemb: 21...we pulled down 2: mighty great Angells, with wings, & divers other Angells, & the 4: Evangelists, & Peter, with his Keies...& about a hundred Chirubims & Angells, & divers superstitious Letters in gold...at Queen's colledge Decemb. 26. We beat downe about 110 Superstitious Pictures besides Cherubims...[69]

King's College got away with preserving its glass, which was very high up, and Dowsing may have arrived at the end of a long and tiring day. Cromwell's army were billeted there, and it has been suggested that he may have responded to the suggestion that the College would see to the destruction of the windows when they could do so more conveniently, judging correctly that the threat would not be fulfilled in the end.[70] It is notable that he seems to have allowed himself to be influenced by presumptions about the stance of the colleges, particularly in the case of Cromwell's own:

> Sidney Colledge Dec: 30, 1643. We saw nothing there to be mended...Emmanuell Colledge, there is nothing to be done.

Dowsing was in reality a naïve idealist. He believed he was doing God's will and fulfilling a divine providential purpose as its instrument. He took it for granted that the righteous puritan cause would triumph and the true Biblical faith be restored. But he saw divisions and bitter rivalries emerge and became disillusioned, withdrawing to private life again.

The 'purge' also marked the high point of Manchester's confident activity in support of the Parliamentarians. Soon after the bloody battle of Marston Moor (1644), he realized – as his worried letter to the Lords already quoted testifies – that the objectives he and others sought were not likely to be achieved by warfare, and any case, his careful arrangements about funding were proving insufficient and his troops could not be paid or even properly fed. He began to see that the King had to win only once to end the matter and punish the rebels, while the rebels would have to fight a war of attrition whose conclusion was by no means certain. He could see the inherent fissiparousness of dissent, the beginning of bitter faction-fighting within and among the interest-groups making up the Parliamentary allies.

Meanwhile the King established his court in Oxford for a time because he could not get back into London against the resistance of Parliamentary forces, and from the mid-1640s until it surrendered in 1646, Oxford was under siege. Oxford, too, then suffered a purge of 'undesirables', in 1648. Undesirableness once more consisted in the appearance of royalist sympathies, tested by asking the suspect to subscribe to the Solemn League and Covenant.

The 'enemy within' or a minor irritant?

How seriously did Cambridge take the purgers? There was a fair amount of nifty footwork. William Sancroft (1617–93) entered Emmanuel College in 1633 and set about preparing for ordination. Until 1637 his own uncle was Master. By 1642 he was a Fellow of Emmanuel and he spent an uncomfortable 'war' in Cambridge, for he was conservative, a royalist, and had nothing against bishops. His way of dealing with the threat of puritan purges[71] reflects the complex loyalties of a University under threat of interference. He, like others, simply tried to stay out of trouble. He arranged to be out of Cambridge at some of the more difficult moments. He stayed sufficiently out of sight when the Master, Richard Holdsworth, Vice-Chancellor of the University and a chaplain to the King, was ejected and forcibly replaced by a presbyterian Master, Anthony Tuckney. He did not long survive the execution of Charles II however, and he retreated to London, to live quietly on his private income and form friendships with like-minded exiles. It was not until after the Restoration that he returned to Cambridge where he was given the Mastership of Emmanuel in 1662, and higher ecclesiastical preferment rapidly followed, culminating in the Archbishopric of Canterbury in 1677. Others went further in seeking to exploit the situation. There are indications that some students deliberately informed on the Fellows of their colleges in the hope that the vacant Fellowships might come their own way.[72]

There were some puritan-minded reformers within, both extremists and moderates, and colleges with 'attitude', ironically perhaps, the two which had taken over the sites of the medieval houses of the Dominicans and Franciscans, respectively. Of Emmanuel College, something has already been said. Sidney Sussex College, founded in the last decade of the sixteenth century, after a battle under the will of Lady Frances Sidney Sussex, took over the Franciscan site. William Bradshaw, author of *English Puritanism* (1605), was an early Fellow and Jeremiah Whitaker another, and moderator of the Westminster Assembly in 1643. Sidney's chief claim to be a 'puritan' college in the eyes of the seventeenth century rested on Cromwell's brief period of study there.

William Dell (1607–69) had been an undergraduate at Emmanuel College and became a friend of John Bunyan. He was among the more idealistic of the reformers, criticizing the Westminster Assembly, calling for assistance for the poor, preaching to the House of Lords and also to the House of Commons in 1646 in terms so controversial that he caused offence, for he reproved the leaders of the revolution for making a personal profit. He eventually became Master of Gonville and Caius College (1649–60), an 'appointment' of the Rump Parliament. A contemporary described him as an 'angry fanatick', no scholar himself and hostile to learning.[73]

A contrast is John Wilkins of Wadham, one of the refugees from Oxford to Cambridge in the Oxford purge of 1648, who became Master of Trinity College, Cambridge, in 1659–60. He married Cromwell's sister in 1655, but was of only moderate puritan persuasion himself.[74]

Some Royalists in Cambridge had a rough ride, but outcomes in the long-term were variable. Robert Brady (c.1627–1700) went to Gonville and Caius College, as a sizar in 1644. He became a scholar there and was close to graduating with a higher degree in medicine when he too found he would have to leave the country for safety's sake. An Edmund Brady had been hanged in Norwich and Robert was erroneously believed to be his brother. So he fled. Robert was able to return to Cambridge in 1652 and graduate in medicine in 1653, but he was still too much under suspicion to be able to go on smoothly to become a doctor of medicine in 1658 as he had planned, and he had to spend six months in prison in Yarmouth. This did not prevent his practising as a doctor, and his royal master granted him an M.D. by royal letters in 1660 at the Restoration. He had not been politically idle. Brady's college chose him as its new Master in the same year. In 1677 he became Regius Professor of Physic, and in 1680 the Royal College of Physicians made him a Fellow. He had apparently had his ambitions in these directions; he had done some manoeuvring to obtain these rewards.

John Smith the 'Cambridge Platonist' benefited from the purge of Cambridge dons who refused to take the Covenant in the early 1640s, for there were vacancies to be filled and he became a Fellow of Queens' College (and mathematics tutor), as did other Fellows of Emmanuel. Whichcote himself, though unwilling to swear allegiance to the Covenant, became provost of King's College in 1644. Smith passed a test of suitability, being examined by the Westminster Assembly.

Ralph Cudworth proved to be something of a timeserver. He belonged to a class of academic of whom we met examples in the sixteenth century, who sought to please Government even if that meant sitting lightly to the issues of principle for which some of their colleagues were prepared to risk their futures and even their lives. At the Restoration, Cudworth became anxious to please the King as he had formerly been to please Cromwell and Parliament. He wrote a poem in Hebrew for the book Cambridge University presented to the King. Some of his colleagues who had remained staunchly loyalist when times were hard regarded this volte-face without enthusiasm, and there was resistance to his keeping the Mastership of Christ's. Gilbert Burnet said as much, remarking that Cudworth had 'great strength of genius, and a vast compass of learning' but 'was a man of great conduct and prudence: Upon which his enemies did very falsely accuse him of craft and dissimulation'.[75] This conduct, however, meant that he lived to write more later, even if it also meant that he died with the reputation of being bad-tempered and isolated. His last illness began while he was out of the city, but he was brought back to die in Christ's College in June 1688.

Restoration: the return of fun but the repression of dangerous conversation

Cambridge found itself in 'war-time' several times in its history, and not only during the Civil War and the repressive Protectorate that followed it. It should not be assumed that that ended its characteristic daily life. Cambridge was probably always notable for its pubs or taverns. The line between accommodation and place of entertainment was not at all hard and fast. 'Wolf College', was teasingly named after the landlord of the Rose Inn on Rose Crescent. This began as a medieval hostel for students and then became an inn with student bedrooms, more than 40 by the early seventeenth century.[76] It flourished through the Civil War and emerged at the other side in good shape. The diariest Samuel Pepys (1633–1703) drank there and also treated it as a hotel in October 1667.[77] (The Rose was still flourishing in 1768 when the King of Denmark slept there and in 1812 when it accommodated Louis XVIII of France.[78])

Pepys was perhaps a little too fond of wine himself as a student, for the Magdalene Order Book has a note that he and a friend of his called Hinde were 'scandalously overseene in drinke' at least once. He became more sober when he was older. Pepys's Diary illustrates well the sense of continuing 'belonging' a former student and a graduate would have. He visited Cambridge in February 1660 in order to go with his father and brother to have his brother admitted to Christ's College. He took the opportunity to revisit Magdalene, where he was 'exceeding civilly received'. He enjoyed 'a very handsome supper' though after some hard drinking 'he could find that there was nothing at all left of the old preciseness in their discourse, specially on Saturday nights'.[79] He visited Cambridge again in July 1660, to see his brother, leaving at 3.00 in the morning and arriving in Cambridge by 7.00. He was 'vexed' to find his brother still in bed in his college at 8.00. He himself went to the service in King's College Chapel where he discovered that some of the restrictions imposed in puritan days had been eased and there were 'the schollers in their surplices with the organs'.[80] On another visit, in October 1662 he took great pleasure in joining in the voting, for on 10 October there was 'a Congregacion for the choice of some officers in the University'. A gown was borrowed for him and a Master of Arts found to take him in and he voted happily for Bernard Skelton 'my old schoolfellow and acquaintance'. He was 'much content' at being able to vote 'which I have long wished for'.[81]

Pepys ultimately became sufficiently prominent in public life to be offered the Provostship of King's College in 1681. His great loyalty was always to Magdalene College, however, although his brother, who had first been entered there, transferred to Christ's before be began his studies. It was to Magdalene where he became a sizar in 1650 that he left his books, fussing over the construction of shelves designed to ensure that the tops of the books all appeared level and of the same height.[82]

In the arena of the academic business of the University, the Restoration of the Monarchy in 1660 did not bring upheaval to an end. There was a Roman Catholic monarch to come, in the person of James II (1685–8), and further disputes about ecclesiastical government. University lectures and the very life of the colleges were almost bound to evince a dangerous combination of free-thinking and free assembly, as we saw in the case of David Owen's tale-telling concerning a conversation about deposing the monarch in the reign of James I.

Among the reasons why this became a serious matter in the eyes of the authorities were that such talk was not confined to academe. A regular meeting was held in Kidderminster on the first Thursday of every month in the 1660s, at Richard Baxter's instigation. A topic was agreed in advance, sometimes a disciplinary matter. The group ate together and after the meal they held their debate. Baxter published some of these disputations and kept records of others among his papers. He gave a lecture each week in addition, after which some of the circle would retire with him to his home to discuss it. Baxter described these as 'comfortable' meetings and he saw them as building up the pastoral community.[83] We can see in them a sense of equality of contribution by everyone who attended, where any 'moderator' or 'lecturer' was not necessarily seen as the leader and everyone felt entitled to express and even publish his thoughts.

This kind of thing had parallels not only in Switzerland but all over Europe, where it was in places the object of official censure. Repression continued into the seventeenth century and if anything it grew more determined. On 12 November 1660, John Bunyan was going to a meeting where he had been invited to give some teaching.

> The justice hearing thereof... forthwith issued out his warrant to take me, and bring me before him, and in the mean time to keep a very strong watch about the house where the meeting should be kept, as if we that was to meet together in that place did intend to do some fearful business to the destruction of the country.

The constable entered the room and as Bunyan reports in his autobiography, he 'was taken and forced to depart the room'.[84] The late seventeenth-century Roman Catholic Church forbade meetings of Quietists, because they involved lay people but also because they were meetings, and therefore provided opportunities for such people to mislead one another.[85] In England, too, the Conventicle Acts of 1664 and 1670 forbade 'Conventicles' as seditious meetings.[86] So the life of the 'intellectual' and 'would-be' intellectual outside the universities was sufficiently influential to cause concern to the authorities in Church and State.

$$* \quad * \quad *$$

John Milton and new trends in Cambridge language study

John Milton, Cambridge graduate, poet, politician and educational reformer

> Yea, our blind Poet, who in his later day,
> Stood almost single; uttering odious truth –
> Darkness before, and danger's voice behind,
> Soul awful – if the earth has ever lodged
> An awful soul – I seemed to see him here

Familiarly, and in his scholar's dress
Bounding before me, yet a stripling youth –
A boy, no better, with his rosy cheeks
Angelical, keen eye, courageous look,
And conscious step of purity and pride.
Among the band of my compeers was one
Whom chance had stationed in the very room
Honoured by Milton's name.
William Wordsworth, *The Prelude III*, 282–95.

John Milton (1608–74) seems to have learned several modern languages as a boy in London as well as the essential Latin and the other two 'Biblical' languages, Greek and Hebrew. Among his tutors was a Scot, Thomas Young, who later returned to Cambridge himself and eventually became Master of Jesus College. Such men took university standards into the schoolrooms of Britain and inevitably taught their pupils with a clear idea of what would be expected of them at Oxford or Cambridge. Milton went to Cambridge in 1625. It was not necessarily expected that a student would begin at the start of the academic year and Milton seems to have arrived in January, though he did not matriculate until April. At Christ's College he was admitted as a 'minor pensioner'. That gave him a status above that of sizar but it did not make him a full fellow-commoner. His tutor was to be William Chappell.

Milton wrote a number of precociously polished verses on Cambridge themes while still a very young student, in his late teens. Only 16, he wrote an elegy for the Vice-Chancellor, a piece elegantly exploiting the *topoi* of death in classical literature, with a *Tuque*, 'you too', for the Vice-Chancellor. At the age of 17 he wrote a Latin elegy on the death of the 'Beadle' [Bedell] of the University.[87] When Hobson the University carrier died in 1631, he wrote that Death had been able to catch up with him only because he had been forced to stay 'so long at home' by the plague and stop his regular weekly journeyings between London and Cambridge.[88] When he was 18 he wrote another Latin elegy, to his former teacher 'serving now as Chaplain among the English Merchants resident in Hamburg'.[89]

Milton's academic exercises survive in some numbers, both those done in college and those done 'in the public schools', that is, in the University. They are disputations, practice for the examination he would eventually take for his degree, on such subjects as 'Whether day is more excellent than night', in which he displays his familiarity with classical rhetorical theory and a sense of the importance of

223

the *captatio benevolentiae.* The pieces are half Quintilian and half scholastic disputation, elegant, graceful, light, but also tightly argued.[90] In 'At a vacation exercise in the Colledge', part Latin and part English, the English part beginning, 'Hail native Language', Milton's conceit is that in this language the 'daintiest dishes shall be serv'd up last', for:

> I have some naked thoughts that rove about
> And loudly knock to have their passage out...[91]

He plays with the ten Aristotelian Categories next, exploiting those which lent themselves to the poetic treatment of Christian theological issues, such as [the] Passion and Time.

Milton's university career was interrupted by a period when he seems to have been sent down, having quarrelled with his tutor Chappell. He was probably allowed to return in the autumn of 1627, and he was given a new tutor, Nathaniel Tovey. *A Second Defence* includes a teasing account of how he was *pulsus*, thrown out of Cambridge, *ob flagitia,* for disgraceful behaviour, and fled to Italy. This cannot be true, says Milton. Why should he have gone to Italy and not to France or Holland?[92] He completed his degree and returned to take his M.A., when he signed the required subscription to the Thirty-Nine Articles. The Milton of these years was an able linguist, a ready poet, sometimes in disgrace. When he finally left the University he seems to have gone to live at home and study further for some years, making a modest name as a poet.

Later, in the context of the Civil War and its aftermath, his political writings led to burning of his books in Oxford. The *Areopagitica* expresses the views of a Milton who has travelled a long way from his student days. Milton was hostile to 'the forcers of conscience under the Long Parliament', for whom

> Men whose Life, Learning, Faith and pure intent
> Would have been held in high esteem with Paul
> Must now be name'd and printed Hereticks.[93]

Milton was not the only 'Cambridge poet' to be drawn into the Civil War. John Dryden (1631–1700) went to Trinity College, Cambridge, in 1650 as one of five scholars from Westminster School. His contemporary Robert Creighton recalled that Dryden

> was reckoned a man of good Parts & Learning while in Coll:
> he had to his knowledge read over & very well understood
> all the Greek and Latin Poets: he stayed to take his Batchelors
> degree; but his head was too roving and active, or what else

you'll call it, to confine himself to a College Life; & so he left it & went to London into gayer company, & set up for a Poet.[94]

He became a civil servant under the Protectorate, along with Milton and Andrew Marvell (1621–78), who was an undergraduate at Trinity.

The line between school and university was not fixed in these centuries, either in terms of the age of transition or in terms of the level of the study expected. Much depended upon where and in which century a student began his studies. Milton saw no need to have a line at all. Milton writes of 'that voluntary Idea, which hath long in silence presented it selfe to me, of a better education, in extent and comprehension farre more large, and yet of time farre shorter, and of attainment farre more certain, then hath been yet in practice'.[95] His idea was to start an 'Academy' in a large house with grounds, 'big enough to lodge a hundred and fifty persons', to be 'at once both School and University' so that the students would not need to attend any other institution unless they intend to be 'practitioners' in Law or 'Physick'.[96] Milton wants to see the boys learn grammar through 'some easie and delightful Book of Education' and with 'Lectures and Explanations upon every opportunity' so that they may be stimulated, enthusiastic and virtuous.[97] The boys are to proceed through a variant of the *quadrivium*, to 'Fortification, Architecture, Enginry, or Navigation'. In natural Philosophy they will study 'the History of Meteors, Minerals, plants and living Creatures as far as Anatomy'.[98] As they grow older they are to learn public speaking, 'whether they be to speak in Parliament or Counsel' or from pulpits. He outlines for them a menu of intellectual pleasures, excursions, periods of 'work experiences' so that they may gradually come to know the world and its ways and find their place in it, without, apparently, needing to acquire a formal qualification at the end of the process.[99]

More languages: cultural awareness of the orient and the new-style polyglot Bibles

Milton stressed the value of formal academic study of languages:

> though a linguist should pride himselfe to have all the tongues that Babel cleft the world into, yet, if he have not studied the solid things in them as well as the words and lexicons, he were nothing so much to be esteem'd a learned man, as any yeoman or tradesman competently wise in his mother dialect only.[100]

It will be remembered that Isaac Barrow also made himself master of oriental languages before equipping himself to be the first holder of the Lucasian Chair of Mathematics.

This represented a significant new phase in the story which began with the arrival of Greek and Hebrew teaching in Renaissance Cambridge. Brian Walton (1600–61) had been a sizar at Magdalene College, Cambridge, from 1616, though he moved to Peterhouse in 1618 before graduating. He acquired a knowledge of the ancient biblical languages, and hit on the idea of producing a polyglot Bible, to add to those produced at Alcalá, Antwerp (1569–72) and Paris (1628–45), a version more up-to-date in its scholarship and more authentic. He also wanted it to be less expensive, so that it might be more widely available.

This was not a university research project but rather a private initiative which sought funding by subscription. Government support was uncertain at first, and gave no financial assistance except allowing free import of the paper which would be needed for the edition. William Laud and Ireland's Archbishop James Ussher were in favour and it was possible to bring in many distinguished scholars at Oxford and Cambridge.[101] Edward Pococke, who serially held the Chair of Arabic and the Regius Chair of Hebrew in Oxford, was also involved in the publication of the polyglot Bible. He did not add much to the compilation but he lent the compilers several manuscripts and read the proofs, sending his comments to Brian Walton. Ralph Cudworth helped too.

The work was printed between 1653 and 1657 in six volumes. Volumes 1–4 contained the Old Testament and Apocrypha, volume 5 the New Testament, and volume 6 the critical appendices, in nine languages. The polyglot Bible received hostile reviews from all 'sides'. It was put on the Roman *Index librorum prohibitorum* at Rome. It was attacked by the Oxford scholar John Owen in *Of the Divine Original of Scripture* and other writings published in 1659. Walton answered him at once with *The Considerator Considered* (1659).

The Bentley interlude

Not every scholar interested in these new areas of study was quietly sitting with his books. The old patterns of internal warfare were still to be observed. Richard Bentley (1662–1742) went as a sub-sizar to St. John's College, Cambridge, on 24 May 1676. After beginning a schoolmaster career and dabbling in scholarly projects, he was admitted as a commoner to Wadham College, Oxford, in 1689, and Oxford duly incorporated him as an M.A. He carried on working as an editor of texts, tackling some immense and demanding projects. Robert Boyle had bequeathed £50 per annum for eight Oxford sermons 'proving the Christian religion against notorious Infidels, *viz.* Atheists,

Theists, Pagans, Jews, and Mahometans', and Bentley was appointed to deliver them in 1692.

In December 1699 Bentley was chosen a Master of Trinity College, Cambridge, where he continued his energetic life, making changes the fellows disliked, not least because he did not consult them as he should have done. He went too far when he arranged for the 'election' of a dubious nephew of the Vice-Master, Wolfram Stubbe, and then expelled two fellows in April 1708. The Fellows petitioned the Visitor in 1709. Bentley asked for a Royal Commission to inspect Trinity.

Conyers Middleton (1683–1750) was a Cambridge graduate who involved himself with enthusiasm in the Bentley affair, energetically writing pamphlets including 'Remarks' and 'Further Remarks' on Bentley's *Proposals for a New Edition of the Greek Testament*, in which the latter tried to make his own case from the text of the New Testament. In 1723 Middleton became involved in a lawsuit against Bentley, resulting from his tract on library administration, written on the occasion of his appointment as University Librarian. In 1726 he offended the medical profession with a dissertation contending that the healing art among the ancients was exercised only by slaves or freedmen. Between the dates of these publications he visited Italy and made certain observations on the pagan origin of church ceremonies and beliefs which he subsequently published in his *Letter from Rome* (1729). This tract probably contributed to the controversy which broke out against him on his next publication (1731).

In the course of all this controversy on many fronts, both academic and academically 'political', Bentley was stripped of his degree. He eventually got it back, but not until 1724, after a lengthy sequence of litigation in the King's Bench, which helped to created the modern system of judicial review of 'administrative action', for the court eventually decided that the University had behaved unlawfully, not because it had not had the powers to take away his degree but because it had not exercised those powers correctly.

New thoughts on 'universal language'

Little of this affected the generality of undergraduate students; it barely entered the syllabus except for advanced students of theology. However, it made for a considerable change of climate in the work of universities on the central principles of the old arts of language. One of the important insights of the early modern period was the realization, now extended to a far wider range of languages, that Augustine had been right, languages differed in complex ways, each having its own idioms, and that this means that there are important academic questions to be addressed about the deep roots of language and whether there is an underlying universal grammar. Academics and private scholars alike explored the implications, as early modern intellectuals unavoidably conducted their *peregrinatio academica* about Europe with a vivid awareness that many different languages were spoken there, each with its own structural peculiarities as well as its own vocabulary.

Yet modern European languages were something for a man to get as a private student as best he could, if he wanted to travel. A correspondent of Milton says that he favours the teaching of modern languages 'as we teach our children English, by words, phrases and constant talk'.[102] They were not yet regarded as appropriate studies to be included in a university syllabus. It seems that the study of modern languages in the eighteenth century in England was disparaged *because* they were not Latin and Greek. They were sometimes offered in dissenting academies, but even there it could by no means be taken for granted that the teachers would be able to pronounce or even speak the languages they offered. One example, who had lived for a few months in France, is held up as exceptional.[103]

The basic presumptions of the Christian tradition were that there had indeed once been a single language, the language in which Adam named the animals,[104] but that this had been fragmented in the episode of the Tower of Babel,[105] so that many, mutually incomprehensible, languages had resulted. This could not be regarded as a good thing since it was a consequence of the Fall, and Pentecost, when suddenly everyone understood what everyone else was saying though it was in all sorts of different languages, was traditionally taken to represent a reversal of this collapse of mutual intelligibility.

Returning to the language of Eden was one desirable option for modern scholars who wanted to work towards a restoration of the way things had been when God gave Adam language. It was assumed that the most ancient and therefore original language would be closest to the language in which Adam and Eve conversed. Inventing a new 'universal' language was a further notion. For both purposes it was an interesting project to compare the patterns of grammar and vocabulary in a variety of languages, especially those which appeared unusual in some way or were thought to survive in a way which might suggest they had been subjected to less modification than most and therefore gave clues to the original (Basque for example).

Interest in the notion of a universal language manifested itself in the sixteenth and seventeenth centuries inside and outside the universities and in various essentially 'interdisciplinary' ways.[106] Some were practical and pedagogical. William Petty published *The Advice of W.P. to Samuel Hartlib* in 1648. It contained proposals for radical reform of the syllabus to give more room for content, substance, especially in natural science. In order to facilitate the students' learning, he recommended that students should be taught a form of shorthand which did not abbreviate words but replaced words with depictions of things. These 'Reall Characters' would be of a universal usefulness and then the students would not have to learn numerous languages to make themselves generally understood.[107] Leibnitz (1646–1716) also thought it might be possible to construct such a 'language' to take the form of an 'algebra' in which all abstract or conceptual thought could be expressed; it was to include symbols, the equivalents of plus and minus and multiplication signs in mathematics, in which the operations involved in the thinking could be noted precisely.

Other thinkers of the seventeenth and eighteenth centuries[108] to explore the notion of creating or recreating a universal language at the theoretical end of the scale included Francis Lodwick and Thomas Urquart (who may have intended a satire, as Voltaire certainly did in his remarks on Pangloss). A fresh wave of interest in a universal language and in signs and thought occurred at the end of the eighteenth century.[109] Joseph Priestley invented a history of the origins of language[110] in search of a universal grammar.[111]

These explorations took thinkers back to the questions of speculative grammar and linguistics which had engaged medieval thinkers, but now they presented new faces and raised new questions in an enlarged forum of language-study in the universities.

A different logic

The value of a training in argumentation was not lost on early modern commentators. Gilbert Burnet, in proposing the founding of a new university, said, 'I wish they may, as soon as they come to the University, be instructed diligently in the Art of Logick, and engaged in the forms of Disputation'. His reason is that this is the best possible training to promote clear and orderly thought and speech. A 'Defect of Logick' leads to 'disjointed and incoherent Conversation'.[112]

But not everyone in the post-medieval period was so enthusiastic about the value of the study of logic for university student. An article in *The Spectator* (16 October 1711) wags a reproving finger at the excessive fondness of lawyers for argument and general disputatiousness.[113] Addison wrote in similar vein on the 'several Methods of managing a Debate' on December 4 of the same year. He gives a short history, from the 'first Races of Mankind' and their 'wild

Logick, uncultivated by Rules of Art', which he compares with the arguments of untaught contemporaries. Then he lists Socrates and his 'Catechetical' method of arguing, and Aristotle, who 'invented a great variety of little Weapons, called Syllogisms... *Socrates* conquers you by Stratagem, *Aristotle* by force'.

The Spectator published critical views on the study of logic in universities in the Middle Ages:

> The Universities of Europe, for many years, carried on their debates by Syllogism, insomuch that we see the Knowledge of several Centuries laid out into Objections and Answers, and all the good Sense of the Age cut and minced into almost an infinitude of Distinctions.

But the universities, says *The Spectator*, warming to its satirical theme, 'found that there was no End of wrangling this way', and invented a new kind of argument. Their method was 'first to discharge their Syllogisms, and afterwards to betake themselves to their Clubs' and knock down their opponents. Erasmus's account of this kind of thing in the battle between the 'Greeks and the Trojans' in Oxford is described.[114]

In the survey of Thomas de Quincey a century later, he identifies as the 'general instruments of study' Logic, Languages, the Arts of Memory to which he adds, metaphysics and mathematics.[115] But in the case of logic, an 'anarchy of errors' 'have possessed this ground from the time of Lord Bacon to the moment at which I write'.[116] These are both a fair and an unfair summary of the syllabus in logic as it was established and developed in the medieval universities and revised and simplified from the sixteenth century.

* * *

From logic to experimental science

The sources of knowledge: probable and necessary arguments again

The most important change making it possible for modern science to develop was the acceptance that however beautiful and 'satisfying' an idea, it would not do unless it would stand up to testing by 'experiment'. This reversed the fundamental principle of ancient and medieval sciences, particularly where Plato's influence was strong. For Plato the highest reality resided in ideas, and there must be a harmony among ideas so that the true would also be good and beautiful. Things in the physical world were mere exemplifications and reflections of these ideas and if their behaviour seemed to put the ideas in question, the physical objects must be at fault. They were capable of change and decay so how could they 'disprove' the ideas which gave them their form and origin? This assumption was powerful and not easily overthrown.

Francis Bacon was taken by the academic world to have been the chief architect of this transition. A parallel set of reflections by René Descartes had an even wider European influence in the seventeenth century. He recognized a principle which had been apparent from the Middle Ages, that self-evident truths are the surest forms of 'knowledge' but that not every branch of study is susceptible of argument by a 'demonstrative' method, as geometry is. He wrote to Mersenne in 1638 to say that only in subjects where it is possible to 'demonstrate' principles of physics by means of metaphysics can this method be applicable and Descartes believes that no 'question of mechanic, optics or astronomy, or any other matter which is not purely geometrical or arithmetical, has ever been demonstrated'... 'To demand that I give geometrical demonstrations in a manner which depends on physics is to demand the impossible'.

Somewhere within this discussion lies Descartes' recognition that at least some areas of knowledge are of an absolute 'kind' and carry their own stamp by way of principles and character, much as Aristotle had argued in the *Posterior Analytics*. That this was so had been a medieval commonplace, but Descartes was now looking at the question differently, asking how this reality affected the mode of study of the subject-matter.

William Paley and 'Evidences'

William Paley (1743–1805) studied at Cambridge as an undergraduate from 1759, on one of the scholarships available for boys from his school. He became a member of the Hyson Club, which had been founded in 1757 by the Wranglers, the top graduates of their year, who shared the views of liberal Christians. This was a drinking club of the most sober kind. 'Hyson' was green tea, and the club was a debating society. Isaac Milner and John Jebb were also members. This was not an exclusively Cambridge club: it expanded until meetings were being held in London. The Club launched a crusade in favour of loosening the requirement to subscribe to the Thirty-Nine Articles which, it claimed, was keeping dissenters out of the Universities and able men out of professional life. Paley was not active in this controversy but he was famously a tolerant man. Utility and expediency were what make something 'right', in Paley's view. The question is whether something 'works', is fit for purpose.

He graduated as Senior Wrangler in 1763. From 1768 he became a fellow of Christ's College, where he and his fellow tutor John Law divided the subject-matter between them, covering Greek Testament, ethics and 'natural philosophy', including the ideas of Joseph Butler (1692–1752), John Locke and Samuel Clarke (1675–1729). He held various Cambridge offices, including that of lecturer in Hebrew, despite the fact that he apparently knew little Hebrew. Paley appears to have been cheerfully unworried by the thought that he was a pluralist or the fact that he was taking income for a sinecure. These were not concerns of his time. In an indirect way, he gave good value for money, was far from idle and proved an energetic thinker and writer. For his Greek New Testament lectures, compulsory for students at his College, he was better equipped than he was for teaching Hebrew, but he still took the opportunity to use the lectures as an opportunity to explore the philosophical and theological methodology appropriate to the study of the Bible. He is reported to have been good at getting students interested.

He was also successful in introducing new textbooks into the syllabus, some of them his own, a considerable achievement in a conservative university world, for example, Clarke's *On the Being and Attributes of God* and Butler's *Analogy of Religion*. His own writings were to find a similar place in a developing syllabus. His *Moral and Political Philosophy*, published in 1785, was based on his personal compilation of material from the sources. In *Horae Paulinae* (1790), he wrote on the Pauline Epistles and Acts of the Apostles, comparing them so as to show that they were in agreement and suggesting that that was evidence of their truth. *A View of the Evidences of Christianity* (1794) won him a doctorate of divinity from Cambridge in 1795.

Paley's *Natural Theology* (1802) is about the argument from design, introduced in the famous opening pages. From the existence of a watch and observance of its mechanism we infer the existence of a watchmaker; so, from the existence of the world and its constituent elements we infer the existence of an intelligent creator. But what kind of revelation was this? Could the account of creation in Genesis be taken literally? The uncovering of the fossil record, with its obvious incompatibility with the story of the Flood, made that seem hard to sustain. Was this a revelation of another sort altogether? The awkward questions about the compatibility of the Biblical narrative with evidence from archaeology and palaeontology and the emergence of evolutionary theory were looming in new forms.

In 1789 Paley was offered the Mastership of Trinity College, Cambridge, but he refused it, hoping perhaps for better offers later.

Problems of reorganizing knowledge in relation to 'mechanics' and manufacturing

Strongly in evidence in the dissenting academies was the view that there was no gulf between theoretical and practical studies, science and metaphysics, when it came to training young men for the ministry in the same institutions as young men entered to study for careers in commerce and industry. In the intellectual climate of the seventeenth and eighteenth centuries, it could even seem that theology and science were faces of the same body of knowledge.

Determining the range of knowledge to be included in the syllabus comes logically before deciding how to teach it, though Joseph Priestley was not alone in finding that the pedagogical challenge arose from having to do both together as the syllabus enlarged and reformed under the pressure of new discoveries and approaches. The cosmos, macrocosm and microcosm, the elements, the nature of heaviness and lightness, falling, motion are the kinds of matter which interested Aristotle and had long detained enquirers in an area where philosophy and science were indistinguishable.[117] Robert Boyle[118] continued to toy with ideas falling between the chemical and the mechanical, such as 'dregs' and 'denseness' and ideas uncertainly poised between natural and supernatural, physical and metaphysical, such as were engaged in some contemporary alchemical studies as well as in the classic philosophy-science problems and concepts.

A quickening of interest is noticeable. There was a sudden early modern realization that the world could be studied in new ways; this was so delightful as to be almost overwhelming, and it did not grow less so with closer familiarity:

> Infinite Goodness is of so communicative a nature, that it seems to delight in the conferring of Existence upon every degree of Perceptive Being. This is shown it is suggested by the way the Creator has made Matter so full of swarming life. And why should there not be numerous ranks of higher being than man, standing between man and the Creator?[119]

exclaimed *The Spectator* in 1711:

> Every part of Matter is peopled: Every green Leaf swarms with Inhabitants. There is scarce a single Humour in the Body of a Man, or of any other Animal, in which our Glasses do not discover Myriads of living Creatures. The surface of Animals

is also covered with other Animals … nay, we find in the most solid Bodies, as in Marble it selfe, innumerable Cells and Cavities that are crowded with such imperceptible Inhabitants, as are too little for the naked Eye to discover … The Author of the Plurality of Worlds draws a very good argument from this Consideration, for the peopling of every Planet, as indeed it seems very probable from the Analogy of Reason, that if no part of Matter, which we are acquainted with, lies waste and useless, those great Bodies which are at such a Distance from us should not be desart and unpeopled, but rather that they should be furnished with Beings adapted to their respective situations.[120]

The task was to position the new kinds of knowledge in this swarm, and to work out their relationship to one another. One danger was the tendency to impute to recent thinkers a degree of originality their ideas did not necessarily possess. 'To the best of my knowledge Des Cartes was the first philosopher who introduced the absolute and essential heterogeneity of the soul as intelligence and the body as matter,' remarks Coleridge (1772–1834), with no apparent sense of the complexities of the centuries of debate about dualism which lay behind Descartes.[121] Similarly, the tracing of chains of influence tended to be restricted to those links which were familiar from more recent times. Coleridge mentions 'Leibnitz's doctrine of a pre-established harmony, which he certainly borrowed from Spinoza, who had himself taken the hint from Des Cartes's animal machines'.[122] There was a new confidence in making connections of thought and expression which seemed to contemporaries quite new and fresh.

Even more profound in their way were the seismic movements affecting the admissibility of 'new' books to the traditional lists and of approaches which were acknowledged to be *parti pris*, whose advocates frankly had axes to grind. For example, some of the Romantic poets' work was soon 'set' for 'translation from English' at Cambridge,[123] including Byron's 'The curse of Minerva' (for translation into Greek tragic Iambics) and some of an English translation of Goethe's *Faust*. Among the axe-grinders were historical revisionists. Even in the sixteenth century, Archbishop Parker would not have been so keen to inventory, collect, and edit medieval English texts if he had not believed that they provided evidence for the original freedom and doctrinal purity of the Church of England.[124] William Chapman joins Englishness, liberty and the pursuit of truth, claiming that the age of Wyclif held 'sacred the cause of truth' but merely as 'the forerunners of a still greater spirit', Wyclif, destined 'to confer the never-dying blessings of liberty upon his country'.

> Wiclif was eminently a patriot...his patriotism was of the highest and noblest type, for he sought, by diffusing light from his own great stores of knowledge, to teach the people to govern themselves.[125]

'All arts and manufactures are derived from science,'[126] claimed Joseph Priestley, in the context of his scientific lectures to the students of a dissenting academy. This was the age of the foundation of the Society of Arts and Manufactures (1754), the product of a café society as much as of its initiator William Shipley. Shipley was an artist rather than a scientist and he brought to his concept a concern with good design in manufacture. The trend, however, was clear. It was unified by the realization that many of the new discoveries in the sciences had an application in the emerging industries. By the time Thomas Carlyle was writing on the 'signs of the times' in the *Edinburgh Review*, a generation after Priestley in 1829, the picture seemed clearer still:

> The school of Reid [Thomas Reid (1710–96)] had also from the first taken a mechanical course, not seeing any other. The singular conclusions at which Hume, setting out from their admitted premises, was arriving, brought this school into being; they let loose instinct, as an undiscriminating ban-dog, to guard them against these conclusions.[127]

This age, he wrote, is

> not an Heroical, Devotional, Philosophical, or Moral Ages, but, above all other, the Mechanical Age. It is the Age of Machinery, in every outward and inward sense of that word; the age which, with its whole undivided might, forwards, teaches and practises the great art of adapting means to ends...On every hand, the living artisan is driven from his workshop, to make room for a speedier inanimate one.[128]

'Nothing follows its spontaneous course, nothing is left to be accomplished by old natural methods. Everything has its cunningly devised implements...it is not done by hand.'[129]

> Thus we have machines for Education: Lancastrian machines; Hamiltonian machines; monitors, maps and emblems. Instruction, that mysterious communing of Wisdom with Ignorance, is no longer an indefinable tentative process, requiring a study of individual aptitudes, and a perpetual

variation of means and methods....; but a secure, universal, straightforward business, to be conducted in the gross, by proper mechanism, with such intellect as comes to hand.[130]

Then we have Religious machines, of all imaginable varieties; the Bible-Society, professing a far higher and heavenly structure, is found, on inquiry, to be altogether an earthly contrivance ... a machine for converting the Heathen.[131]

'Experience' to experimental method

A way of 'knowing' fashionable in the early modern period was by reflecting on the evidence of the senses, and on one's 'experience' in general, including the working upon one's 'understanding' of perceptions, and of observations of things, including things that happen. Within this strand or tradition stood Butler's *Analogy*:

> We know we are endued with capacities of action, of happiness and misery, for we are conscious of acting, of enjoying pleasure and suffering pain. Now, that we have these powers and capacities before death, is a presumption that we shall retain them through and after death; indeed a probability of it abundantly sufficient to act upon.[132]

It became a matter of debate whether there could or should be systematic ways of 'using' experience through experimentation, which is a form of systematic testing by contriving experiences within artificially controlled situations.

The great shift which had to take place to justify the use of an experimental method was from the presumption that the elegance and authoritativeness of an idea were testimonies to its soundness, to the complete reversal contained in the acceptance that an idea or hypothesis had to be tested by trying it out in nature and seeing if its behaviour repeated itself in like circumstances. Beyond lay the question whether universities should begin to teach in this way.

The Irish satirist Jonathan Swift (1667–1745) describes a group of 'scientists' met by Gulliver on his 'travels', conducting their enquiries about him on this basis. They are puzzled to find what appears to them to be a tiny creature behaving like one of themselves. They are 'surprised at so much wit and good sense in so diminutive an Animal':

> The King, although he be as learned a Person as any in his Dominions and had been educated in the Study of Philosophy, and particularly Mathematicks; yet when he observed my Shape exactly, and saw me walk erect, before I began to

speak, conceived I might be a piece of Clock-work ... contrived by some ingenious Artist. But when he heard my Voice, and found what I delivered to be regular and rational, he could not conceal his Astonishment.[133]

'His Majesty sent for three great Scholars who were then in their weekly waiting (according to the Custom in that Country). These Gentlemen, after they had a while examined my Shape with much Nicety ... all agreed that I could not be produced according to the regular Laws of Nature; because I was not framed with a capacity for preserving my Life, either by Swiftness, or climbing of Trees, or digging Holes in the Earth.' They inspected his teeth and saw that he was carnivorous, 'yet most Quadrupeds being an Overmatch for me; and Field-Mice, with some others, too nimble, they could not imagine how I should be able to support myself, unless I fed upon Snails and other Insects; which they offered by many learned Arguments to evince that I could not possibly do'. They deduced his age by peering at the 'Stumps' or his beard through a magnifying glass. They observed and reasoned until they reached the conclusion that he was a sport of nature, 'a Determination exactly agreeable to the Modern Philosophy of Europe: whose Professors, disdaining the old Evasion of occult Causes, whereby the Followers of Aristotle endeavour in vain to disguise their Ignorance; have invented this wonderful Solution of all Difficulties, to the unspeakable Advancement of human Knowledge'.[134]

The scholars were contemptuous of Gulliver's attempts to explain that where he came from everyone was his size and the plants and animals were in proportion. The King then sent for the Farmer who had brought him to Court and there was a return to common sense.[135]

A further problem was that it was necessary not only to coax the study of science into the syllabus (where it could locate itself under philosophy without too much disturbance), but also bring in an expectation that there would be experiments and students would learn an experimental method.[136] Another aspect of the difficulty was to refine the understanding of the connotation of the vocabulary of 'experience', 'experiential', 'experiment'. It meant anything senses could experience at least until the eighteenth century. It did not necessarily imply actually doing experiments.[137]

Conducting experiments

Joseph Priestley reflected in the early 1790s on the difficulty he had faced in preparing his lectures on 'experimental philosophy':

> I contrived to bring within that compass as much of the subject of experimental philosophy as I well could, and especially to include the whole of what is called chemistry, to which so much attention is now given, and which presents so many new fields of philosophical investigation.[138]
>
> I think it most advisable not to trouble beginners with more than a large outline of any branch of science ... in future life they may pursue any of them as much farther as their inclination may dispose.[139]

He tried to determine where to draw the line between physics and metaphysics for this purpose within the conspectus of the theologically inclined syllabus of the students before him:

> Experimental philosophy is an investigation of the wisdom of God in the works and the laws of nature, so that it is one of the greatest objects to the mind of man, and opens a field of inquiry which has no bounds; every advance we make suggesting new doubts and subjects of further inquiry ... [140]

The dissenting academies are perhaps the most startling in their willingness to teach modern science alongside theology, and to do so in the confidence that scientific studies were advantageous and not dangerous. Joseph Priestley preached a Sermon on 'Wisdom the principal thing' more than once. It was given by Priestley, according to notes in his own hand, at Leeds in October 1790, Birmingham 1791, Warwick 1792, Hackney, November 1792. He himself judged this particular sermon to be 'middling'.[141] This was close to the time he was preparing his chemistry lectures with their frank reflections on the difficulty of teaching such a new subject in a manner students would find helpful. Priestley was accused of dabbling too much in theology and not concentrating on his work in the natural sciences and he was defending himself on this point in print about this time.[142] He is sensitive on the point in the sermon, in what was possibly an added passage:

> I will venture to say there is no man who has divided his attention between natural science and studies of a theological nature, such as Newton and others, who have not given a decided preference to the latter, especially in riper years, when the judgement is the soundest.[143]

It is notable that his concern is merely to be seen to get his priorities right; he was not concerned about the inherent incompatibility of theology and science.

His method in the sermon is essentially the same as that used by medieval university preachers: to break down the theme into sub-topics and support each assertion by a quotation from the Bible. He is interested in the moral impact of the possession of wisdom.

> Though wisdom, in the sense of Solomon, stands for every qualification of the mind that is truly valuable, it is chiefly of a *moral* nature, consisting of those principles and habits of virtue which constitute the glory and perfection of human nature. True wisdom... is twofold; consisting of mental accomplishments in general, and of virtuous and religious attainments in particular... In the first place, wisdom is excellent, and worthy of our study and pursuit, as it consists in the improvement of our reason, and in the attainment of useful knowledge... Reason is the distinguishing property and the chief glory, of human nature... with no more senses than brutes naturally have, we are capable of receiving pleasures and gratifications vastly more noble, and infinitely more various... [therefore] the improvement of our reason, by adding to our stock of knowledge, is the improvement of our natures and that which must qualify us to answer, in the most effectual manner the great ends of our being; a duty incumbent on all persons who are capable of a sense of moral obligation.

Everyone does not have the same capacity for this.

> But certainly where a person has capacity, opportunity, and leisure, for thus improving his mind, by any valuable acquisition of knowledge, whether a more intimate acquaintance with the works of God, in the laws of nature; with the world we inhabit and the history of it, that is, with the dispensations of divine providence respecting it; or with any branch of natural science whatever; to such a one it is a proper *duty*... for by these means men become capable of being more eminently useful, of doing more essential service to themselves, their friends, their country and the world.[144]

Coleridge had memorable comments on all this at a date when the battle for experimental science was in reality already won but the rationale was still being thought through.

> No man, [he says,] can confidently conceive a fact to be
> *universally* true who does not with equal confidence anticipate
> its *necessity*, and who does not believe that necessity to be
> demonstrable by an insight into its nature, whenever and
> wherever such insight can be obtained.[145]

He gives as an example the Linnaeus system of classification, 'a scheme
of classific and distinctive marks, by which one man's experience
may be communicated to others, and the objects safely reasoned on
while absent, and recognised as soon as and wherever they are met
with':[146]

> With the knowledge of law alone dwell Power and Prophecy,
> decisive Experiment, and, lastly, a scientific method, that
> dissipating with its earliest rays the gnomes of hypothesis
> and the mists of theory may, within a single generation, open
> out on the philosophic Seer discoveries that had baffled the
> gigantic, but blind and guideless industry of ages.[147]

*   *   *

Enlightenment or marking time?

Cambridge enjoyed two centuries full of intellectual light and ambition
during the Tudor and Stuart periods. But it began to slip behind in the
eighteenth century, as others seized the torch of innovation and ran
ahead with it. Eighteenth-century Cambridge kept up intellectually and
made its contributions, but that was not the same thing. It was going
to be a duller and more second-rate university for a time, though no
less inwardly argumentative.

Yet Cambridge was not without its reforming attitudes. In 1769 the
undergraduate round cap became square.[148] The radical John Wilkes
stirred up a protest against John (Horne) Tooke being allowed to take
his M.A. in 1771, with the result that the two houses of Regents and
Non-Regents had to vote about it (they let him graduate).[149] A Bill of
1783 sought to enable heads of colleges to marry.[150] In 1787 disputants
at Trinity were heard by the Lord Chancellor.[151] In 1788 a petition of
the University was got up against the slave trade.[152]

The eighteenth century had begun with showy entertaining. In
1705 Queen Anne visited Cambridge. The University borrowed £500
for the entertainment of the Queen, passing a Grace for the purpose.
The City Corporation then resolved to borrow £100 to provide a

PLATE 26 – In this portrait by Hans Holbein, Desiderius Erasmus (1466?–1536) is seen writing at his desk. It is not difficult to imagine him in his short period of lecturing at Cambridge trying to interest his students in the study of Greek grammar.

PLATE 27 – Sir Thomas More (1478–1535) was another of the circle of leading humanists of the early sixteenth century who had contact with Cambridge (although he himself studied at Oxford and at the Inns of Court). He was High Steward of the University and an active defender of the interests of both universities in the testing times of Henry VIII's reign.

PLATE 28 – The playwright and tragedian Christopher Marlowe (1564–93) is one of the most enigmatic figures of the Elizabethan age. Killed in mysterious circumstances in a tavern brawl in Deptford, Marlowe may well have been one of the first 'Cambridge Spies'. In 1587 the Privy Council ordered the University to award Marlowe his MA, despite his long absences, indicating that he had been away from Cambridge on unspecified 'matters touching the benefit of his country'. This portrait, thought likely to be of the young poet, is reproduced by kind permission of the Master, Fellows and Scholars of Marlowe's college, Corpus Christi.

PLATE 29 – This is a modern impression of the 'town' and 'gown' fights which frequently broke out in Cambridge's early centuries and sometimes became riots. Injuries could be serious and blood was shed. Resentments lingered and one side was often ready with its fists to 'pay back' the other for an insult.

PLATES 30 and 31 – John Fisher and Margaret Beaufort were instrumental in bringing about the changes which turned Cambridge from a medieval into a modern university. Before he moved into politics, and lost his way during the King's Affair which led to Henry VIII divorcing Catharine of Aragon, John Fisher (c. 1459–1535) was a student at Cambridge and then (from 1505 to 1508) President of Queens' College. Margaret Beaufort (1443–1509), mother of King Henry VII, became one of Cambridge's most important patrons when the University was emerging from its medieval doldrums. Encouraged in her benefactions by Fisher, she helped found Christ's and St John's Colleges in their modern form and established the Lady Margaret Chair in Divinity. She was renowned for her extreme piety even when visible expression of religious sentiment was thoroughly expected from the ruling classes.

PLATE 32 - The old Faculty of Divinity was leased from St. John's College across the road. Its Victorian interior contained rooms named after the great figures of nineteenth-century Cambridge theology. Lightfoot's heavy-eyed portrait supervised the seminars held in the Lightfoot Room. There were busts of other great men on the stairs. The Faculty now has a new building on the Sidgewick site.

PLATE 33 - The chapel of St. John's is the work of a Victorian architect, George Gilbert Scott. It was built in 1866–9 to take the place of the medieval chapel which had stood there since the thirteenth century but was considered too small. St. John's choir rivals that of King's College, though their chapels form a strong contrast of architectural style.

PLATE 34 - St. John's 'bridge of sighs' is not much like its Venetian inspiration but it is a testimony to Victorian romanticism. It was built after the construction of New Court in 1831 made it necessary to link the part of St. John's across the river with its older part.

PLATE 35 - Newnham College stands here as a monument to the desire to build a residential community for women students. The first building for the College on its present site was erected in 1875. The main building shown here is planned on a 'corridor' rather than a 'staircase' arrangement, which was something new.

PLATE 36 – Selwyn College chapel stands here at the end of its lawns, a severe reminder of Victorian seriousness and the spirit in which the College was founded.

PLATE 37 – Magdalene College, originally a combined lodging for young monks from several houses, is seen from the river through a row of bicycles.

PLATE 38 – Cambridge is full of bicycles. Flocks of cyclists overflow the streets between lectures and when the City Council attempted to pedestrianize part of the centre of the city, there were complaints that the University would not be able to function. Here a lone cyclist rides into the city centre along Garrett Hostel Lane.

PLATE 39 – A few yards on from the end of Garrett Hostel Lane and round one or two corners the cyclist would come into Senate House passage, which runs between Gonville and Caius College and the Senate House and is shown here in an early drawing. At the end, looking right, the cyclist would be able to see St. Mary's the University Church and the top of King's Parade and the front of King's College.

PLATE 40 – Several Oxford and Cambridge Colleges have notable sundials. Gonville and Caius College has this double aspect sundial above its Gate of Honour (1575).

PLATE 41 – The University Library, built in the 1930s, is monumental in scale and on a site large enough to allow room for expansion, a good deal of which has now been used.

PLATE 42 – The Fitzwilliam Museum was opened in 1848 in a building designed in grand classical style by George Basevi (who died before it was finished) and C.R. Cockerell (1788–1863).

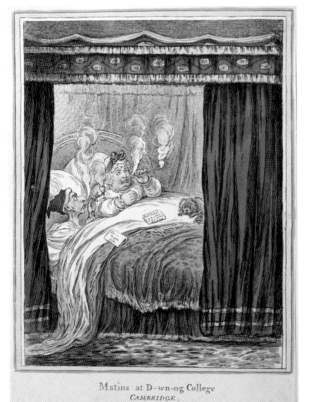

Matins at D–wn–ng College
CAMBRIDGE.

PLATE 43 – In an era with a taste for classical elegance in buildings, low comedy and sexual romps were as much the fashion in the Universities as in the wider world. Here is a satirical cartoon of the scene in an undergraduate's room one morning at the beginning of the nineteenth century.

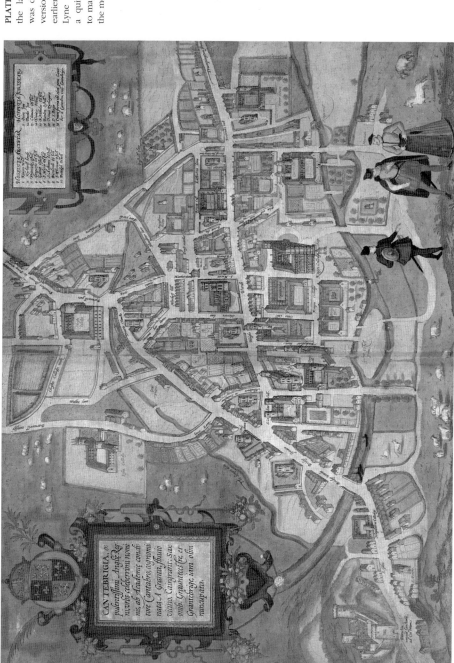

PLATE 44 – This map of the late sixteenth century was drawn in a decorative version with figures, from an earlier map made by John Lyne in 1574. It illustrates a quite different approach to map-making from that of the modern geographer.

PLATE 45 – A supply of fine wine and humbler alcoholic refreshment has historically been important to the University's contentment.

PLATE 46 – Thomas Rowlandson drew this sketch for his book of Oxford caricatures, published in 1821, but he could equally well have set it in Cambridge. It shows students smuggling in a local prostitute. There was always a contrast between the expectations of celibacy and good behaviour and the realities of the student taste for sexual adventure and the records of the University's courts contain many examples of problems arising for the University in dealing with the local prostitutes.

rival entertainment.[153] Cooper notes another instance of corporate entertaining in his *Annals,* when in 1706 the University of Frankfurt on the Oder invited Cambridge to come and help it celebrate its jubilee; it had been founded 200 years earlier.[154] This was celebration of past achievement.

The reign of Queen Anne marked significant developments for the University, which ought to have been more of a stimulus than they were, among them the Copyright Act of 1710 and its effects on the University Library's collections.[155] The Copyright Act followed on the Printing Act of 1662, which had had subsequent versions (the Licensing Acts). These had had among their purposes an intention of imposing censorship. The expiring of the last 'licence' in 1695 had meant that the libraries of Oxford and Cambridge no longer had the right to legal deposit copies until the passing of the Copyright Act. Cambridge seems to have been lackadaisical about seeking to ensure continuity in the building of its collections. Cambridge's acquisitions and accessions were not impressive during the eighteenth century partly because no one in the Library took the trouble to enforce rights and chase up copies 'owed'; it was found to be more convenient to have occasional parcels delivered than regular and frequent arrivals of consignments.[156]

The Lysons, describing in 1808 the position at the end of the eighteenth century, comment in describing the Old Schools:

> The whole of the upper story of this building, a great part of which was formerly divided into schools for different sciences, is now occupied by the university library, which, in its infancy, was deposited only in the upper apartment of the east side, and afterwards extended over the north side also. In 1648, the sum of 2000L. was voted by Parliament for repairing the library at Cambridge. The principal acquisition to this library was...when King George I, having purchased a very large collection of books, of the executors of Dr. Moore Bishop of Ely, amounting to upwards of 30,000 volumes...gave them to the university of Cambridge, and contributed the sume of 2000L towards fitting up rooms for their reception...Before this time there has been but one librarian. Who was called keeper of the University Library. The place of the principal librarian. Then newly created, was given to the celebrated D. Conyers Middleton [1683–1750] on account, it is said, of his having, when at Rome, successfully maintained the honour and dignity of the university...All members of the Senate,

and all the bachelors of law and physic in the university, are entitled to have books at any time to their own apartments, not exceeding 10 volumes, unless by a particular dispensation: under-graduates are allowed also to have books on the recommendation of a privileged person.[157]

The election of the Librarian could be contentious, as in 1783,[158] but the general tenor of Library development was slow. A fresh Copyright Act was passed in 1814, in the midst of a wrangle by pamphlet orchestrated by Basil Montagu, a former friend of Coleridge and Wordsworth and William Godwin and once a student at Christ's. He was a lawyer by profession and he noticed that a volume of law reports had not arrived in the University Library as it should have done.[159]

The *Reporter* of 7 June 1961, p.1811, includes the Annual Report of the Library Syndicate for 1959–60, which tells a tale indicating a lack of care in library matters in this earlier period:

> Mr. Oates has continued his researches towards the compilation of a History of the Library. He has recently written some 5,000 words on the events of 1815–18, when the Library extricated itself from a situation in which it might easily have lost its Copyright privilege. The brief facts are as follows:
>   1. Down to September 1815 the Library sold to the local booksellers all Copyright accessions which were thought to be not worth keeping (including nearly all fiction).
>   2. On 26 February 1816 the Syndics decided to abandon this practice but came to no decision about what to do with these 'rejected' books in future.
>   3. On 1 July 1816 on the motion of Sir Egerton Brydges the House of Commons ordered the Copyright libraries to make return of books claimed under the Act of 29 July 1814, showing which had been placed in their libraries and which had been otherwise disposed of, and how.

The return was made in alphabetical order, 'the imposture was thus effectively concealed, and the Select Committee on the Copyright Acts in 1818, though it asked the University's representatives a number of very awkward questions, never quite got to the point of discovering it'.

Colleges were actively acquiring libraries during these centuries, too. For example, Edward Stanhope who studied at Trinity and graduated in 1563, founded the College library. He gave money (his will was proved 1608) 'for the construction and fitting up' and books and manuscripts and also 'gave the college permission to change books which they had for any of his which were of a later impression or more fitly bound' and provided 'one very great book of large vellum' to have in it all the coats of arms of the college founders and its own 'this book to be kept for a public register book' of the holdings of the college library (to be chained with the rest).[160]

Downing: did Cambridge need a new college?

The foundation of Downing College, Cambridge,[161] involved a wrangle of many decades, beginning with Sir George Downing's will in 1717 and ending with the grant of a royal charter in 1800. The founding of this college was to happen only in the unlikely eventuality of all the serial beneficiaries of Downing's will dying,[162] as eventually occurred. It was more than 200 years since anyone had founded a new college and some thought this new venture was timely and would help to bring the University up to date. But in the event it was rather a flop, attracted few students and a good deal of opprobrium. It did however have a leading part in re-establishing a proper academic standard for the two laggard 'higher degree' subjects of the original medieval three, theology having gone from strength to strength in the intervening centuries. There was to be a Downing Professor of the Laws of England and a Downing Professor of Medicine, the sixteenth-century Regius Professor of Physic having failed to keep the subject's end up.[163]

Did Cambridge need new Professorships?

New Chairs began to appear in a flurry towards the end of the eighteenth century, partly to meet teaching needs identified in connection with the new trends. John Norris, who had been at Trinity, died in 1777, leaving a will under which a Norrisian Professorship of Materia Medica was to be established. This was to be held for no more than five years at a time, and the Professor was to give 50 lectures in the year for which he was not allowed to charge a fee. If he had an audience of fewer than six, the lecture did not count. A Professor who did not fulfil his obligations was to be fined. These were no doubt rules designed to prevent this becoming another Professorial sinecure. The lectures were to be based chiefly on the Bible 'particularly the Prophecies and the Evangelical History'.[164] There was also a Chair of Natural Experimental Philosophy which was founded by a Fellow of Trinity in 1782. This Professor had to give only 36 lectures though he also had to perform 30 experiments in anatomy, animal economy, chemistry botany, agriculture or the materia medica. Isaac Milner was the first to hold it although his qualifications were not as extensive as the brief.[165]

The eighteenth century brought the number of Professorships in the University up from the five of the sixteenth century plus the Lady Margaret Professorship of Divinity, with the four more added in the seventeenth century, to twenty, doubling the provision.[166] It has been suggested that this partly provoked a sense of crisis about the college teaching provision, which still emphasized the personal guidance of a student's reading by a tutor.[167]

Student life

> IT was a dreary morning when the wheels
> Rolled over a wide plain o'erhung with clouds,
> And nothing cheered our way till first we saw
> The long-roofed chapel of King's College lift
> Turrets and pinnacles in answering files,
> Extended high above a dusky grove.
> Advancing, we espied upon the road
> A student clothed in gown and tasselled cap,
> Striding along as if o'ertasked by Time,
> Or covetous of exercise and air;
> He passed – nor was I master of my eyes
> Till he was left an arrow's flight behind.
> As near and nearer to the spot we drew,
> It seemed to suck us in with an eddy's force.
> Onward we drove beneath the Castle; caught,
> While crossing Magdalene Bridge, a glimpse of Cam;
> And at the 'Hoop' alighted, famous Inn.
> My spirit was up, my thoughts were full of hope;
> Some friends I had, acquaintances who there
> Seemed friends, poor simple schoolboys, now hung round
> With honour and importance: in a world
> Of welcome faces up and down I roved;
> Questions, directions, warnings and advice,
> Flowed in upon me, from all sides; fresh day
> Of pride and pleasure! to myself I seemed
> A man of business and expense, and went
> From shop to shop about my own affairs,
> To Tutor or to Tailor, as befell,
> From street to street with loose and careless mind.
> I was the Dreamer, they the Dream; I roamed
> Delighted through the motley spectacle;
> Gowns grave, or gaudy, doctors, students, streets,
> Courts, cloisters, flocks of churches, gateways, towers:

> Migration strange for a stripling of the hills,
> A northern villager.
> Wordsworth, *The Prelude, Book III*, Residence at Cambridge

William Wordsworth (1770–1850) arrived in Cambridge in 1787, where he became a student at St. John's College. Wordsworth's first impressions, recorded in *The Prelude* is of a university as crowded and busy as a modern university is likely to seem in Freshers' Week. Wordsworth wrote nostalgically of the flavour of student life as he experienced it:

> Companionships,
> Friendships, acquaintances, were welcome all.
> We sauntered, played, or rioted; we talked
> Unprofitable talk at morning hours;
> Drifted about along the streets and walks,
> Read lazily in trivial books[168]

Henry Gunning, a close contemporary, had entered Christ's College as a sizar in 1784, moved up to a scholarship and graduated very creditably as Fifth Wrangler in 1788, only to become Esquire Bedell almost at once (1789) and remain in that office for 64 years, until he died. This was an ancient office in the University, beginning in the thirteenth century, but its precise duties have always been somewhat fuzzy. They have mainly been ceremonial, involving leading processions carrying the mace. He wrote reminiscences of his life, including a vivid account of the habits of his Tutor Parkinson, who had a beautiful fiancée living 18 miles away, whom he was always anxious to go and see:

> We were lectured immediately after chapel, and generally in a very hasty manner, as Parkinson not unfrequently was equipped with boots and spurs, which his gown but ill concealed, and his servant was waiting with his horse ready to take him into Suffolk.

He tried to be kind and approachable and he encouraged his students to come to him if they were in difficulty. But then he became peevish. 'I cannot make it any plainer, Sir.' Gunning stopped trying and 'frankly told' his tutor of his intention 'to give up reading altogether'. His tutor released him from attending his lectures. But Gunning generously explains that poor Parkinson was very frustrated. He had expected to get the Mastership of Christ's in 1780, which would have allowed him to marry. Now he was getting into debt trying to provide his lady with the style of life she wanted and to pay his bills to the college cook.[169] His reminiscences abound in such tales, how Jemima Watkins 'lived in expensive lodgings, where she was in the habit of receiving some of the most fashionable men in the University',[170] how the Commencement, the great summer Degree Ceremony, used to be a great social occasion, with the nobility taking their 'honorary' degrees and a fair on 'Midsummer Green' called the 'Pot Fair' with stalls of pictures, china and millinery which were raffled each evening, and on the Saturday evening 'the greatest assemblage of company', including 'the gentry in the town and neighbourhood' with as many as 20 private carriages in waiting. There was a Commencement Ball and high spirited behaviour among the young gentlemen 'who had evidently dined'.[171] Gunning manifestly loved all this.

Wordsworth, altogether a more buttoned-up character, had an underlying awareness of serious things in the atmosphere of Cambridge:

> Imagination slept,
> And yet not utterly. I could not print
> Ground where the grass had yielded to the steps
> Of generations of illustrious men
> Unmoved. I could not always lightly pass
> Through the same gateways, sleep where they had slept,
> Wake where they waked, range that inclosure old,
> That garden of great intellects, undisturbed.[172]

He could fancy even Isaac Newton a mere fellow-student in the ghostly company thronging Trinity College's courts:

> Even the great Newton's own ethereal self,
> Seemed humbled in these precincts[173]

In his studies, he consciously made the most of the freedom a student still had at the end of the eighteenth century to read as he chose:

> many books
> Were skimmed, devoured, or studiously perused,
> But with no settled plan. I was detached
> Internally from academic cares[174]

He wonders in retrospect whether to blame himself for this loose application to his work, but only to point out that such a time of lying fallow gave him room to learn things he did not know he was learning at the time:

> Yet who can tell –
> Who knows what thus may have been gained, both then

> And at a later season, or preserved;
> What love of nature, what original strength
> Of contemplation, what intuitive truths
> The deepest and the best, what keen research,
> Unbiassed, unbewildered, and unawed?[175]

And even where he paid attention to the syllabus he was able to find in them more than the designers of the syllabus had required. Wordsworth speaks of the philosophical insights Euclid prompted:

> The pleasure gathered from the rudiments
> Of geometric science. Though advanced
> In these enquiries, with regret I speak,
> No farther than the threshold, there I found
> Both elevation and composed delight
> With Indian awe and wonder, ignorance pleased
> With its own struggles, did I meditate
> On the relation those abstractions bear
> To Nature's laws, and by what process led,
> Those immaterial agents bowed their heads
> Duly to serve the mind of earth-born man;
> From star to star, from kindred sphere to sphere,
> From system on to system without end.[176]

Meanwhile, at undergraduate level, social patterns were changing. The main meal of the day in colleges was taken in the middle of the day and in the evening informal bread-and-cheese suppers in students' rooms were the norm, though they complained of overcharging by the college kitchens. Students were easy meat for local shopkeepers and the providers of various goods, who were delighted to offer them credit and allow them to get into debt. The Hyson tea-drinking society had rivals among coffee-drinkers. In an age of coffee-houses, students spent their evenings there rather than in taverns, for that was where the gossip was to be had. That does not mean that there was not a student drinking problem too.[177]

How important was it to get a degree?

It was possible, but not very common, for a slightly more 'mature' student (over 24 years of age) to obtain a higher degree without first graduating as a B.A. and then an M.A. This could be achieved by a student of theology who spent ten years nominally in study, though not necessarily actually resident, before becoming a Bachelor of Divinity. These were known as 'ten year men',[178] and there was a certain amount of controversy about the propriety of this practice. In

247

1679 there were 'disputes' in Cambridge about conferring honorary degrees 'without time or exercise' upon baronet and knights. The matter was referred to the King, who ruled that it should continue to be allowed for those 'qualified by the statute in that case provided'.[179]

For the regular student, there were expectations which had to be met before gaining a degree, though not all those who went to Cambridge and subsequently made their names completed their degrees. Some had to leave because of poverty and some because of politics. Some simply did not bother to finish. A degree was not a required 'qualification' for future professional life in every field and not all the young gentlemen entering colleges had their livings to earn in any case.

What does success in an examination demonstrate – that the student knows and can do certain specific things or that the student is an 'educated person', equipped to turn his hand to many things and learn whatever he needs to know for the purpose if it turns out that it was not on the syllabus? This dilemma was going to be much discussed in the nineteenth century, and became visibly sharper with the emergence of a new type of examination. For there was major stock-taking at the end of the eighteenth century when the form and conduct of the examinations was radically reconsidered, the medieval disputation finally abandoned, and the 'essay' type of examination gradually introduced:

> Every University must have a criterion whereby to judge of the respective merits of the candidate for Degrees; hence the necessity of a public examination, and of certain sciences to be made the ground-work of that examination.[180]

Yet,

> Examination [remains] but an imperfect test of knowledge, and a still more imperfect test of capacity, while it tells us next to nothing about a man's power as an investigator.[181]

The medieval reason for conducting examinations had been twofold. The degree (*gradus*) was originally confined to members of the body which awarded it, the guild or *universitas*. The graduate was admitted to a standing among the member of the *universitas*. It marked the body's recognition of a status within that body. And the licence to teach (*licentia docendi*) granted within the university could, if the university was of sufficient standing, lead to a *ius ubique docendi* (a licence to teach anywhere), so it had in part the complexion of a professional qualification too. A full member of the guild entitled (and required) the holder to share in its governance, for guilds were autonomous corporations.

Edward Gibbon (1737–94) recognized that the early modern system was a legacy of these historical underpinnings:

> The use of academical degrees, as old as the thirteenth century, is visibly borrowed from the mechanic corporations: in which an apprentice, after serving his time, obtains a testimonial of his skill, and a licence to practise his trade and mystery.[182]

How to conduct an examination

The medieval method of examining candidates for a degree had involved a live public examination in which they displayed their skills in formal argumentation in a disputation, still conducted in Latin until the end. Long after Latin was the usual vehicle of academic discourse, and well beyond the period when teaching was partly conducted through disputations, young English gentlemen were expected to display a competence in both in order to obtain a degree. In eighteenth-century Cambridge,[183] the traditional *disputatio* was still held in much the way it had been in the Middle Ages, with some pragmatic modifications to make it still feasible when many students were idle young gentlemen who did not much care whether they took their degrees or not.[184] The colleges sent in lists of their third-year students with an indication which ones had been reading hard (or even adequately), and a list was drawn up of those who seemed likely to be capable of being 'respondents'. These were sent a notification of their date for performing. The 'respondent-to-be' sent in three subjects in the form of questions or 'propositions' to the 'moderator' selected to preside over the debate.[185]

One Cambridge figure, Thomas Johnson of Magdalene, compiled a manual of such *quaestiones philosophicae* (Cambridge, 1735), for the 'academic youth', 'the person taking the leisure for philosophical studies' (*philosophicis studiis vacanti*), 'so that you may have in your hands a book' capable of giving pleasure and also providing 'subject-matter for disputations' (pp.ii–iii). (He admits that he is no longer at Cambridge himself, so he was not offering this crib as a tutor.) The questions are grouped under headings, relating to natural history, chemistry, meteorology, mechanics, hydrostatics, optics, astronomy, logic, metaphysics and ethics. There is an appendix 'On the rules of disputation' (*De legibus disputandi*), to remind the student of the rules of the formal debate.

The Senate House was completed in 1730 and then became the venue for what was thereafter known as the final 'Senate House Examination'. Once a student had completed the required exercises, he could take this Examination, which lasted three days. This was the test which eventually became the Mathematical Tripos. This had the character of an intellectual wrestling match, out of which someone emerged as Senior Wrangler. William Whewell (1794–1866) himself had come out of his final Examination in 1816 as Second Wrangler.

By 1740 the content of the examination in Cambridge was intended to be mathematical or philosophical rather than classical, but Johnson's little manual indicates that propositions or questions for debate might include topics which would now be classified as metaphysical as well as those more strictly scientific in modern terms, and could embrace the theological too. There were also questions on logic and ethics, and the debate would include the citation of classical authors in support of various arguments. Is there such a thing as perpetual motion (*Utrum motus sit aeternus?*) (p.65) and 'Whether God is the author of motion and keeps it in being (*Utrum Deus sit auctor et conservatur motus?*)' (p.67) exemplify very well the close cousinship of many of the acceptable types of question with those which are to be found in late medieval disputations.

Under the heading of each question Johnson collects conveniently together, exactly as a medieval master would have done in training his pupils, a list of authorities which support one side and a list of authorities which support the other (though he gives sources with fuller references than could be offered in the Middle Ages). Questions and authorities could be selected from such comparatively modern authors as Descartes or Locke or Newton. There is a happy mixture of ancient and modern, Descartes for, and Aristotle and Newton against, the view that motion is maintained by divine power, for example.

Logical questions were also allowed, interestingly raising for-and-against possibilities with reference to a number of matters which might have been expected to be the subject of examination with a view to establishing whether the student knew the 'right' answer. 'Is the best method of definition by genus and differentia?' has its *pro* and its *contra* (p.174). Sometimes a question seems to have been thought capable of arguing about only one way. Among his ethical questions, Johnson asks whether 'A good intention is sufficient to make an action good?' (*Utrum bona intentio ad bonitatem actus sufficiat?*) (p.227). Only two negatives appear below, from Sanderson and Pudendorf, no affirmatives.

The respondent being examined by this ordeal of 'disputation' was to meet three 'opponents' who were also selected from the colleges' lists. On the day, he read out his 'thesis', an essay 'proposing' his theme lasting perhaps ten minutes, and the opponents then countered it, couching their ripostes in syllogisms. The process was described in an account written for a friend early in 1815 by William Whewell (who graduated as Senior Wrangler in 1816 and whom we shall meet in the next chapter as a leader of Cambridge's scientific revolution). It consisted

> in a person getting up into a box to defend certain mathematical and moral questions, from the bad arguments and worse Latin of three men who are turned loose into an opposite box to bait him with syllogisms.[186]

William Whewell wrote a later letter from Trinity College, Cambridge, in October 1819, describing what was involved in what had now become his own sometimes tedious 'duties of presiding in the disputations in the Schools and examining the candidates in the Senate House'. The disputations

> are one of the most marked relics in their form of the ancient discipline of the University. They are held between undergraduates in pulpits in opposite sides of the room, in Latin and in a syllogistic form.

He despaired of the quality of both the logic and the Latin:

> The syllogisms are such as would make Aristotle stare, and the Latin would make every classical hair on your head stand on end.

But he did not think the exercise was without value:

> it is an exercise well adapted to try the clearness and soundness of the mathematical ideas of the men, though they are of course embarrassed by talking in an unknown tongue.[187]

The more able might have to do this twice as respondents and six times as opponents. Other students were let off more lightly. But from these practice-sessions a list of students in order of excellence would begin to emerge for the year. Gradually this final examination became more important than the disputations or 'questions' which had previously been what really ranked a man in the lists. By the time Whewell described it, the 'effect on a man's place in the tripos' had diminished.

From 1772, John Jebb had been active in pressing for reform, with mixed success. Jebb had been a student at Trinity College, Dublin, where he had been faced with regular examinations. He thought it would be a sound plan to require Cambridge undergraduates to face annual examinations and to be tested in a wider range of subjects, to include history, philosophy, international law as well as classics, to complement the mathematics on which Cambridge was by now placing an almost exclusive emphasis. Jebb failed to carry all his points about the need for reform of the whole system, but he had prepared the ground by raising questions and at last, in 1822, Cambridge agreed to introduce a Previous Examination. The Previous Examination tested not only knowledge of the classics (at least the languages) but also Paley's *Evidences of Christianity,* as a nod to the importance of theology (and in recognition of the need to try to ensure that ordinands had some acquaintance at least with these matters). An additional Tripos in Classics was also added in 1822, which might be taken by those who had successfully completed the examination in mathematics. But until 1849 when those who had only an ordinary degree in the first part of the Mathematical Tripos were allowed in, they had to have achieved Honours in Mathematics first.[188]

These first moves in reforming the examination system were to be followed by others, some of them focused upon the particular needs of specific subjects. Professor T.W. Körner told part of the story elegantly in a speech in the Senate-House in 2009:

> In 1769 the Smith Prize Examination was instituted in order to encourage the study of subjects more advanced than those in the standard undergraduate course. As part of the 1883 reforms, its position was taken by an exam called Part III and the Smith essay prize instituted. In 1886, Part III was renamed Part II (with the degree result determined by Part I) and, as part of the ever to be remembered 1909 reforms, this became Part II, Schedule B. Finally, in 1934, Part II, Schedule B became Part III again. Throughout all these name changes and various changes of regulations, the exam has retained its original purpose of providing the best students with an experience taking them well beyond normal undergraduate study ... Only a small handful of students took the Smith's prize examination in the nineteenth century. When Karl Pearson took the examination in 1879, the examiners were Stokes, Maxwell, Cayley, and Todhunter and the examinees went on each occasion to the examiner's house, did a morning paper,

had lunch there, and continued their work on the paper in the afternoon... Carathéodory described Göttingen during the days of its glory as the 'seat of an international mathematical congress permanently in session'. With Part III, Cambridge has become the seat of an international mathematical kindergarten permanently in session.'[189]

For the ordinary student who did not aspire to these higher studies, there was a need for reform as late as the mid-twentieth century, to get rid of what the chief architect of change saw as the wrong kind of examination for the wrong kind of purpose:

> 'Honours examinations'... pride themselves particularly on their traditions and their "standards". To these examinations are subjected a heterogenous mass of students of entirely disparate attainments, and the examination purports to sort out the candidates and to label them according to the grade of their abilities. Thus in the old Mathematical Tripos there were three classes, each arranged in order of merit, and in the new there are three classes and two degrees of marks of special distinction... It is not, and prides itself that it is not, merely a useful test of industry, intelligence and comprehension. It purports to appraise, and... to some extent, though very imperfectly, it does appraise, higher gifts than these... It is these examinations... which I would destroy if I had the power.[190]

Cambridge at the end of the eighteenth century was in the doldrums, in need of reform and revitalization in many respects, overtaken by the dissenting academies in the areas of its natural supremacy, the teaching and development of the new sciences. It was awaiting the transformation which was about to begin.

5 THE NINETEENTH-CENTURY TRANSFORMATION

Students have fun

Clubs for students had probably always existed, especially for sport, gambling or just for drinking, and they must always to some extent have reflected the social expectations of their members. They were not necessarily formal arrangements. Thomas Adkin from Norfolk, who graduated in 1782, took a suite of rooms opposite the entrance to Trinity at the White Bear Inn, where Heffer's book shop now stands. Adkin was so hospitable that his rooms became known as Adkin College, until he overreached himself and became embarrassed financially.

Then there were grown-up clubs, which might want to attract students from the influential classes, to the concern of the university authorities. The Pitt Club was founded in 1837 to honour William Pitt and to work for the election of would-be Tory members of Parliament. It eventually had its own club house in Jesus Lane. This had opened in 1863, built by the Roman Bath Co. with the intention of providing Cambridge with a public bath the size of a swimming pool; but Cambridge found it did not want a Roman Bath and various attempts to coax the townspeople in with free offers failed, so the building became available for the club. The club fell into disrepute over allegations of bribing voters, and William Whewell, Master of Trinity, gave it to understand that it was not considered appropriate for undergraduates to attend its dinners.[1]

Serious and high-minded student clubs became fashionable. Here the informal associations of their elders which we have already seen turning into 'learned societies' had junior counterparts. The Cambridge Apostles began in 1820 as an example of this new trend in student societies. The Society regarded itself as 'secret' though its existence was widely known. It was a particularly 'Trinity College' group, but not exclusively so. It was a privilege to be elected to it, and the duties of membership were taken seriously. The members met every Saturday evening for serious debate, with the evening's 'paper' given by the appointed member, who traditionally stood on the hearth-rug to deliver it. There was an element of rhetorical display but hard debate followed.[2]

The Apostles tended to go into public service or the academic or literary worlds. They were not, for the most part, nature's businessmen, though some of them tried and a few succeeded. Henry Romilly was to become a merchant in Liverpool and others went into the expanding industries of the time, shipping, textile manufacturing, bleaching and dyeing, insurance and finance.[3] Henry Sidgwick (1838–1900), whom we have met as a maverick don supporting the cause of women in Cambridge, dictated to his wife on his deathbed his own sense of the guiding spirit of the Society:

> I can only describe it as the spirit of the pursuit of truth with absolute devotion and unreserved by a group of intimate friends, who were perfectly frank with each other and indulged in any amount of humorous sarcasm and playful banter, and yet each respects the other when he discourses, tried to learn from him and see what he sees. Absolute candour was the only duty that the tradition of the society enforced.[4]

Societies began to be formed for the purpose of pursuing hobbies or special interests. F.C. Burnand, an Old Etonian, had made quite a name for himself at school in 'theatricals':

> In the October term of 1854, my first term at Trinity, the notion occurred to me how much more amusing than cars, drinking, and supper, would be amateur theatricals...so it became known and accepted, at college, that I was an authority in theatricals, and before the term was out, we had contrived a capital little stage in our rooms, opposite Trinity College, over a grocer's shop, now swept away...Lads...slim and guiltless of whisker or moustache, downy fledglings...could easily "make up" for the female characters, and represent them admirably, voice excepted.

He notes that 'at that time the "moustache movement" had barely commenced'.[5] The first production was a success and it was decided to move into a real theatre, the one at Barnwell, half an hour's walk away. Burnand was told that this would require permission from the Vice-Chancellor. 'I had not an idea what a Vice-Chancellor was like. I didn't believe in him, any more than did Mrs. Prig in Sairey Gamp's Mrs. Harris. I thought he was a sort of Guy Faux figure on a woolsack. I had no reverence.'[6] 'I had said in my heart, There is no Vice-Chancellor;[7] and, in fact, I did not, at that time, realize the full extend of University authority'.[8]

> We were not at all sure what penalty might be incurred for acting stage-plays without a licence ... we might be 'gated' for the test of the term, and as that meant a most severe restriction on our liberty, no one cared to run such a risk, especially those who lived outside college, and who when 'gated' would have no companions to share their imprisonment, and no cheerful quadrangle, or cloisters, to lounge in.[9]

He describes his visit to the Vice-Chancellor to ask for the necessary permission. The Vice-Chancellor, he found, was

> a short, wizened, dried-up, elderly gentleman, with little legs and a big head, like a serious Punch doll, wearing his academical cap, and with his gown hitched up under his elbows, which gave him the appearance of having recently finished a hornpipe before I came in.[10]

He had mislaid his glasses and was due at a meeting and was under the impression that his visitor was a Fellow of a College, or at least a graduate; he envisaged a Greek play, perhaps? In the end he was persuaded to lay the general question before the Heads of House. 'This was the first step taken towards obtaining official recognition for an amateur University performance.' Whatever the confused Vice-Chancellor actually said to the heads is not known, but they said no. Then the Athenaeum Club 'which was *the* University club' put on a show of their own and authority did nothing.[11] Burnard's club took courage. It performed. 'Terence was magnificently arrayed in bright check trousers, a very white waistcoat, a light dustcoat, and glossy white hat. This wasn't the sort of "Terence" whose classical works Vice-Chancellor Guest would have had on our boards'.[12]

The maintenance of an often precarious balance between seriousness and fun runs through the century in the lives and activities of students, though Burnand, for one, doubted if it could quite be managed by dons 'There is no such creature, properly speaking, as a young Don. If a man is a Don by nature, he is never young. There are no such comfortable places anywhere as those held by the college Dons in residence. Their life is simply a luxurious development of bachelor existence in club and chambers' ... 'Dons ... probably, never partook of the generally hilarious undergraduate's temperament – the healthy outburst of youth and the overflow of animal spirits, peculiarly

English in its boisterous character, and turned off into various channels of harmless recreation'.[13] A description of a debate in the Cambridge Union on 28 November 1889 hits the characteristic mix before:

the enormous throng which assembled to hear Mr. Hyndman on Tuesday...[The] debate...resolved itself into something like a game of Aunt Sally, Mr. Hyndman personating the lady in questions while the other orators did the duty of marksman at his devoted head'.

He was too rigid about his programme of reform.[14] In the vastly energetic strivings of nineteenth-century Cambridge to adjust itself to the new industrial world, the students took a limited part. Yet to a considerable extent, it was meant for their benefit, and we shall see students being taken on educational walks and trips by tutors who wished to share with them their own discoveries in the new arena of 'academic research'.

*   *   *

The early nineteenth-century call for reform

Robert Southey's *Letters from England*,[15] published in 1807, pretend to look at England as a stranger might. This was a fashionable genre of social commentary at the time, and Southey's device of pretending to be a foreigner himself had literary precedent; the letters could claim a place in a type of travel writing about England, sometimes by Englishmen, with a few examples by genuine foreigners. Nor did he think it necessary that all his researches should be his own and original. He made use of the observations friends passed on to him and there is evidence that he was expressing quite widely held views. The 'letters' were published with the fiction that they had been translated from Spanish originals written by one 'Don Manuel Alvarez Espriella'. He had some challenging things to say about the universities of the day.

In Letter 45 he describes a visit to Cambridge. Southey makes use of the opportunity to discuss the purpose of a university education. He sees it, in the person of the fictional Spaniard, as affording a time of socially approved leisure for intellectual pursuits, *otium cum dignitate*. *Otium cum dignitate* was the kind of thing Cicero had longed for as a busy Roman civil servant, the chance to write philosophy books in retirement, and it was largely the privilege of those who could afford the leisure in the first place. But no, Don Manuel is told, university is often a mere social episode in the life of rich young men. The practical benefit to society is real enough though. It consists in the acquirement of a general awareness of the way the world wags, its ideals and expectations, once learnt never to be lost:

> I inquired what were the real advantages of these institutions to the country at large, and to the individuals who study in them. 'They are of this service,' he replied, 'to the country at large, that they are the great schools by which established opinions are inculcated and perpetuated...A knowledge of the world, that is to say or our world and the men in it, is gained here, and that knowledge remains when Greek and geometry are forgotten'.

A social need is being met, if not an intellectual one. On this understanding, a student's time at university is a period of acclimatization or acculturation. In a sense this is what Wordsworth says he found, except that he did not feel under pressure to use his time as a student to become a good citizen and to prepare to make a useful practical contribution to the national economy. He was learning to be a poet.

Other outside observers of the scene were pressing for reform for reasons which were as much social as academic and which reflect a similar stirring of the notion that universities ought to redesign their teaching and examining, to the benefit of society. Richard Lovell Edgeworth (1744–1817) (Oxford and Dublin) was the father of Maria Edgeworth (1768–1849), his eventual collaborator, and probably the cleverer of the two. Richard Edgeworth's *Essays on Professional Education* (London, 1809)[16] lists a series of 'professions' so broadly conceived as to include mere 'ways of life' and mingled in no particular order with those requiring preliminary study: clerical, military and naval, medical, being a country gentleman, law, being a statesman, being a prince. Edgeworth begins from the presumption that parents will consider their children's natural aptitudes and ensure that their early education seeks to improve on innate ability. He has some sensible suggestions about ways of teaching history, for example, and thinks a little less Latin and Greek and a little more of other things might be beneficial in schools preparing boys for life. Clerical and military/naval education are discussed principally in terms of the appropriate character and mode of life which fit a man for one of these professions. He argues that the universities ought to take much more seriously the need to teach a broader range of subjects, including what would be of practical usefulness.

The review of Edgeworth's book which appeared in the influential *Edinburgh Review* in 1809[17] had surprising and long-term consequences. It set various hares running, for the reviewer agreed with Edgeworth that it was time to do something to curb 'the excessive abuse of classical learning in England'. Edgeworth notes, as Southey does, that an established system can become self-perpetuating and self-validating if no challenge shakes up its complacency:

> The routine of tuition established in colleges in some degree obliges professors to pursue the course of their predecessors; and their natural indolence and love of authoritative superiority perhaps increase the attachment to ancient forms and dogmas. Let them act candidly and they will not lower their real authority.[18]

Edgeworth argued, again as Southey had done, that when a university's courses become fossilized, it ceases to be enquired why things are done thus and thus; it is enough to insist that they have traditionally been done that way: 'Nobody doubts, that there are parts of most college courses, which are useless in the business of the world, and ridiculous in the present state of society, but which gothic custom has retained.'

By 'gothic' Edgeworth means the system of instruction which was now disparaged as 'scholastic', but which had put a spine of bony firmness into the medieval curriculum with its insistence on a mastery of advanced logic. 'The common sense of mankind now duly appreciates the logic of the schools [i.e. at a low level of esteem],' says Edgeworth. At the same time, he recognizes that logic can still serve a useful purpose because there are professional fields such as law, where it remains a necessary practical skill:

> But we must separate the cumbersome and useless apparatus of scholastic logic from its serviceable rules and principles. It is peculiarly necessary for a lawyer to be expert at logic: he must know both its use and its abuse, that he may reason accurately itself and may expose the sophistry of his opponents... The disputes of lawyers frequently depend upon verbal distinctions, and upon the various and inaccurate significations annexed to general terms.[19]

His proposal was that there should be a fearless review of current assumptions and practice, that the best should be retained, new emphases introduced, and everything tested against the criterion of usefulness to the student and benefit to society, with no preconceptions that one area of study was inherently better or higher than another:

> New schools, that are not restricted to any established routine, should give a fair trial to experiments in education, which afford a rational prospect of success…Destroy nothing – injure none – but let the public try whether they cannot have something better.

The *Edinburgh Review* drew attention to another aspect of what he was saying.[20] It was Edgeworth's contention that 'Greek and Latin are insensibly become almost the only test of a cultivated mind' (which would be lopsided) and that the more obscure its researches the greater the respect they have come to command (which puts them beyond the reach of most people):

> A learned man! – a scholar! – a man of erudition! Upon whom are these epithets of approbation bestowed?…the epithet of Scholar, is reserved for him who writes on the Œolic reduplication, and is familiar with Sylburgius his method of arranging defectives.

So an awed respect for high classical scholarship may have the effect of causing society to undervalue other areas of intellectual endeavour: 'It is suggested that "the greatest chemist, or the greatest mechanician, or the most profound political economist of his time" would not be rated "equal in dignity of understanding."'[21]

We may be glimpsing in such remarks an early appearance of a cult of anti-élitism which came to take a peculiarly British form. It was compounded of disparagement of the 'learnedness' of the specialist whose knowledge is so obscure that few people can understand it, of no practical value (and by the same token, useless to the majority of the population), and acquired – it is alleged – only by the privileged. Two kinds of élite, the social and the intellectual, are conflated, and a link created in the popular mind between advanced and disinterested learning and social privilege, tainting the first with resentment of the second. This was to prove an immensely important thread of influence by the late twentieth century, and it remains so.

So, it was proposed, the overhaul of assumptions should include an emphasis on the presumed equality of all disciplines, a readiness to introduce new ones, and an emphasis on useful knowledge, in a revised sense of 'useful':[22] 'In a place of education, we would give to all knowledge an equal chance for distinction; and would trust to the varieties of human disposition, that every science worth cultivation would be cultivated.'

The belief that all studies are to be treated as though they are of equal value was to be of great long-term importance as the curriculum broadened and the question of vocational and applicable learning grew more and more challenging:

> Looking always to *real utility* [emphasis added] as our guide, we should see, with equal pleasure, a studious and inquisitive mind arranging the productions of nature, investigating the qualities of bodies, or mastering the difficulties of the learned languages. We should not care whether he were chemist, naturalist, or scholar, because we know it to be as necessary that matter should be studied, and subdued to the use of man, as that taste should be gratified, and imagination inflamed.[23]

'How modern!' the reader may exclaim at this point.

The 'Oxford controversy' about the future shape of higher education attracted interest in Cambridge circles, too, as Coleridge's reference to it attests. Samuel Taylor Coleridge (1772–1834) mentions it being talked about in Cambridge. He himself had been at Cambridge from 1791 to 1794. The presumptions in Cambridge had been different in recent generations, but appeared just as fixed in their way, and, it began to be argued, possibly just as much in need of a thorough shake-up. In the record of Coleridge's *Table Talk* for April 1811 is a note of an occasion when there was discussion of the current controversy about what universities should be teaching. At this date this was a way of asking whether the most appropriate balance was being struck with mathematics at Oxford, not whether the classics should be abandoned: 'We then got upon the Oxford controversy...He wished some portion of mathematics was more essential to a degree at Oxford, as he thought a gentleman's education incomplete without it.'[24]

The progressive implementation of the 'Edgeworth agenda' was a consequence of developments both inside the world of the universities and in society at large as the academic and industrial sciences came into being and the Industrial Revolution created a need for what would now be called a 'skilled workforce'.

The three developments in the 'intellectual' life of nineteenth-century universities which were needed before this could have its full impact were the emergence of the notion of academic 'research'; some hard new thinking about the distinctive characteristics of 'scientific method'; and the identification of distinguishable 'sciences' to use it on. While Cambridge's academics were considering all this, an 'Industrial Revolution' was taking place in Britain and factories needed skilled workers up to the level of 'industrial chemists' and individuals who knew enough about geology to direct the digging of the canal network. The trick was going to be to bring the two sides of the educational enterprise together.

There were prejudices to be overcome at the other end of the social scale, too, and important considerations to be addressed about the level at which the employees of the future should be educated in order to make their contribution in the 'Mechanical Age'. Did the disadvantaged deserve society's help to better themselves intellectually? Henry Mayhew (1812–87) (who ran away to sea from Westminster School and was not himself a university man), took an active part in the 1840s in getting newspaper coverage for the concerns he felt. In *London Labour and the London Poor* (London, 1851), he published a collection of his articles on the problem of poverty. In Chapter 1, he discusses the educational attainments of the children of the costermongers. Few of them are sent to school at all. One mother he encountered who happened to be able to read had tried to teach her children to read too, but this seemed extremely unusual. The children are taught to live by their wits and get their livings on the streets like their parents, who can in most cases envisage no more ambitious possibility for them. Some of the Christian Socialists supported him, including the two 'Cambridge' men Charles Kingsley (1819–75) and F.D. Maurice (1805–72); nevertheless, he had his active critics, who tended to the traditional view that few of the poor were 'deserving'. But even if the poor did not deserve it, should they be offered better educational opportunities to become a more useful workforce in the national interest?

The 'social agenda' of Cambridge was, then, going to change in the course of the nineteenth century.

* * *

Scientific research becomes an academic activity with industrial outreach

William Whewell's review of the need for reform

William Whewell (1794–1866) was born to a father who was a carpenter, but he was able to enter Trinity College, Cambridge, in 1812, with an Exhibition (a form of student financial support) to fund his studies. He had all-round abilities. He won a medal for poetry in 1814 and was a sufficiently good mathematician to graduate as Second Wrangler in 1816. He became a Fellow of Trinity in 1817 and remained there until in 1841 he became Master of the College. He held that office until his death. Meanwhile he held more than one Cambridge Professorship, again covering a considerable span of subjects – Mineralogy from 1828 to 1832 and Moral Theology (1838–55). Politically astute, energetic, afraid of nothing intellectually, he had an immense effect on the development of intellectual life in Cambridge during his lifetime. He was highly conscious of the need to review both the method and the content of what was taught in the University and to bring together the innovatory and original 'research' work of the scientists and the needs of students.

Whewell's review of the past of universities

Whewell was prompted to write a letter to the Editor of the *Edinburgh Review* in 1837, and to write an 'Edgeworth' of his own. The *Review* of 1837 had carried a review of the new edition of Francis Bacon's works.[25] Whewell's *On the Principles of English University Education* included an appendix 'Thoughts on the study of mathematics as part of a liberal education' and the letter to the Editor of the *Edinburgh Review* prompted by the review there of the first edition of *Thoughts*. *On the principles* is divided into three sections, 'Of the subjects of university teaching'; 'Of direct and indirect teaching' (on the important question whether study at universities should be geared primarily to the passing of examinations); 'Of discipline' (concerned with moral 'formation').

By then significant change was under way in Cambridge, and Whewell considered it high time for some further stocktaking. Yet Whewell puts the benefits of the existing state of affairs very high, at least as regards the past. He argues that there may be good reason for radical review in the present generation, but universities have done a good job for the world so far:

> The cultivated world...has been bound together...by living upon a common intellectual estate...all the civilized world has been one intellectual nation; and it is this which has made it so great and prosperous a nation.[26]

Yet it is his contention that the continuation of merely theoretical studies is likely to lead to stagnation; when it comes to scientific study there has to be a practical application or learning grinds to a halt: 'The progress of science corresponds to the time of practical teaching;

the stationary, or retrograde, period of science, is the period when philosophy was the instrument of education.'[27]

He argues from history that this has always been the pattern. The Greeks saw philosophy as the highest form of intellectual culture 'till civilization itself sickened and declined. It was so, too, among the Neoplatonists, the schoolmen, the theologians of the Middle Ages'.

He suggests (mistakenly as to the facts of course, but that does not invalidate his general point) that the situation was rescued by the pragmatic monastic tradition, for 'in the monasteries there again grew up a method of practical teaching from which the system of the English universities had its origin'.[28] Then the academic mind was drawn irresistibly to the theoretical once more and the practical usefulness of learning diminished: 'In vain do the schoolmen of the middle ages build system upon system, as the schoolmen of Athens and Alexandria had done before. The centuries roll on, and bring no day.'

Once more the situation had to be 'rescued'. His understanding is that the 'religious orders' in the person of 'a Franciscan friar' (Roger not Francis Bacon) had insisted on review. This Bacon 'lifts up his voice against the saw of Aristotle, and points to the far-off temple of science, declaring that mathematics is its gate and its key'.

Bacon's announcement is found to be true: 'The universities of Europe assume a form in which such a training goes on...and we reach the present condition of the civilized world.'

But the German universities returned to the speculative method, complains Whewell, and another dead end loomed. The student 'is not disturbed by any demands on his mind' and the result is

> 'such men as [are] utterly incapable even of comprehending and appreciating the most conspicuous examples of the advance of science...Hegel and Schelling, cannot understand that Newton went further than Kepler had gone in physical astronomy, and [they] despise Newton's optical doctrines in comparison with the vague Aristotelian dogmas of Göethe respecting colors'.

'Thus the experiment on education...appears to be quite...consistent in its result' (looked at historically), he concludes with satisfaction.[29] The question is not whether he was right in his historical analysis, but whether his contemporaries were influenced by this argument, which chimed so well with what Edgeworth had said. From a Cambridge vantage-point this meant encouraging a movement away from pure mathematics to the sciences more broadly conceived. From an Oxford point of view it meant deciding where and how to introduce more mathematics and science.

Whewell starts a debate

Whewell's *Thoughts*, rather to his surprise, prompted an energetic response in the *Edinburgh Review* on exactly this question. He had meant to write only about the best mode of conducting mathematical examinations in Cambridge, but he had been taken up by his critics on the subject of the way the balance should be struck between pure and applied mathematics. Whewell had suggested that one of the educational benefits of the study of mathematics was that it is, as a 'mental discipline', 'an example and exercise of exact reasoning'. 'Nothing is more common than to hear persons urge very foolish arguments in support of very just opinions.' This means, he admits, that there is a 'chance of being practically right and speculatively wrong' but he urges that 'this is not a state of mind in which those can acquiesce contentedly whose object is the mental culture of man'.[30]

He contrasts the two main methods of training reasoning in use in the universities of the day (logic and mathematics), particularly in Cambridge where mathematics is taken very seriously. He makes the point that mathematics is inherently a practical method, since the student can see that he is getting the answers right and learns what 'works':

> He is accustomed to a chain of deduction, where each link hangs from the preceding; and thus he learns continuity of attention and coherency of thought... and thus he acquires a just persuasion of the importance of principles... and of the necessary and constant identity of the conclusions legitimately deduced from them.[31]

Whewell was as well aware as medieval university teachers had been that geometry may be argued to be a special case, perhaps unique in its capacity for using the demonstrative method. He explores some of the implications[32] in an extended discussion which reflects the debate of contemporary fellow mathematicians on this point. His idea is that the application of the practical benefits of a mathematically-based training of powers of reasoning will best be realized by giving the student Mechanics and Hydrostatics to study, for those involve 'the most simple branches of mathematics, after Plane Geometry': 'The great practical utility of these sciences would weigh with many persons, and their application to a vast variety of questions which come under the notice of everyone, and often demand our thoughts even in the course of common life.'[33]

He weakens his position here in an important respect, of which he was at least dimly aware. Before offering these two subjects, he explores some of the difficulties which arise as soon as the mathematically trained student, with his exacting standards of reasoning, begins to attempt to apply mathematical or demonstrative reasoning in the burgeoning new sciences of the time. The danger is that he will confuse 'arbitrary' definitions with true first principles: 'If he be left to suppose that mathematical truths depend ultimately upon the evidence of the senses, he will look in other subjects for evidence equally palpable' and 'the habit of ever aiming at extreme generality' could also be dangerously misleading.[34] Whewell was tiptoeing unknowingly towards the complex of questions to be raised by Thomas Kuhn and Karl Popper, but still partly steering himself by the approach of the Middle Ages and Roger and Francis Bacon.

*   *   *

Forming the academic sciences and making them intellectually respectable

It was not a foregone conclusion that in the course of the nineteenth century modern science was going to become a province of 'academic' activity, with its research headquarters in universities. In much of Europe, the new research institutes which were being founded remained separate from universities, which continued to concentrate on the provision of courses for students seeking degrees and other accredited qualifications. This division has continued to affect the framework of European university education. The story was different in England partly because of the way a few individuals, among whom Whewell was to be prominent, ensured that the ancient universities, particularly Cambridge, took control of scientific study.

In the seventeenth and eighteenth centuries, academics who happened to share their enthusiasms were not regarded by the independent 'gentlemen of science' as being more entitled to regard themselves seriously as working at the edge of science. That was about to change. At the beginning of the nineteenth century not to complete one's degree was still no great bar to being taken seriously. Charles Babbage (1791–1871) entered Trinity College, Cambridge, in April 1810, though he left it for Peterhouse two years later. He had a lively time as a student, but although his intellectual powers were obvious, he did not get an honours degree. The thesis about God which he tried to 'defend' in the preliminary examination designed to rank the candidates was considered by the examiners to be blasphemous and he never took his final examination. This meant he could not seek a college Fellowship.

He left Cambridge and set off on a continental tour lasting a year, during which he met European scientists and saw what they were doing in laboratories and workshops. Back in London he began on the 'lecture circuit', and his lectures at the Royal Institution, only a year or so after he had left Cambridge under a cloud, won him the Fellowship of the Royal Society in 1816. He joined his Cambridge friend John Herschel in founding the Astronomical Society.

Cambridge 'recognized' him at last by electing him Lucasian Professor of Mathematics in 1828. He hardly ever appeared in Cambridge during the years he held the Chair (which he did until 1839) and he did not give any lectures. But he wrote and published busily, across the same phenomenal range of subjects as a number of his contemporaries in this last period when it was possible to be a scientific polymath and be taken seriously. And like others, he took an active interest in the industrial application of modern science. His *On the Economy of Machinery and Manufactures* first published in 1832, brought together his knowledge of what was going on in factories and workshops in England and on the Continent. It is perhaps from this area of his interests that there emerged his invention of an 'engine' for calculating, which has made him famous as the 'father of the computer'. Ada Lovelace, Lord Byron's daughter (1815–52), a natural mathematician, who would today perhaps have become a pioneering computer programmer, became interested in his attempt to design an 'analytical engine', which would have been an early computer. Babbage called her 'the enchantress of numbers'.

Meanwhile, John Herschel (1792–1871), son of the astronomer William Herschel, became a student at St. John's College, Cambridge, in 1809. As an undergraduate he had started a society (of which Charles Babbage was a member) to press for revolutionary reform of mathematics, which intended to move decisively on from Isaac Newton. He graduated as Senior Wrangler in 1813 and he was elected to the Royal Society at once. But he was already too controversial a figure for Cambridge to welcome him among its mathematical academics, although he nearly got elected to the Professorship of Chemistry in 1815. After briefly considering reading for the Bar, he went back to Cambridge to a junior lecturing post. He found he did not like having to deal with pupils but he could not leave mathematics, and the work he did in the next few years was important enough to win him the Copley Medal of the Royal Society in 1821. Nor did he stop working on Chemistry. He was also interested in Astronomy, founding another Society in 1820 for the purpose – a body which matured in 1831 into the Royal Astronomical Society.

He travelled in Europe, which made him the ideal choice to be the 'foreign secretary' of this new society. With his father's encouragement Herschel was to concentrate on astronomical observation from the 1820s until 1838. He was publishing steadily, not only on specific research topics but also, in 1830, an influential *Preliminary Discourse on the Study of Natural Philosophy*. This was translated into several European languages and was important in the formation of many of his British contemporaries, including William Whewell in Cambridge.

Despite the success of these challenging figures in defying the need to behave themselves intellectually and conform with the University's expectations, the lack of an agreed ladder to professional standing could turn out to be a disadvantage. David Brewster (1781–1868) had an uncomfortable experience in trying to get evidence of his scientific credentials in order to improve his chances of an appointment to a Professorship at Edinburgh. He set about 'qualifying' himself with considerable determination, with the aim of becoming a Professor. The method of the day was to solicit open 'testimonials' from well-known referees. Brewster provided him with letters of introduction and he travelled to meet the people he needed to impress. His visit to Cambridge was particularly important in gaining him the supporters he was going to need, for there he met Whewell and Adam Sedgwick among others. When the Chair of Natural Philosophy at Edinburgh became vacant he organized his support with energy until he had 59 testimonials, which he had printed under the title *Testimonials in Favour of James D. Forbes ... as a Candidate for the Chair of Natural Philosophy in the University of Edinburgh* (Edinburgh, 1832). Forbes, the son of an Edinburgh banker, got his Chair.

* * *

The 'learned societies' adjust their standards

For some decades of the nineteenth century academe and the 'societies', still operating as parallel universes, jostled to become the accepted forum for serious science. (Governments could take an interest too. A Geological Survey was set up in 1835, one of a series of Government 'initiatives' throughout the nineteenth century, but the really important wrestling match was that which engaged the universities and the societies.)

There seems to have been a good deal of mutual backscratching by way of exchange of 'recognition' among would-be serious scientists once the advantages of gaining an 'accepted reputation' of the sort Forbes found he needed began to be recognized. The societies had expectations about the maintaining of standards. The scientific fraternities liked to think that they conferred membership only on those of appropriate knowledgeableness and proven good character. John Philips (1800–74) sent a 'signed obligation to good behaviour' with his ten guinea subscription to the Geological Society in January 1828.[35] Nevertheless, several examples of election to the Royal Society in extreme youth noted in this chapter involved young men with influential connections. Sir Humphrey Davy (1778–1829), President of the Royal Society in London from 1820 to 1827, wrote to William Harcourt (1789–1871) in January 1824 to express his pleasure in being elected to the Yorkshire Philosophical Society and to promise that Harcourt will be 'proposed as a Fellow of the Royal Society at the next meeting'.[36] Some effort was made to capture leading figures and famous names as members. 'I enclose an epistle from our Secretary to the geologist Smith, signifying his election as an honorary member of our Institution,' wrote Conybeare of the Bristol Institution to Harcourt with a request to forward it.[37]

It began to be asked whether the local or specialist scientific societies should remain independent or work together in some way. Responses to this idea were mixed. Local officers were anxious to retain control of their own affairs and not have them swallowed up in the activities of a larger body. 'It is not thought practicable at the Bristol Institution to enter into any *regular compact* with any other body as to lectures,'[38] wrote William Conybeare (1787–1857) of the Bristol Institution and the Bristol Philosophical and Literary Society, to William Harcourt, who had helped to found the Yorkshire Philosophical Society in 1822, having been awakened to the interest of geology by hearing William Buckland lecture at Oxford (19 April 1824). Nevertheless, he thought that without their entering into any 'regular compact' it would be 'very desirable' that some 'mutual understanding should be established between the managing committees on this subject': 'it is believed that if [and] when the Birmingham Council have determined on applying to A or B to lecture there they would communicate their intention and vice-versa.'

This could be mutually advantageous 'but any more general treaty is not considered advisable'. In an earlier letter of 17 January, he had commented to Harcourt: 'In many respects I much like your plan of circular lecturers, if practicable, though it smacks strongly of being borrowed from the itinerant preachers of the Methodist Conference,' he adds teasingly.[39]

The chief problem, as Conybeare saw it, was how 'the collective body of the different institutions [was] to agree?'... 'When, where and how is it to be convened? Suppose it assembled: will not each district have some promising protégé of its own to support?'[40]

Lectures delivered to the societies sometimes took the form of making public some piece of research an individual had completed or the gleanings of 'study' travels and field-work. This would be new work, at the 'cutting edge' of knowledge. In late 1826 Harcourt wrote to Roderick Murchison (1792–1871) to say, 'I was much gratified to hear of the success of your researches and of your intention to communicate them to the public'.[41] Such public launchings of discoveries might be no more than the expression of a simple wish to share them with the world for the common good, but they could also be a means of ensuring that ownership of the idea could not subsequently be disputed. They were naturally also a further route to fame and the building of a reputation.

There were 'conferences' too, though it was discovered that organizing a conference brought its difficulties, in this same area of striking a balance between exclusiveness and popular education.[42] Was anyone who wished to be allowed to come? 'The efficiency of the society will be destroyed if "the terms of admission" be too "lax"', it was suggested.[43] The dependence of societies upon the goodwill of volunteers to run them was put under strain by their very success. Managing Committees even of small local societies (whose members were mostly interested volunteers, active would-be scientists themselves), could find themselves with a considerable load of work. William Conybeare's description of the tasks which fell to him as convenor of the first meetings of the Bristol Philosophical and Literary Society shows how heavy the administrative burden could be. He 'was attending numerous committees' 'getting ready lists of all donations', 'answering arrears of letters', as well as preparing a 'paper' on 'the origin and history of philosophical associations'.[44]

Societies liked to publish 'Proceedings' to record the success of their endeavours, and this also made it possible for individuals to see their work in print, but – as in the case of the early issues of the *Transactions of the Royal Historical Society*[45] – an editor or editorial committee could find himself with a drawerful of contributions of dubious lasting value because of the mixed character of addresses to meetings. There were some who thought it was important to restrict voting membership of scientific societies to serious scientists, who were to be known by the fact that they had 'written on scientific subjects'.

So getting one's paper published in the *Proceedings* of a respected society could be important to the building of one's reputation.

> I think therefore the German regulation an exceedingly good one. All interested in science are admitted and enrolled and attend all meetings and take part in the discussions; but whenever any matter comes to a vote in the general meeting – that is upon all matters connected with the laws and regulations of the society – only those who have written on scientific subjects vote.[46]

Further 'positioning' which was bound to affect the development of academic science was the call for popularization. Sometimes a 'course' of lectures would be given on behalf of a 'society', for which the lecturer would expect to be paid, and which might have a different, more 'popular' purpose. John Philips (1800–74), who had his living to earn, wrote to the Yorkshire Philosophical Society in January 1826 to say that for the money offered he could give only seven lectures. 'If the Council are disposed to stretch their expenditure to £40' he can offer eight, including a final one on 'a connected view of the whole modern system of geology'.[47] Such lectures could be pitched at a popular level for interest only, or make a serious attempt to take a scholarly overview of the state of knowledge in a general area of study in a way the general listener could understand. Popular science was proving attractive:

> All knowledge ... is fitted to attract; for the mere gratification of curiosity is itself a pleasure: but some kinds of knowledge are so much more easily apprehended than others ... that they may be rendered interesting to a class of readers far more sluggish or volatile than ever think of opening books of instruction.

The book being reviewed here came from *The Library of Entertaining Knowledge. Vol. I. Part I. The Menageries-Quadrupeds Described and Drawn from Living Subjects*: 'the purpose is to teach zoology analytically, by proceeding from particular instances to general laws'.[48]

Charles Babbage was nervous of a danger to standards if science thus lowered itself to the level of the 'popular'. He favoured exclusiveness. The bold perversity which had got Babbage into trouble in his final examinations as a Cambridge student prompted an attack on the scientific establishment which was forming in England. In *Reflections on the Decline of Science in England* (1830) he criticized the Royal Society, annoying even some of his closest friends, such as Herschel. Learned societies can, he argues, help with the costs of printing a discoverer's findings, which is beneficial to science, but it is important that they should limit their membership so that 'it becomes an object of ambition to be admitted on their list'.[49] England is letting too many in to the Royal Society.[50] The proliferation of smaller, specialist, societies ought to be a sign of the health of science, but not if they are badly run. Worst run of all, claims Babbage, is the Royal Society itself. Standards have slipped and all is patronage and rivalry.

The universities take charge: the British Association for the Advancement of Science

The universities took charge of serious science only from the middle of the nineteenth century, not closing down the 'learned societies' but to some degree sidelining them and turning them into clubs for the bestowal of honours and approval through admission to their membership. Two developments were probably most important here. One was the take-over by Cambridge academics in the 1830s of the newly-created British Association for the Advancement of Science. The other was the demand created by the new and multiplying civic universities and the local industrialists who were funding them and wanted them to produce industrial scientists to work in their factories.

The British Association for the Advancement of Science had its beginnings in a wish to keep up with Europe in launching a grand scheme, which would have the additional benefit of providing aspiring scientists with a route to personal professional standing which would be internationally recognizable. David Brewster wrote to Charles Babbage in February 1829: 'I am quite delighted with your plan of a great European Academy. It holds out singular advantages to science, and I wish you would set your shoulders to the scheme.'[51] Brewster wrote again, this time to Henry Brougham (1778–1868) in March 1829, to try to forward the project:

> Mr. Babbage has written to me about the establishment of a great scientific association or society embracing all Europe. The idea has sprung out of the Congress of Philosophers at Berlin...and has been warmly embraced by many leading continental philosophers. The power of such a body to promote science, and give respectability to the various classes of men who sustain the intellectual character of the age is obvious...Mr. Babbage and I would take the oar if you would touch the helm.[52]

In tension with such ambitious plans was the conviction shared by Brewster and Babbage that, far from being ready for such a giant leap, science in England was in decline. Brewster wrote an article on this hypothesis for the influential *Quarterly Review* in 1830.[53] In preparation, he did his research, journalistically speaking, sending a letter to Babbage in which he asked for information on such matters as 'the scientific institutions, offices etc which ought to be filled by men of science'; whether the academicians of Berlin are paid by the Government; whether the Royal Society derives its income apart from subscriptions; whether progress on the 'machine' Babbage is working on is 'stopped by withdrawal of former allowances'; how Herschel and his telescope were funded; whether there are any known 'instances of liberality to scientific men during the present reign, unconnected with politics'; what is known of 'the state of science in Russia'; whether there are any 'examples of science being patronised in England since the time of Newton'.[54]

Brewster's motivation for this campaign was at least partly personal. He wrote to Babbage in February 1829:

> You will probably have heard that the practical astronomy chair in Edinburgh is vacant, and that the professor will have charge of the Observatory... I am desirous to have some certificates of my general scientific qualifications for such an office in case of their being needed, I therefore hope you will oblige me by one, and you would add generally to the favour if you would ask Mr. Herschel to confer upon me the same obligation.[55]

After years of unsuccessful attempt to get a university post, of which this was but a recent example, he was a man with a grievance against the scientific establishment in the universities (though it would perhaps have been more logical to resent the urban patrons who controlled appointments in Scotland until the mid-century).[56] Charles Babbage found that he shared his concern, and this 'heartbreaking subject' became the subject of an exchange of correspondence between them.[57] He too had personal animus to drive him. In 1829 Babbage had published *Reflections on the Decline of Science in England, and on Some of its Causes*[58] among which he identified as a cause the behaviour of the group which now had control of the Royal Society. John Herschel, to whom he showed a draft, advised him to 'burn it, or rewrite it'.[59] It contained personal attacks on the 'party' which had control of the Royal Society,[60] though Babbage begins by expressing a distaste for such things:

> I feel as strongly as anyone, not merely the impropriety, but the injustice of introducing private character into such

discussions. [But] The public character of every public servant is legitimate subject of discussion, and his fitness or unfitness for office may be fairly canvassed by any person.[61]

Ethical questions were arising in other connections too. Babbage describes four modes of scientific fraud, hoaxing ('no such animal exists'), forging ('the forger... records observations which he has never made'), trimming ('clipping off little bits here and there'), cooking (selective use of evidence).[62]

The 'decline' dispute, however, diminished in retrospect by what can be seen of the personal resentments of those who led it, did help to ensure that the Royal Society was not universally considered to have filled already the place in the British scientific world which it was now proposed should be occupied by the British Association for the Advancement of Science. Brewster used the opportunity to propose the Association as a means of 'reviving science' in England.[63] The plan for a British Association was mooted by Brewster in a letter to Babbage in February 1831. He had heard from a friend who had been at the recent conference in Hamburg[64] what the 'German Naturalists' were achieving, and this had 'strongly impressed' him 'with the opinion that the cause of science in England would derive great benefit from a meeting of British men of science at York in July or August next'.[65]

Brewster now had his enemies, however. Such a campaign is not quickly forgotten in academe. It was recognized that the project had a better chance 'if the plan appeared to come from London rather than from Edinburgh'.[66] The Cambridge scientists, led by William Whewell, refused to attend the meeting at York. He wrote distastefully to James Forbes (1809–68) on 14 July 1831:

I should feel no great wish to rally round D. Brewster's standard after he has thought it necessary to promulgate so bad an opinion of us who happen to be professors in universities...he has now chosen to fancy that we are all banded together to oppose his favourite doctrine of the decline of science[67]

It became a bitter irony that the very abuse of allowing the nation's scientific affairs to be dominated by an oligarchy which had led to the attempt to replace the Royal Society by a new British Association for the Advancement of Science (BAAS) had emerged in exactly the same way in the running of the Association, while the same corruptions by patronage and nepotism which had stood in Brewster's way, he believed, in his attempts to get a university post, had assisted Forbes. However, the oligarchy which came to run the BAAS, once Whewell decided to involve himself, was led by Cambridge academics, Whewell himself and a number of others, who were joined by their Oxford counterparts.[68] These universities largely took over control of British science and thus helped to ensure that the routes to acknowledged greatness, funding and influence ran through academe for the future.

* * *

'Call him a scientist'

One of the results of the mass interest in the sciences which emerged as a result of the work of the British Association for the Advancement of Science was the realization that 'science' had now become 'the sciences' and it was going to be necessary to specialize if one was to do work of value. John Herschel, who had been drawn into the controversy partly at Whewell's instigation, commented that 'No man can now hope to know more than one part of one science'.[69] The *Quarterly Review* of 1834 commented on[70]

> the want of any name by which we can designate the students of the knowledge of the material world collectively. We are informed that this difficulty was felt very oppressively by the members of the British Association for the Advancement of Science, at their meetings...in the last three summers...Philosophers was felt to be too wide and too lofty a term...savants was rather assuming...some ingenious gentleman proposed that, by analogy with artist, they might form scientist, and added that there could be no scruple in making free with this termination when we have such words as sciolist[71], economist, and atheist but this was not generally palatable.

William Whewell had a practical suggestion. 'We need very much a name to describe a cultivator of science in general. I should incline to call him a Scientist.'[72] But Cambridge was not thinking of offering degrees which would label graduates as scientists. (Indeed it is still a B.A. not a B.Sc. with which science students graduate from Cambridge.) Only when a sufficient body of recognized expertise could be pointed to could science become a 'profession'. In a profession there develops a critical mass 'which powerfully tends to repress conduct that is injurious either to the profession or to the public,' suggests Charles

Babbage.[73] Peer review is important. 'Few estimations will be found generally more correct than the opinion of a whole profession on the merits of any one of its body.'[74] These realizations were crucial, an indication of the increasing recognition of the significance of achieving something like a professional standing as a scientist.

Yet the briefest review of the trends in the terms used to describe the emerging scientific disciplines identified in the entries in the *Oxford English Dictionary* shows how uncertain it all remained. In 1735 Geology could be taken to include zoology because it included everything on earth.[75] For William Whewell in 1837, Geology had 'a strong resemblance...to philosophical archæology'.[76] In the mid-nineteenth century Archaeology began where Geology left off, chronologically speaking, though not in terms of the materials for study. ('The closing epoch of geology is that in which archæology has its beginning.'[77]) In 1876 Mineralogy looked like a 'branch' of Geology. In 1876 Geology was expected to concentrate on the rocks which form the earth's crust, while in the same decade archaeology was to concentrate on 'old structures and buried relics of the remote past'. Other 'subjects' did not, for some reason, get adopted for formal academic study, although they might lay claim to be sciences as well as arts. Architecture was captured, partly by Oxford's Ruskin and Pugin, as a Fine Art. Some were to remain *bona fide* areas of academic study, but their groupings varied. Some of the labels proposed for these new areas of scientific study did not last long. It was suggested in 1878 that Botany and Zoology together might form a 'science of living nature'. Within disciplines, too, there was a growing awareness that technical terms were important and might make for a helpful exactness. Charles Kingsley has a character in a novel complain that 'the rationalist's shallow and slipslop trick of using the word "natural" to mean in one sentence "material" and in the next, as I use it, only "normal and orderly"'.[78]

Whewell's *Novum Organum Renovatum* has a section on 'the language of science' (Book IV) in which he discusses 'Technical Terms', some of which are 'words adopted from common language, but rendered precise and determinate for purposes of science'.[79] In Botany, 'the formation of an exact descriptive language...was...the first step in that systematic construction of the technical language of science, which is one of the main features in the intellectual history of modern times'.[80] He sees other sciences as following when they saw the scientific advantages of a 'systematic improvement' of the language they used. In Mineralogy, for example, 'Werner's innovations...were the result of great acuteness, an intimate acquaintance with minerals, and a most methodical spirit: and were in most respects great improvements'. But in the case of Mineralogy the effect of clarifying the language was not the same. It 'was far from regenerating that science'. Whewell puts this down to the fact that in this case, 'scrupulous attention to most minute differences...fetters the mind, rather than disciplines it or arms it for generalization'.[81] By contrast, modifications to the 'language of Chemistry' led to definite progress.[82]

Whewell was noticing that the emerging sciences had distinctive features, affecting the ways in which they could most usefully be discussed and in what terms, if the discussion was to lead to advancement in the sciences. He made an attempt to formulate some axioms of general applicability, nevertheless. The principle that '[i]n framing scientific terms, the appropriation of old terms is preferable to the invention of new ones' (Axiom III), he takes from Bacon, who put it more floridly.[83] 'When common words are appropriated as technical terms, their meaning and relations in common use should be retained as far as can conveniently be done.'[84]

Calling a halt? Was science going too far?

There were voices expressing anxieties about this scientific free-for-all. Particular ideas were regarded as threatening even after the subsidence of the acute alarm of the educated world about the challenge geology posed – eventually successfully – to acceptance of the historical veracity of the story of the Flood as it is told in Genesis. The anxiety that the progress of science would undermine the Christian faith did not end with the concession that geology and genesis did not match. In Charles Kingsley's (1819–75) *The Water Babies* (1862–3) there are references to the issues Darwin had been raising, and although at the time of the great debate in the University Museum at Oxford[85] Kingsley was just beginning his time as Regius Professor of Modern History in Cambridge, he was certainly already interested in the implications. His inaugural lecture was entitled 'The limits of exact science applied to history'. Kingsley's connection with Cambridge had begun in 1844, when, after a period of study at King's College, London, he went to Magdalene College, planning to be ordained. He spent a period of pastoral ministry in Hampshire before he was invited back to Cambridge to be Regius Professor in 1860, apparently at least partly on the slender warrant of some historical novels for children which had pleased Prince Albert and gained his recommendation.[86]

In Chapter VI of *The Water Babies*, Charles Kingsley reviews the history of mankind, from happy innocence, through stages of increasing sophistication, until the way people live begins to affect their appearance and their very constitution, ending with a satirical paradox:

> 'But there is a hairy one among them,' said Ellie.
>
> 'Ah!' said the fairy, 'that will be a great man in his time, and chief of all the tribe.'
>
> And, when she turned over the next five hundred years, it was true.
>
> For this hairy chief had had hairy children, and they hairier children still; and every one wished to marry hairy husbands, and have hairy children too; for the climate was growing so damp that none but the hairy ones could live: all the rest coughed and sneezed, and had sore throats, and went into consumptions, before they could grow up to be men and women.
>
> Then the fairy turned over the next five hundred years. And they were fewer still.
>
> 'Why, there is one on the ground picking up roots,' said Ellie, 'and he cannot walk upright.'
>
> No more he could; for in the same way that the shape of their feet had altered, the shape of their backs had altered also.
>
> 'Why,' cried Tom, 'I declare they are all apes.'

So the section ends with a reference to Darwin's theory, coupled with a touch of the Hermetic tradition, with its ancient warning that those who behave like animals will grow more beastly:

> 'Yes!' said the fairy, solemnly, half to herself, as she closed the wonderful book. 'Folks say now that I can make beasts into men, by circumstance, and selection, and competition, and so forth. Well, perhaps they are right; and perhaps, again, they are wrong. That is one of the seven things which I am forbidden to tell, till the coming of the Cocqcigrues; and, at all events, it is no concern of theirs. Whatever their ancestors were, men they are; and I advise them to behave as such, and act accordingly. But let them recollect this, that there are two sides to every question, and a downhill as well as an uphill road; and, if I can turn beasts into men, I can, by the same laws of circumstance, and selection, and competition, turn men into beasts. You were very near being turned into a beast once or twice, little Tom.'

It is evident that public interest and concern ran high and continued for a considerable time. Browning wrote to F.J. Furnivall in October 1881 to explain his exact position on Darwin. He is not, as has been said, hostile to Darwin's theory. Furnivall had done him the courtesy of 'disbelieving' that he was 'strongly against Darwin, rejecting the truths of science and regretting its advance'. But he does not go all the way with Darwin. Tortoises never 'saw their own shells, top or bottom'; 'and the insects; this one is coloured to escape notice, this other to attract it, a third to frighten the foe – all out of one brood of caterpillars hatched in one day. No, I am incredulous'. 'I believe in the cue pushed by a hand,' he says.[87]

The vivisection debate

In this climate where it was bound to appear threatening to old certainties, science began to be disliked as arrogant, ruthless, unwilling to consider the harm it might do in the pursuit of truth. Ethical questions started to be raised. For example, there were debates about the way animals should be treated.

The Penny Magazine of the Society for the Diffusion of Useful Knowledge, Saturday, 3 January 1835, describes the sloth. A Mr. Waterton kept one in his room for some months to observe its behaviour. This was of interest because scientists were trying to explain to themselves, in a spirit 'Darwinian' before its time, 'the adaptation of the structure of the sloths to their peculiar mode of life' (the title of one of Buckland's own papers given in March 1833).[88] Was this sort of thing kind to sloths? Was it acceptable for scientists to go further and conduct painful experiments on animals to satisfy their curiosity? How was this different from small boys pulling the wings off flies for sheer devilment, to see what happened?

The term 'vivisection' was not new in the nineteenth century and neither was the practice. The *Oxford English Dictionary* records several occasions of the use of the term in the eighteenth century. In 1707 experiments on living creatures to watch the twitches of muscles when nerves are touched are described as 'vivisections'.[89] It is noted in 1736 that there is an inherent difficulty, in that one cannot put a portion of one's experimental animal under the microscope without removing it from the living creature which defeats the whole purpose of 'vivisection' because it will no longer be alive.[90] A medical dictionary of 1842 defines 'vivisection' as 'the act of opening or dissecting living animals'.[91] And the growing frequency of the practice in recent years is remarked on in 1852.[92]

Charles Kingsley may be referring obliquely and ironically to the practice in his disapproving strictures on the way physicians and mother 'torture' living children in *The Water Babies* in 1862–3:

> And first she called up all the doctors who give little children
> so much physic (they were most of them old ones; for the

young ones have learnt better, all but a few army surgeons, who still fancy that a baby's inside is much like a Scotch grenadier's), and she set them all in a row; and very rueful they looked; for they knew what was coming.

And first she pulled all their teeth out; and then she bled them all round: and then she dosed them with calomel, and jalap, and salts and senna, and brimstone and treacle; and horrible faces they made; and then she gave them a great emetic of mustard and water, and no basons; and began all over again; and that was the way she spent the morning.[93]

There is a distinct hint of disapproval of causing pain for trivial and unworthy reasons:

And then she called up a whole troop of foolish ladies, who pinch up their children's waists and toes; and she laced them all up in tight stays, so that they were choked and sick, and their noses grew red, and their hands and feet swelled; and then she crammed their poor feet into the most dreadfully tight boots, and made them all dance, which they did most clumsily indeed; and then she asked them how they liked it; and when they said not at all, she let them go: because they had only done it out of foolish fashion, fancying it was for their children's good, as if wasps' waists and pigs' toes could be pretty, or wholesome, or of any use to anybody.[94]

The Cruelty to Animals Act of 1876 was passed at the instigation of Lord Carnarvon. Darwin had been actively involved in the promotion of the Bill, though he himself believed that there were circumstances in which vivisection was justified:

You ask about my opinion on vivisection. I quite agree that it is justifiable for real investigations on physiology; but not for mere damnable and detestable curiosity. It is a subject which makes me sick with horror, so I will not say another word about it, else I shall not sleep to-night.[95]

Vivisection was not decisively discouraged by the passing of this Act, though it was brought under control to a degree. The *Westminster Gazette* of 26 February 1894 speaks of 'the atrocious character of many vivisection experiments'.

As with other branches of scientific research and practice, the implications spilled over and opened questions in adjacent fields. One of the areas of enquiry these debates prompted was the capacity of members of the animal kingdom not only to suffer but to think. Do animals have souls? Can souls, of beasts or people, be studied by experimental science? Robert Browning's short narrative poem *Tray* (1879) describes an occasion when a dog dived to save a beggar-child who had fallen into a river and then dived again and brought up her doll, which she had dropped. No one had told the dog to go back for the doll. Why did the dog think this was important?

> Purchase that animal for me!

concludes the poem:

> By vivisection, at expense
> Of half-an-hour and eighteenpence,
> How brain secretes dog's soul, we'll see!'[96]

The underlying concern, shared by Browning and Charles Kingsley among others, was still to fix the boundary beyond which scientific explanations could not, and should not attempt to, go:

> And at that Tom cried so bitterly that the salt sea was swelled with his tears, and the tide was .3,954,620,819 of an inch higher than it had been the day before: but perhaps that was owing to the waxing of the moon. It may have been so; but it is considered right in the new philosophy, you know, to give spiritual causes for physical phenomena–especially in parlour-tables; and, of course, physical causes for spiritual ones, like thinking, and praying, and knowing right from wrong.
> *The Water Babies*, Chapter 6.

So the theological problems science had been raising had not receded.

* * *

Must science exclude theology?

In 1832 Adam Sedgwick gave the sermon at the annual service in Commemoration of Benefactors, held in the chapel of Trinity College, Cambridge. Adam Sedgwick was reluctant to separate science and religion and inclined more towards Paley than Darwin though he did gradually relinquish the insistence on the literal truth of the Flood as a datable incident in the formation of the earth's crust. He took as his subject a theme which was eventually expanded until his sermon became a book, *A Discourse on the Studies of the University*, a volume which continued to grow through several editions and appeared in an even lengthier form in 1850. Its considerable popularity is the less surprising perhaps in the light of the excitement which had attended the reviews of Edgeworth. *The Times* discussed it on 10 January 1834, and the *Quarterly Review* spoke well of it in the same year, though John Stuart Mill disliked it in an article in the *London Review* in 1835.[97]

It is a heavy and earnest effort, which contrives never to forget that it began as a sermon, and one especially addressed to pious undergraduates, even while it was expanding and acquiring its extensive and equally ponderous notes. The first branch of 'the studies of this place' to which Sedgwick addresses himself is 'the study of the laws of nature, comprehending all parts of inductive philosophy'.[98] This was a natural place for him to begin as Woodwardian Professor of Geology.[99]

Sedgwick clearly expected his student congregation to be exercised about the novel ideas of the day, for they would perforce have read their Paley's *Evidences;* and to stand in need of active correction and guidance from the pulpit. Sedgwick has strong critical things to say of Paley's theological arguments in his sermon, though he tries to be fair about the 'homely strength and clearness of style' which is bound to make him 'popular'.[100] But he himself saw no reason not to argue the 'theology' of geology, the way geological evidence has now made it clear that a 'thousand ages' have passed in geological time even though it can still be held that man 'was called into being within a few thousand years of the days in which we live – not by a transmutation of species [did Darwin read these words?]...but by a provident contriving power'.[101] Genesis and science can still be held together, he seems to be saying, but no longer without energetic argument and considerable effort.

The second area of university studies Sedgwick discusses in his sermon is 'classical studies'. He approves of doing this properly: 'Whatever is taught in this place ought to be taught profoundly: for superficial information is not merely of little value, but is a sure proof of bad training.'[102]

But he fears that a high literary standard is being achieved at the expense of reading the classics for the kernel of their content and the moral training they can offer, and that takes him to his third area of university education, the moral and religious. An Appendix suggests that the expression of his concerns in this area reflected deep professional grievances about exactly the controversies in which he had just been defending the Bible:

> The recent attacks on physical science, and the gross misapprehension of its moral tendency, have been singularly

wanton and ill-timed. The living philosophers of this country are a set of sober-minded men, who have betrayed no hostility to revealed truth. An exclusive devotion to one subject inevitably makes a man narrow minded; and a successful career of intellectual toil, may make a man proud and full of self.[103]

The truth was – and it is reflected everywhere in the general contemporary discussions of universities and their purposes – that it was proving difficult to detach purely pedagogical questions from moral and religious ones. The student was to be formed not only intellectually but as a moral being, and a Church of England Christian moral being at that. This emphasis was inescapable when the career pattern of academics still normally involved ordination and a life as a clergyman, practising or not; anyway society tended to support the assumption. John Stuart Mill was as merciless with this 'Discourse' as he was in his criticism of William Whewell. Sedgwick's 'intellectual pretensions... are high. Not of him can it be said that he aspires not to philosophy; he writes in the character of one to whom its loftiest eminences are familiar.'[104]

It is evident again and again in nineteenth-century debates that the place of religion, especially Christian belief, and most particularly that of the Church of England, was a constant preoccupation, and one hard to separate from the notion that study should be edifying, and form the man as well as the mind in the man. It could hardly be otherwise in Oxford and Cambridge, where until late in the nineteenth century, Fellowships still normally led to the grant of a College living and the disappearance of young tutors to become parish clergy when they married. Moreover, the anguishing about emerging conflict with a literal reading of the Bible was a great driver of scientific debate in the early decades, particularly in such subjects as Geology, where it was gradually having to be accepted that the evidence was against there having been an actual Flood. The beginning of the book of Genesis had for centuries provided a convenient row of pegs on which to hang discussion of optics (at the creation of light) and other matters.[105] But now, as Sedgwick's sermon-lecture illustrated,[106] the grating of one set of ideas upon another was becoming new and urgent. It was to prove a productive friction.

In October 1858, Whewell wrote a letter about an article he had seen in the *Athenaeum* of 18 September. He mentions a speech of Isaac Barrow (made in 1652) discussing the 'Cartesian hypothesis' that 'all natural phenomena may be accounted for by matter and motion', against which Barrow argues. 'I have no doubt Bacon's works were familiar to all Cambridge men of Newton's time,' Whewell asserts.[107]

In November Whewell was referring in another letter to 'Robert Leslie Ellis, one of the editors of the new edition of Bacon's works'[108] which was to appear progressively from 1857 to 1874.

This edition was of seminal importance. As its joint-editor James Spedding noted in his introductory remarks of 1857,[109] Francis Bacon had 'had no confidence in the permanent vitality of English as a classical language' and had therefore arranged for all his works which were not originally written in Latin to be translated into Latin; he had thus created an authoritative version in that 'universal language'. Decisions had been taken to meet the needs of readers in English in the mid-nineteenth century, which included keeping to a chronological arrangement and not including the Latin versions (though these had been carefully compared with the English and discrepancies noted).

Robert Leslie Ellis contributed a General Preface to Bacon's philosophical works. He was aware that Bacon had not completed his planned later parts of the *Novum Organum,* but undeterred he had tried both to piece together the intention of the whole and to distil the essence of what Bacon had wanted to say: 'Absolute certainty, and a mechanical mode of procedure such that all men should be capable of employing it, are…two great features of the Baconian method' (pp.23–4).

Philosophy had for centuries been enmeshed with theology. It remained so for Bacon. Ellis comments in his General Preface: 'When, not long before Bacon's time, philosophy freed itself from the tutelage of dogmatic theology, it became a grave question how their respective claims to authority might be most fitly coordinated.'

Bacon, he claims, saw no conflict: 'Next to his determination of the true end of natural philosophy ad of the relation in which it stands to natural and revealed theology, we may place among Bacon's merits his clear view of the essential unity of science.'[110]

It was not so simple, however. The change our nineteenth-century academics were grappling with was the one identified in part by Charles Kingsley in his lecture on Agriculture. 'Questions of moral right and wrong are beyond' the 'sphere' of science, not because ethical questions are not important in ensuring that it is honest science, but because the science itself cannot determine such questions. Nor can the study of the kind of evidence which, by Kingsley's time, science was clear was its province, lead to conclusions about the supernatural.

The underlying questions had been debated even in the ancient world and they were not going to go away. Alfred North Whitehead (1861–1947) was a student at Trinity, and then taught mathematics in

Cambridge. He left Trinity in 1910 in protest when one of the Fellows was dismissed because his adultery had become known. Whitehead belonged to the generations of Cambridge academics who took theology seriously (there were many clerics in his family though he regarded himself as an agnostic for many years). He put theology in the picture when considering scientific questions, which he approached much as the seventeenth century did, partly as philosophical questions. He was one of the inventors of a 'process philosophy' which had a considerable influence on the 'process theology' of the twentieth century. His *Process and Reality* was published in 1929.

* * *

Professorships and the emergence of academic specialization

Intellectual disciplines do not develop on their own. They are taken forward in the minds of their students, and through exchanges among those who have an interest in the subject. On the other hand, it is not possible to establish clear requirements about specialist expertise until it is apparent what specialisms there are to become expert in. The emergence of acknowledged specialists and professionals was slow partly because the subject-matter itself was in flux. In the nineteenth century, there was a great sense of academic freedom to rethink things from first principles, but with that went the difficulty of knowing how to classify and label areas of study and their purpose. A body of knowledge had to be identified as an entity possessing some form of intellectual integrity and not a mere hotch-potch of miscellaneous information. This was a problem Aristotle had addressed in the *Posterior Analytics* by floating the notion that every true 'discipline' rested on its innate first principles.[111] The nineteenth century tended to press for a broader 'Baconian' idea that scientific studies should be of a sort which permitted of inductive reasoning from experiments. Rigour was then required in the establishment of the parameters of the study of the 'discipline', textbooks had to be found, and teachers competent to teach it. In Cambridge the arrival on the scene of new subjects in the form of experimental lectures was to lead to the establishing of a series of scientific Triposes. It took rather longer to move to the expectation that those who would teach them ought to be specialists.

Oliver Goldsmith (1730–74) was already aware in 1761 of the problem that the increasing scale and variety of the body of 'knowledge' was creating a need for specialists who could not talk to one another knowledgeably about the work each was doing:

> A man of letters of the last age should he leave his cell to mix among the scholars of a more modern education, would find himself entirely thrown out from the practiced circle of study. About thirty years ago, for instance, no man thought himself learned in nature without being able to account for all its appearances.[112]

It was abundantly evident in the seventeenth and eighteenth centuries that the holder of a Chair could not necessarily be taken to have special expertise in the subject in question, or even a lasting loyalty and commitment to the subject of the sort modern 'specialization' requires. Edward Clarke (1769–1822) had already lectured in Mineralogy at Cambridge and he was given the Professorship when it was created in 1808. But John Henslow (1796–1861), who gained the Chair of Botany in 1825, had dabbled in Geology, Mineralogy and Chemistry as well as making a reputation as a mathematician.

William Whewell is an example of the range of influence an individual could have in encouraging change in syllabus and approach, within the freewheeling life of the academic in nineteenth-century Oxford and Cambridge. He wrote on logic, aiming to modernize its content and approach, a *History of the Inductive Sciences*, the first edition of which came out in three volumes in 1837 and moved on in due course to *The Philosophy of the Inductive Sciences*. He wrote on Geology. He translated Goethe into English hexameters. No one said he was spreading his net too wide or should confine himself to his proper area of expertise. New disciplines benefited from the attentions of those who could take a view of the options available for studying them most effectively. He was very far from being a 'specialist' but that was not held against him.

Charles Darwin (1809–82), student at Edinburgh then Cambridge, was also able to think about the *Origin of Species* as a whole, and not only within the framework of a limited specialization. He was not confined to barnacles. Frederick Pollock (1845–1937), who became a member of the famous debating society 'the Apostles' in 1865, is an example of an intellectual who felt quite free to take up anything, even very late in the nineteenth century. 'You do so many things that I never know whether to expect a drama, a law book, a symphony or a system of philosophy,'[113] wrote Mr. Justice Holmes in 1883. Sir William Hardy (1864–1934) could still be appointed to a university lectureship in Physiology in Cambridge in 1913, having published in the fields of colloid chemistry and the physics of friction.[114] There could scarcely be clearer testimony of the continuing fluidity of disciplinary boundaries although the tide was running strongly in the direction of fixing them enough to require specialist knowledge in those who taught or otherwise practised them.[115]

The range of knowledge studied in academe reached the point in the later nineteenth century where scholars *had* to become specialists; no one could know it all. Yet it was not regarded as necessarily an uncontroversially good thing that experts and specialists should emerge. It was going to be divisive. There also began to be signs of the emergence of protectionist academic rivalries amongst those defending what they regarded as their own territory:

> I have, I believe, discovered two entirely new laws of my own, though one of them, by-the-bye, has been broached by Professor Brown since in his lectures. He might have mentioned my name in connection with the subject, for I certainly imparted my ideas to him two years at least before the delivery of those lectures of his. Professor Brown is a very great man, certainly, and a very good man, but not quite so original as is generally supposed. Still, a scientific man must expect his little disappointments and injustices.[116]

The most important consequence of these developments for the intellectual life of Cambridge was perhaps that at some point in the nineteenth century, it ceased to be possible for the individual to command a range of knowledge sufficiently broad and varied to make possible (or at any rate likely) personal breakthroughs such as Isaac Newton was able to achieve.

That did not automatically answer the question how the new professional academic was to set about establishing that he had a specialist expertise. The purpose of a university was going to be defined in the Oxford and Cambridge Act of 1877 as the fostering of 'education, religion, learning and research'. Yet it had by no means been assumed from the beginning of universities in the Middle Ages that it was part of their job to foster the advancement of knowledge or do 'research'. That idea arrived with early modern times,[117] with the introduction of serious inquiry into the activities of a university.

It was still not clear that this necessarily meant sustained and serious research activity. A researcher might go on a journey to study a phenomenon, as the geologists did in their early nineteenth-century field trips. It took time for it to be recognized that that was a quite different thing from going on the sort of tour of Europe engaged in by young men in the eighteenth century, sending back letters to friends about amusing incidents with a scattering of comment of serious potential scientific interest: 'With respect to philosophy, I am become a complete Academic. I am persuaded, that in all questions purely speculative there is just as much to be said on the one side as the other.'[118]

When Thomas Love Peacock (1785–1866) wrote this in a letter in 1811, he was referring to the 'academic' of the classical world, who believed that it was impossible to be sufficiently sure about anything to take a firm view on it. Cicero touches on the point twice in discussing the 'Old' and 'New' Academies (*Academica*, I.xii.45, II.v.14). This is the 'academic' whose label seems to have passed by transferred usage to members of the modern 'profession' who evince the characteristics just listed.

There is more to it still. The cultivation of a lack of prejudice and a fundamental intellectual honesty was seen, before the beginning of the nineteenth century, to be essential to the clarity of thought and mastery of his subject-matter that an academic would also need.

> It is admitted to be the mark of a good genius, to reduce a complicated subject to a few plain principles, or to exhibit a just representation of it, in some one striking point of view. But many, we know, are apt to fail in such attempts...if their minds are warped by strong prejudice...and adventure to interpose their decisions in matters which they have not deliberately and dispassionately considered.[119]

That these general features of the breed should be as widely accepted as they were was by no means a foregone conclusion. These 'fundamentals' had to be identified.

Even a Cambridge leader in such matters like William Whewell was still unconvinced in the mid-nineteenth century that any formal system could be devised for finding things out by systematic research: 'An Art of Discovery is not possible. At each step of the investigation are needed Invention, Sagacity, Genius – elements which no art can give.'[120] And, 'We can give no Rules for the pursuit of truth which shall be universally and peremptorily applicable.'[121]

Student awareness of the progress of specialist Cambridge sciences

Ordinary students in the universities might become aware of some of what was happening in these early ventures into modern academic science. Nevertheless, there appear to have been remarkable opportunities for those who were specially interested. Charles Darwin (1809–82) provides evidences of the contact an interested undergraduate might have with such topics. When Darwin was a student, he went to the lectures of John Henslow, Professor of Botany and his tutor, and accompanied him on nature walks. Henslow held informal seminars on Friday evenings which Darwin also attended, along with Adam Sedgwick and William Whewell and other senior figures. Darwin even went with Sedgwick on one of his field-trips as a student in August 1831, at Henslow's suggestion.[122]

Specialist laboratories and museums

One of the most lasting indications that there was serious investment in the sciences was the provision of laboratories and museums. Cambridge had made a promising early start in building to meet the needs of science. Cambridge's Botanical Garden was created in 1760–2 by Walker, Vice-Master of Trinity. This was a physic garden. He had medicinal study of plants in mind as well as botany. The Botanical Garden moved from its first site to the larger space it now occupies, as a result of an agreement in 1831. Geology had a room in the Old Schools from 1735 but there was scant awareness of the need for museum space for display or laboratories for experimental work until the first quarter of the nineteenth century. In 1822–4 Cambridge built itself an Observatory for Astronomy on the Madingly Road. By 1850 Cambridge had the Observatory, the Fitzwilliam Museum, the Botanic Garden and a Botanic Museum. In 1851 the Natural Sciences Tripos began and Robert Willis began to plan for the new buildings with some laboratories nearby on what is now the New Museums site.

Then began extended wrangles about locations and division of requirements among the emerging sciences. After much debate and modification, and in the climate of uncertainty about the way science was going to develop, the result was the huddle of museums and lecture-rooms on the New Museums site.[123] By the 1860s the New Museums Site had museums for comparative anatomy and for zoology. The Cavendish Laboratory in Cambridge was founded in 1871, simultaneously with the appointment of James Clerk Maxwell as the first Cavendish Professor.

James Clerk Maxwell

James Clerk Maxwell (1831–79) was, like Herschel, introduced to the study of science by his father, who used to take him to meetings of the Royal Society of Edinburgh and the Royal Scottish Society of Arts. He had an uncle, too, who took him to the laboratory run by William Nicol, who invented a prism which would polarize light. When he was 16 he went to Edinburgh University and was soon writing publishable scientific papers.

In 1850 he was to move on Cambridge, going first to Peterhouse but soon (in the first term) moving on to Trinity College. He came with recommendations to William Whewell as a star mathematical student. He read Whewell's books on the history and philosophy of science. He made himself ill with overwork and graduated as only Second Wrangler in 1854. He was elected a Fellow of Trinity only on his second attempt. While still a student, in 1852–3, he was elected to the Apostles' club. This took him into theological discussions and Frederick Denison Maurice's Christian socialist movement.

He removed himself to a post in Aberdeen in 1856, to be closer to his father, who died before he could take up the post. In March 1855, Cambridge's Adams Prize for 1857 was advertised as a study of 'the motions of Saturn's rings'. This was something of a fashionable question. Whewell had set a question on Saturn's rings in 1854, in which candidates for the same prize were to demonstrate that the rings were not solid. The subject was topical because of the publications of Pierre Simon Laplace and Joseph Plateau and the work of George Bond. Maxwell won the prize and the work he did set him off on new lines of enquiry of his own, including studies in electricity and magnetism. In 1860 Maxwell moved again, to the Professorship of natural philosophy at King's College, London, working on the theory of colour and taking forward Newton's own work. By 1865 he had given up the London post and was living privately in Scotland, but continuing to work, for this was still a period where a scientist was not dependent on laboratories or funding. But that was about to change. Cambridge invited him to act as an examiner in the Tripos and he had been trying out questions in the fields of electricity and magnetism in the late 1860s.

It began to seem a good idea to found a Professorship in these areas, and with the aide of a benefaction from the Chancellor, then the Duke of Devonshire, to provide a laboratory and a salary. Maxwell was appointed to the Professorship of experimental physics in 1871. The Cavendish Laboratory was opened in 1874 containing equipment some of which he had paid for himself.

* * *

Teaching: should new 'useful' subjects replace the classics?

The word 'syllabus' seems to have come into use in English in the nineteenth century to describe the *content* of a course of study.

Sir Walter Scott uses it in the context of a 'syllabus of lectures' in 1818[124] and by the end of the century (1889), it became an accepted term for a programme of study in a school or university.[125] 'Curriculum', with its stronger sense of 'course' was in use from the 1820s, when it described the curriculum in German universities and also at Glasgow.[126] If a curriculum is a 'course' of study it must have a sequential character. The student lives and studies a day at a time. Is there a single sequence of study, of increasing difficulty, with each student stepping off at the level where he or she enters employment? Might there be different routes of study leading to different employments and how, and what point will it be decided which one the student should follow? If this proves to be a wrong turning, can the student go back and try another way? It was a long time before the content of a degree course was thought of other than in terms of a list of approved set books.

Classics make the man

The main decision the nineteenth-century Cambridge with its new scientific ambitions had to make was what was to be done about the teaching of the classics, the Greek and Latin writings which had formed the main content of the curriculum since the end of the Middle Ages (with, in the case of Cambridge, a particular emphasis on the mathematical studies of the day, also studied in the ancient texts), now that other subjects were jostling for a place in the syllabus. What were the justifications in nineteenth-century minds for continuing the study of the classics? There was the theory that 'moral' and 'intellectual' education ought to go together; the belief that the study of the classics still provided the most secure foundation for study even in the new 'sciences'; and above all the claim that here supremely and perhaps uniquely a 'liberal' education was to be had.

From the beginning of theorizing about the purpose of education in the medieval Christian West it had been taken for granted that there was a disciplinary element, a purpose of moral formation, as well as one of intellectual formation. Classical texts contained useful material for the formation of character. By the nineteenth century this had mutated in some quarters into the view that an educated man would merely have been 'socialised', turned into an acceptable member of society, and that might mean only a modest civilizing process. Thackeray's *Pendennis* gives several chapters to the career of young Pendennis at university, where he distinguishes himself for fine living and 'Pen the superb, Pen the wit and dandy, Pen the poet and orator' is eventually 'plucked', failing his final examinations.[127]

A rearguard response, as Huxley put it, came from those 'educated Englishmen' who believe that 'culture is obtainable only by a liberal education; and a liberal education is synonymous, not merely with education and instruction in literature, but in one particular form of literature, namely, that of Greek and Roman antiquity'.[128]

The benefit of the study of the classics was considered to be not only the socializing and civilizing of the young (which it failed to achieve for Thackeray's 'Pendennis'), but more profoundly and more seriously, the enrichment of mind and the development of skills of language and the deployment of arguments which were (in modern terminology) the general and 'transferable' skills of the educated. John Collingwood Bruce was still thinking in this way in 1834:

> It is respectfully suggested that the object of a liberal education is not only to make the youth a successful man of business, but so to cultivate the moral and intellectual powers that he may be an intelligent and honourable and useful member of general society; hence, while especial reference is had to those pursuits which will be more immediately useful in his intended professions, other branches may at the same time be prosecuted with much ultimate advantage.[129]

Others set the bar higher and thought education should be edifying, and raise man above the level of the beasts. William Whewell had something to say about that:

> Even the brutes have practical powers of thought; they have a practical notion of space and force; a practical sense of things good and bad, of things which they may and which they may not do; but man alone has a geometry and a mechanics, an idea of happiness and a moral law.[130]

A broader view, that the study of classics and other serious reading could lead to a considerable variety of types of 'trained mind' is to be found at the end of the century, and it is here that we should look for the evolution of a Cambridge awareness of intellectual styles.

New set books

New candidates to become set books had to emerge, find their level and prove that they would be of lasting value. Some books and their authors became famous and entered the syllabus for a time and then dropped out of it. In the first examination Charles Darwin was required to take in 1830 – the 'Little Go' or Previous Examination,

293

instituted in 1822 – one of the set books was William Paley's *Evidences of Christianity,* published as recently as 1794, but already accepted as representing a major contribution to an important contemporary debate.[131] The speed with which this had made its way onto the elementary syllabus seems to gainsay the claims that the syllabus was stagnant.

Yet it was not easy to know how to 'rate' the newcomers in the forum of great minds. Thomas Babington Macaulay (1800–59) wrote to William Whewell on 1 December 1856 about the respective merits of the various figures being canvassed as suitable to be honoured by a new statue in the ante-chapel at Trinity College.

> An equal of Bacon and Newton it cannot be ... We must chuse some second rate man to be the associate of our two first rate men. 'Dryden's most enthusiastic admirers will hardly put him so high as third among our poets. Barrow did many things well, but nothing, I think, preeminently well.'[132]

Should new subjects oust the old?

As the nineteenth century wore on and more and more subjects were added to the range taught in the universities, it became necessary to make a positive case for continuing to insist on a requirement to study Greek, in the way Oxford and Cambridge had previously taken to be essential. If they were not going to have to study Greek when they arrived, was there any need to continue the requirement that university entrants should demonstrate a proficiency in Greek as a condition of entry? Such an expectation was bound to exclude a considerable proportion of the young population from university education.[133] Did the young scientist-to-be really need a knowledge of ancient Greek in any case? What was Europe doing about this question? Matthew Arnold's researches into the way things were done in the rest of Europe were published in Matthew Arnold, *Schools and Universities on the Continent, First Written as a Report to the Schools Inquiry Commission* (1865–7). This made him an obvious port of call when Cambridge found itself wondering whether to end the teaching of Greek. 'In Germany a degree may be taken without examination in Greek,' wrote Arnold rather formally to the Vice-Chancellor of Cambridge in June 1879:

> But an admission to the University is given only to those who have passed the Leaving Examination of the Classical public Schools, and as for this Examination Greek is required, the German universities are not open to those who have not studied Greek. The High School open to such persons is the

Polytechnicum ... In France the degree of bachelor of Sciences is given to those who can pass an examination in the matters taught in the 2nd year class of Elementary Mathematics at the Lycées. Among these matters Greek is not included.[134]

Matthew Arnold commented on the same question whether a foundation in classics was necessary for university entrance for potential scientists:

In England we have no institution which answers to a German Polytechnicum. I should be glad if students following the mathematical or natural science could be admitted to the University by an examinations without Greek and could also take an honour degree in those Sciences by an Examination without Greek.[135]

Yet it was recognized that a discipline of thinking and writing went with the mastery of the two classical languages and the formal training in thinking.[136]

Another possible solution was to begin with a common foundation, after which the student would choose a special direction? In that case, could – or should – the student give up the study of what has been mastered as soon as he or she reaches an agreed level and moved on to specialized employment-related, vocational or professional studies? One of the proposals of the 1852 Commissioners for Oxford was that professional training might be included within the Oxford degree course by allowing students to give up their preliminary studies in the classics and move on:

All students after giving satisfactory evidence of classical knowledge at the Intermediate Examination, should be relieved from the necessity of continuing the studies of the Grammar School, and should be at liberty for the latter period of their career, to devote themselves to pursuits preparatory to their future professions.[137]

More arts subjects

When the tailor hero of Charles Kingsley's novel *Alton Locke* (1850) sets out to study at Cambridge, he knows he wants to be a poet. Discussing his course of 'reading' (as a student) with the Dean he is told,

'You must study some science. Have you read any logic?' I mentioned Watts's 'Logic' and Locke 'On the use of the Understanding'.[138]

These books the Dean dismisses as 'merely popular'. Aristotle and Kant are the thing.

The somewhat hit-or-miss process of adjusting the reading lists for undergraduates to reflect their tastes and the changing interests of the times and the advancement of knowledge, seemed unsatisfactory to some of those involved in these developments. They wanted to see something more systematic. But that threw up questions about the boundaries of the disciplines which reached across from the new sciences into the arts.

William Whewell saw the need for a 'history' of the 'sciences'. He describes this idea in the dedicatory letter of 1837 at the beginning of his *History of the Inductive Sciences from the Earliest to the Present Time* as the fruit of conversations he and John Herschel (1792–1871) had had as students. His book is '[t]he result of trains of thought which have often been the subject of our conversation, and of which the origin goes back to the period of our early companionship in the University.'[139]

It is an irony that it is Herschel's name which is much the better known to posterity, while Whewell stayed in Cambridge, monitoring, defining and encouraging the changes which transformed the intellectual content of early nineteenth-century university life, partly through such dull but essential activities as writing elementary textbooks. Herschel had gone off to the southern hemisphere to make astronomical observations, and in a further note added in 1846, Whewell refers to these in congratulating him on the publication of his *Observations in the Southern Hemisphere*: 'I cannot refrain from congratulating you upon having had your life enobled by the conception and happy execution of so great a design.'[140]

Whewell had realized that it was going to be important to link the old work with new work of the kind Herschel was doing, and to consider whether the new science was a development of the old or something entirely different.

Herschel was a somewhat intense individual. Maria Edgeworth's *Letters* include one to Harriet Butler written on 3 December 1843. She describes his shyness and reserve and comments: 'when vexed in friendship or when scientific things go wrong he betakes himself to darkness and solitude and in abstraction shuts himself up from the external universe. Very very dangerous!'[141]

Whewell found it easier to command detachment and stand back. His 'history' of the taxonomy of knowledge, as he conceived it, was to be:

> not merely the narration of the facts in the history of Science, but a basis for the Philosophy of Science ... it seemed to

me that our study of the model of discovering truth ought to be based upon a survey of the truths which have been discovered.[142]

He was already of the view that 'the history of each science forms a whole in itself'[143] and arranged his material accordingly, beginning in the first volume with the 'physical sciences'. So Whewell was becoming clear in his own mind where the boundaries of the sciences lay, at least from the point of view of their conceptual or philosophical underpinnings, such categories as 'Sound and Light and heat; and Magnetism and Electricity and Chemistry...the ideas of Force and Matter, of Mediums by which action and sensation are produced.'[144]

Whewell speaks of coupling 'narration of the facts in the history of Science' with an attempt to establish 'a basis for the Philosophy of Science' in his 'history'. His idea was that a study of the past might usefully inform future work. Historiographically speaking, these were sophisticated and novel thoughts for their time, for History was not yet an academic subject, and modern historiography, the theory of the way to write it, was in its infancy.

With new and newly defined subject-areas entering the syllabus the conceptual division of the arts and humanities from the 'sciences' was by no means a foregone conclusion. Here was to be the first great branching of the new fast-flowing river of knowledge and it is worth pausing over its implications for the future framing of study in universities. The Society of Arts and analogous societies elsewhere in Europe made no rigid separation, as Oliver Goldsmith had remarked in 1761: 'About three years since there was established at Berne a society for the promotion of agriculture, arts and commerce, probably in imitation of that set up at Stockholm, Dublin or Florence.'[145]

A century later, T.H. Huxley put the emphasis on striking the right balance:

> It is not a question whether one order of study or another should predominate. It is a question of what topics of education you shall select which will combine all the needful elements in such due proportion as to give the greatest amount of food, support, and encouragement, to those faculties which enable us to appreciate truth.[146]

He did not consider that 'arts' should be kept out of the 'science' curriculum or *vice versa:* 'I think that sound and practical instruction in the elementary facts and broad principles of Biology should form part of the Arts Curriculum.'[147]

The constant moving of boundaries of content and subject classification prompted an awareness – which might not otherwise have been so sharp – that there were fundamental questions to be answered. What is a 'subject'? What is 'science'? When is a subject a 'science'? What must be true of an area of study if it is to be regarded as a science or a discipline worthy of serious study, both in the sense of inclusion in a syllabus and of research? Are there features of true disciplines which mark them out as fundamental, possessing ground-rules peculiar to themselves, and incapable of being confused with other disciplines, as Aristotle had argued?

These were questions which had last been considered with a degree of educational and scholarly urgency in the twelfth century when universities were first emerging. The underlying idea was that these disciplines or 'subjects' were fundamental in rather the way Aristotle envisaged in the *Posterior Analytics*, where he discusses the idea that for every truly distinct area of knowledge there are first principles, self-evident truths and other truths derived from these, which are distinctive to the branch of knowledge concerned. Although the *Posterior Analytics* itself was not available in Latin or apparently read in the West before the mid-twelfth century, these ideas were certainly abroad. Gilbert of Poitiers discusses something very like them when he suggests that while all disciplines have their distinctive first principles (including 'ethics'), grammar may be different, since the grammatical rules are not the same for every language.[148]

Some would say, John Stuart Mill observes, that

> it is not the office of an University to give instruction in single branches of knowledge from the commencement. What the pupil should be taught here (they think), is to methodize knowledge: to look at every separate part of it in its relation to other parts, and to the whole, combining the partial glimpses which he has obtained of the field of human knowledge at different points into a general map, if I may so speak, of the entire region; observing how all knowledge is connected, how we ascent to one branch by means of another, how the higher modifies the lower and the lower helps us to understand the higher.[149]

Mill seems to have believed that subjects had the characteristic of having general features and detailed ramifications, and that a good grasp of the former would enable anyone to master the latter:

> To have a general knowledge of a subject is to know only its leading truths, but to know these not superficially but

thoroughly, so as to have a true conception of the subject in its great features; leaving the minor details to those who require them for the purposes of their special pursuit.[150]

In 1867 John Stuart Mill did not think every branch of 'general' knowledge should be included in the curriculum. Modern languages are, he believes, something which should be 'acquired by intercourse with those who use them in daily life', though no one can be deemed a 'well-instructed person' without sufficiently fluent French to 'read French books with ease', and some German. Nevertheless, the study of languages is important to the training of the mind, for it includes learning how not to mistake words for things.[151] History and Geography, he thinks, should be studied by private reading. He was keen, too, on the student working from original sources: 'How little we learn of our own ancestors from Hume, or Hallam, or Macaulay, compared with what we know if we add to what these tell us, even a little reading of contemporary authors and documents!'

He thinks the Philosophy of History is a fit subject for university study. There

> Professors who not merely know the facts but have exercised their minds on them, should initiate [the student] into the causes and explanation, so far as within our reach, of the past life of mankind in its principal features. Historical criticism also – the tests of historical truth – are a subject to which [a student's] attention may well be drawn at this stage of his education.[152]

The study of the classics Mill excepts from these reservations, for those he regards as laying the foundations for the study of modern language and literature and history alike. In the study of the classics, the original sources are met with directly.[153]

Once the door was open, new branches of knowledge began to proliferate and have continued to do so, with new juxtapositions and sub-divisions and renamings. The speed and fluidity of these changes took some time to build a momentum. In Cambridge English and Modern Languages, for example, were Tripos subjects which became established only in the period of the First World War and they too have had staying power, although the range of languages and their groupings has shifted, with oriental languages forming a group of their own for a time, and linguistics making its own space.

History began to be studied too, though Oxford was the trail-blazer there. Cambridge's own history attracted fresh interest. Charles Henry

Cooper's *Athenae Cantabrigienses* (Cambridge, 1858 and 1861) was a conscious attempt to provide for Cambridge what Anthony Wood had provided for Oxford, a biographical resource which would 'reflect great lustre' on the University of Cambridge as Wood's had done for Oxford. He decided to make his list under headings which classified areas of distinguished endeavour in which Cambridge graduates had shone: authors; cardinals and other 'church dignitaries'; statesmen and their like; judges and other lawyers of note; 'sufferers for religious or political opinions'; 'persons distinguished for success in tuition' eminent physicians; 'artists, musicians and heralds'; heads of colleges; benefactors. 'This scheme is more comprehensive than Wood's,' he notes.[154] He began at 1500 and proceeded chronologically. He also compiled the *Annals of Cambridge* whose anecdotes and documents remain an important source for historians of the University.[155]

*   *   *

Cambridge reconsiders its duty to society: the long legacy of Prince Albert's Chancellorship

> Prince Albert intervenes
> This day, when Granta hails her chosen Lord,
> And proud of her award,
> Confiding in the Star serene,
> Welcomes the Consort of a happy Queen.
> AIR–(CONTRALTO)
> Prince, in these Collegiate bowers,
> Where Science, leagued with holier truth,
> Guards the sacred heart of youth.

William Wordsworth's rather laboured 'official' verses welcomed Prince Albert as Cambridge's Chancellor in 1847. He accepted a commission which had defeated Tennyson. Whewell wrote to ask Tennyson to compose an Ode for the Installation and Tennyson wrote back to say he had wasted a day in the attempt 'but the work does not seem to prosper in my hands'.[156]

The first attempt to interfere with the financial affairs of Oxford and Cambridge 'for the public good' came speedily after, in the 1850s, partly at the instigation of Prince Albert, Chancellor and Royal Consort (1819–61). Albert fancied himself as an educationalist. He had spent an interrupted academic year 1837–8 at University in Bonn before his marriage to Victoria and he had had the best tutors.

Prince Albert's letters show that he began to take an active interest in questions of higher education and 'University Reform' when he became Cambridge's Chancellor. William Whewell had had the idea of proposing him, and Albert turned out to be almost too willing to take his duties seriously. He wrote to the Vice-Chancellor on 14 October 1847, the year he was installed as Chancellor, 'naturally anxious to trace the course of studies and scientific enquiries pursued at Cambridge' and asking that he should be 'furnished with a comprehensive table, showing the scheme of tuition in the Colleges separately and in the University for the ensuing year'. He was seeking detailed information:

> The subjects to be taught in the different colleges, the authors to be read there, the subjects for examination, those selected for competition and prizes, and the lectures to be given by the different professors in their different branches.[157]

The response he received showed him, to his concern, that not all the Professors were giving the lectures they should and that even those who did might have scant audiences among the undergraduates.

Albert's close scrutiny continued when it came to the question whether he wished to continue the Chancellor's medals. He did. He wanted to add a further medal, for a historical essay. 'In the absence of all historical lectures this stimulus to the study of history appears to me of some importance.' The English poetry medal should be for a poem of a subject from 'Northern mythology', and in awarding the classical medal he wanted to 'encourage the young men to go rather deeper into the spirit and meaning of the classical languages and authors' rather than to 'learn appointed books by rote'.[158]

But Albert's interest in improving things at Cambridge went far beyond the requirements for the award of a few medals for students. In his first autumn as Chancellor he invited Philpott the Vice-Chancellor to Windsor, so that they could discuss the important question of the introduction of new subjects, particularly the sciences, into the syllabus, a matter on which William Whewell had already been in correspondence with his new Chancellor.[159]

Royal Commissions were in the air, plans for one to look into the affairs of schools and colleges with royal founders, and perhaps something for the Universities too. The question of the more institutional aspects of the reform needed at Oxford and Cambridge was the subject of active consideration in the middle of the century, leading in due course to Royal Commissions in the 1850s and again in the 1870s, and to statutory interference. Lord John Russell (1792–

1878), an Edinburgh graduate, was one of only a handful of British Prime Ministers who have not been Oxford or Cambridge graduates themselves. In an article written 15 months after the first set of Commissioners reported, he was to warn Oxford and Cambridge that they had only been spared for a time from Parliamentary Reform on the express condition of their labouring to reform themselves in directions which would be of social benefit.[160] The irreducible minimum would include, as Russell put it,

1. The removal of restrictions on elections to Fellowships so that they shall become real rewards of merit.
2. An efficient alteration of the governing body of the University.
3. A great extension of the University to classes hitherto excluded.
4. The application of some portion of the college endowments towards the adequate payment of professors, that thus the Universities may be enabled to command the services of a body of really intelligent instructors.[161]

The idle rich Fellows of Magdalen College, Oxford, it was complained, were educating 22 students a year and even those are not performing very well and these Fellows are not publishing an impressive number of books to show they are making good use of their time in other ways. Good feeling 'must be kept alive [socially] by opening easy means of transition for the promising youth of one class to rise into another'.[162]

In an attempt to hold off outside interference, Cambridge set up an internal Syndicate to report on the burning questions of the moment. Whewell was to be one of the members. The Syndicate recommended the establishment of new Triposes in Moral Sciences and Natural Sciences, and there was to be a requirement that students should actually attend the Professorial lectures provided. These proposed internal reforms did not satisfy the Government. It had its sights on improving Oxford too, and in April 1850 Lord John Russell as Prime Minister decided that there must be a Royal Commission. He put this to the Commons without proper consultation with Prince Albert, or with the two universities themselves, to their considerable indignation.

The Commissioners were thorough, insisting on the compilation of a set of *Documents Relating to the University and Colleges of Cambridge, Published by Direction of the Commissioners Appointed by the Queen to Inquire into the State, Discipline, Studies, and Revenues of the Said University and Colleges* (London, 1852), 3 volumes, including the 1570 statutes and the charters and statutes of the colleges in foundation order ending with Downing. One of the principal objectives was to force a transfer of funds from the colleges to the two universities, so that there would be sufficient money to pay the salaries of the Professors who were going to be needed if the range of subjects was to be extended and if students were to be adequately taught by the University as well as within their colleges. But the debates indicate that concerns went wider and included the ending of other kinds of exclusion, including that of non-Anglicans, and encountered objections from those who did not want to see a precedent set for Parliamentary interference with property rights.[163]

Albert's awakened interest in higher education matters extended beyond Cambridge. As its Chancellor he took an expansive view of contemporary needs. On a visit to Ireland he had been drawn into the debate about the future of University education in Ireland. Sir Robert Peel had fallen into an advisory role with the Prince on educational matters. 'The great question to decide now,' Albert wrote to Peel, 'is, whether the Colleges or the United University are to confer the degrees and guide the Examinations'.[164] In September he was writing to Stockmar linking the 'plan for the establishment of a free University for Ireland' in conjunction with colleges having no religious restrictions (the 'godless colleges') with 'another plan for a 'World Industrial Exhibition' which was to grow into the Great Exhibition of 1851.

Prince Albert's speeches were published by the Society of Arts in 1857, at the Queen's wish.[165] In June 1843, he had become President of the Society (founded in 1754 'for the Encouragement of Arts, Manufactures and Commerce'). To this, too, he had brought a young man's energies, promoting the Scientific Societies Act of 1843[166] ('the Prince Consort's Act') to exempt the land and the buildings of such societies from paying rates as long as they depended on voluntary contributions, at least in part. 'Land and Buildings occupied by Scientific and Literary Societies [provided that they]...shall be supported wholly or in part by annual voluntary contributions.' The Society's current officers, with Albert's enthusiastic backing, decided to promote the holding of exhibitions to show off British manufacturing achievements, on the model of exhibitions held in France and Germany. After holding a modest 'national' exhibition in 1847, they began to plan the much grander 'international' one which was to become the Great Exhibition of 1851.

Albert seems to have been personally responsible for the planning memorandum which asserted that 'Machinery, Science, and Art...are of no country, but belong, as a whole, to the civilised world', with the embedded idea that British manufactures would stand up well to international comparison or 'fair competition', and the result would benefit the national economy.

On 21 March 1850, he gave a speech at a banquet whose guests included the Royal Commissioners of the 1851 Exhibition. Theirs, he cries, is a 'period of most wonderful transition':

> Whilst formerly the greatest mental energies strove at universal knowledge, and that knowledge was confined to the few, now they are directed on specialities... but the knowledge acquired becomes at once the property of the community at large; for, whilst formerly discovery was wrapped in secrecy, the publicity of the present day causes that no sooner is a discovery or invention made than it is already improved upon and surpassed by competing efforts. The products of all quarters of the globe are placed at our disposal, and we have only to choose which is the best and cheapest for our purposes, and the powers of production are intrusted to the stimulus of competition and capital.[167]

The combination of high idealism with this commercial pragmatism is apparent in the ringing: 'Gentlemen – the Exhibition of 1851 is to give us a true test and a living picture of the point of development at which the whole of mankind has arrived.'[168]

Raising the money for the Great Exhibition, which would require a building to be constructed to hold it in, proved to be hard work, however; Albert worked at it, put in money himself and got the Queen to do so. The result was the 'Crystal Palace'.

George Price Boyce went to see the Great Exhibition for the first time on 27 May 1851, aged 25, where he went

> through the India, China, Africa, Persia and Turkey departments – these displaying the requisite knowledge and feeling for colour and its right application, and also of greater ingenuity and propriety of design as applies to coloured fabrics and objects than any other in the Exhibition.

Boyce, from a well-off family, was articled as an architect after completing his education in France but had soon decided to become a landscape painter instead.[169]

The thinking which drove the Great Exhibition was inseparable in Albert's mind from the arguments he was marshalling in his capacity as Cambridge's Chancellor. Britain needed to be industrially competitive, so it needed a skilled workforce and highly qualified industrial scientists. That meant more mechanics' institutes and a radical review of the purposes of the existing universities. The Great Exhibition had made a large profit and Albert was ambitious to use it to forward the complex of projects whose interrelationship he so clearly saw. One result was to be the cluster of buildings and institutions in South Kensington including the museums and Imperial College.

Lectures on the Results of the Great Exhibition (1852) included a call by Lyon Playfair for all the provincial technical schools to be integrated and linked to a London-based 'university of mines and manufactures' which would be able to grant degrees. He himself had an unusually good grasp of the needs to be met. He had been educated at the University of St. Andrews and University College, London, and then in Germany, where he obtained a doctorate of philosophy in 1841 at Giessen. Playfair briefly became an industrial chemist and manager of a dye works in the early 1840s and then chemist to the Geological Survey in 1845. In November of 1851 he was appointed to the Professorship of Chemistry at the School of Mines, from which vantage point he criticized the manufacturers of Britain for their unwarranted assumption that because of the success of the Great Exhibition they could claim superiority in world business circles. Prince Albert encouraged him to undertake a tour of the universities and technical colleges of Europe to see what they were teaching. On his return Playfair gave a lecture at the School of Mines on 'Industrial instruction on the continent'. A debate began on the future of technical education in Britain and in 1853, in a new Government Department Science and Art, Playfair was appointed as Secretary for Science.

Prince Albert worked, too, at other aspects of education in the national interest and for the benefit of society. In a speech given at a banquet for the occasion of the laying of the foundation stone of the Midland Institute, 22 November 1855 (Founded by Act of Parliament in 1854 'for the Diffusion and Advancement of Science, Literature and Art amongst all Classes)', he was claiming that 'the value and dignity of human labour will receive a manifold increase when guided by the light of scientific knowledge'.[170]

He made a speech at the opening of the Conference on National Education, 22 June 1857 (on schools). As President of the British Association for the Advancement of Science for the year he made a speech at Aberdeen on 14 September 1859:

> This Association is a popular Association, not a secret confraternity of men jealously guarding the mysteries of their profession, but inviting the uninitiated, the public at large, to join them, having as one of its objects to break down those

imaginary and hurtful barriers which exist between men of science and so-called men of practice.[171]

The demand for industrial scientists

It was apparent to others than Albert that science might be economically fruitful, that even early 'collections' had, potentially, a practical industrial use. In America, Thomas Paine (1737–1809), reflected on the 'advantages' to a 'new country' such as his own of collections of objects of scientific interest, like the 'cabinet of fossils' 'in the possession of the Philadelphia Library Company', linking them with industrial applications:

> The same materials which delight the Fossilist, enrich the manufacturer and the merchant. While the one is scientifically examining their structure and composition, the others, by industry and commerce, are transmuting them to gold. Possessed of the power of pleasing, they gratify on both sides; the one contemplates their natural beauties in the cabinet, the others, their re-created ones in the coffer.[172]

The 'duality' debate, which struggled then (and struggles now) with the question whether higher education should have a cultural or a practical purpose, developed an additional dimension when it came to the need to make provision for the education not merely of the scientists of the future, but also the entrepreneurs, managers and workmen manufacturing industry needed.[173] The civic universities which were being created in the great manufacturing towns of Victorian England were heavily reliant on funding by local industrialists who wanted graduates who could come and work in their factories as industrial scientists. The *British Quarterly Review* of May 1846 distinguished three kinds of university: 'the aristocratic, for *liberal accomplishment*…the sacerdotal, for *truth*' *and a third, to improve 'practical ability'*.[174] The first two needs were being met in the existing system. It was realized that the third was not. Industries needed industrial chemists, laboratory technicians, book-keepers and accountants and secretaries and even managers.

One of the prompters for the foundation of the British Association for the Advancement of Science had been the anger Brewster expressed when he could not get the financial reward he believed he was entitled to from the invention of the kaleidoscope, which he had patented in 1817. He railed against the current patent law and the way it tended to 'stab the inventor'.[175] He was not the only early member who felt like this; it was decided at the outset that there should be a subcommittee on the 'mechanical arts', though this did not get properly off the ground at first; it was the only committee which failed to report to the subsequent meeting of the Association held in Oxford. This was partly because Charles Babbage, expected to take the lead but distracted by other preoccupations, failed to write the requested paper outlining ways in which the serious sciences might be made useful in practical applications.[176] There were ambitious proposals, but they were dropped. By 1834 the committees of the Association officially included scarcely any aspect of the mechanical arts.

This began to change in 1835, when the Association met in Dublin and there was a sufficiently numerous group of interested individuals to take the matter seriously and make a link with the fact that the Association was to meet in a series of industrial towns. Babbage thought letting commercial motivation influence the direction of research might be doing harm to science. Encouragement of research by financial reward 'from the sale of the commodity' which results was a topic of considerable sensitivity to his friend Brewer, but Babbage robustly points out that 'all abstract truth is entirely excluded from reward under this system'.[177] Moreover, at this time, those capable of making new discoveries outnumbered those capable of applying them:

> Unless there exist peculiar institutions for the support of such inquirers, or unless the Government directly interfere, the contriver of a thaumatrope may derive profit from his ingenuity, whilst he who unravels the laws of light and vision, on which multitudes of phenomena depend, shall descend unrewarded to the tomb.[178]

It may be argued that 'sufficient encouragement is already afforded to abstract science' in the universities, but Babbage suggests that 'the lectures which are required from the Professor are not perhaps in all cases the best mode of employing the energies of those who are capable of inventing'.[179] If there is to be real advancement of knowledge, research needs freedom and funding. Governments ought to assist more with the funding of science, but with 'prudence and economy'.[180]

The difficulty continued, however, of determining the proper place for applied scientists in the hierarchy of the Association's endeavours. It was to be a subordinate one, and uncertain.[181] In 1831 there were six subcommittees, the last in the 'mechanical arts'. In 1832 there were four, and mechanical arts was not mentioned. In 1833, the first section covered mathematics and physico-mathematical sciences (and which 'mechanical arts' appeared again at the end of a long list of sub-sections). Mechanical arts had disappeared again in the list of six committees for 1834, but in 1835, there as a 'mechanical science' subsection for mathematics and physics.[182] There was criticism in the Report of the Mechanical Arts Section of the British Association held at Bristol in 1836. Excitement over the railways had, it was suggested:

> for several years so engrossed public attention, that other means of facilitating the operations of commerce and expediting the social intercourse of distant masses of people, less fascinating, but not less important, have been overlooked.[183]

Sections lists were associated with a general sense that there was a hierarchy of the sciences. From 1833 the British Association was able to make research grants.[184] There was also active lobbying of Government, with the potential to release more funding for approved projects Section A work (mathematics and physics) benefited disproportionately.[185] Another effect of these developments was to encourage collaborative projects, and team-work began to replace the pilot endeavours of interested individuals.

In 1879 Rayleigh, the Cavendish Professor in Cambridge, began to hold 'laboratory teas' in the afternoons (a novel time for tea, which had previously been a drink for the evenings), at which students and researchers and interested members of his family could meet and talk science. His wife sometimes came. His sister-in-law, who came too, was Eleanor Sidgwick, herself at work as a serious scientist trying to fix the basic units of electricity. These were at first Professorial social occasions but the benefits of being able to talk about work in progress were so apparent that 'staff rooms' began to be arranged for.[186] The Cambridge botanists of 1908 launched a magazine which they called the *Tea Phytologist*,[187] though it was not until the last third of the twentieth century that it became a matter of routine in some teams to keep a record of lab talk.[188]

James Muspratt (1793–1886) set up chemical works in Liverpool in 1823, which emitted poisonous clouds of hydrochloric acid; nevertheless, he was considered an educational benefactor; he helped to found the Liverpool Institute in 1825 and the Liverpool College of Practical Chemistry in 1848 (with his son Sheridan).[189] In the late 1870s Liverpool was swept by an enthusiasm for starting something locally to rival what had been done in Manchester, with meetings of civic worthies and support forthcoming from a range of local business and industry, willing and able to raise funds to endow chairs (the shipowners, for example, raised the money for a Chair in mathematics). Sir John Tomlinson (1842–1919) endowed three Chairs. The public gave and the corporation gave. Industrial benefactors and shipping magnates provided laboratories (Muspratt, Brunner, Gossage were among the leading names in this region). Industrial sponsorship went, then as now, with control of the uses to which the money was put, here often to meet the needs of local industries.

Industrially-minded local politicians saw the advantages of an expansion of higher education as clearly as politicians at national level. As the nineteenth century went on and the industrial 'base' expanded, there were calls for local universities to be set up specifically to meet the needs of local employers. Owens College was set up in Manchester (1846) by John Owens, who left the money needed in his will. From the colleges begun by local steelmasters came the University of Sheffield. The biscuit-manufacturing Palmers made possible the foundation of Reading's University.[190]

At Sheffield there was an understandable wish to specialize in metallurgical sciences, since local industry was dominated by the manufacture of steel. Sheffield had an ambitious Professor of metallurgy in Oliver Arnold, who had entered academic life from the role of chemist at a steelworks. His research was of the most practical kind, designed to introduce improvements which would be beneficial to industry, such as new alloys, electric furnaces (introduced from Sweden) and machines for measuring the stresses induced in steel by vibration. For a time after the University got its royal charter in 1880, Manchester University formed a 'federation' along with University College, Liverpool (which joined it in 1884) and the Yorkshire College in Leeds (1887). Liverpool became a University in its own right after it left the federation in 1903 and Leeds did the same in 1904. These were responses to the pragmatic discovery what constituted a critical mass.

Not all these industrialists were looking for industry-university collaboration or 'employer-led' courses. Some dreamed of starting new Oxfords and Cambridges. But those who did think industrially had the support of Hastings Rashdall, who gave a series of addresses pressing his view that the first universities had seen their purpose in the most pragmatic and vocational terms. It was to send out the graduates of their day into the contemporary professional workforce, then consisting of lawyers, physicians and the clergy. On the other hand, his conception of an employable graduate still stood squarely within the tradition where culture was important. Universities' 'greatest service to mankind was simply that they placed the administration of human affairs – in short, the government of the world – in the hands of educated men'.

Indeed, industrial benefactors could be particularly energetic in pressing for radical reform of the syllabus to ensure students emerged qualified to meet local employers' needs. Some of those involved in education planning in Birmingham wanted a new balance to be struck between science and technology on the one hand, and a liberal education on the other. Josiah Mason (1795–1881), self-taught local businessman and manufacturer and philanthropic founder of a local orphanage, was also an educational benefactor.

Resentment of privilege and the resulting policy development

The call for the universities to make adequate provision to produce the graduates the nation was going to need in science and technology, led to uncomfortable and searching questions for those who were already living the academic life, and particularly for Oxford and Cambridge. T.H. Huxley commented on the groundswell of popular and political resentment of what was seen as the privileged position of the two ancient English universities in 1874: 'Change is in the air...It insists on reopening all questions and asking all institutions, however venerable, by what right they exist.'[191]

He pointed out that even those enjoying the privileges are beginning to ask such questions: 'And it is remarkable that these searching enquiries are not so much forced on institutions from without, as developed from within. Consummate scholars question the value of learning.'

It is not difficult to detect in these debates threads which reflect prejudices, particularly against the two old universities, their ancient privileges, the perceived élitism of what they did and its alleged uselessness to the 'ordinary' person and the national economy. As Mark Pattison observed in 1868:

> Our lower middle class is now, for the first time, brought face to face with Oxford...the public, as soon as it looks into our affairs thoroughly, will immediately discover...that we are not the right sort of school for its purposes [and] that such a school as it wants could be conducted for probably a fourth of the cost.[192]

T.H. Huxley mentioned the matter in his inaugural address as Rector of the University of Aberdeen in 1874, sure of the sympathy of his audience if he argued that local Scottish institutions and their students were financially disadvantaged by current policy in comparison with the ancient English universities: 'In Aberdeen...endowments are numerous, but so small that, taken together, they are not equal to the revenue of a single third-rate English college'.[193]

And,

> I feel inclined to ask, whether the rate-in-aid of the education of the wealthy and professional classes, thus levied on the resources of the community, is not, after all, a little heavy?...And when I turn...to the real vision of many a brave and frugal Scotch boy, spending his summer in hard manual labour, that he may have the privilege of wending his way in autumn to this University.[194]

An aspect of the resentment of the perceived disproportionate generosity of the endowments of Oxford and Cambridge was the belief that it was somehow at the expense of making funding available to meet the growing national need for types of education (scientific and technical) which Oxford and Cambridge were not providing, or at least not sufficiently and not to a wide enough range of students, and which would meet needs now being felt in different places and for different social classes.

The Royal Commission on Scientific Instruction and the Advancement of Science (the Devonshire Commission, 1870) was meeting at the time when these arguments about funding were astir. Witnesses before the Devonshire Commission left it with a strong general impression that the quality of students opting for the sciences at Oxford and Cambridge was not high; they were ill-prepared by their (privileged) schooling; they were taught by Professors whose teaching load was now interfering with their research, partly because they had to cover the elementary education in the sciences for these students which the schools were failing to provide.[195]

Sir John Lubbock, who was a member of the Devonshire Commission, was inclined to blame the universities for not making bursaries available for would-be students of science coming from disadvantaged backgrounds. He saw the problem of getting children to study science at university as deriving in part from the fact that 'there is not the same number of awards for it in universities', so the schools do not prepare children by teaching them science, and that in its turn is why the universities do not make awards in the sciences, for the candidates are not coming forward.[196]

It was admitted in evidence to the Devonshire Commission that the study of the sciences at Oxford and Cambridge was not flourishing at student level (with only three students of mineralogy).[197] The Devonshire Commission made recommendations accordingly:

> The principal professions for which extensive preliminary scientific studies are required are the professions of medicine, consulting and manufacturing chemistry and civil, mechanical and telegraphical engineering. It is our opinion, therefore, that the universities should provide to the fullest extent for theoretical instruction of such professional students.[198]

The Commission accordingly blamed the universities. In a 'Memorandum of Suggestions for enlarging the System of State Aid to Scientific Instruction', which had been drawn up in 1867 under the auspices of the Lords of the Committee of Council on Education, one suggestion was that 'nothing can have much effect on the government schools and middle-class schools of the country, generally, until the universities...allocate a fair proportion of their endowments to the award of scientific studies'.[199]

The 1870s saw the second of the series of Royal Commissions of the nineteenth century and early twentieth century which enquired into Oxford and Cambridge. In 1871 each of two Vice-Chancellors received a letter, asking for 'the free and full assistance' of the Universities and the Colleges. The Oxford and Cambridge Act 1877 s.16 requires the colleges to make contributions to their respective Universities 'with a view to the advancement of art, science, and other branches of learning', and to make payments directly under the supervision of the University, 'for the giving of instruction, the doing of work, or the conducting of investigations within the University in any branch of learning or inquiry connected with the studies of the University.'

The Act of 1877 s.16(8) allows the Commissioners to make statutes: 'For altering the conditions of eligibility or appointment or mode of election or appointment to any professorship of lectureship, and for limiting the tenure thereof.' And 16(13) allows the Commissioners to make statutes for modifying trusts, endowments, foundations or gifts 'affecting any professorship, lectureship, scholarship, office, or institution, in or connected with the University'. The 1877 Oxford and Cambridge Act thus allowed the State to take control of funding given to the two universities and their colleges in earlier times and held in trust and redirect the way it was to be applied.

Revising the terms of old trusts was one thing. Winning new endowments was another, and new universities looked to a different kind of benefactor, the philanthropic industrialist. The new civic universities were, for the most part, well aware of the financial benefits of having 'links with industry', for their start-up funding and their continuing support frequently depended on the goodwill of local businessmen.[200] Huxley, speaking mainly of the secondary school level, reflected: 'I suppose the best of all possible organizations is that of a school attached to a factory, where the employer has an interest in seeing that the instruction given is of a thoroughly practical kind'.[201]

This was to be the trend of the future.

* * *

Applying science: Cambridge and the industrial uses of university research

Cambridge and early links with industry

Prince Albert's high profile efforts were an important sign of the times and not without their direct influence in strengthening the trend. Lyon Playfair spoke on 'Industrial competition and commercial freedom', in a discussion at the National Liberal Club, April 1888, on the importance to the national interest of the creation of an educated workforce:

> we must prepare to keep our position in the increasing struggle of nations. We must give more of a trained intelligence to our producers, intelligence to the rank and file, high technical education to the officers of our industrial armies. What is technical education? It is simply the rationale of expert empiricism...

The working men of technical skill and trained intelligence seek more education for themselves and their children because they know it both 'dignifies' and 'fructifies' their 'labour'[202]

There was uncertainty as to whether Oxford and Cambridge saw the benefits of fostering links with industry at first, though they gradually began consciously to do so. *The Cambridge University Reporter* of June 1899, reproduces a flysheet calling for 'A Proposed Appointments Association', W.H. Shaw suggested:

> there is reason to think that many openings would be available for capable men...in Banks or other business houses, in Metallurgical and other industries requiring a knowledge of Chemistry...and in the various branches of Engineering.

A meeting was held in the Senate House in November 1899 to which came leading representatives of commerce and industry[203] and Cambridge set up an Appointments Association. Addressing the inaugural meeting, the Vice-Chancellor said:

> The University from one point of view might be regarded as a large manufacturing concern. Every year in June it turned out a number of students with trained capacity and willing to work if work could only be found for them.[204]

Speakers expressed concern that the world was failing to realize how useful these graduates could be because of a vague notion that study at Cambridge took place 'far removed from the world'. One (Mr. G.S. Gibb) who knew something of the railway business said that he had made efforts to bring university men into it'.[205]

At a meeting held in Trinity College, Cambridge in 1903 one speaker urged: 'We ought to pay far more regard to the future careers of our students, and interest them by making them feel that what they learn would serve them in after life. A contempt for trade is not justifiable.'[206]

Francis Cornford comments slyly on this attitude in Chapter IX of his *Microcosmographia Academica* of 1908, 'On acquiring influence':

> Or, perhaps, you may prefer to qualify as a Good Business Man. He is one whose mind has not been warped and narrowed by merely intellectual interests, and who, at the same time, has not those odious pushing qualities which are unhappily required for making a figure in business anywhere else. He has had his finger on the pulse of the Great World – a distant and rather terrifying region, which it is very necessary to keep in touch with, though it must not be allowed on any account to touch you ... All business men are good; and it is understood that they let who will be clever, provided he be not clever at their expense.

Were Oxford and Cambridge out of line with the industrial links? Less than 20 per cent and often a bare 10 per cent or so of Oxford graduates went into business-related occupations in the 1900s.[207] Cambridge tried to make links with industry by getting its students into employment. Graduates must be encouraged to enter the workforce.

*   *   *

Widening access

Of College labours, of the Lecturer's room
All studded round, as thick as chairs could stand,

With loyal students, faithful to their books,
Half-and-half idlers, hardy recusants,
And honest dunces – of important days,
Examinations, when the man was weighed
As in a balance! of excessive hopes,
Tremblings withal and commendable fears,
Small jealousies, and triumphs good or bad –
Let others that know more speak as they know.
Such glory was but little sought by me,
And little won. Yet from the first crude days
Of settling time in this untried abode,
I was disturbed at times by prudent thoughts,
Wishing to hope without a hope, some fears
About my future worldly maintenance.
William Wordsworth, *The Prelude,* III, 64–9.

'Aspiration': Changing expectations of 'access' to higher education

'The ordinary man's ideas about institutions are apt to be governed by the models which he has before his eye,' remarked H.A.L. Fisher in an address he gave in 1927 when University College, London was celebrating its hundredth anniversary.[208] In the 1820s, he suggested, this was likely to include 'pleasant groves, streams and gardens', in which are educated 'boys from gentle homes'. The 'ordinary man' then

> conclude[d] that gentlemen are created to go to a University, and that a University is created to turn out gentlemen. To a mind so attuned...the idea that a University might be erected in the gaunt wastes of Gower Street for the sons of poor parents...came with the startling ring of a paradox.[209]

At first University College, London, stood to Oxford and Cambridge 'in the relation not of a child but a rebel,'[210] suggested Fisher. In a century much had changed, but not without a certain amount of struggle. Among the significant changes he was able to point to was the removal of the requirement that undergraduates at Oxford and Cambridge should be practising members of the Church of England, which had been one of the prompters to the launch of London and other colleges to meet the higher educational needs of dissenters. Modern universities aim, he suggests, 'to offer, a generous education in the higher learning divorced from religious tests and open to all, irrespective of creed, race, class or sex'.[211] But the perception that the ancient universities were of higher *standing* socially and intellectually did not die with such success stories, and the notion has persisted into the twenty-first century that they have been unfairly reserved for the socially privileged. This was however a perception of relatively recent origin.

Are able potential students discouraged from trying to study by social or financial disadvantage? If so, should society be trying to help? These are not new modern questions. Medieval universities were remarkably 'class-free' and so were the Oxford and Cambridge of the early modern centuries. Many of their most famous and successful graduates had come from poor homes or were the first in their families to go to university, as we have seen. Charitable 'funding' or the support of a patron or a religious order, 'sizarships' and 'servitorships',[212] were all broadly the equivalent of the modern bursary, grant or loan. Gentleman commoners were waited on by poor students who were 'servitors', and who ate what was left from the common table and got their education almost free. During the two succeeding centuries this system decayed and increasingly only gentlemen were admitted, with minor gentry and clerical offspring rather than the truly disadvantaged taking up such scholarships as were available.[213] So perhaps in the nineteenth century there was more merit in the claim that something needed positively to be done to widen access.

On the other hand, Oxford and Cambridge undergraduates in the 1820s seem to have included more sons of professional men and clergy and not such a preponderance of gentlemen's sons as had been the case in the eighteenth century.[214] And once the nineteenth-century creation of more and more institutions began, the social range of opportunity grew exponentially with them. The question then became how readily those who gained a higher education would be able to move within society so as to become accepted as the equals of those born to more privileged positions, how far social mobility would continue to be possible with a widening community of students of different sorts, studying a broadening range of subjects for an expanding variety of purposes. The ladder was no longer a simple structure leading upwards. To use a somewhat neo-Gothic image, it was becoming a scaffolding on a building which developed new wings and turrets and corridors, leaving the ambitious unsure where to put their feet. One might emerge in the servants' quarters when one had hoped to arrive in the drawing room.

Social mobility and social ease

The wish to establish a link between self-betterment through education and a general freeing up of the possibilities of social mobility early became embedded in the ambitions of social reformers. Samuel Taylor Coleridge (1772–1834) met Southey on a visit to Oxford in June 1794.

Together, in a fever of excitement, they devised the notion of creating a new settlement in North America which was to be run on egalitarian lines and known as a 'Pantisocracy'. Southey was an eager recruiter drawing in members of his family and his circle of friends much as Bernard of Clairvaux had done in an early twelfth-century explosion of early Cistercian enthusiasm. A sense of excitement and of new possibilities emanates from Southey's letters (12 October 1794): 'This Pantisocratic system has given me new life new hope new energy. All the faculties or my mind are dilated. I am weeding out the few lurking prejudices of habit and looking forward to happiness.'[215]

The theoretical underpinnings of this enterprise owed something to William Godwin's *An Enquiry Concerning Political Justice* (1793), a work with all the optimism of its time that society could be improved by rational adjustment of the activities of its members. This need not imply any class distinction between, or different expectations of, different groups in society. It was airily optimistic that 'change management' offered open-ended possibilities of improvement. Chapter VIII of the 1797 version is entitled 'Human Inventions susceptible of perpetual improvement':

> Let us carry back our minds to man in his original state, a being capable of impressions and knowledge to an unbounded extent, but not having as yet received the one or cultivated the other; let us contrast this being with all that science and genius have effected.

The proposers of Pantisocracy were never able to raise the money to put their scheme into operation, but it had a flavour which reflects contemporary trends and aspirations. It reflected the classical ideals of balance, of 'healthy mind in healthy body', restyled for a social experiment. 'The varied day of toil'[216] in a life which balanced intellectual and practical endeavours, was one objective, glimpsed even at this planning stage:

> My mind is never at rest not even for a moment. One grand object has fully possessed my soul...When Coleridge and I are sawing down a tree we shall discuss metaphysics; criticize poetry when hunting a buffalo, and write sonnets whilst following the plough. Our society will be of the most polished order...This prospect is only clouded by some slight shadows – My Aunt knows nothing of it[217] and we have money to raise.[218]

However, balancing the two in a reformed society raised some difficult questions for the would-be higher education reformer. The idea

317

that the class structure is something to be protected was persistent. The middle classes pose a problem. 'It is not to be expected that farmers and tradesmen should send their children to be the playfellows of the children of day-labourers in the parish schools.'[219] But such parents often pay for schools run by unqualified teachers where the standard of instruction is less satisfactory than that at a parish school. 'All who wish it ought to have a classical education to prepare them for the Universities and the learned professions.'[220] 'There will soon be no deserving boy in the kingdom in the lowest rank who may not, if his talents fit him for such promotion, win the highest University education by his industry.'[221]

In the later nineteenth century, it still tended to be the better-off and socially advantaged who could hope to enjoy the luxury of such varied and well-balanced lives. In the 1860s Mark Pattison expressed a wish to see the same educational system made available to all: 'We wish to restore the road, and maintain one broad-gauge line of refining education, along which all our youth, the aspiring and enterprising...shall be willing to travel.'[222]

T.H. Huxley's remarks of 1877 when he was a member of the London School Board were much quoted for some decades: 'I said our business was to provide a ladder, reaching from the gutter to the university, along which every child in the three kingdoms should have the chance of climbing as far as he was fit to go.'[223]

'Society' has done what it ought:

> When every working lad can feel that society has done as much as lies in its power to remove all needless and artificial obstacles from his path; that there is no barrier, except such as exists in the nature of things, between himself and whatever place in the social organisation he is fitted to fill.[224]

This takes the objective of opening the highest levels of learning to everyone, rich or poor, and links it with the possibility of upward social mobility for the graduate.

Mark Pattison noted the emergence in his generation of a new kind of educational need, not obvious when Southey and Coleridge fancied themselves as Pantisocrats. This was to educate for a new kind of work, industrial and 'business':

> [Until 1815] the aristocratical, political, professional, and clerical sections of society had been everything in social consideration...The career of English life lay...through the grammar-schools and universities. But the enormous development of commerce and manufactures since 1815

has opened a new world to energy. The career opened by commercial enterprise to the middle class is a far more tempting career to ambition than those opened by the old road of the professions and public life. The thousands who tread this path go without any education properly so called... these moneyed classes, containing the better half of the nation's wealth and life, lie outside the pale of our educational system.[225]

It was natural for nineteenth-century parents to hope that their sons would return from university with their characters 'formed' as well as their minds. The notion that a student ought not only to have knowledge and 'skills' but also be a particular kind, of person did not offend against contemporary expectations. There were, however, important questions about the exact 'kind of person' study at university should produce. Should he necessarily be religious? A gentleman? A good citizen? Cultured? Inventive and challenging? A good employee? And how far was it really possible for a boy to travel in his understanding and character if he wanted to move upward socially not merely in terms of professional status and earning power but also in matching the 'boy from a good home' in subtler accomplishments?

There survives among the Coleridgean 'anecdotes' an amusing example of the way in which the uneducated could move from mockery of things intellectual, to interest in them, which nicely illustrates how wide the gulf could be between the educated and the uneducated classes. Among some serving soldiers a 'misfit' was observed:

'The officers hastened into the room, and enquired of one and another, about that "odd fish" at the door' then 'it is believed, the surgeon... told them he was actually a "stray bird" from Oxford, or Cambridge.

'Ah, said one of the officers, 'we have had, at different times, two or three of these "University birds" in our regiment.' This suspicion was confirmed by one of the officers... who observed that he had noticed a line of Latin, chalked under one of the men's saddles'... 'The officers now kindly took pity on the "poor scholar" and had Mr. C. removed to the medical department, where he was appointed assistant to the regimental hospital'.

This misplaced graduate then began to talk to his comrades of military matters, in the form of stories from ancient history. 'He told them of the Peloponnesian War' and 'still more excited their wonderment, by recapitulating the feats of Archimedes.' But this was found to be too demanding, so he 'changed his subject, and told them of a famous general, called Alexander the Great'. The men hung on his stories: ' "Ah," said one man, whose open mouth had complimented the speaker, for the preceding half hour; "Ah" said he, "Silas, this Alexander must have been as great a man as our Colonel!" '[226]

A high hurdle for boys like the soldier with the open mouth was the difficulty of acquiring the social confidence of those boys born to upper-class life. The misfit soldier shows a sharp appreciation of the need to fit his tales to his audience but the appreciative comment is limited to finding a comparison which makes sense from a much narrower range of experience.

It had long been a presumption that the graduate became a gentleman at the end of his time at university:

> Where else can he learn so quickly in three years, – what other men will perhaps be striving for through life, without attaining, – that self-reliance which will enable him to mix at ease in any society and feel the equal of its members.[227]

But how easy was it for a boy to achieve ease, confidence, self-reliance in any company, if he did not spend his childhood in a gentleman's home? Charles Kingsley's *Alton Locke* contains depictions of university life and the standards of teaching which Kingsley later thought he might have exaggerated. But, written as it was in a white heat of fervour about social injustice, the very exaggerations are evidence of the social and cultural barriers an aspiring working-class boy would face. The hero's cousin George arrives, in the highest good spirits at having just taken a double first-class at Cambridge, airily proposing 'to get ordained as fast as ever I can', for he has patrons, one of whom has promised him a living as soon as he is 'in priest's orders'. Has he 'seen much of what a clergyman's work should be?' Has he 'read much for ordination'?

> Oh, as for that, you know it isn't one out of ten who's ever entered a school, or a cottage even, except to light his cigar, before he goes into the Church; and as for the examination, that's all humbug – any man may cram it all up in a month.[228]

There is the all social confidence of the graduate.

The hero's own visit to Cambridge is described so as to underline the near impossibility of an outsider's breaking into the social life of the place. He finds himself 'wandering up and down noble courts and cloisters, swarming with gay young men, whose jaunty air and dress seemed strangely out of keeping with the stern, antique solemnity of the Gothic buildings around.'[229]

He observes the confident young 'half a dozen powerful young men, in low-crowned sailors' hats and flannel trousers...some smoking cigars, some beating up eggs in sherry.'[230]

There were reformers – including Kingsley himself – who were keen to make the experiment of helping young men to bridge the gap. Some notion of the 'noble savage' lingered among the enthusiasts for winning a new 'dignity' for ordinary labour who were also, often, enthusiasts for lifting young people out of the class they were born into, by means of education:

> I should choose, by preference, a man of your class for experiments, not because the nature is coarser, or less precious in the scale of creation, but because I have a notion...that you are less sophisticated, more simple and fresh from nature's laboratory, than the young persons of the upper classes, who begin from the nursery to be more or less trimmed up and painted over by the artificial state of society – a very excellent state, mind, Mr. Locke. Civilisation is, next to Christianity, of course, the highest blessing, but not so good a state for trying anthropological experiments on.[231]

The barriers to social mobility were, however, as subtle as they were strong. We find the fictional clerk Leonard Bast in E.M. Forster's *Howard's End* reading Ruskin for self-improvement. (Forster was born in 1879 and was himself a Cambridge man. He had begun to write for the left-wing *Independent Review* in 1903. *Howard's End* was published in 1910.) Leonard Bast reads Ruskin on Venice: 'Leonard was trying to form his style on Ruskin: he understood him to be the greatest master of English Prose. He read forward steadily, occasionally making a few notes.'

Forster quotes a particularly convoluted sentence of Ruskin. Bast asks himself whether there is 'anything to be learned from this fine sentence? Could he adapt it to the needs of daily life? Could he introduce it, with modifications, when he next wrote a letter to his brother, the lay-reader?'

> And the voice in the gondola rolled on, piping melodiously of Effort and Self-Sacrifice, full of high purpose, full of beauty, full even of sympathy and the love of men, yet somehow eluding all that was actual and insistent in Leonard's life.

Leonard perceives that it does not speak to his condition. Yet,

> he felt that he was being done good to, and that if he kept on with Ruskin, and the Queen's Hall concerts, and some

pictures by Watts, he would one day push his head out of the grey waters and see the universe.[232]

He had glimpsed the world which he aspired to enter at a concert earlier, where he had fallen into conversation with the Schlegel family over an umbrella. As he listens to them 'discoursing at ease' he reflects 'With an hour at lunch and a few shattered hours in the evening, how was it possible to catch up?'[233]

Edgeworth's influential treatise of 1809 makes it clear that the range of careers deemed appropriate for the upper classes was still relatively limited in the extent to which is foresaw what was beginning to happen and where it was likely to lead. The nineteenth-century expansion of the need for technical skills and technical education greatly complicated the question what it was fitting for a gentleman to do for a living or an occupation. A clergyman was always a gentleman. A lawyer or a doctor might be a gentleman. It was not so clear that a craftsman or tradesman could become a gentleman when he 'qualified'.

The rise of anti-élitism?

The ancient universities were also sometimes seen as bastions of something else 'inaccessible' to 'ordinary people', an intellectual élitism, a culture which it was harder to acquire if one had not absorbed it in childhood. Glimpses of disapproval of intellectual privilege are to be had in nineteenth-century writing and comment. In view of Fisher's remarks, at its centenary, it is an irony that University College London has since become one of the 'top' institutions against which this criticism is levelled: 'When a degree in the professions can be taken only by men of independent fortune, the number of candidates in learning is lessened, and consequently the advancement of learning retarded.'[234]

'A waste of time?' The drop-out rate

If 'access' is 'widened' so that students from disadvantaged backgrounds can attend a range of new kinds of institution to study a broader range of subjects, will a higher proportion drop out or fail to complete the course? Student comments on their 'experience' of student life suggest that the reasons for dissatisfaction of 'dropping out' were probably more complex than can be accounted for in such crude terms. Not all students completed the course they began, even when they were 'gentlemen' studying at Oxford or Cambridge. For some the reason to depart was of a gentlemanly sort – boredom or an embarrassment of debts. William Makepeace Thackeray (1811–63) wrote to his mother to rationalize a decision to leave Cambridge without taking his degree, which had probably been prompted as much by his gambling debts as by the sentiments he expresses to her. His 'official' reason is that he has come to feel that taking a degree is a waste of time. What he was learning appeared to him to be irrelevant to his future needs:

> You seem to take it so much to heart, that I gave up trying for Academical honours – perhaps Mother I was too young to form opinions but I did form them – & these told me that there was little point in studying what could after a certain point be of no earthly use to me.

He spells this out. His 'opinions' told him:

> that subtle reasonings and deep meditations on angles and parallelograms might be much better employed on other subjects – that three years industrious waste of time might obtain for me mediocre honours which I did not value at a straw…I believe that study at the University is almost waste of time.[235]

In November 1818, Thomas Babington Macaulay wrote a letter to Hannah More as a Cambridge undergraduate, which is probably the one she is known to have sent on enthusiastically to his parents, calling it 'incomparable'. He compares the pleasures of 'association at this seat of the muses' with 'the cheerful blaze of a domestic hearth, the reciprocation of varied conversation and mixed company'. He finds he is 'no great admirer of this monastic life':

> This I look upon as the mere armoury of literature and of professional skill. The weapons which it furnishes for the contest of life are necessary to engage in it with distinction or utility…Whenever I forget the purposes of education, and cease to look upon classical and mathematical acquirements as the means of something better and nobler, may I become that pitiable being an old fellow of a college.[236]

So Macaulay, who was naturally studious, was able to look beyond the enjoyment of the moment and ask whether what he was learning was going to be useful to him in later life, and also whether study was really a fitting occupation for a lifetime.

By the April following his admission to Cambridge, Tennyson (1809–92) was writing gloomily to his Aunt:

> I am sitting Owl-like and solitary in my rooms [in Trinity]…The eternal riot of this place, the wear and tear of

mind and body are a very insufficient balm to the wound of recollection. When my dearest Aunt may I hope to see you again? ...the country is so disgustingly level, the revelry of the place so monotonous, the studies of the University so uninteresting... 'There is no pleasure like proof' cries the Mathematician. I reverse it, 'There is no proof like pleasure'.[237]

* * *

Entrances and exits

Alfred Lord Tennyson (1809–92) had an easy passage into Cambridge. In a letter of 5 December 1827, he wrote: 'I found no difficulty in my admission – I was examined by my tutor Mr. Whewell and the Dean [Henry Parr] who both said that I was fully competent to enter the University.'[238] Let us now look at some different experiences.

O.C. and the Crammer

Alfred Henry Lawrence (1859–1900) wrote his *Reminiscences of Cambridge Life* as 'O.C.' published in London, 1889.[239] He graduated from Trinity, and eventually became a barrister. He describes how he got into Cambridge, after a period of preparation with a crammer, 'one of the Resident masters of Arts, who took pupils, to be prepared for the Trinity Entrance Examination'.[240] He was earnest and not gifted with eloquence but his account of his experiences is painstakingly detailed. On his first visit to the University he was very much impressed by a glimpse of the University cricket ground on the way from the railway station. Once arrangements were made with his prospective tutor, he walked with his uncle 'through the courts built by Dr. Whewell a former Master of Trinity College', which he found keenly disappointing he says; he 'had often pictured it to myself and now these *little* courts were to be the fulfilment of my dreams'.[241] He changed his mind as he walked through them and was impressed after all.

He describes his impressions of the town, gained during the three months he spent at his crammer with a friend called Lowe, who was also in need of coaching if he was to reach the required entrance standard. They went for regular walks in their afternoon break from the intensive study imposed by their master, though Lowe was the more ambitious as to distance and would head out to Grantchester, Trumpington and Cherry Hinton. 'At times I had to consult a little map

I had purchased,' he explains. He identified the colleges and found the Fitzwilliam Museum and, of much greater interest, the Trinity College cricket ground. 'Another day when with my friend by Parker's Piece I said, "where by the bye is the river?" Neither of us knew, but having asked once or twice, soon made our way to it, crossing over Christ's Piece and Midsummer Common... Afterwards a walk by the Cam was my favourite way of spending the afternoons. I was much interested in the rowing and did not greatly notice the unpleasant smells which I was told hung about the river... after going down as far as the railway bridge or a little further, I used to return home quite satisfied.' He keenly watched boat races when he could.[242]

He was able to get a taste of the richness of the cultural life Cambridge had to offer. 'About the end of November, a Greek Play was performed at the Theatre' (Aristophanes' *The Birds*). It quickly sold out and an extra performance had to be put on. He comments that 'the Theatre was crowded with a fashionable assembly'.[243] He explains that non members of the Union could enjoy its facilities for a week if a member of the University entered their names as 'Strangers'. Their tutor gave his pupils this opportunity and O.C. went to hear a debate. 'The resolution was on the question of Confidence in H.N.Government'. 'The Debate was not over until about 11 o'clock, and it resulted in a victory for the Conservatives by 5 votes.' 'I longed for the time when I should be able to join with the others in the Debates'.[244]

The entrance examination arrived. O.C. says that he and his friend Lowe went to look at the examination hall the day before

and saw the places assigned to us for the morrow... the number of those competing was, as far as I recollect, 144... On the eventful morning, Lowe and I taking a little circuit, approached the exam. Room. A number of young men were strolling about with their Parents and Guardians, many looking very 'blue' indeed.

He took his papers, including the optional one on advanced mathematical topics, 'the subjects set being Higher Algebra, Trigonometry, etc'.[245] He got his place.

There was no 'gap year' to follow. He went back to the crammer's for 12 more weeks of preparation to begin his undergraduate career, 'being what is euphemistically surnamed by Undergraduates a "Beast"', for he was neither a member of the University nor entirely an outsider now.[246] There was a new pupil at the crammers who took him on the river to steer for him whilst he sculled, but this entertainment came to an end when O.C. developed 'a neuralgic headache' which he put down to his hat having fallen off into a ditch one day and got wet, so that it had an adverse effect on his head afterwards.[247]

The preparation he was undertaking now was for Little-Go, the first University examination, and he notes that 'at that time there was a great deal of discussion in the Senate' about this examination, 'with the view of adding fresh subjects, in order to make the examination harder than it has hitherto been'. The crammer taught to the examination, not requiring his pupils to do extra work 'until a decision had been come to on the question'.[248] The Little-Go took a week and proved a particularly testing one. 'The percentage who were "weeping and gnashing their teeth," was far in excess of the ordinary'.[249] However, the crammer, Mr. J.H. Taylor was one of the examiners and his former pupil did well, despite the introduction of the new requirement that 'unprepared Latin pieces' should be attempted.[250]

'O.C.' took lodgings for his new life as an undergraduate 'over Cave's, the boot shop in Sidney Street', 'the sitting room being of good size, close to the College, and having a private door'.[251] When he came into residence he bought all sorts of things on his first day, including engravings for his room. 'I believe the shops that I entered were legion'. He put on his cap and gown and went to see his tutor at Trinity, V.H. Stanton. Stanton spoke most kindly 'and gave him a copy of the rules of the University'.[252]

Matriculation came next. 'The order was sent round for us to be at our Hall by 9. a.m. Trinity's Praelector' took a register and 'we were all marched off to the Senate House'. O.C. explains that Matriculation is not an examination.

> It consists solely of paying a fee and subscribing one's name in full to the following declaration. *I promise to observe the Statutes and Ordinances of the University so far as they concern me, and to pay respect and obedience to the Chancellor and other Officers of the University.*[253]

He glimpsed something of the dignity of Cambridge ceremonial at the installation of a new Master of Trinity,

> The new Master, having arrived at the great gate which was closely shut and barred, knocked for admission, when the gate was opened by the head porter, to whom Dr. Butler handed the letters patent, and then the door was again

closed. The porter immediately carried the letters to the Combination Room, and delivered them to the Vice-Master, who proceeded at once with the other Fellows in order of seniority, to the great gate, which was at once thrown open...the new Master was then escorted to the chapel, where the authorised declaration was subscribed.[254]

O.C., now he was a student, joined clubs: 'the First Trinity Boat Club, the Trinity Cricket Club; the University Cricket Club; and the Nonconformist Union' (for its Sunday evening debates). He lists, wistfully, other clubs he might like to have joined, 'social ones', such as the Athenaeum and the Pitt Club and the Amateur Dramatic Club (mentioning Burnard its founder, who became Editor of 'Punch').[255] He was visited by his aunt and uncle, who were able to enlarge his circle of contacts in ways likely to be of use to him in later life. They encountered the MP for Cambridgeshire and O.C.'s uncle, who was also an MP, introduced him. He received an offer of a mount, if he should fancy hunting with the local hunt.[256] He made the most of the environs too.

> The country round is too tame to be really pretty, but, in the Spring, a walk through Grantchester meadows, with the river flowing at the bottom, is not uninteresting. The best drives are round by Madingley, passing the red brick Quadrangle of Girton on the Huntingdon Road, or by Trumpington and Shelford.[257]

In the winter, he 'saw the skaters enjoying their pastime on the upper part of the Cam. In the following week the frost suddenly broke up the paths and streets being as may be imagined in a great state of mud and slush'.[258]

But Little-Go was not the end of it for the undergraduate who wanted to take 'honours' and not just a Pass degree. There were mathematical 'Additionals' to be passed. O.C. took yet more extra coaching but came to the reluctant conclusion that he was not going to qualify. 'I "funked it"'.[259] He did not give up hope at once and asked to be allowed to study History alongside his mathematical preparations, discovering the interest of that and related subjects. 'Mr Fawcett was the Professor of Political Economy in the University. I attended his first lecture of the term, and though those present were far from numerous, the subject was treated in a most interesting manner'.[260] He had better opportunities of using the library than earlier generations. 'The University Library (to which, however, Undergraduates cannot take visitors) for anyone interested in seeing a vast accumulation of books'... 'Undergraduates are admitted in the afternoon in Academical costume'.[261]

The end of a somewhat undistinguished career left him with a strong incipient nostalgia. 'Before I left I had my rooms photographed, that I might possess a lasting memento of my Cambridge habitation.'[262]

Transitions

> Still there is wanting in England, upon almost every object of science, public means of acquiring information, free from unnecessary obstructions, and the pitiful sale of tickets for admission,[263]

lamented Edgeworth in 1809. The suggestion that the general public should not meet 'obstructions' if they wanted to keep up with new discoveries was revolutionary when he made it but, like other things in his book, it turned out to be forward-looking. This was the road which was to lead towards the modern notion of a 'knowledge society' in which it is deemed to be in the public interest for knowledge to be as widely disseminated as possible, but where that carries costs which have to be met by students themselves.[264]

In the nineteenth century it no longer appeared socially acceptable for some students to work their way through their university education as servants to others, as had been the earlier route for the poorer student.[265] Some were arguing that higher education should not continue to be the preserve of the wealthy and privileged it had now become. If not, how could the poor afford to become students? Should universities be free to everyone? If so, how would the cost of tuition and living costs for such students be covered?

School to university: Thomas Babington Macaulay

Francis Bacon argued that certain studies properly belonged at university not school level: 'Scholars in universities come too soon and too unripe to logic and rhetoric, arts fitter for graduates than children and novices. For these two, rightly taken, are the gravest of sciences, being the arts of arts'.[266]

What should a well-prepared student know, and to what standard at the beginning of a degree course? This was a question to be answered in one way in the case of a student who was going on to a traditional course in classics, who would be expected to know quite a lot of Greek and Latin on arrival, and in another if new subjects altogether were to be studied. But there was a central consideration in both cases. At what point – in terms of age and attainment – should school study end and university study begin in the nineteenth century? 'A young man passes from our public schools to the universities, ignorant almost of the elements of every branch of useful knowledge,' accused Charles Babbage (1792–1871) in 1830,[267] but his idea of 'usefulness' would not have been universally shared.

The transition was experienced very differently by different schoolboys as they became students. Not all were crammed like 'O.C.' Among the letters of Thomas Babington Macaulay are his homesick letters to his mother from the school he was sent to at Little Shelford near Cambridge in 1813. The schoolmaster was Thomas Preston, an evangelical clergyman. Macaulay worked extremely hard, getting up at five in the morning and 'fagging'. He discusses his methods of study when it comes to mathematics. 'I find, upon the whole, that to understand a proposition and know it are the same thing.'[268] Later he writes that when he translates Greek and Latin: 'the 1st time of going over I shall mark the passages which puzzle me, and then return to them again.'[269]

In April he was writing that he had 'already begun to season [himself] for working at the examination, the subjects for which will be given out in four weeks'.[270] A boy might reach an impressive standard academically in such a school. The examination included 'Mathematics, Euclid from the beginning as far as we have done. Lyrics, The burning of Muscow [sic] with a list of set texts and a 'declamation' on 'the Question of the Crusades' to be prepared'.[271] It seems that the school was organized in classes within which boys were placed with reference to their standard in a given subject rather than their age. So Macaulay, then only 12, is in the fourth class for some subjects, the third or the second for others, but in the first for French because his mother has taught him well.[272] A Fellow of Magdalene, George Hodson (1788–1855) took seriously the importance of helping the boy aspire to enter University; he took Macaulay to Cambridge for a short visit in April 1813.[273] Macaulay's Sundays ('quite a day of rest') were spent with 'pleasure' learning 'a chapter in the Greek Testament', going to church and reading. The only thing of which the small Macaulay complains is that he may have only one book at a time, and that he must finish it before he is allowed another.[274]

By 1818 Macaulay was an undergraduate at Trinity College, Cambridge. He was supplied with an excellent college tutor. He wrote home, this time to his father, that 'Cambridge is a strict exemplification of the old maxim, magna urbs, magna solitudo, and that I live among my small circle of friends as familiarly and as quietly as if we were in a desert island.'[275]

Going to a mechanics institute instead

The question where the boundary should lie between secondary and tertiary education, was much complicated by the advent of the new universities, and the mechanics' institutes, and the new subjects taught in them. In a lecture given as early as April 1783 on 'A Plan for the Improvement and Extension of Liberal Education in Manchester', Thomas Barnes DD had argued that the school leaver is 'unfurnished'. 'Few can afford to go to a college or a university' and 'so very few of those young men who are destined for trade enjoy any advantages beyond those of the grammar school. His hope was that means might be found of 'connecting together liberal science and commercial industry':

> The course of study he advocated was not to be a mere continuation of what had been given in school, but the application of school learning to superior objects. There were to be natural science, mathematics, languages ancient and modern, English literature, law ad commerce, mental and moral philosophy... The object of the scheme was to afford a training for the learned professions as well as for commerce.[276]

The surviving Birkbeck examination papers of the late nineteenth century suggest that the existence and location of this boundary was only gradually becoming clearer after some generations of students had made the transition, and now some were mature students and some were part-time. A considerable range of types of examination question is to be found in the Birkbeck *Syllabus of Classes and Examinations for the Session 1873–4 with the Results of the Examinations and the Examination Papers of the Year 1873* (Witherby and Co., London), with substantial variation in the level of difficulty. For 1873 the examination in Political Economy is very difficult and Universal History is absurdly easy (requiring mere descriptions and the listing of memorized answers).

The Arithmetic examination is designed to be a practical test of an applied and useful sort. The candidate for 1873 is invited to make out a bill for 44 lbs. 7 oz. beef, at 10 1/2d, and for 7327 tons rails, at £9 15s. There are questions to test facility in operations. A fraction is reduced to a decimal. Miles per hour are converted into feet per second. Calculations have to be done in both metric and imperial measures. There are scenarios of a sort likely to arise in actual commercial and business life. 'I sell certain articles at a profit of 57 per cent. on the selling price. What is the profit on the cost price?' In 1873,

Mathematics goes from simple arithmetic up to advanced, where the 'class is limited in number'. In the advanced class the syllabus seems to have been extremely flexible. 'Students may take up any branches of Mathematics they may wish to study. Text books may be ascertained on application to the Professor.'[277]

So there was a long and complex process of evolution and planning to be gone through if standards were to be agreed at which a student was considered to be studying at degree level rather than at 'school' level; and in 'mixed economy' institutions which prepared for the London University degree examinations as well as providing a wide range of courses not intended for would-be graduates the transition was not necessarily simply a move from 'school' to 'university' at all.

Indeed, with the advent of new types of institution the question of gaining admission took on a new complexion. For some courses one need only enrol.

University Examinations

Arthur Hilton was at Cambridge from 1869 to 1872. Hilton's undergraduate magazine, the *Light Green* (Cambridge, 1872) contains a jesting poetical description of an examination room in which some, but not all, are eager to come top:

> And the tables will be dotted o'er with paper, ink and
> quill,
> And some will do their papers quick, and run away
> to play[278]

And:

> There's not a man about the place but doleful
> Questionists:
> I only wish to live until the reading of the Lists.
> I wish the hard Examiners would melt and place
> me high.
> I long to be a Wrangler, but I'm sure I don't
> know why.[279]

The recent modern suggestion is that the classification of degrees is no longer useful.[280] It was far from uncontroversial even when it was first introduced at the beginning of the nineteenth century. There was robust exchange of views, as in *A Letter to the Rector of Lincoln College*, from 1807 which expresses strong views about 'the proposed method of classing the Candidates according to their merit'[281] ('You have absolutely lampooned the University; you have ridiculed its Governors not only in the sight of the young men, thereby weakening the due respect which they ought to pay to their Tutors; but in the face of the whole world have drawn an invidious comparison between this and a Sister University, so as to make the distance greater between them, and increase that unhappy jealousy which exists on each side.'[282]) 'Now the arrangement by classes would, in my opinion, be a most excellent plan,' concludes the author.[283] The Oxford Statute of 1809 accordingly says that

> those persons who shall appear to excel the rest of the candidates... to such a degree as to be thought worthy of some marked commendation, are to be entered in the first class... and in the second those who appear to have made a laudable though not distinguished progress.[284]

An *Ordo Senioritatis* was used in Cambridge in the eighteenth century to grade the best of the B.A.s.[285] The supreme Cambridge distinction was to be the Senior Wrangler of the year, a mathematical honour, but a title derived from the lingering medieval notion that an examination was essentially a disputation.

However, one of the most important developments of the nineteenth century in encouraging the setting of testing standards in examinations was the introduction of the Civil Service examinations. Getting a university place might not be just a matter of passing a qualifying examination to demonstrate an adequate level of preparatory education. Here the debate about the merits of competitive examinations which had been so fierce in connection with entry to the Civil Service[286] proved relevant once more. Indeed, *Propositions Made by the Head Masters of Schools to the University of Cambridge* survive in the name of Henry Latham, noting (p.3) that the advent of the Civil Service examinations has had the effect of causing parents 'to withdraw boys from schools and place them in the hands of tutors'.[287] This is expensive and bad for their morals.

The Passmen

At Padua, it was said in the eighteenth century, even the cattle might have doctorates: *so dottorono i bo.*[288] Nineteenth-century universities consciously faced the problem of what to do about the intellectually less able student. Below the classes of those taking what were now to be known as degrees with 'Honours', lurked the Passmen. 'Pass degrees' became the Oxford and Cambridge solution to the problem which presented itself in the persons of the less able offspring of the gentry. These 'poll men' were the subject of agitated debate in the 1860s, as Cambridge, badly shaken by its experiences with the first Royal Commission, tried to adjust its standards.[289] Pass degree candidates might come up from school in a cloud of ignorance about mathematics, as some Cambridge lecturers complained to the Public Schools Commission which reported in 1864.[290] Cambridge was reluctant to set an entrance examination but the Previous Examination was imposed as a required hurdle for everyone and easy though it was, the dimmer students (sometimes half the entry) 'were plucked outright'.[291] Ordination candidates could perform the worst of all.

It was also argued that the 'motley' collection of new options gave the student such a wide choice that it was possible to 'obtain a degree on very easy terms' by avoiding the hard core of the 'older subjects, which really are the back-bone of the Arts Curriculum'.[292] To counter this awkward possibility, it came to be accepted that all subjects were going to be regarded as equal. The new science subjects were not necessarily easier, insisted William Whewell, even if they were accessible to students who had not begun with the traditional classical education:

> Elementary mechanics, like elementary geometry, is a study accessible to all: but...it is a study which requires effort and contention of mind...there is no Popular Road to these sciences...The art of exact thought can be acquired only by the labour of close thinking.[293]

Perhaps the most important presumption to be established in the course of these rearrangements was this presumption of the equality of subjects. 'No question as to their relative importance, or as to the superiority of one to the other, can be seriously raised,'[294] suggested T.H. Huxley in 1872, discussing the relative merits of subjects for study. It followed that a graduate in one 'subject' must not be considered superior to a graduate in another. This was held to despite a concurrent wry recognition that this might not be true: 'The easiest way of obtaining a Degree is to take an Aegrotat in Botany. Always go in for the English Poem.'[295]

* * *

Cambridge graduates: good men, good citizens

Should the graduate still be a good man and preferably a practising member of the Church of England?

The requirements about wearing gowns meant that students and their conduct were visible to the University's disciplinary officers, the Proctors, at least at certain times of day and in the course of certain activities. But this visibility merely presented the surface of deeper questions about appropriate student behaviour which were being asked throughout the nineteenth century. William Godwin had believed moral improvement could be achieved by application and practice much like getting better at an art or a science:

> Such was man in his original state, and such is man as we at present behold him. Is it possible for us to contemplate what he has already done without being impressed with a strong presentiment of the improvements he has yet to accomplish? There is no science that is not capable of additions; there is no art that may not be carried to a still higher perfection. If this be true of all other sciences, why not of morals? If this be true of all other arts, why not of social institution?... This is the temper with which we ought to engage in the study of political truth. Let us look back, that we may profit by the experience of mankind; but let us not look back as if the wisdom of our ancestors was such as to leave no room for future improvement.[296]

Victorian England found it difficult to think of moral goodness except in the context of being a sound practising Anglican. This tendency was strengthened by the continuation for much of the century of the restriction that only members of the Church of England might be admitted to Oxford or Cambridge. Adam Sedgwick's analysis of the moral purposes of a Cambridge education in his day fitted, to his mind, perfectly naturally into the sonorous periods of a lengthy sermon, and when he turned the sermon into a book and added copious notes he did not see a need to change the tone. But others, no less sincerely pious, were able to adjust the proportions of their concerns and dwell more firmly on purely intellectual aspects of the continuing controversy.

A striking contemporary exception to the pervasive approval of Anglicanism is Benjamin Disraeli, who published his novel *Coningsby* in 1844. His 'object', he said in a dedicatory note to Henry Hope was 'to scatter some suggestions that may tend to elevate the tone of public life'.[297] Among them was the desire to persuade his readers to reexamine their assumptions about Judaism, 'and to meet in a spirit worthy of a critical and comparatively enlightened age, the position of the descendants of that race who were the founders of Christianity', as he wrote in a new preface in 1894.[298] Other novelists were at best equivocal in their attitudes to Jews; Trollope, for example, in *The Way We Live Now* makes his villain Melmotte a

Jew and the characters struggle to approve of even a 'good' Jew as a marriage partner for a well-born young woman.[299]

But Disraeli, too, took it for granted that 'the renovation of the national spirit' was an appropriate objective for those who would influence the education of the young. His hero Coningsby and his friends at Eton share 'a reigning inclination for political discussion'.[300] Coningsby arrives at Cambridge 'neither a prig nor a profligate; but a quiet, gentlemanlike, yet spirited young man, gracious to all...and giving always an impression in his general tone that his soul was not absorbed in his university'.[301]

Disraeli suggests that though he had 'already acquirements' which would 'ensure him at all times his degree', there was no need for a Coningsby to bother with honours. He merely 'chalked out for himself that range of reading which, digested by his thought, should furnish him in some degree with that various knowledge of the history of man to which he aspired'.[302]

So here is a literary 'hero' who could have been one of Adam Sedgwick's own students when he preached his important sermon,[303] eager to form his mind and his morals but not strictly within the Christian mould Sedgwick would have approved. This is a long way from the clerisy of early Cambridge and the embattled years of the puritan revolution, but before the University Tests Act of 1871.

The 'gentlemanlike' but 'spirited' Coningsby looks beyond the university for his career. Should universities prepare graduates for public service, and adapt their syllabus and teaching for the purpose?

* * *

Enter the Cambridge University Reporter

The first issue of the *Cambridge University Reporter*, Michaelmas Term, 1870, was published on 19 October. It contains a declaration of purpose. It was to provide a way of bringing together conveniently between covers on a regular basis all the loose leaves in different sizes on which the University's business was currently printed and to ensure that important happenings such as the withdrawal of a Grace are properly and officially recorded and not just mentioned in a public newspaper.[304] It was thus to become the official consolidated record of the University's proceedings. But it was also to be something more, an 'unofficial' forum. It:

> [w]ill have no party purpose to serve. Political questions which are out of place in a University will be excluded

from its columns. The following was among the principal objects of its publication: To afford an opportunity for open discussion on all subjects fairly connected with the interests of the University.

The *Reporter* was to include a letters column. There were also little articles, such as the one by G.M. Humphry in the first issue. He had taken two eminent Professors, one English and one German, on a tour. The German said he thought the money spent on 'the many grand' buildings would have been better spent on 'promoting scientific education'. If it had, 'how very different would now be the position of Cambridge and England with regard to science,' he claimed. He also said he thought it could not be good for the young to live in college, cooped up together, fed and looked after. He thought it would 'tend more to the development of their character and energies and the sharpening of their faculties, at that time of life, to rub more against the outer world, and provide for and take care of themselves'. His final thought, after a good dinner at Trinity, was that wealthy benefactors ought to be encouraged to build a laboratory. 'There are plenty of riches here, why are not more laboratories built for your University?' It is to be assumed that the intention was indeed to prompt debate in the University by publishing in its new formal historical record reflections on such clearly important and potentially far-reaching matters, and it seems that contributors behaved responsibly. Their comments were, after all, to be laid before their colleagues with unprecedented efficiency of distribution within the University.[305]

Active use was made of the letters column (which evolved almost at once into 'letters and reviews'). It was a means of raising a topic of concern in an informal manner. For example, on 8 February 1871 there was a letter from C. Trotter about the question of financial support from colleges to enable the University to pay its way, a matter which was central to the work of the Commissioners and to the ensuing 1877 Act.[306] This was followed on 15 February by a crisp letter from W.H.H. Hudson of St. John's:

> The needs of the University may be roughly classified under two heads. First: the supply and maintenance of buildings and apparatus. Secondly: teachers. I urge that the men for the latter ought to be supplied by the colleges. This was, in effect, to propose a form of joint appointment. 'It may be presumed that the higher stipend and the distinction of a Fellowship would be more attractive than the £150 a year which the University proposes to give.' And the College would benefit

because 'one of its Fellows would have definite University work to do'.[307]

On 22 February of that first year, there were letters on the Previous Examination, Academic teachers, Celibacy in the University, the need for more punctual circulation of Flysheets, the separation of Law and History at Oxford, and the Hitchin College for Women.[308] Henry Sidgwick's letter on academic teachers as those who 'alone can keep the machinery of teaching ever on a level with the advance of knowledge',[309] also appeared.

We are back where we began, at the beginning of the modern University. The reader may observe with interest in the pages of the online Reporter today the current progress of events.

CONCLUSION

> How are we to provide for the maintenance and transmission of all this rich treasure of knowledge which has been painfully accumulating in the past? Can a more proper place for the purpose be found than in our Universities? A University is ... 'a corporation which has charge of the interests of knowledge as such, the business of which is to represent knowledge by the acquirements of its members [and] to increase it'.[1]

To tell the tale of Cambridge's life for the 800 years of its history is to tell this much bigger story. Here in microcosm is the intellectual life of Europe, and from early modern times, of the world. The tale of the way academics have led the development of ideas and scientific understanding, and helped to ensure that knowledge has a practical application and benefits the world economy, is not of course confined to Oxford and Cambridge. But for many centuries they were a main engine of such developments in England and a considerable force much more widely.

One must not pretend that the contributions of Oxford and Cambridge can be wholly separated. Their narratives interweave, and at times they form a single thread. Many of the leading intellectuals involved with one over the centuries have spent time at the other. This book and its companion volume on Oxford both glance across the English Midlands from time to time, with an amused deference to the required rivalry.

Yet Cambridge, like Oxford, has adapted to the changing atmosphere and expectations of changing times while remaining distinctively itself. Sometimes it has been inward-looking and self-absorbed but it has always had within it individuals who were thinking thoughts and writing books and in due course doing experiments which would change the world.

The institutional development of Oxford and Cambridge was at the outset 'of a piece' with what was happening elsewhere in Europe in the other early universities. They formed small democracies of academics.

These little latter-day versions of Greek city states persisted in this method of self-government long after universities in other parts of Europe had been taken over by secular and ecclesiastical authorities. They have worked out a way of running themselves which has often been dysfunctional. Internal squabblings appear many times in these pages; but these were mostly healthy arguments, and the evolving democratic constitution has so far proved a strong and flexible structure – and by the measurement of international league-tables even today, a resoundingly successful one.

So these twin studies have sought to do something new in placing Oxford and Cambridge in this wider context of their contribution to history, particularly to intellectual history, and, where appropriate, the always significant place of their doings in contemporary politics.

NOTES

1   Cambridge in living memory: the last hundred years

1. Robert Willis, *The architectural history of the University of Cambridge* (Cambridge, 1886), 3 vols., Vol. I, pp.1ff.
2. Ibid., pp.89ff.
3. F.A. Reeve, *The Cambridge that never was* (Cambridge, 1976), p.5.
4. Ibid., p.6.
5. Ibid.
6. Ibid., p.9.
7. Ibid., p.6.
8. Andrew Sinclair, *My friend Judas* (London, 1959), p.138.
9. Frederic Raphael, *The glittering prizes* (London, 1976), p.53.
10. John Cowper Powys, *Autobiography* (New York, 1934), pp.145–6.
11. Ibid., p.167.
12. Ibid., p.147.
13. John Cowper Powys, *Letters of John Cowper Powys to his brother Llewelyn* (London, 1975), Vol. I, pp.22–3.
14. Powys, *Autobiography*, p.151.
15. Ibid., p.167.
16. Francis Cornford, *Microcosmographia academica* (1908), Gordon Johnson, ed., *University politics: F.M. Cornford's Cambridge and his advice to the young academic politician* (Cambridge, 1994), p.13.
17. W.C. Lubenow, *The Cambridge Apostles, 1820–1914* (Cambridge, 1998), p.297, quoting Strachey papers, BL Add, MS 60707,ff. 96–96v.
18. Francis Cornford, *Microcosmographia academica* (1908), and see the new ed. by Gordon Johnson with a detailed introduction (Cambridge, 1994).
19. Raphael, *The glittering prizes*, p.26.
20. Ibid., p.36.
21. H.A.L. Fisher, 'Our universities', address given to mark the centenary of University College, London, on 30 June 1927, p.21.
22. Cornford, *Microcosmographia*, in *University Politics*, ed. Johnson, II.
23. Ibid., IV.
24. Ibid., VIII.
25. Ibid.
26. Ibid, I.
27. See pp.255–6.
28. Irene Lister, *Cambridge characters* (Cambridge, 1978), p.47.
29. Gwen Raverat, *Period piece: a Cambridge childhood*, first published 1952(Bath, 2003), p.47.
30. Ibid., p.273.
31. Ibid., p.78
32. Ibid., p.46.
33. Ibid., p.16.
34. Josephine Kamm, *Hope deferred* (1965), Chapter XVIII.
35. Cornford, *Microcosmographia*, in *University Politics*, ed. Johnson, III.
36. 1818–1863, historian.

37. See, too, *Reporter* (1896–7), pp.749–51.
38. Camhist, Vol. IV, p.325.
39. *Reporter,* 26 March 1897, p.791.
40. Ibid., p.793.
41. Ibid., p.761.
42. Ibid., p.750
43. On this, see too, ibid., pp.765 and 783.
44. Ibid., p.775
45. Ibid., p.742.
46. Cornford, *Microcosmographia,* in *University Politics,* ed. Johnson, p.35.
47. Ibid., pp.16–17.
48. This picture is reproduced in Gordon Johnson, *University Politics,* plates.
49. *Poems by Frances Cornford* (Cambridge, 1910).
50. Rupert Brooke, *Letters,* ed. Geoffrey Keynes (London, 1968; November 1909), pp.196–7.
51. Ibid., p.190.
52. Ibid., p.186.
53. Christopher Hassall, *The prose of Rupert Brooke* (London, 1956) prints some examples.
54. Ibid., pp.72–3.
55. Virginia Woolf, *The early journals,* ed. Mitchel A. Leaska (London, 1990), p.223.
56. Ibid.
57. Gordon Johnson, *University politics* (Cambridge, 1994), p.2.
58. Leonard Woolf, *Sowing: an autobiography of the years 1880–1904* (London, 1967), p.97.
59. Ibid., p.104.
60. Ibid.
61. Ibid., p.135.
62. *Reporter,* 1920–1, pp.60–8. 1921 Commission on women issue, Camhist, pp.326–7.
63. *Reporter,* 28 October 1921, p.193.
64. Camhist, p.326.
65. Virginia Woolf, 'A woman's college from outside', *The complete shorter fiction of Virginia Woolf,* ed. Susan Dick (London, 1985), p.141. Camhist, Vol. IV, p.328.
66. Debate of 24 July 1907 col. 1526–33.
67. Ibid., Gore, col. 1526.
68. The separate Oxford and Cambridge Acts of the 1850s and the Oxford and Cambridge Act of 1877.
69. House of Lords Debate of 24 July 1907 col. 1526–33, Gore, col. 1527.
70. Ibid., col. 1529.
71. Ibid., col. 1530.
72. Ibid.
73. Ibid., col. 1531.
74. Ibid., Gore, Bishop of Birmingham, col. 1532.
75. Ibid., Bishop of Bristol, col. 1533.
76. Ibid., Bishop of Bristol, col. 1533 and 1538
77. Ibid., Lord Ellenborough, col. 1539.
78. Ibid., Lord Ellenborough, col. 1540.
79. Ibid., Lord Ellenborough, col. 1540.
80. Ibid., Lord Ellenborough, col. 1542.
81. Ibid., Bishop of Hereford, col. 1546–7.
82. Ibid., Earl of Crewe, col. 1555.
83. The Old Vicarage, Grantchester, *Café des Westens,* Berlin, May 1912, http://www3.amherst.edu/~rjyanco94/literature/rupertchawnerbrooke/poems/grantchester/grantchester.html
84. 24 February 1915, *The Cambridge mind: ninety years of the* Cambridge Review,1879–1969, ed. Eric Homberger, William Janeway and Simon Schama (London, 1970), pp.31–3.
85. Camhist, p.331.
86. *Reporter,* 20 May 1919, p.752, Needs of the University.
87. Ibid., 28 March 1918, pp.546ff.

88. Ibid., p.547.
89. Ibid., 7 October 1918, p.50. Discussed 29 October 1918, *Reporter*, p.149.
90. Ibid., 4 February 1918, p.434.
91. Ibid., 3 April 1919, p.572, Research students' work approved.
92. J.B. Priestley, Foreword to Thomas Thornley, *Cambridge memories* (London, 1936).
93. Under the Education Reform Act 1988, s.202.
94. Bodleian MS Asquith 139, Top. Oxon. B.104–9.
95. Ibid., p.33.
96. Ibid.
97. Ibid., p.35.
98. *Hugh Dalton, Robert Young, J.L. Stocks,* 2 July 1920.
99. MS. Asquith 139, p.96.
100. Ibid., p.100.
101. Ibid., p.104.
102. Ibid., p.965.
103. Ibid., pp.119ff.
104. Ibid., p.67.
105. Ibid., p.58.
106. Ibid., pp.179ff.
107. Ibid., pp.32, 43–4.
108. Ibid., p.32, p.4.
109. Ibid., p.32, p.73.
110. Ibid., p.68.
111. Ibid., p.237, p.250.
112. Ibid., p.35.
113. Ibid., p.169.
114. Ibid., p.172.
115. Ibid., p.39.
116. Ibid., p.40.
117. Ibid., p.37.
118. Ibid., p.38.
119. Ibid., p.37.
120. Ibid.
121. Virginia Woolf, *A room of one's own,* ed. S.P. Rosenbaum (Oxford, 1992), Vol. I.
122. MS. Asquith 139, p.41.
123. Ibid.
124. Ibid., p.48.
125. Ibid., p.53.
126. Ibid., pp.54–5.
127. Ibid., p.158.
128. Ibid., p.237.
129. Ibid., p.159.
130. Ibid., p.160.
131. Ibid., p.32, pp.47–8.
132. Statute D, XII, 8.
133. Statutes identify administrative officers, including the Chancellors, the Vice-Chancellor, the High Steward, the Proctors, Orator, Registrary, Assistant Registrary, Librarian, Treasurer, Director of the Fitzwilliam Museum, Esquire Bedell, Censor of Non–Collegiate Students (Statute D,II,1) They can be sacked (D,II,9) if 'not satisfactorily performing the duties or fulfilling the conditions of tenure of his office'.
134. Christopher Andrew, 'Cambridge Spies', *Cambridge contributions,* ed. Sarah J. Ormrod (Cambridge, 1998), pp.208–223, pp.209–10.
135. Ibid., p.213.
136. Ibid., pp.208–223, p.214.

137. Harry Hinsley, *Proceedings of the British Academy*, 120 (2003), pp.264–5, and see Andrew, 'Cambridge Spies', pp.208–223, pp.208–9.
138. *The Cambridge mind*, p.59.
139. http://nobelprize.org/nobel_prizes/medicine/laureates/1962/watson–speech.html
140. Letter to the Editor, 23 October 1931, *The Cambridge mind*, p.47.
141. *Reporter* 9 December 1936, on Statute B,VI,2, see p.360. The plan was to move from the old 'six [wise] men *sex viri* who had sat with the Vice–Chancellor as an internal court of appeal, to the *septemviri* (who do so now)'.
142. *Reporter,* 9 June 1936, p.1105.
143. Ibid.
144. Ibid., 21 April 1936, pp.880–1.
145. Ibid., 7 November 1932, pp.294–7.
146. Ibid., 28 July 1939, p.1290.
147. Ibid., p.1291.
148. Ibid., 31 October 1939, p.212.
149. http://www.ivpbooks.com/275. Timothy Dudley-Smith, *John Stott* (Leicester, 1999), Vol. I, Chapter 3.
150. Donald Keene, in *Fifty years of Japanese at Cambridge, 1948–98*, ed. Richard Bowring (Cambridge, 1998), p.20.
151. *Reporter*, 27 February 1940, p.593.
152. Ibid., 12 March 1940, p.648,
153. Ibid., 24 November 1943, pp.207–8.
154. Keene, in *Fifty years of Japanese at Cambridge*, p.20.
155. *Reporter,* 2 December 1941, p.264, on Report of, p.200 about extending his tenure of office.
156. William Skillend, in *Fifty years of Japanese at Cambridge,* pp.11–12.
157. *Reporter,* 12 October 1948, p.204.
158. Ibid., 28 October 1948, p.282.
159. Skillend, in *Fifty years of Japanese at Cambridge*, p.10.
160. Ibid., pp.12–3.
161. Keene, in *Fifty years of Japanese at Cambridge,* p.28.
162. Ibid., p.31.
163. *Reporter*, 1943–4, p.402.
164. Ibid., 3 December 1946, p.358, Memorial published on pp.269, 294.
165. Ibid., 11 November 1947, pp.295–6, on the *Report of the Syndicate appointed to consider the status of women in the University* (published) (Cambridge, 1946), p.234.
166. *Reporter*, 25 May 1948, pp.1229ff. Discussion of *Second report of the Syndicate appointed to consider the status of women in the University,* p.1148.
167. Ibid., 8 March 1967, p.1011, for example. See, too, Tullberg, *Women at Cambridge* (Cambridge, 1998), p.180.
168. Sinclair, *My friend Judas*, pp.9–10.
169. Andrew Sinclair, *In love and anger: a view of the sixties* (London, 1994), pp.9–10.
170. Ibid., pp.6–7.
171. Ibid., pp.12–3.
172. Ibid.
173. Sinclair, *My friend Judas*, p.224.
174. Tom Sharpe (d.1928, Pembroke) Porterhouse Blue (1974) (London, 2002), pp.1–2.
175. Ibid., p.11.
176. Ibid., pp.1–2.
177. Ibid., p.31.
178. Ibid., p.160.
179. Cf. Education Act 1994 Part II.
180. Hinsley, *Proceedings of the British Academy*, 51 (1965), pp.418ff.
181. Ibid., *Proceedings of the British Academy*, 61 (1975), pp.439ff. and 457–9.
182. Sinclair, *In love and anger*, p.29.

183. Ibid., p.16.
184. *Cambridge commemorated: an anthology of University life,* ed. Laurence and Helen Fowler (Cambridge, 1984), p.21.
185. Martin Thompson, 'The lure of landscape', *CAM,* 55 (2008), pp.14–17.
186. *Reporter,* 13 March 1962, p.1111.
187. Ibid., 1961–2, pp.1073–1150, p.1104.
188. Ibid., 10 February 1948, p.721.
189. Ibid., 13 March 1962, p.1107.
190. Raphael, *The glittering prizes,* p.22.
191. A Report Discussed on 20 January 2009.
192. According to the anecdote, Crick had agreed to become a Fellow on the basis that no chapel be placed in Churchill. A majority of Fellows voted the other way when a donation was offered to enable them to build one. He replied with a letter containing a cheque for £10 for the provision of a brothel, for no Fellow need use it unless he chose.
193. *Report of the Committee on Higher Education* (Robbins) (1963), Appendix 4, Section 3, para.73.
194. See Oxhist VIII, pp.603–5.
195. *Report of the Committee on Higher Education* (Robbins) (1963).
196. *Reporter,* 8 May 1968, p.1931.
197. http://www.qaa.ac.uk/reviews/institutionalAudit/handbook2006/default.asp.
198. *Reporter,* 10 October 1962, p.231.
199. Ibid.
200. Ibid., (1967–8), 6 December 1967, pp.716–727, p.720.
201. *Times Higher Education Supplement* and *Times Higher Education,* back page.
202. *Reporter,* 24 October 1961, p.337.
203. Ibid., 3 October 1968, p.297.
204. Ibid., p.297.
205. As early as 1961, Mr. A. Hyde spoke against the idea 'that a Grace' should lie upon a table 'for a stated number of days, and if no notice of non-placet is given, it should be automatically considered as having been agreed', *Reporter,* 24 October 1961, p.337. The 'procedure' Hyde deplored whereby 'Graces of the Regent House are published and are deemed to have been approved in the absence of objection by a prescribed date' had been only 'recently adopted' in 1967. Graves Report, *Report to the Council of the Senate on the administrative organization of the University* (*Reporter* (1967–8), 13 October 1967, pp.333–67, p.337).
206. Cf. the Franks Commission in Oxford in the 1960s.
207. Graves Report, 13 October 1967, pp.333–67, p.336.
208. *Reporter* (1967–8), 1 November 1967, pp.454–501.
209. Ibid. (1967–8), 6 December, 1967, pp.716–727, p.720.
210. Ibid., pp.716–727, p.722.
211. Ibid., pp.716–727, p.727.
212. University car parking problems are a good example, 'University car parking problems and policy', *Reporter* (1967–8), 13 October 1967, pp.333–67, p.340. Long Discussion, pp.635–41.
213. *Reporter* (1967–8), 6 December 1967, pp.716–727, p.713.
214. Ibid., pp.716–727, p.717.
215. Ibid., pp.716–727, p.720.
216. Ibid.
217. HL 468 col. 1058ff., HL 470, col. 1138ff.
218. Hansard, 123 (1987–8), HC Debates of 1 December 1987, col. 779.
219. Standing Committee J, col. 1653–4.
220. Ballot of 27 and 28 October 1988, flysheets printed in the *Reporter* on 2 November, pp.132–6.
221. Cf. *Reporter,* 1984–5, p.511.
222. Ibid., 19 May 1989, p.619.
223. Ibid., 21 June 1989, p.779.
224. See Statute A,V,1 and 6.

225. A Statute had been included among the 1926 statutes (then K,4), which allowed a representation to be made to the Vice–Chancellor that something had been done *ultra vires*, specifically in breach of the University's Statutes and Ordinances. This continued in existence, though now it is Statute K, 5. As a corrective if one turned out to be needed, mechanisms of accountability were proposed. Topics of Concern were to take the place of the old Matters of Concern. These 'topics' could be raised for Discussion in the Senate House by members of the Regent House.

226. *Reporter,* 21 June 1989, p.778, The 'speeches' on this occasion were not published verbatim or even in reported speech but were summarized for publication.

227. Ibid., 1988–9, p.616.

228. http://www.admin.cam.ac.uk/reporter/2000–01/weekly/5822/22.html, Reporter, 18 October 2000.

229. http://www.publications.parliament.uk/pa/cm199899/cmselect/cmsctech/17/9020104.htm

230. Ibid.

231. Ibid.

232. Ibid.

233. http://www.cam.ac.uk/univ/nobelprize.html

234. http://www.publications.parliament.uk/pa/cm199899/cmselect/cmsctech/17/9020104.htm

235. http://www.admin.cam.ac.uk/reporter/1999–2000/weekly/5795/23.html, *Reporter*, 15 December 1999.

236. The University of Cambridge and MIT will create the Cambridge–MIT Institute (CMI) which will support academic collaboration in four broad areas: undergraduate education; a programme of integrated research; professional practice programmes in innovation and entrepreneurship; and the creation of a National Competitiveness Network of the Enterprise Centres recently announced by the Government, *'Reporter,'* 8 November 1999, p.130.

237. http://www.admin.cam.ac.uk/reporter/1999–2000/weekly/5790/2.html, The Council and the Board will publish a Joint Report later in the current academical year, containing detailed proposals necessary to establish CMI and to effect the academic collaboration, *Reporter,* 10 November 1999, p.130.

238. http://www.admin.cam.ac.uk/reporter/1999–2000/weekly/5806/21.html, *Reporter*, 22 March 2000.

239. http://www.admin.cam.ac.uk/reporter/1999–2000/weekly/5806/21.html, *Reporter*, 22 March 2000.

240. On impressions in the USA, see http://tech.mit.edu/V122/N7/col07wasfy.7c.html http://tech.mit.edu/V122/N9/col9kttan.9c.html

241. http://www.q–flo.com/profiles/profile–ahw.pdf

242. http://www.cambridge–mit.org/. There was a slightly desperate air about the claim on the website that now, in its dying months: 'building on past successes, and anchored in the 2003 strategic review, CMI is launching a series of bold experiments designed to test key hypotheses about the knowledge exchange process. We will set these experiments in the context of research programmes, the outcomes of which will flow to our educational programmes, and will be made available for uptake by UK industry, government and educational institutions through our strategic networks.'

243. Dr. M.R. Clark: 'I have voiced considerable concerns over the University's proposed policies on intellectual property rights, in particular over how changes in policy might impact in a detrimental way on our academic freedoms and on our personal rights. Freedom to tell the truth as you see it. Freedom to say anything in teaching? Freedom to publish. Freedom to research anything. The freedom to pursue knowledge wherever it leads and seek the truth even if it turns out to be unpopular. (*Reporter*, 30 October 2002–3, 5901, p.16)

244. http://www.admin.cam.ac.uk/reporter/2002–03/weekly/5901/16.html

245. Professor William Cornish, a leading intellectual property rights lawyer, set out the history of the matter in Cambridge in a speech in Discussion:
'In 1977 Cambridge refused to join the general rush of higher educational institutions to assert their ownership of patent rights in the results of research by their staff. Subsequently the University was obliged to take power to do so where the funding was from a Research Council. This policy was contained in a Notice published in 1987. Its effect was broadened by Grace 6 of 21 March 2001, in light of similar conditions being required by research charities and industry. In that Grace, where research

funding was external, University ownership was asserted not only of patents but in an additional range of IPRs. Revenue from the technology transfer was to be shared on the basis specified in the Grace', Discussion, 21 October 2003 (*Reporter*, 2003–4, pp.123–37), http://www.admin.cam.ac.uk/reporter/2002–03/weekly/5919/5.html.

246. http://www.admin.cam.ac.uk/reporter/2002–03/weekly/5919/5.html, http://www.admin.cam.ac.uk/reporter/2003–04/weekly/5938/18.html,

247. *Report* of the Discussion (*Reporter*, 30 October 2002).

248. Cambridge first made moves with the Report of the General Board on the ownership of intellectual property rights generated by externally funded research (*Reporter*, 31 January 2001) and Notice (*Reporter*, 21 March 2001). Then came the Report of the Joint Working Party on Copyright, Section 4 'Exploitation of copyright material created by staff and students' (*Reporter*, 17 October 2001), followed by The Joint Report of the Council and the General Board on the ownership of intellectual property rights (*Reporter*, 24 July 2002). Cornish referred in his account of the story so far to the 'Report of the Joint Working Party on Copyright, written in 1999 and eventually published in 2001', which he had also chaired: 'That Report recommended that copyright in research results should belong initially to the researchers, save in limited special cases. It emphasized not just our long–established practice in the matter, but equally its vital importance as a guarantee of freedom of academic expression.'

249. Anderson Discussion took place on 21 October 2003 (*Reporter*, 2003–4, pp.123–37).

250. Discussion, 21 October 2003 (*Reporter*, 2003–4, pp.123–37), http://www.admin.cam.ac.uk/reporter/2002–03/weekly/5919/5.html.

251. 'I can testify from experience that the operating practice of the TTO has often been to take crucial decisions without full consultation with the inventor. These changes in working practice seem to have been sanctioned by the Director of the RSD.' (The Technology Transfer Office had been created within the RSD).

252. Discussion, 21 October 2003 (*Reporter*, 2003–4, pp.123–37), http://www.admin.cam.ac.uk/reporter/2002–03/weekly/5919/5.html

253. http://www.admin.cam.ac.uk/offices/secretariat/, http://www.admin.cam.ac.uk/offices/secretariat/ipr/ipr_appeal.pdf.

254. The Thirteenth Report of the Board of Scrutiny commenting on this was published in August 2008. http://www.admin.cam.ac.uk/reporter/2007–08/weekly/6119/17.html

255. *Reporter*, 2004–5, p.1047.

256. http://www.admin.cam.ac.uk/reporter/2005–06/weekly/6039/21.html

257. http://www.admin.cam.ac.uk/offices/secretariat/ipr/ipr_appeal.pdf

258. http://www.admin.cam.ac.uk/reporter/2007–08/weekly/6119/17.html

259. http://www.admin.cam.ac.uk/reporter/2000–01/weekly/5822/22.html

260. Ibid.

261. 'The consequence of all this was grave disruption of the work of Faculties and Departments, where nobody could place orders or pay bills, and a period of intense stress for the University's computer and administrative staff, who were left stranded with an unfamiliar accounting system that would not work, and a help-desk that was unable to provide sufficient help.' http://www.admin.cam.ac.uk/reporter/2000–01/weekly/5822/22.html

262. http://www.admin.cam.ac.uk/reporter/2000–01/weekly/5822/22.html

263. Notice in response to the Discussion held on 10 October 2000: CAPSA and its implementation, 20 November 2000.

264. http://www.admin.cam.ac.uk/reporter/2001–02/weekly/5861/

265. http://www.admin.cam.ac.uk/reporter/2001–02/weekly/5867/28.html.

266. 'The Board was deeply concerned when, on trying to issue its initial statement on the CAPSA report through the Press Office, the Press Office first tried to censor the statement and then to suppress it. The Board was also disturbed, when, on 5 November 2001, the Press Office published a statement about the current state of CAPSA which the Board believed to be misleading, and in its interim statement on the implementation of CAPSA on 21 November the Board criticized it for doing this. The June/July 2002 issue of the Newsletter quotes a footnote to the Board's Report on CAPSA, but without dealing with the main thrust of the Report.' 7th Report of the Board of Scrutiny, Reporter, 7 August 2002, http://www.admin.cam.ac.uk/reporter/2001–02/weekly/5895/20.html

267. http://www.admin.cam.ac.uk/reporter/2000–01/weekly/5827/6.html, *Reporter,* 22 November 2000.

268. 'Who was closely involved with the implementation of CAPSA – the then unestablished Directors of Management Information Services and Finance (who have of course since "left" the University). We are being asked to consider a Report where the "proposed" administrative structure has been tested, and has been proved to be lacking, or to be more precise, a total disaster. A review of the Discussions over CAPSA indicate that there were warnings. Where did they come from? The academic and academic–related staff, whose input and, most importantly, oversight is to be marginalized and sidelined by the current "proposals"'? said Stephen Cowley, http://www.admin.cam.ac.uk/reporter/2000–01/weekly/5842/19.html, 10 May 2001.

269. http://www.admin.cam.ac.uk/reporter/2001–02/weekly/5873/4.html, *Reporter,* 6 February 2002.

270. Ibid.

271. The Council are publishing a Consultative Paper (p.508) to carry forward these issues. *Reporter,* 6 February 2002, http://www.admin.cam.ac.uk/reporter/2001–02/weekly/5873/4.html

272. http://www.admin.cam.ac.uk/reporter/2001–02/weekly/5890/, p.946.

273. *Reporter,* 2001–2, p.508.

274. http://www.admin.cam.ac.uk/reporter/2001–02/weekly/5890/, p.946.

275. *THES,* 8 March 2002.

276. http://www.jabberwocky.com/carroll/walrus.html

277. *Reporter,* 1988–9, p.615.

278. http://www.admin.cam.ac.uk/reporter/2001–02/weekly/5890/

279. http://www.admin.cam.ac.uk/reporter/2002–03/weekly/5901/16.html
http://www.admin.cam.ac.uk/reporter/2007–08/weekly/6087/22.html, http://www.admin.cam.ac.uk/reporter/2007–08/weekly/6108/42.html, http://www.admin.cam.ac.uk/reporter/2008–09/weekly/6122/4.html

280. http://www.admin.cam.ac.uk/reporter/current/weekly/6130/1.html,
http://www.admin.cam.ac.uk/reporter/current/weekly/6130/4.html

281. http://www.joh.cam.ac.uk/college_life/societies/may_ball/

282. http://www.cam.ac.uk/admissions/undergraduate/profiles/index.html

283. http://www.hughlaurie.net/footlights.html

284. http://www.independent.co.uk/arts–entertainment/comedy/features/the–cambridge–footlights–first–steps–in–comedy–1517691.html

2　How it all began

1. 'Ideals pass into great historic forces by embodying themselves in institutions', Hastings Rashdall, *The universities of Europe in the Middle Ages,* ed. F.M. Powicke and A.B. Emden (Oxford, 1936), Vol. I, p.3.

2. When the new diocese of Oxford was created in 1542 and the chapel of Christ Church became the cathedral.

3. Bede, *Ecclesiastical history,* ed. B. Colgrave and R.A.B. Mynors (Oxford, 1969), Vol. IV, 9, pp.361–2.

4. Orderic Vitalis, *Historia ecclesiastica,* II.185 (Oxford, 1969), Vol. IV, p.218.

5. Roger of Wendover, *Flores Historiarum,* ed. H.G. Hewlett, Rolls Series 84 (London, 1886–9), Vol. II, p.51.

6. Matthew Paris, *Historia Anglorum,* ed. F. Madden, Rolls Series (1866), pp.ii, 120.

7. Mark Pattison, *Suggestions on academical organization* (Edinburgh, 1868), p.128.

8. Peter Abelard, *Historia Calamitatum,* ed. J.Monfrin (Paris, 1967).

9. A.B. Emden, *Biographical register of the University of Cambridge to 1500* (Cambridge, 1963), pp.241, 272, 315, 560, and cf. his *Biographical register of the University of Oxford to AD 1500* (Oxford, 1957–9), 3 vols.

10. *Nisi sit legittime et publice et in generali conventu examinatus et approbatus et licentiatus quod possit in sua scientia ubique legere. Studia e sculoa in Arezzo durante il medioevo e il rinascimento: I documenti d'archivio fino al 1530,* ed. Robert Black (Arezzo, 1996), pp.184–5.

11. Hastings Rashdall, *The Universities of Europe in the Middle Ages,* ed. F.M. Powicke and A.B. Emden (1936), Vol. II, p.8, suggests this had one of the earliest codes of statutes, made by the Doctors.

12. *Quod prefata civitas aretina consueverit ab antiquo habere studium generale et auctoritatem doctorandi seu doctorari faciendi in iure canonico et civili et quadam alia facultate et in eadem civitate longo tempore studium viguerit iuxta imperialia privilegia [which have lapsed because of time of war] he regrants the old powers, Studia e sculoa in Arezzo durante il medioevo e il rinascimento: I documenti d'archivio fino al 1530,* ed. Robert Black (Arezzo, 1996), p.194.

13. Robert Black, *Education and society in Florentine Tuscany* (Leiden, 2007), p.203.

14. F.A. Reeve, *The Cambridge nobody knows* (Cambridge, 1977), pp.15–16.

15. Emden, *Biographical registers.*

16. Raymond Williamson, 'The plague in Cambridge', *Medieval History,* 1 (1957), pp.51–64.

17. Ibid., 52.

18. Paris, *Historia Anglorum,* pp.iii, 47 and 306.

19. Charles Henry Cooper, *Annals of Cambridge* (Cambridge, 1842ff.), 5 vols., Vol. I, p.52.

20. Ibid., Vol. I, p.55.

21. Ibid., Vol. I, p.147.

22. Ibid., Vol. I, pp.120–5.

23. Camhist, I, p.224.

24. See J.C.T. Oates, *Cambridge University Library* (Cambridge, 1986), Vol. I, to the reign of Queen Anne, and David McKitterick, *Cambridge University Library* (Cambridge, 1986), Vol. II, to the nineteenth century.

25. Peter Denley, 'The collegiate movement in Italian universities in the late Middle Ages', *History of Universities,* 10 (1991), pp.29–91, pp.33–4.

26. Ibid., p.35.

27. *The Late Medieval English College and its context,* ed. Clive Burgess and Martin Heale (York, 2008).

28. W.G. Searle, M.A., *The history of the Queens' College, 1446–1560,* Cambridge Antiquarian Society (Cambridge, 1867), pp.3–17.

29. Denley, 'The collegiate movement in Italian universities', pp.29–91.

30. Thomas Cranmer, *Miscellaneous writings,* Parker Society (Cambridge, 1846), Vol. 15, pp.396–9.

31. Mavis Batey, *The historic gardens of Oxford and Cambridge* (London, 1989).

32. *Cambridge commemorated,* pp.14–15.

33. Ibid.

34. Williamson, 'The plague in Cambridge', pp.53–4. Cooper, *Annals,* I, pp.132–4.

35. Cooper, *Annals,* I, p.196.

36. Williamson, 'The plague', p.54.

37. Camhist, I, p.41.

38. Ibid., p.42.

39. Ibid., p.43.

40. Ibid. p.40.

41. Cooper, *Annals,* I, pp.262–70.

42. Examples of twelfth-century trees of knowledge are reproduced in R.W. Southern, *Medieval humanism* (Oxford, 1970).

43. See R.B.C. Huygens, *Accessus ad auctores* (Leiden, 1970).

44. Robert Sanderson, *Logicae Artis Compendium,* ed. E.J. Ashworth, *Instrumenta rationis* (Bologna, 1985), Vol. II, p.XVII.

45. W. and M. Kneale and Kneale, in their definitive, *The development of logic* (Oxford, 1962), deal only very cursorily with this important period of transition.

46. Boethius, *De Hebdomadibus,* I, *Theological Tractates,* ed. H. Stewart, E.K. Rand and S.J. Tester (Harvard, 1973), p.41.

47. See G.R. Evans, *Alan of Lille* (Cambridge, 1983).

48. See *The University of Oxford: A New History* (London, 2010).

49. Camhist, I, p.93, referring to Hackett, pp.297–9.

50. Simon of Tournai, *Disputationes,* ed. J. Wariches, Spicilegium Sacrum Lovaniense, 12 (1932) and Peter Abelard, 'Commentary on Romans', ed. M. Buytaert, *Corpus Christianorum Continuatio Medievalis,* XI (1969), pp.113–18.

51. *Determinatio est unus honorabilis gradus attingendi magisterium* [1284 Chart. Univ. Paris. I. I], No. 515.

52. On examinations, see, pp.249ff.

53. Gilbert Burnet, *A dialogue concerning education,* Tracts and discourses (1704), p.326.

54. Charles Burnett, 'Give him the white cow: Notes and note-taking in the Universities in the twelfth and thirteenth centuries', *History of Universities,* 14 (1995–6), pp.1–30.

55. Ibid., p.3, 21.

56. Ibid.

57. See pp.233ff.

58. Burnett, 'Give him the white cow', p.7.

59. J. Hamesse, 'Le Vocabulaire de la transmission orale des textes', *Vocabulaire du livre* (Louvain-la-Neuve, 1989), pp.168–94, pp.189–90.

60. Burnett, 'Give him the white cow', pp.8, 22.

61. *Studium Upsalense: specimens of the oldest lecture notes taken in the Mediaeval University of Uppsala*, ed. Anders Piltz (Uppsala, 1977), pp.11–13.

62. Ibid, p.16.

63. Ibid., p.29.

64. Ibid., pp.30–1.

65. Ibid., p.205.

66. *Circa inicium exercicii veteris artis movetur talis questio primo: 'Utrum logica arcumentacionis considerativa sit pocius censenda practica aut verius speculativa', Studium Upsalense,* p.225.

67. Ibid., pp.210ff.

68. *Primum que sit Vtilitas huius libri; secundum quis sit titulus; tercium intentio Atistotilis in hoc libro; quartum cui parte philosophie presens liber vel noticia supponatur; quantum que et quot sunt cause huius libri vel sciencie.*

69. *Studium Upsalense,* p.277.

70. *Et iterum dixerunt: Nota, quod pigritantibus orientalibus ecclesiis Latini iterum ac sepe repetent ammoniciones, nam in ewangelio de nupciis filii regis primo invitatis neglexerunt venire, sed compulsi assidua monicione Latinorum reiterancium Alleluia intrabunt ad nupcias, Studium Upsalense,* p.207.

71. William J. Courtenay and Katherine H. Tachau, 'Ockham, Ockhamists, and the English–German nation at Paris, 1339–1341', *History of Universities,* II (1982), pp.53–96, pp.54–5.

72. Ibid., pp.54–5.

73. Ibid., p.57.

74. Ibid., p.63.

75. F. Smahel, 'The Kuttenberg Decree and the withdrawal of the German students from Prage in 1409: a discussion', *History of Universities,* 4 (1984), pp.153–61.

76. John M. Fletcher, 'Change and resistance to change: a consideration of the development of English and German universities during the sixteenth century', *History of Universities,* I (1981), 1–36, p.6.

77. Ibid., pp.14–16.

78. Ibid., pp.4–5. Prince Albert as Prince Consort and Cambridge Chancellor in the mid-nineteenth century may have got the idea from this practice.

79. Duns Scotus, *Philosophical writings: a selection,* ed. Alan Wolter (London, 1962), provides a convenient short introduction to his work. *Opera Omnia* ed. C. Balíc et al. (Vatican, 1950).

80. Oxhist, 1, p.426.

81. Oxhist, 1, p.558.

82. Oxhist, 1, p.499.

83. Williamson, 'The plague', p.53.

84. See Oxhist, I, p.600 n.75 on the St. Catherine's statutes and their stipulation.

85. Cooper, *Annals,* I, p.128.

86. Ibid.

87. See p.105.

88. Camhist, I, p.221, cf. *Fasciculi Zizaniorum,* ed. W.W. Shirley, Rolls Series (London, 1858), p.311.

89. Decisions of the Masters creating domestic legislation.

90. Damian Riehl Leader, 'Philosophy at Oxford and Cambridge in the fifteenth century', *History of Universities,* 4 (1984), pp.25–46.

91. Sermon 9, *The sermons of John Donne,* ed. G.R. Potter and Evelyn M. Simpson (Berkeley, 1953–1962), 10 vols., Vol. I, p.310.

92. Sermon 6, *The sermons of John Donne,* Vol. IV, p.168.

93. Heiko A. Oberman, 'Via Antiqua and Via Moderna: late medieval prolegomena to early Reformation thought,' *Journal of the History of Ideas,* 48.1 (Jan–Mar 1987), pp.23–40, p.24.

94. Ibid., p.25.

95. Valla, *Opera Omnia*, 1 (Basle, 1540, reprinted Turin, 1962), pp.117ff., and see Heiko A. Oberman, 'Luther and the Via Moderna: the philosophical backdrop of the Reformation breakthrough', *Journal of Ecclesiastical History*, 54 (2003), pp.641–70.

96. *Conclusiones philosophicae, cabalasticae et theologicae* (Rome, 1486).

97. Cooper, *Annals*, III, p.353.

98. R. Weiss, *Humanism in England during the fifteenth century* (Oxford, 1967), pp.160–1.

3 Cambridge and the tudor revolution

1. William Wordsworth, *The complete poetical works*, ed. John Morley (London, Macmillan, 1888, 1850 text), III.486–7.

2. *Erasmus and Cambridge: the Cambridge letters of Erasmus*, tr. D.F.S.Thomson (Toronto, 1963), p.188.

3. William Wordsworth, *Ecclesiastical Sonnets* (1821–2), 43, Inside of King's College Chapel, Cambridge.

4. Thomas Baker, *History of the College of St. John the Evangelist, Cambridge* (Cambridge 1869), 2 vols. He refers to himself as 'Ejected Fellow'.

5. Among its early students were Richard Croke, Robert Wakefield, George Day, Ralph Baynes, John Redman, John Seton, Thomas Watson, John Cheke, Roger Ascham, John Christopherson.

6. Wordsworth, *The Prelude*, III.46–52.

7. Fletcher, 'Change and resistance to change', pp.1–36, pp.10–11.

8. John of Salisbury, *Metalogicon*, ed. C.C.J. Webb (Oxford, 1929), II.10.

9. Camhist, p.250.

10. Examples are John of Salisbury and Peter of Blois.

11. Though the *Oxford English Dictionary* suggests that the noun 'intellectual' gained currency with this modern meaning only in the nineteenth.

12. Mark Curtis, 'The alienated intellectuals of Early Stuart England', *Past and Present*, 23 (1962), 25–41.

13. Constance M. Furey, *Erasmus, Contarini, and the religious republic of letters* (Cambridge, 2006), p.165.

14. Some secular authors (*secula*) were studied still, he concedes, but *verum ut rariores, ita inferiores*. Erasmus, *Antibarbarorum liber*, ed. K. Kumaniecki, *Erasmi Opera Omnia*, I.1 (1969), pp.1–138, p.129.

15. The chief model seems to have been the *De Oratore*.

16. Erasmus, *Antibarbarorum liber*, pp.1–138.

17. Camhist, I, p.292.

18. See p.162.

19. *Erasmus and Cambridge*, p.183.

20. Ibid., p.115.

21. Ibid., p.131.

22. Ibid., p.183.

23. Félix Nève, *La Renaissance des lettres en Belgique* (Louvain, 1890).

24. Georges Minchamp, *Le Cartésianisme en Belgique* (Brussels, 1886). The same is true of the system of Copernicus and the trials of Galileo, see Georges Monchamp, *Galilée et la Belgique* (Brussels, 1892).

25. *Erasmus and Cambridge*, Letter 6.2, mentions Greek being studied in Cambridge without the resistance encountered in Oxford.

26. Ibid., p.109.

27. Ibid., p.110.

28. Ibid., p.199.

29. Erasmus, *De ratione studii*, ed. J. Margolin, *Erasmi Opera Omnia,* I.2 (1971), pp.79–152, p.83.

30. Ibid., p.125.

31. Erasmus, *De pueris statim ac liberaliter instituendis*, ed. J. Margolin, *Erasmi Opera Omnia*, I.2 (1971), pp.1–78, p.23.

32. Ibid., p.55.

33. Thus embodying the two *viae*. Fletcher, 'Chance and resistance to change', pp.1–36, p.4.

34. Sachiko Kusukawa, 'Law and Gospel: the importance of philosophy at Reformation Wittenberg', *History of Universities*, XI (1992), pp.59–74.

35. Where in 1557 he took part in the deliberations concerning the university statutes.

36. *Supplementa Melanchthoniana* (1510–28), ed. O. Clemen (Leipzig, 1926), Vol. I.

37. Corpus Reformatorum (CR), XI, p.10.

38. Ibid., pp.5ff.
39. Ibid., pp.15ff.
40. Ibid., pp.15ff., col. 17.
41. Ibid., pp.15ff., col. 18.
42. Ibid., pp.15ff., col. 22.
43. Philipp Melanchton, *De corrigendis adulescentiae studiis*, CR, XI, pp.15ff, tr. *The Reformation in its own words*, ed. Hans J. Hillebrand (London, 1964), pp.58–9.
44. CR, XI, col. 52.
45. CR, XI, col. 52, 55–6.
46. *Urkundenbuch det Universitat Wittenberg*, I, 1502–1611, ed. W. Frieensburg (Magdeburg, 1926), pp.267ff. See too Kusukawa, 'Law and Gospel', pp.33–57.
47. Allan G. Chester, *Hugh Latimer* (Philadelphia, 1954), p.11.
48. Ibid., p.14.
49. Ibid., Chapter 3, note. 3.
50. By Foxe.
51. Hugh Latimer, *Sermons*, ed. G.E. Corrie, Parker Society (Cambridge, 1844), Sermons 334–5.
52. Thomas More, *Complete works* (Yale, 1990), Vol. 7, p.xvii.
53. Carl S. Meyer, 'Thomas More and the Wittenberg Lutherans', *Concordia Theological Monthly*, 39 (1968), pp.246–56.
54. More, *Complete works*, Vol. 7, pp.13–15.
55. *Cobbett's Parliamentary history of England* (London, 1806), I, col. 487.
56. More, *Complete works*, Vol. 7, p.xxiii.
57. *Records of Convocation VII, Canterbury, 1509–1603*, ed. Gerald Bray, Church of England Record Society (Boydell, 2006), p.152.
58. *Constatque universitates illas Oxoniensis et Cantabrigiensis fontes esse, unde rivuli omnium scientiarum profluxuerunt, qui quidem fonts, si fuerint corrupti, si errorum et haeresum maculis conspurcati fuerint, quantum timendum est, ne ex illis fontibus prodeant, qui universum regnum suis haeresibus inficiant,* Records of Convocation VII, Canterbury, 1509–1603, p.174.
59. State Papers 1.384.
60. Cranmer, *Miscellaneous writings*, 1.305.
61. See *Narrative of the days of the reformation with two contemporary biographies of the Archbishop Cranmer,* ed. John Gough Nichols (1859).
62. Ibid., pp.218–19.
63. British Library, Ms. C.81.f.2.
64. More, *Complete works*, Vol. 7, pp.xxiii–xxv.
65. Coverdale, *Remains,* ed. G. Pearson, Parker Society (Cambridge, 1846), p.492.
66. *Writings and translations of Myles Coverdale,* ed. George Pearson (Cambridge, 1844), pp.491ff.
67. Wittenberg designed its syllabus on Reformation principles so decisively that it became, ironically, somewhat fixed, did not keep up with the times, and its reputation had decayed by the eighteenth century. It was closed in 1815, and what remained of it was merged with the University of Halle in 1817.
68. John Twigg, 'The limits of "reform": some aspects of the debate on university education during the English Revolution', *History of Universities*, 4 (1984), 100–14, and see Camhist, I, pp.332–3.
69. Arthur Engel, 'The emerging concept of the academic profession at Oxford, 1800–1854', *The University in Society* (Princeton, 1975), 2 vols, Vol. I, pp.305–52, p.305.
70. Lucia Felici, 'The Erasmusstiftung and Europe: the institution, organization, and activity of the Foundation of Erasmus of Rotterdam from 1538–1600', *History of Universities*, 12 (1993), pp.36–43, 25.
71. His idea was already set out in the first version of his will in 1527 and in the final version of 1536 he bestowed his entire estate for the poor, so his ideas may have developed.
72. Felici, 'The Erasmusstiftung and Europe', p.31.
73. Ibid., p.32.
74. Ibid., pp.36–43.
75. *Correspondence of Archbishop Parker*, Letter XIII–V, ed. John Bruce, Parker Society (Cambridge, 1853), pp.16–18.

76. Ibid., Letters XVI–XXI, pp.22ff.
77. Ibid., Letters XVI–XXI, p.25.
78. Ibid., Letters XVI–XXI, p.27.
79. Ibid., Letters XVI–XXI, p.28.
80. Ibid., Letters XVI–XXI, p.29.
81. Chantries and Colleges Act, Hen VIII c.4 sec. 6.
82. An Act for the Dissolution of Colleges Stat. 37 Henry VIII. C.4, s.6.
83. Cooper, *Annals,* I, pp.429ff.
84. *Chantry Certificates,* ed. Rose Graham, *Oxfordshire Record Society,* 1 (1919), pp.viii–x, and see document 1, p.1.
85. Cooper, *Annal,* I, pp.430b–431.
86. *Correspondence of Archbishop Parker,* pp.34–6.
87. James Heywood, ed., *Collection of Statutes for the University and the Colleges of Cambridge* (London, 1840), pp.4–5, pp.1–41, which are the same as Gibson *Statuta Antiqua* Latin for Oxford. Heywood, p.342, *Visum est nonnullas leges, in hoc volumine inscriptas, quas nos in maximum vestrum commodum tulimus et sancivimus, illis dare, ut vobis tradant, ut, antiquitatis semibarbaris vestris et obscuris statutis, et, propter vetustatem, iam plerumque non intellectis, regiis deinceps legibus, et nostro latis auspicio, pareatis* (Strickland, *Statuta Antiqua,* pp.342–3).
88. *Chantry Certificates,* pp.viii–x.
89. Thomas Cranmer, *Letters,* Parker Society, *Epistola* XIII, p.15.
90. *et nos piam synodum congregare negligemus, ut errores refutare, dogmata repurgare et propagare possimus?*
91. *docti et pii viri, qui alios antecellunt eruditione et judicio.*
92. Cranmer, *Letters, Epistola* XIV, p.16.
93. Ibid., pp.16–17.
94. Ibid., *Epistola* VII, p.9.
95. Cranmer, *Miscellaneous writings,* Parker Society, 2.433.
96. Bucer in *Cambridge University Transactions,* I, pp.352–3.
97. Cooper, *Annals,* II, p.76.
98. Ibid., II, pp.77–8.
99. Ibid., II, p.80.
100. Ibid., II, p.113.
101. Ibid., II, p.116.
102. Ibid., II, p.119.
103. W. and M. Kneale, *The development of logic,* pp.298–9.
104. Abraham Fraunce, *The Lawiers Logike* (London, 1588), p.120.
105. Luther, *Werke,* Weimar Ausgabe, Vol. 39.
106. *Writings and disputations of Thomas Cranmer,* ed. J.E. Cox, Parker Society (Cambridge, 1884), p.389.
107. Nicholas Ridley, *Works,* ed. Henry Christmas, Parker Society (Cambridge, 1841), pp.363–4.
108. Ibid., p.171.
109. Ibid.
110. Cooper, *Annals,* II, p.86.
111. Erasmus, *Opera Omnia* (1882), IX.1, p.443.
112. *Early writings of John Hooper DD.,* ed. Samuel Carr, Parker Society (Cambridge, 1843), p.101.
113. *Writings and disputations of Thomas Cranmer,* p.9.
114. Ibid.
115. Ibid., p.21. Transubstantiation held that the bread and wine became the real body and blood of Christ.
116. John Bradford, *Writings,* ed. Aubrey Townsend (Cambridge, 1848), pp.441–7.
117. Jennifer Summit, *Memory's Library* (Chicago, 2008), p.105.
118. Andrew, 'Cambridge Spies', p.208.
119. *Cambridge University transactions during the Puritan controversies of the sixteenth and seventeenth centuries,* ed. James Heywood and Thomas Wright (London, 1854), 2 vols., Vol. II, p.18.
120. Furey, *Erasmus, Contarini,* pp.91–3.
121. Roger Ascham, *The Scholemaster,* Book II.2 (Cambridge, 1904).
122. Patrick Collinson, *Elizabethan essays* (London, 1994), pp.191–2.

123. Letter 1, *Zurich letters*, ed. Hastings Robinson (Cambridge, 1842), p.1.

124. Matthew Parker, *Correspondence,* No.45, p.54.

125. Henry Norbert Birt, *The Elizabethan religious settlement* (London, 1907), p.262.

126. Cooper, *Annals,* II, p.173.

127. Philip Melanchthon, *On Christian doctrine: Loci communes,* 1555, tr. and ed. Clyde L. Manschreck (New York, 1965), p.3.

128. *Locorum theologicorum … quibus et Loci Communes, p. Melanchthonis explicantur* (1599), p.21.

129. Calvin, *Works, tracts and treatises on the Reformation,* Vol. I, p.71.

130. *Correspondence of Archbishop Parker,* Letter CLXXX, pp.238–8.

131. *quorum duo quinque Mosis volumnia Hebraice scripta complectuntur, multis doctissimorum hominum commentariis illustrata; tertius vero manuscriptus quatuor Evangelistas Graeco–Latinos continet, cum Actis Apostolorum. Ex quibus omnibus facile existimar potest quam honorifice de academia Cant. sentias,* Heywood, *Transactions,* Vol. I., pp.352–3.

132. Cooper, *Annals,* III, p.455.

133. *Works of John Whitgift,* ed, John Ayre, Parker Society (Cambridge, 1851), Vol. I, p.7.

134. Ibid., Vol. III, pp.567ff.

135. J. Heywood, *Early Cambridge University and College statutes in the English language* (London, 1855), pp.4–5.

136. *Cambridge University Transactions,* I, p.61.

137. Ibid., I, p.63.

138. Ibid., I, p.65.

139. Ibid., I, p.89.

140. Ibid., I, p.113.

141. Ibid., I, p.121.

142. Ibid., I, p.137.

143. Ibid., I, pp.124–5.

144. Ibid., I, p.140

145. Ibid., I, pp.141–3.

146. Ibid., I, p.145.

147. Cooper, *Annals,* II, p.322.

148. *Cambridge University Transactions,* I, p.353.

149. Ibid., I, p.358.

150. Ibid., I, p.359.

151. Ibid., I, p.361.

152. Ibid., II, p.19.

153. Ibid., I, pp.315–21.

154. *Cambridge University,* I, pp.21ff., and see Camhist, II, pp.294–5, on the sixteenth-century enlargement of the personal powers of Heads of House enabling them more easily to misappropriate college funds.

155. William Whitaker, *A disputation on Holy Scripture against the Papists,* Parker Society (Cambridge, 1849), p.14.

156. Ibid., p.16.

157. Ibid., prefatory letter to Burghley, April 1588.

158. *Cambridge University Transactions,* II, p.4.

159. Ibid., II, p.16.

160. Ibid., II, p.7.

161. Ibid., II, pp.158ff.

162. *Cambridge commemorated,* pp.24–5.

163. Ibid.

4 Seventeenth- and eighteenth-century Cambridge: puritans and scientists

1. Camhist, p.109, note 46.

2. Cooper, *Annals,* III, p.11.

3. Ibid., III, p.15.

4. *Cambridge University Transactions,* II, p.287.

5. Ibid., II, pp.278–91.

6. Ibid., II, pp.269–70.

7. Ibid., II, p.277.

8. Ibid., II, p.271.

9. Ibid., II, p.337.

10. 'Never at rest. A biography of Isaac Newton', by Richard S.Westall (Cambridge, 1980), title page.

11. David A. Reid, 'A science for polite society: British dissent and the teaching of natural philosophy in the seventeenth and eighteenth centuries', *History of Universities,* 21 (2006), 117–158,

12. Gerrard Winstanley, 'The law of freedom in a Platform', *The law of freedom and other writings,* ed. Christopher Hill (Cambridge, 1973), pp.348ff.

13. Tim Fulford, Debbie Lee and Peter J. Kitson, *Literature, Science and exploration in the Romantic Era* (Cambridge, 2004), p.2.

14. Isaac Barrow, 'Of industry in general', *The theological works of Isaac Barrow* (Oxford, 1830), 8 vols., iii.230–1.

15. Samuel Taylor Coleridge, *Biographia Literaria,* Chapter 1, ed. G. Watson (London, 1906), pp.5–6.

16. Henry More, *A collection of several philosophical writings* (London, 1662), p.V.

17. Ibid., p.VI.

18. Descartes to More, 15 April 1649, *The philosophical writing of Descartes,* tr. John Cottingham et al. (Cambridge, 1991), pp.380–1.

19. L.J. Beck, *The Metaphysics of Descartes* (Oxford, 1965), p.271.

20. Descartes to More, August 1649, *The philosophical writing of Descartes,* pp.370–1.

21. Ibid.

22. *Tracts ... containing new experiments touching the relation betwixt flame and fire* (1672).

23. *The magical writings of Thomas Vaughan* were edited by A.E. Waite in 1888. His miscellaneous Latin and English verses are included in Vol. II of A.B. Grosart's Fuller Worthies Library edition of the *Works* of Henry Vaughan (1871). A manuscript book of his, with alchemical and autobiographical jottings made between 1658 and 1662 forms Brit. Mus. Sloane Ms. 1741.

24. John Evelyn, *Diary,* ed. E.S. de Beer (London, 1959), p.341.

25. *Letters of Sir Robert Moray to the Earl of Kincardine, 1657–73,* ed. David Stevenson (Ashgate, 2007), p.43.

26. Ibid., p.102.

27. Descartes, *Philosophical Writings,* tr. John Cottingham et al. (Cambridge, 1985), Vol. I, p.186.

28. Samuel Butler, *Prose observations,* ed. Hugh de Quehen (Oxford, 1979), pp.82–3.

29. Descartes to More, 15 April 1649, *The philosophical writing of Descartes,* pp.380–1.

30. Ibid., August 1649, pp.370–1.

31. Ibid., August 1649, pp.370–1.

32. Alfredo Dinis, 'Giovanni Battista Riccili and the science of his time', *Jesuit Science and the Republic of Letters,* ed. M. Feingold (Cambridge, MA, 2003), pp.195–224, pp.211ff.

33. *A letter of advice to young gentleman at the University to which are subjoined, directions for young students* (London, 1701, reprinted 1721), p.7.

34. See p.238.

35. Cambridge University Library, MS 3996, fols. 88–135 for the 45 headings he used to keep his new philosophical thoughts in order.

36. Ibid.

37. King's College, Cambridge., Keynes MS 130.10, fol. 2*v.*

38. Cambridge University Library, Add. MS 3968.41, fol. 85.

39. Ibid.. MS 4004, fols. 10–15, 38*v.*

40. Cooper, *Annals,* III, p.223,

41. Williamson, 'The Plague', pp.57, 59.

42. *The Correspondence of Isaac Newton,* ed. H.W. Turnbull (Cambridge, 1959), 1.92–102, published in *Philosophical Transactions,* 6 (1671/2), pp.3075–87.

43. *The Correspondence of Isaac Newton,* ed. H.W.Turnbull (Cambridge, 1960), 2.133–5).

44. Ibid., 2.288ff.

45. Smithsonian Institution, Washington, Dibner Collection, Burndy MS 16.

46. *The Correspondence of Isaac Newton*, 1959, 1.362–4.

47. Ibid., 1.364.

48. *The Correspondence of Isaac Newton*, 1960, 2.182–3.

49. Ibid., 2.20–32, 110–61.

50. Turnbull, *Samuel Hartlib*, 5.

51. Oxford, 1637.

52. Reid, 'A science for polite society', p.125. 'Communicatio' having a religious signification, since it was the Latin rendering of the Greek 'koinonia' or 'shared communion', *Dictionary of National Biography*.

53. Oliver Cromwell, *Letters and Speeches*, 1904, letter 1.

54. Abraham Cowley, *Collected works*, ed. Thomas O. Calhoun et al. (Delaware, 1989), Vol. I, 3.

55. John Twigg, *A history of Queens' College, Cambridge, 1444–1986* (Woodbridge, 1987), pp.88ff.

56. *Camden Miscellany*, VIII (1883), item 4, Camden 1891, 1890, 1879.

57. Cowley, *Collected works*, Vol. I, lines 15–16.

58. Ibid., Vol. I, lines 19–23.

59. Ibid., Vol. I, line 54.

60. *The arraignment of persecution* (1645) in *Tracts on Liberty in the Puritan Revolution*, ed. W. Haller (Columbia, 1934), Vol. 3, pp.211–12.

61. *Camden Miscellany*, VIII, 3.

62. John Twigg, *The University of Cambridge and the English Revolution* (1990).

63. Daniel and Samuel Lysons, *Magna Britannia: Cambridgeshire* (Wakefield, 1808), p.6.

64. J.D. Twigg 'The Parliamentary Visitation of the University of Cambridge, 1644–1645', *The English Historical Review*, 98 (1983), pp.513–528, p.513.

65. Cooper, *Annals*, III.372. Twigg, *The University of Cambridge and the English Revolution*, pp.93, 98–9.

66. Twigg, *The University of Cambridge and the English Revolution*, p.95.

67. Oxford, Bodleian Library, MS Tanner 61 and 62.

68. *Querela Cantabrigiensis* (1647), pp.17–18.

69. *The Cambridge Journal of William Dowsing, 1643,* transcribed by A.C. Moule (1926)

70. *Carola Hicks, The King's Glass* (London, 2007), pp.199–201.

71. Camhist, II, p.476.

72. Ibid., II, p.477.

73. Twigg, *The University of Cambridge and the English Revolution*, p.230.

74. *Letters and Speeches* (1904), 3.267, 31 December 1649.

75. *Bishop Burnet's history of his own time*, ed. G. Burnet and T. Burnet, 2 vols., 1724–34, Vol. 1.187.

76. Reeve, *The Cambridge nobody knows*, pp.21–2.

77. *The Diary of Samuel Pepys*, ed. Robert Latham and William Matthews (London, 1970), Vol. VIII, p.468.

78. Reeve, *The Cambridge nobody knows*, pp.21–2.

79. *The Diary of Samuel Pepys*, Vol. I, pp.66–7.

80. Ibid., Vol. II, pp.134–5.

81. Ibid., Vol. III, pp.217–18.

82. Irene Lister, *Cambridge characters* (Cambridge, 1978), pp.23–4.

83. *Reliquiae Baxterianae*, 1.85, 1.119.

84. John Bunyan, *Grace abounding and other spiritual autobiographies*, ed. John Stachniewski and Anita Pacheco (Oxford, 1998), p.98.

85. Owen Chadwick, 'Indifference and morality', *Christian Spirituality: essays in honour of Gordon Rupp*, ed. Peter Brooks (SCM, London, 1975), pp.203–231, p.217.

86. See R.L. Greaves, *Deliver us from evil: the radical underground in Britain, 1660–1663* (Oxford, 1986).

87. John Milton, *Works*, ed. Frank Allen Patterson et al. (New York, 1931), I, p.176.

88. Ibid., I, p.32.

89. Ibid., I, p.84.

90. Ibid., XII, pp.19ff.

91. Ibid., I, p.19.

92. Ibid., VIII, p.112.

93. Ibid., I, p.71.

94. Trinity College, Cambridge Muniments, 'The great volume of miscellany papers III', no. 42.

95. John Milton, *Of education, complete prose works,* ed. D. Bush et al. (Yale, 1959), vol. II, p.364.

96. John Milton, *Of education, Works,* ed. Frank Allen Patterson et al. (New York, 1931), IV, p.280.

97. Ibid., IV, pp.281–2.

98. Ibid., IV, pp.283.

99. Ibid., IV, pp.286–7.

100. Ibid., IV, p.277.

101. On Ussher see Alan Ford, *James Ussher, theology history and politics in early-modern Ireland and England* (Oxford, 2007).

102. Letter of Roger Williams, 12 July 1654, in John Milton, *Apophthegmata, Works,*Vol. xviii, p.369.

103. Yusef Azad, 'The limits of University: the study of language in some British Universities and Academies 1750–1800', *History of Universities,* VII (1988), pp.118–147, pp.138–9.

104. Genesis 2.19–20.

105. Genesis 11.9.

106. Prompted partly by the writings of Johannes Trithemius (1462–1516), and see James Knowlson, *Universal language schemes in England and France 1600–1800* (Toronto, 1975).

107. Rhodri Lewis, 'A Babel off Broad Street: artificial language planning in 1650s Oxford', *History of Universities,* XXI (2005), pp.108–46.

108. George Dalgarno (*Ars signorum*, 1661); John Wilkins, *An essay towards a real character and a philosophical language* (1668).

109. Knowlson, *Universal language schemes in England and France,* pp.161–82.

110. Azad, 'The limits of University', pp.118–47.

111. Joseph Priestley, *A course of lectures on the theory of language* (Warrington, 1762), and see Horne Took, *Diversions of Purley* (London, 1798 and 1805).

112. Gilbert Burnet, *A dialogue concerning education,* p.326.

113. *The Spectator,* 197, 16 October 1711, ed. Donald F. Bond (Oxford, 1965), II, pp.271–2.

114. Ibid., 239, 4 December 1711, II, pp.428–32.

115. *Letters to a young man whose education has been neglected,* II, first published in *London Magazine,* VII (February, 1823), pp.189–94, *The works of Thomas de Quincey,* ed. Frederick Burwick (London, 2000), Vol. III, pp.50–58, pp.51, 57.

116. Ibid., p.52.

117. M. Clagett, *Science and mechanics in the Middle Ages* (London, Oxford, Madison, 1959).

118. *The works of Robert Boyle,* ed. M. Hunter and E.B. Davis, 7 vols. (1999–2000).

119. *The Spectator,* 518, 16 October 1711, ed. Donald F. Bond (Oxford, 1965), IV, pp.347–8.

120. Ibid., IV, p.346.

121. Coleridge, *Biographia Literaria,* Chapter VIII, p.75.

122. Ibid.

123. Michael Hofstetter, 'The Classical Tripos and the Romantic Movement at Cambridge', *History of Universities* XIX (2004), pp.221–239, pp.232–3.

124. *History of Scholarship,* ed. C.R. Ligota and J.-L. Quantin (Oxford, 2006), p.8, referring to T. Graham and A.G. Watson, *The recovery of the past in early Elizabethan England* (Cambridge, 1998).

125. William Chapman, *The Life of John Wiclif: the herald of the Reformation.* (London, No publisher, 1883), pp.20, 34–5.

126. Joseph Priestley, *Heads of lectures on a course of experimental philosophy, particularly including chemistry, delivered at the New College in Hackney* (Dublin, 1794), p.2.

127. Thomas Carlyle, 'Signs of the times', *Critical and Miscellaneous Essays* (London, 1899), II, p.64.

128. Ibid., II, p.59.

129. Ibid., II, p.60.

130. Ibid., II, p.61.

131. Ibid.

132. Joseph Butler, *Analogy,* I.i.2, ed. with an appendix by Henry Morley (London, 1884), p.10.

133. Jonathan Swift, *Gulliver's Travels,* ed. Colin McElvie (1976), p.96.

134. Ibid., pp.96–7.
135. Ibid., p.97.
136. Gert Vanpaemel, 'Experimental physics and the natural science curriculum in eighteenth century Louvan', *History of Universities, 7* (1988), pp.175–196, pp.190–1.
137. Ibid., p.177.
138. Priestley, *Heads of lectures*, p.iv.
139. Ibid., pp.iv–v. See too, D.A. Reid, 'Technical knowledge and the mental universe of the early cotton manufacturers', *Canadian Journal of History*, 36 (2001), pp.284–304.
140. Priestley, *Heads of lectures*, p.2.
141. Sermons in shorthand in MNC Priestley MSS Box 1.
142. Joseph Priestley, *Experiments and observations, etc., in three volumes* (Birmingham, 1790), Vol. I, pp.xxxii–xliii.
143. Joseph Priestley, Sermon on 'Wisdom the principal thing', given by Priestley according to notes in his own hand, at Leeds, October 1790, Birmingham 1791, Warwick, 1792, Hackney. November 1792. Sermons in shorthand in MNC Priestley MSS Box 1.
144. Ibid.
145. Samuel Taylor Coleridge, *The Friend, Essay IV, Collected Works,* 4, ed. Barbara E. Rooke (Princeton, 1969), p.466.
146. Ibid.
147. Ibid., p.470.
148. Cooper, *Annals,* IV, p.355.
149. Ibid., IV, p.362.
150. Ibid., IV, p.407.
151. Ibid.. IV, p.424.
152. Ibid., IV, p.426.
153. Ibid., IV, p.71.
154. Ibid., IV, p.75.
155. Ibid., IV, p.79.
156. Basil Montagu, *Enquiries and observations respecting the University Library* (Cambridge, 1805), p.[1]. McKitterick, *Cambridge University Library*, Vol. II, pp.27, 30.
157. Daniel and Samuel Lysons, *Magna Britannia: Cambridgeshire* (1808), p.102, Virginia F. Sterne, *Gabriel Harvey, his Life, marginalia and Library* (Oxford, 1979).
158. Cooper, *Annals,* IV, p.409.
159. McKitterick, *Cambridge University Library,* Vol. II, pp.394ff.
160. Cooper, *Annals,* III, p.471.
161. Ibid., IV, p.467.
162. Tim Hochstrasser, '"A college in the air": myth and reality in the foundation story of Downing College, Cambridge', *History of Universities,* 17 (2001–2), pp.81–120.
163. D.A. Winstanley, *Early Victorian Cambridge* (Cambridge, 1940), pp.1ff.
164. D.A. Winstanley, *Unreformed Cambridge* (Cambridge, 1935), p.174.
165. Ibid., p.177.
166. Ibid., p.181.
167. Ibid..
168. Wordsworth, *The Prelude,* III.46–51.
169. Henry Gunning, *Reminiscences of Cambridge*, selected and ed. D.A. Winstanley (Cambridge, 1932), pp.5–8.
170. Ibid., p.23.
171. Ibid., p.24–5.
172. Wordsworth, *The Prelude,* III.257–64.
173. Ibid.
174. Ibid.
175. Ibid., VI.35–41.
176. Ibid., VI.116–29.
177. Winstanley, *Unreformed Cambridge*, pp.206–12.

178. Ibid., pp.68–70.
179. George Dyer, *The privileges of the University of Cambridge* (London, 1824), 2 vols., p.371.
180. *A letter to the Rector of Lincoln College*, by Philalethes (1807) G.A. Oxon b.19 (356), 383, p.8.
181. 'Universities: actual and ideal', inaugural address as rector of Aberdeen, *T.H. Huxley on Education*, ed. Cyril Bibby (Cambridge, 1971), p.139 (1874)
182. Gibbon gave an answer in his *Autobiography*, 29 (1794)
183. On Cambridge examinations, see Peter Searby, *A history of the University of Cambridge*, Vol. III (Cambridge, 1997), pp.154–63.
184. *Disputatio* is discussed in Christopher Stray, 'From oral to written examinations: Cambridge, Oxford and Dublin 1700–1914', *History of Universities*, XX/2 (2005), pp.76–130, pp.79–83.
185. See Thomas Johnson, *Quaestiones* (Cambridge, 1735), for an example.
186. Isaac Todhunter, *William Whewell* (London, 1976), 2 vols., Vol. I, p.5.
187. Ibid., Vol. II, pp.35–6.
188. Searby, *A history of the University of Cambridge*, Vol. III, pp.163–202.
189. http://www.admin.cam.ac.uk/reporter/current/weekly/6138/16.html
190. G.H. Hardy, 'Presidential address: the case against the Mathematical Tripos', *The Mathematical Gazette*, 32.300 (July 1948), pp.134–145, p.135. http://www.jstor.org/pss/3609929.

5 The nineteenth-century transformation

1. Reeve, *The Cambridge nobody knows*, pp.15–16.
2. W.C. Lubenow, *The Cambridge Apostles, 1820–1914* (Cambridge, 1998).
3. Ibid., pp.125ff.
4. Ibid., p.33.
5. F.C. Burnand, *Personal reminiscences of the Univerity Amateur Dramatic Club, Cambridge* (London, 1880), pp.2–4.
6. Ibid., pp.5–6.
7. Compare Psalm 14:1.
8. Burnand, *Personal reminiscences*, pp.5–6.
9. Ibid., pp.6–7.
10. Ibid., p.8
11. Ibid., pp.24–5.
12. Ibid., p.113.
13. Ibid., pp.18–19.
14. H.M. Hyndman and J. Ellis McTaggart, 'A debate on socialism at the Union', in *The Cambridge mind: ninety years of the* Cambridge Review, 1879–1969, ed. Eric Homberger, William Janeway and Simon Schama (London, 1970), p.25.
15. Robert Southey, *Letters from England*, ed. Jack Simmons (London, 1951).
16. Richard Lovell Edgeworth, *Essays on professional education* (London, 1809).
17. *Edinburgh Review*, xv (1809), pp.40–53.
18. Edgeworth, *Essays on professional education*, pp.229–30.
19. Ibid., pp.318–19.
20. *Edinburgh Review*, xv (1809), p.43.
21. Ibid., pp.46–7.
22. Ibid., pp.51–2.
23. Ibid.
24. Coleridge, *Table talk*, ed. Kathleen Coburn Collected Works, 14 (Routledge, 1990), 2 vols., Vol. 1, p.8, 20, April 1811.
25. The works of Francis Bacon, Lord Chancellor of England. A new edition. By Basil Montagu, Esq., *Edinburgh Review*, 65.132 (July 1837), p.1.
26. William Whewell, *On the principles of English University education* (London, 1929), p.35.
27. Ibid., p.22.
28. Ibid.
29. William Whewell, *On the principles of English University education* (London, 1837), pp.24–5.

30. Ibid., pp.146–7
31. Ibid., p.144.
32. Ibid., pp.150ff.
33. Ibid., p.180.
34. Ibid., p.149
35. *Gentlemen of science: early correspondence of the British Association for the Advancement of Science*, ed. Jack Morrell and Arnold Thackeray, Royal Historical Society, Camden Fourth Series, 30 (1984), p.21.
36. Ibid., p.16.
37. Ibid., p.17.
38. Ibid.
39. Ibid., p.15.
40. Ibid.
41. Ibid., p.189.
42. Ibid., p.38.
43. Ibid., p.41.
44. Ibid., p.15.
45. See the earliest issues beginning in 1872.
46. *Gentlemen of science*, p.41.
47. Ibid., p.18.
48. The Library of Entertaining Knowledge. Vol. I. Part I. The menageries–quadrupeds described and drawn from living subjects. Published under the Superintendence of the Society for the Diffusion of Useful Knowledge, *Edinburgh Review*, 49.97 (March 1829), p.150.
49. Charles Babbage, *Reflections on the decline of science in England and on some of its causes* (London, 1830), p.29.
50. Ibid.
51. *Gentlemen of science*, p.22.
52. Ibid., p.23.
53. David Brewster, 'Decline of science in England', *Quarterly Review*, xliii (1830), 305–42.
54. *Gentlemen of science*, pp.28–9.
55. Ibid., p.22.
56. See p.269.
57. 12 February 1830, *Gentlemen of science*, p.24.
58. Jack Morrell and Arnold Thackeray, *Gentlemen of science* (Oxford, 1981), pp.47–51.
59. March 1830, quoted in ibid., p.48.
60. Babbage, *Reflections on the decline of science in England*, p. xiv.
61. Ibid., p.xi.
62. Ibid., pp.174–83.
63. March 1830, quoted in Morrell and Thackeray, *Gentlemen of science*, p.50.
64. James Johnston (1796–1855).
65. *Gentlemen of science*, p.33.
66. Ibid., p.37.
67. Ibid., p.42.
68. Listed in Morrell and Thackeray, *Gentlemen of science*, p.449.
69. Quoted in ibid., p.424.
70. *Quarterly Review*, LI (1834), 59.
71. 'A superficial pretender to knowledge; a conceited smatterer', *Oxford English Dictionary*.
72. William Whewell, *The philosophy of the inductive sciences*, I, Introduction (1840), p.113.
73. Babbage, *Reflections on the decline of science in England*, p.10.
74. Ibid., p.10.
75. See references in *Oxford English Dictionary* under 'geology'. References to the *OED* are given in *OED* format.
76. William Whewell, *History of the inductive sciences* (1837), XVIII. v. §1 'Theoretical geology ... has a strong resemblance ... to philosophical archæology'.
77. Daniel Wilson, *Prehistoric annals of Scotland* I. i. 27 (London and Cambridge, 1863), 'The closing epoch of geology is that in which archæology has its beginning'.
78. Charles Kingsley, *Alton Locke* (1850) (Nelson, 1924), p.461.

79. William Whewell, *Novum Organun Renovatum* (London, 1858), pp.257ff., 259.
80. Ibid., p.272.
81. Ibid., pp.273–4.
82. Ibid., p.275.
83. Ibid., p.278.
84. Ibid., p.279.
85. See *The University of Oxford: A New History*, forthcoming.
86. He had been invited to preach before the Queen and Prince Albert at Buckingham Palace in 1859.
87. *The letters of Robert Browning*, ed. Thurman L. Hood (London, 1933), pp.198–200.
88. *Monographs by the very Rev. Dr. Buckland, Oxford Bodleian Library, Bod.18811 d.31.*
89. 1707 SLOANE *Jamaica* I. 2 How sensible those nervous parts are, need not be told any who have seen vivisections, where the least ... touches ... will cause a sensible motion, *Oxford English Dictionary*.
90. 1736 *Phil. Trans.* XXXIX. 260 Small parts of large objects cannot easily be applied to the microscope without being divided from their wholes which in the case of vivi section defeats the experiment, *Oxford English Dictionary*.
91. 1842 Dunglison *Med. Lex.* 735 *Vivisection* ... the act of opening or dissecting living animals, *Oxford English Dictionary*.
92. 1852 Lewis *Meth. Obs. & Reas. in Pol.* I. 161 Of late years in particular vivi~section, or anatomical investigation of the living subject, has often been practised upon some of the smaller mammalia, *Oxford English Dictionary*.
93. Charles Kingsley, *The water babies*, Chapter VI (1862–3).
94. Ibid.
95. Letter of 22 March 1871 to Professor Ray Lankester, Darwin, *Correspondence. Selected letters of Charles Darwin*, ed. Frederick Burkhardt, Alison Pearn and Samantha Evans (Cambridge, 2008).
96. Browning, *The Poems*, ed. John Pettigrew (Yale, 1981), Vol. I, p.605.
97. Adam Sedgwick, *A discourse on the studies of the University* (1833 version), intr. Eric Ashby and Mary Anderson (Leicester University Press, 1969), p.8.
98. Ibid., p.9.
99. In the first half of the nineteenth century, 'The brethren of the hammer fused Enlightenment cosmopolitanism to Romantic Wanderlust and Nature worship. They mountaineered, read Scott and Wordsworth, grew beards and mannerisms, [were] like a German students' Confraternity, and celebrated their Arthurian adventures in heart romances and masculine drinking songs', Roy Porter, 'The natural sciences tripos and the "Cambridge School of Geology", 1850–1914', *The History of Universities*, II (1982), pp.93–216, pp.195–6.
100. Sedgwick, *A discourse on the studies of the University*, p.49.
101. Ibid., pp.22–3.
102. Ibid., p.31.
103. Ibid., p.107.
104. John Stuart Mill, *Essays on ethics, religion and society*, ed. J.M. Robson (Toronto, 1969), p.36.
105. For example by Robert Grosseteste in the thirteenth century and Henry of Langenstein some generations later.
106. See p.282.
107. Todhunter, *William Whewell*, p.414.
108. Ibid., Vol. II, p.415.
109. Bacon, *Works* (1857–74), Vol. I, p.xi.
110. Ibid., pp.64–5.
111. Fulford et al., *Literature, science and exploration in the Romantic era*, p.2.
112. *New essays by Oliver Goldsmith*, Essay VIII, 'New fashions in learning', from *The Public Ledger*, 22 August 1761, ed. Ronald S. Crane (Chicago, 1927), p.59.
113. *The Pollock-Holmes Letters*, ed. Mark De Wolfe Howe (Cambridge, 1942), Vol. I, p.22.
114. C.N.L. Brooke, *The history of the University of Cambridge* (1970–90), (Cambridge, 1993), Vol. IV, p.151.
115. It has been suggested that 'before the professionalisation of disciplines in the later nineteenth century, there were few hard-and-fast barriers between intellectual discourses and fewer blanket designations'. Fulford et al., *Literature, science and exploration in the Romantic era*, p.2.

116. Kingsley, *Alton Locke*, p.206.
117. For example with the inclusion of 'research' in the purposes of a university in the Oxford and Cambridge Act 1877.
118. Thomas Love Peacock, *Letter to Thomas Forster*, February 1811, *Works*, ed. Nicholas Joukovsky (Oxford, 2001), Vol. 1, p.62.
119. Daniel MacQueen, *Letters on Hume's history of Great Britain* (1756), Letter II, reprinted with introduction by John Vladimir Price (Thoemmes, 1990), p.36.
120. Whewell, *Novum Organun Renovatum*, p.v.
121. Ibid., p.142.
122. Darwin, *Correspondence*, Vols. 6.178 and 1.123.
123. Brooke, *The history of the University of Cambridge*, Vol. IV, p.153.
124. Sir Walter Scott, *The heart of Midlothian*, ed. Andrew Lang (London, 1932, first edition 1818), p.i.
125. *Higher education in London, Parliamentary Papers* (1889) (C. 5709), XXXIX, 323, p.ix.
126. *Glasgow University Calendar* (1829), 39.
127. William Maekpeace Thackeray, *Pendennis*, ed. Peter Shillingsburgh (New York and London, 1991), pp.161–92, p.192.
128. T.H. Huxley, 'Science and culture, an address delivered at the opening of Sir Josiah mason's Science College, Birmingham, 1880', *Collected essays, iii, science and education* (London, 1905), and *T.H. Huxley on Education*, ed. Cyril Bibby (Cambridge, 1971), p.182.
129. 'An outline of the system of education pursued in the Percy Street Academy', John Collingwood Bruce, 1834, quoted in Gainsford Bruce, *The life and letters of John Collingwood Bruce* (Edinburgh, 1905), p.54.
130. William Whewell, *On the principles of English University Education* (London, 1837), p.17.
131. *Camhist*, III, p.310.
132. G.M. Macaulay, *Letters*, ed. Thomas Pinney (Cambridge, 1981), Vol. VI, p.68.
133. Oxhist VII, p.554.
134. In an appendix to his *The Scottish Universities and what to reform in them* (1857), Alexander Kilgour gives extracts from Edward Robinson's *A concise view of the Universities (and the state of theological education) in Germany* (republished by Clark, Edinburgh, 1835), but written from the vantage-point of a Professor in the USA, at the Theological Seminary at Andover, Alexander Kilgour, *The Scottish Universities and what to reform in them* (Edinburgh, 1857), pp.54ff.
135. *The Letters of Matthew Arnold*, 18 June 1879, ed. Cecily Y. Lang (Virginia University Press, 1996–2001), Vol. V, pp.39–40.
136. See Chapter 3.
137. *The universities in the nineteenth century*, ed. Michael Sanderson (Routledge 1975), p.94.
138. Kingsley, *Alton Locke*, p.202.
139. William Whewell, *History of the inductive sciences from the earliest to the present time* (1837, third edition, London, 1857), Vol. I, Dedication, p.v.
140. Ibid., Vol. I., p. vi.
141. Maria Edgeworth, *Letters from England* (1813–44), ed. Christina Colvin (Oxford, 1971), p.597.
142. Whewell, *History of the inductive sciences*, Vol. I., pp.vii–viii.
143. Ibid., Vol. I., p.x.
144. Ibid., Vol. I., p.338.
145. *New essays by Oliver Goldsmith*, Essay X, 'The progress of the arts in Switzerland, from *The Public Ledger*, 29 August 1761, ed. Ronald S. Crane (Chicago, 1927), p.59.
146. 'Science and art in education', *T.H. Huxley on education,* ed. Cyril Bibby (Cambridge, 1971), p.195 (1883).
147. 'Universities: actual and ideal, inaugural address as rector of Aberdeen', *T.H. Huxley on education,* ed. Cyril Bibby (Cambridge, 1971), p.136 (1874).
148. Gilbert of Poitiers, *Commentaries on Boethius*, ed. N.M. Haring (Toronto, 1965), p.189.
149. John Stuart Mill, inaugural address delivered to the University of St. Andrews, 1867, *Essays on equality, law and education*, ed. John M. Robson (Toronto, 1984), pp.217–257, p.219.
150. Ibid., p.223.
151. Ibid., p.225.
152. Ibid., pp.224–5.

153. Ibid., p.227.
154. Charles Henry Cooper, *Athenae Cantabrigienses* (Cambridge, 1858 and 1861), p.vii.
155. Cooper, *Annals*.
156. William Wordsworth, *Ode on the installation of his Royal Highness Prince Albert as Chancellor of the University of Cambridge, July, 1847*, and see Winstanley, *Early Victorian Cambridge*, p.200, note 2, for Tennyson's response.
157. *Letters of the Prince Consort*, ed. Kurt Jagow and tr. E.T.S. Dugdale (London, 1938), p.130.
158. Ibid., pp.134–5.
159. See Winstanley, *Early Victorian Cambridge*, pp.200–1.
160. Report and evidence upon the recommendations of Her Majesty's Commissioners for inquiring into the State of the University of Oxford. Presented to the Board of Heads of Houses and Proctors, December 1. 1853. Oxford: at the University Press. 1853, *Edinburgh Review*, 99.201 (January 1854), p.160.
161. Ibid., p.174.
162. Ibid., p.161.
163. Hansard 3rd series, Vol. 111, pp.491 and 1151–3, see too 3rd series, Vol. 110, pp.691–765, and 3rd series, Vol. 125, pp.543–9 for the debate on Education, 4 April 1853.
164. *Letters of the Prince Consort*, ed. Kurt Jagow and tr. E.T.S. Dugdale (London, 1938), p.152.
165. *The principal speeches and addresses of His Royal Highness the Prince Consort*, sixth thousand (London, 1862).
166. http://hansard.millbanksystems.com/acts/scientific-societies-act-1843
167. *The principal speeches and addresses of His Royal Highness the Prince Consort*, p.111.
168. Ibid., p.112.
169. *The Diaries of George Price Boyce*, ed. Virginia Surtees (Norwich, 1983), p.1.
170. *The principal speeches and addresses of His Royal Highness the Prince Consort*, p.162.
171. Ibid., p.204.
172. *The Writings of Thomas Paine*, ed. Moncure Daniel Conway (New York and London, 1894), Vol. I, pp.20–25, originally published in the *Pennsylvania Magazine*, February 1775.
173. See Chapter 1.
174. *British Quarterly Review*, 3 (1 May 1846), p.364.
175. Brewster, 'Decline of science in England', p.333.
176. Morrell and Thackeray, *Gentlemen of science*, p.257.
177. Babbage, *Reflections on the decline of science in England*, pp.14–15.
178. Ibid., p.19.
179. Ibid.
180. Ibid., p.24.
181. Morrell and Thackeray, *Gentlemen of science*, pp.259, 261.
182. Ibid., p.453.
183. Report of the proceedings of the Section of the British Association on the Mechanical Arts, at the meeting held at Bristol, in September, 1836, *Edinburgh Review*, 65.131 (April 1837), p.119.
184. The British Academy was not established by Royal Charter until 1902, when it became the 'national academy' for the humanities and social sciences, on a similar basis of self-governing and independence.
185. Morrell and Thackeray, *Gentlemen of science*, p.500.
186. James A. Secord, 'How scientific conversation became shop talk', *Transactions of the Royal Historical Society*, Sixth Series, 17 (2007), pp.129–156, p.152 and see P. Gould, 'Women and the culture of university physics in late nineteenth-century Cambridge', *British Journal of the History of Science*, 30 (1997), pp.127–49.
187. Secord, 'How scientific conversation became shop talk', p.153.
188. Ibid., pp.130, 151ff. S. Woolgar, *Laboratory life: the social construction of scientific facts* (Beverly Hills, 1979). M. Lynch, *Art and artefact in laboratory science: a study of shop work and shop talk in a research laboratory* (1985). See too T.W. Heyck, *The transformation of intellectual life in Victorian England* (1982).
189. See M.D. Stephens, 'The Muspratts of Liverpool', *Annals of Science* (1972), pp.282–311.
190. On these see Michael Sanderson, 'The English Civic Universities and the "Industrial Spirit", 1870–1914', *Historical Research*, 61 (1988), pp.90–104, p.91.

191. 'Universities: actual and ideal, inaugural address as rector of Aberdeen', *T.H. Huxley on education,* ed. Cyril Bibby (Cambridge, 1971), p.130 (1874).

192. Pattison, *Suggestions on academical organization,* p.136.

193. 'Universities: actual and ideal, inaugural address as rector of Aberdeen', p.131.

194. Ibid., p.132.

195. Quoted in G.W. Roderick and M.D. Stephens, 'Scientific studies at Oxford and Cambridge, 1850–1914', *British Journal of Educational Studies,* 24 (1976), pp.49–65, p.55.

196. Ibid., p.53, and Royal Commission on Scientific Instruction and the Advancement of Science (Devonshire Commission, 1870), Vol. I, p.321.

197. Roderick and Stephens, 'Scientific studies at Oxford and Cambridge', pp.53–4.

198. Devonshire Commission (Vol. III.liv–lv), Quoted in Roderick and Stephens, 'Scientific studies at Oxford and Cambridge', p.55.

199. Roderick and Stephens, 'Scientific studies at Oxford and Cambridge', p.53.

200. See p.256.

201. 'Address on behalf of the national association for the promotion of technical education' (1887), *T.H. Huxley on Education,* ed. Cyril Bibby (Cambridge, 1971), p.201.

202. Lyon Playfair, 'Industrial competition and commercial freedom, discussion at the National Liberal Club, April 1888'.

203. Michael Sanderson, *The Universities and British Industry* (1850–1970) (London, 1972), p.55.

204. Michael Sanderson, *Universities in the nineteenth century,* pp.230–1.

205. Arthur Shipley (1861–1927) was one of the leaders. He had won a scholarship to study natural sciences at Christ's College, Cambridge, in 1880, concentrating on zoology in the second part of the Tripos. He progressed through an academic career at Cambridge from a Demonstratorship to a lectureship to a readership. By 1891 he was secretary to the Museums and Lecture Rooms Syndicate which acquainted him closely with the practical infrastructure requirements of the sciences.

206. Cambridge University Library, Cambridge University Archives, MS report of a conference held on 18 June 1903, Sir George Darwin's papers, printed in Michael Sanderson, *Universites in the nineteenth century,* p.234.

207. Michael Sanderson, *The Universities and British Industry* (1850–1970) (London, 1972), pp.31ff. A depressing account in Sanderson not necessarily accurate in view of evidence in an earlier chapter. The gulf seems to be not in the excitement of the original work or the consciousness of its educational interest and importance but in actually ensuring that Fellowships were available in colleges in these subject-areas.

208. The pressure now being exerted by state-driven expectations of public funding includes a drive to encourage the disadvantaged to 'aspire' not only to university education but to the 'top' universities. This assumes that intellectual hunger and curiosity alone will not be enough, that for 'the poor' to 'learn' requires state intervention.

209. H.A.L. Fisher, 'Our universities', address given to mark the centenary of University College, London, on 30 June 1927, p.10.

210. Ibid., p.8.

211. Ibid., pp.8ff.

212. For example, the University of Liverpool.

213. M.H. Curtis, *Oxford and Cambridge in transition* (Oxford, 1959), pp.49–51. See. too, the references in Twigg, 'The limits of reform', pp.99–114. See too John Webster, *Academiarum Examen* (London, 1963).

214. Mark Girouard, *The return to Camelot: chivalry and the English gentleman* (Yale, 1981), p.232.

215. *New letters of Robert Southey,* 12 October 1794, ed. Kenneth Curry (New York and London, 1965), Vol. I, pp.81–2.

216. Ibid., p.73.

217. She turned him out of the house and cut him off when she did.

218. *New Letters of Robert Southey,* August 1794, Vol. I, p.72.

219. Report and evidence upon the recommendations of Her Majesty's Commissioners for inquiring into the State of the University of Oxford. Presented to the Board of Heads of Houses and Proctors, December 1. 1853. Oxford: at the University Press. 1853, *Edinburgh Review,* 99.201 (January 1854), p.169.

220. Ibid., p.172.
221. Ibid., p.173.
222. Pattison, *Suggestions on academical organization*, p.102.
223. 'Technical Education', *T.H. Huxley on education*, ed. Cyril Bibby (Cambridge, 1971), p.163 (1877).
224. Ibid.
225. Pattison, *Suggestions on academical organization*, p.102.
226. *Anecdotes from Coleridge, Table talk II*, p.475.
227. 'Cuthbert Bede' [Edward Bradley], The adventures of Mr. Verdant Green (London, 1853), Vol. I, pp.10–11.
228. Kingsley, *Alton Locke*, p.274.
229. Ibid., p.158.
230. Ibid.
231. Ibid., p.204.
232. E.M. Forster, *Howard's end* (Penguin, 200), p.42.
233. Ibid., p.34.
234. Oliver Goldsmith, *An enquiry into the present state of polite learning in Europe*, Vol. 1, p.334.
235. William Makepeace Thackeray, letter to his mother, 31 December 1830, from Weimar, William Makepeace Thackeray, *The letters and private papers*, ed. Gordon N. Ray (Oxford, 1945), 4 vols., Vol. I (1817–1840), pp.138–9.
236. *The letters of Thomas Babington Macaulay*, ed. Thomas Pinney (Cambridge, 1974), pp.106–7.
237. Alfred Lord Tennyson, *The Letters*, ed. Cceil Y. Lang and Edgard F. Shannon (Oxford, 1982), Vol. I, pp.22–3.
238. Ibid., p.20.
239. Henry Lawrence (1859–1900) wrote his ('O.C') *Reminiscences of Cambridge Life* (London, 1889).
240. Ibid., p.23.
241. Ibid., p.7.
242. Ibid., pp.17–20.
243. Ibid., pp.20–1.
244. Ibid., pp.22–4.
245. Ibid., pp.26–7.
246. Ibid., p.31.
247. Ibid., p.32.
248. Ibid., p.34.
249. Ibid., p.56.
250. Ibid., p.56.
251. Ibid., p.41.
252. Ibid., pp.46–8.
253. Ibid., p.58.
254. Ibid., pp.150–1.
255. Ibid., pp.46–8.
256. Ibid., pp.62–3.
257. Ibid., p.81.
258. Ibid., p.161.
259. Ibid., p.66.
260. Ibid., p.71.
261. Ibid., pp.79–80.
262. Ibid., p.172.
263. Edgeworth, *Essays on professional education*.
264. As in the case of buying tickets for Birkbeck lectures, see p.330.
265. L. Stone, 'The Oxford student body', *The University in Society*, ed. L. Stone, (1975), 2 vols., Vol. I, pp.72–3.
266. Francis Bacon, *The Advancement of Learning*, Book II (12).
267. Babbage, *Reflections on the decline of science in England*, p.3.
268. 30 March 1813, Thomas Babington Macaulay, *Letters*, ed. Thomas Pinney (Cambridge, 1974–81), 6 vols., Vol. I, p.24.

269. Ibid., 8 May 1813, pp.30–1.
270. Ibid., 12 April 1813, p.25.
271. Ibid., 17 May 1813, p.32.
272. Ibid., 12 April 1813, pp.26–7.
273. Ibid., 20 April 1813, pp.27–8.
274. Ibid., 26 April 1813, pp.28–9.
275. Ibid., 23 October 1818, p.101.
276. Joseph Thompson, *The Owens College: its foundation and growth; and its connection with the Victoria University, Manchester* (Manchester, 1886), pp.2–3.
277. *Syllabus of classes and examinations for the Session 1873–4 with the results of the examinations and the examination papers of the year 1873* (Witherby and Co., London).
278. *The works of A.C. Hilton together with his life and letters,* ed. Robert P. Edgcumbe (Cambridge, 1905), p.177.
279. Ibid., p.179.
280. The Burgess Group Final Report, http://www.universitiesuk.ac.uk/Publications/Documents/Burgess_final.pdf.
281. *A letter to the Rector of Lincoln College*, by Philalethes (1807) G.A. Oxon b.19 (356), 383, p.9.
282. Ibid., p.7.
283. Ibid., p.9.
284. 1809 Oxford Statute 'Of examining candidates for degrees', Tit. IX, sec. 2.
285. Christopher Stray, 'From oral to written examinations: Cambridge, Oxford and Dublin 1700–1914', *History of Universities,* XX.2 (2005), pp.76–130, p.86.
286. See *The University of Oxford*, forthcoming.
287. On the Civil Service Examinations, see futher p.000.
288. Brendan Dooley, 'Science teaching as a career at Padua in the early eighteenth century: the case of Giovanni Poleni', *History of Universities*, iv (1984), pp.115–151, p.115.
289. D.A. Winstanley, *Later Victorian Cambridge* (Cambridge, 1947), pp.144–50.
290. *Report of the Public Schools Commission* (1864), I, p.26, II, pp.24–30.
291. Winstanley, *Later Victorian Cambridge*, p.146, and see W.H. Girdleston, *The Poll Course* (1862), pp.5–6.
292. Robert Sangster Rait, *The Universities Commission: a review* (Banff, January 1898), p.13.
293. Whewell, *Novum Organum Renovatum*, p.228.
294. 'Universities: actual and ideal, inaugural address as rector of Aberdeen', *T.H. Huxley on education,* ed. Cyril Bibby (Cambridge, 1971), p.134 (1874).
295. *The works of A.C. Hilton*, p.195.
296. William Godwin, *An enquiry concerning political justice,* 1793, Chapter VIII.
297. Benjamin Disraeli, *Coningsby* (1844), p.7.
298. Ibid., p.9.
299. See Johnson, *University Politics*, p.13.
300. Disraeli, *Coningsby*, p.117.
301. Ibid., p.273.
302. Ibid., p.273.
303. See p.87.
304. *Cambridge University Reporter*, 19 October 1870, p.1.
305. Ibid., p.26.
306. Ibid., pp.181–2.
307. Ibid., pp.192–3.
308. Ibid., pp.203–7.
309. See p.87.

Conclusion

1. Mark Pattison, 'Address on education', published in *Transactions of the National Association for the Promotion of Social Science* (London, 1877), pp.61–2.

SELECT BIBLIOGRAPHY

A letter of advice to young gentleman at the University to which are subjoined, directions for young students (London, 1701, reprinted 1721).

Abelard, Peter, *Commentary on Romans,* ed. M. Buytaert, *Corpus Christianorum Continuatio Medievalis,* 11 (1969).

Abelard, Peter, *Historia Calamitatum,* ed. J. Monfrin (Paris, 1967).

Albert of Saxe-Coburg, *Letters of the Prince Consort,* ed. Kurt Jagow and tr. E.T.S. Dugdale (London, 1938).

Albert of Saxe-Coburg, *The principal speeches and addresses of his royal highness the Prince Consort* (London, 1862).

Andrew, Christopher, 'Cambridge Spies', *Cambridge Contributions,* ed. Sarah J. Ormrod (Cambridge, 1998).

Arnold, Matthew, *The letters of Matthew Arnold,* 18 June 1879, ed. Cecil Y. Lang (Virginia, 1996–2001), 6 vols., Vol. V.

Ascham, Roger, *The Scholemaster* (Cambridge, 1904).

Aston, M., *Lollards and reformers. Images and literacy in late medieval religion* (London, 1984).

Azad, Yusef, 'The limits of University: the study of language in some British universities and academies 1750–1800', *History of Universities,* 7(1988), 118–47.

Babbage, Charles, *Reflections on the decline of science in England and on some of its causes* (London, 1830).

Bacon, Francis, *The works of Francis Bacon,* ed. James Spedding, Robert Leslie Ellis and Douglas Denon Heath (London, 1857–84), 14 vols.

Baker, J.H., *The third university of England,* Selden Society Lecture, 1990 (London, 1990).

Baker, Thomas, *History of the College of St. John the Evangelist, Cambridge* (Cambridge, 1869), 2 vols.

Barbara S. Tinsley, *Pierre Bayle's reformation* (Susquehanna, 2004).

Barrow, Isaac, 'Of industry in general', *The theological works of Isaac Barrow* (Oxford, 1830), 8 vols.

Batey, Mavis, *The historic gardens of Oxford and Cambridge* (1989).

Beck, L.J., *The metaphysics of Descartes* (Oxford, 1965).

Bede, *Ecclesiastical history,* ed. B. Colgrave and R.A.B. Mynors (Oxford, 1969), Vol. IV.

Birt, Henry Norbert, *The Elizabethan religious settlement* (London, 1907).

Black, Robert, *Education and society in Florentine Tuscany* (Leiden, 2007).

Black, Robert, ed., *Studia e sculoa in Arezzo durante il medioevo e il rinascimento: I documenti d'archivio fino al 1530* (Arezzo, 1996).

Blair, Ann, 'Ovidius Methodizatus: the Metamorphoses of Ovid in a sixteenth century Paris College', *History of Universities,* 9(1990), 73–118.

Blair, Ann, 'The teaching of Natural Philosophy in early seventeenth century Paris: the case of Jean Cécile Frey', *History of Universities,* 12(1993), 95–158.

Boethius, *De Hebdomadibus,* I, *Theological Tractates,* ed. H. Stewart, E.K. Rand and S.J. Tester (Harvard, 1973).

Boute, Bruno, 'Academics in action. Scholarly interests and policies in the early Counter Reformation: the reform of the University of Louvain, 1607–1617', *History of Universities,* 18(2003), 34–89.

Bowring, Richard, *Fifty years of Japanese at Cambridge, 1948–98* (Cambridge, 1998).

Boyle, Robert, *The works of Robert Boyle,* ed. M. Hunter and E.B. Davis (1999–2000), 7 vols.

Bradford, John, *Writings,* ed. Aubrey Townsend (Cambridge, 1848).

Bradley, Edward, writing as 'Cuthbert Bede', *The adventures of Mr. Verdant Green* (London, 1853).

Brewster, David, 'Decline of science in England', *Quarterly Review,* 43(1830), 305–42.

British Quarterly Review, 3(1 May 1846), 364.

Brockliss, L.W.B., 'Philosophy teaching in France, 1600–1740', *History of Universities,* 1(1981), 131–68.

Brooke, C.N.L., ed., *A history of the University of Cambridge* (Cambridge, 1988–93), 4 vols.

Brooke, Rupert, *Letters*, ed. Geoffrey Keynes (London, 1968).

Browning, Robert, *The poems,* ed. John Pettigrew (Yale, 1981), Vol. I.

Browning, Robert, *The letters of Robert Browning*, ed. Thurman L. Hood (London, 1933).

Bruce, Gainsford, *The life and letters of John Collingwood Bruce* (Edinburgh, 1905).

Bunyan, John, *Grace abounding and other spiritual autobiographies,* ed. John Stachniewski and Anita Pacheco (Oxford, 1998), p.98.

Burgess, Clive and Martin Heale, *The late medieval English college and its context* (York, 2008).

Burnand, F.C., *Personal reminiscences of the University Amateur Dramatic Club, Cambridge* (London, 1880).

Burnet, G., *Bishop Burnet's history of his own time*, ed. G. and T. Burnet (London, 1724), 2 vols. Oxford.

Burnett, Charles, 'Give him the white cow: notes and note-taking in the universities in the twelfth and thirteenth centuries', *History of Universities*, 14(1995–6), 1–30.

Butler, Joseph, *Analogy*, ed. with an appendix by Henry Morley (London, 1884).

Butler, Samuel, *Prose observations*, ed. Hugh de Quehen (Oxford, 1979).

Calvin, John, *Works, tracts and treatises on the Reformation*, tr. H. Beveridge (Edinburgh, 1958), Vol. I.

Cambridge Antiquarian Society, *Proceedings* (Cambridge, 1840).

Cambridge commemorated: an anthology of university life, ed. Laurence and Helen Fowler (Cambridge, 1984).

The Cambridge mind: ninety years of the Cambridge Review, 1879–1969, ed. Eric Homberger, William Janeway and Simon Schama (London, 1970).

Carlyle, Thomas, 'Signs of the times', *Critical and miscellaneous essays* (London, 1899), Vol. II.

Chadwick, Owen, 'Indifference and morality', *Christian spirituality: essays in honour of Gordon Rupp,* ed. Peter Brooks (London, 1975).

Chapman, William, *The life of John Wiclif: the herald of the Reformation.* (London, No publisher, 1883).

Chester, Allan G., *Hugh Latimer* (Philadelphia, 1954).

Clagett, M., *Science and mechanics in the Middle Ages* (London, 1959).

Cobbett, William, *Cobbett's Parliamentary history of England* (London, 1806), Vol. I.

Coleridge, Samuel T., *Biographia Literaria,* ed. G. Watson (London, 1906).

Coleridge, Samuel T., *The friend, essay IV, collected works,* ed. Barbara E. Rooke (Princeton, 1969), Vol. 4.

Coleridge, Samuel T., *Table talk,* ed. Kathleen Coburn, *Collected works* (London, 1990), 2 vols., Vol. 14.

Collection of statutes for the University and the Colleges of Cambridge, ed. James Heywood (London, 1840).

Collinson, Patrick, *Elizabethan essays* (London, 1994).

Cooper, Charles Henry, *Athenae Cantabrigienses* (Cambridge, 1858 and 1861).

Cornford, Frances, *Poems by Frances Cornford* (Cambridge, 1910).

Cornford, Francis, *Microcosmographia Academica* (1908), and new ed. by Gordon Johnson with detailed introduction (Cambridge, 1994).

Courtenay, William J. and Katherine H. Tachau, 'Ockham, Ockhamists, and the English-German nation at Paris, 1339–1341', *History of Universities*, 2(1982), 53–96.

Coverdale, Miles, *Remains,* ed. G. Pearson, Parker Society (Cambridge, 1846).

Coverdale, Miles, *Writings and translations of Myles Coverdale,* ed. George Pearson (Cambridge, 1844).

Cowley, Abraham, *Collected works,* ed. Thomas O. Calhoun (Delaware, 1989), vol. I.

Cranmer, Thomas, *Letters*, Parker Society.

Cranmer, Thomas, *Miscellaneous writings*, Parker Society (Cambridge, 1846).

Cranmer, Thomas, *Writings and disputations of Thomas Cranmer,* ed. John E. Cox, Parker Society (Cambridge, 1844).

Cromwell, Oliver, *Letters and speeches* (London, 1904).

Curtis, M.H., *Oxford and Cambridge in transition* (Oxford, 1959).

Curtis, Mark, 'The alienated intellectuals of early Stuart England', *Past and Present,* 23(1962), 25–41.

Darwin, Charles, *The correspondence of Charles Darwin*, ed. Frederick Burkhardt and Sydney Smith (Cambridge, 1985).

Davies, Joan, 'Student libraries in sixteenth century Toulouse', *History of Universities*, 3(1983), 62–86.

Denley, Peter, 'The collegiate movement in Italian universities in the late Middle Ages', *History of Universities,* 10(1991), 29–91.

De Quincey, Thomas, 'Letters to a young man whose education has been neglected', Vol. II, first published in *London Magazine,* 7(February, 1823), *The works of Thomas de Quincey,* ed. Frederick Burwick (London, 2000), Vol. III.

De Rosa, Stefano, 'Studi sul'universita di Pisa. I, Alcune fonti inedited: Diari, Lettere e Rapporti dui Bidelli (1472–1700)', *History of Universities,* 2(1982), 97–125.

Deacon, Malcolm, *Philip Doddridge of Northampton, 1702–51* (Northamptonshire Libraries, 1981).

Descartes, René, *The philosophical writings of Descartes,* tr. John Cottingham, Robert Stoothoff and Dugald Murdoch (Cambridge, 1984–91), 3 vols.

Dick, Susan, ed., 'A woman's college from outside', *The complete shorter fiction of Virginia Woolf* (London, 1985).

Dinis, Alfredo, 'Giovanni Battista Riccili and the science of his time', *Jesuit Science and the Republic of Letters,* ed. M. Feingold (Cambridge, MA, 2003).

Disraeli, Benjamin, *Coningsby* (London, 1844).

Doddridge, Philip, *Calendar of the correspondence of Philip Doddridge DD* (1702–51), ed. Geoffrey Nuttall (London, 1979).

Donne, John, *The sermons of John Donne,* ed. G.R. Potter and Evelyn M. Simpson (Berkeley, 1953–1963), 10 vols.

Dooley, Brendan, 'Science teaching as a career at Padua in the early eighteenth century: the case of Giovanni Poleni', *History of Universities,* 4(1984), 115–51.

Dowsing, William, *The Cambridge Journal of William Dowsing, 1643,* transcribed by A.C. Moule (1926), *The diaries of George Price Boyce,* ed. Virginia Surtees (Norwich, 1983).

Duns Scotus, John, *Opera Omnia,* ed. P.C. Balíc et al. (Vatican, 1950–)

Duns Scotus, John, *Philosophical writings: a selection,* ed. Alan Wolter (London, 1962).

Dyer, George, *The privileges of the University of Cambridge* (London, 1824), 2 vols.

Edgeworth, Maria, *Letters from England* (1813–44), ed. Christina Colvin (Oxford, 1971).

Edgeworth, Richard Lovell, *Essays on professional education* (London, 1809).

Elisabeth Leedham-Green, *A concise history of the University of Cambridge* (Cambridge, 1996).

Emden, A.B., *Biographical register of the University of Cambridge to 1500* (Cambridge, 1963).

Emden, A.B., *Biographical register of the University of Oxford to AD 1500* (Oxford, 1957–9), 3 vols.

Engel, Arthur, 'The emerging concept of the academic profession at Oxford, 1800–1854', *The university in society* (Princeton, 1975), 2 vols.

Erasmus, *Antibarbarorum liber,* ed. K. Kumaniecki, *Erasmi Opera Omnia,* I–1(1969).

Erasmus, *De ratione studii,* ed. J. Margolin, *Erasmi Opera Omnia,* I–2(1971).

Erasmus, Desiderius, *Opera Omnia* (1882).

Evans, G.R., *Alan of Lille* (Cambridge, 1983).

Evans, G.R., *Inside the University of Cambridge in the modern world* (Lampeter, 2004).

Fasciculi Zizaniorum, ed. W.W. Shirley, Rolls Series (London, 1858).

Felici, Lucia, 'The Erasmusstiftung and Europe: the institution, organization, and activity of the Foundation of Erasmus of Rotterdam from 1538–1600', *History of Universities,* 12(1993), 25–63.

Fisher, H.A.L., 'Our universities', address given to mark the centenary of University College, London, on 30 June 1927.

Fletcher, John M., 'Chance and resistance to change: a consideration of the development of English and German universities during the sixteenth century', *History of Universities,* 1(1981), 1–36.

Ford, Alan, *James Ussher, theology history and politics in early-modern Ireland and England* (Oxford, 2007).

Forster, E.M., *Howard's end* (Penguin, 1941).

Fraunce, Abraham, *The Lawiers Logike* (London, 1588).

Fulford, Tim, Debbie Lee and Peter J. Kitson, *Literature, science and exploration in the Romantic era* (Cambridge, 2004).

Furey, Constance M., *Erasmus, Contarini, and the religious republic of letters* (Cambridge, 2006).

Gassendi, Pierre, *Exercises in the form of paradoxes against the Aristotelians, the selected works,* ed. and tr. Craig B. Brush (London, 1972), from the *Opera Omnia* (Lyons, 1658, reprinted Stuttgart, 1964).

Gilbert, George, *The reminiscences of George Gilbert* (1796–1874), ed. John Shirley (London, 1938).

Gilbert of Poitiers, *Commentaries on Boethius,* ed. N.M. Haring (Toronto, 1965).

Girdleston, W.H., *The poll course* (Cambridge, 1862).

Girouard, Mark, *The return to Camelot: Chivalry and the English gentleman* (Yale, 1981).

Glasgow University Calendar (Glasgow, 1829).

Godwin, William, *An enquiry concerning political justice*, ed. K. Carter (Oxford, 1971, first published 1793).

Goldsmith, Oliver, *An enquiry into the present state of polite learning in Europe,* ed. David Masson (London, 1895), Vol. 1.

Goldsmith, Oliver, *New essays by Oliver Goldsmith*, Essay X, 'The progress of the arts in Switzerland', from *The Public Ledger,* 29 August 1761, ed. Ronald S. Crane (Chicago, 1927).

Gould, P., 'Women and the culture of university physics in late nineteenth-century Cambridge', *British Journal of the History of Science,* 30(1997), 127–49.

Graham, Rose, ed., *Chantry certificates, Oxfordshire Record Society,* 1(1919).

Graham, T. and A.G. Watson, *The recovery of the past in early Elizabethan England* (Cambridge, 1998).

Graves Report, *Report to the Council of the Senate on the administrative organization of the University, Reporter,* 1967–8, 13 October 1967.

Greaves, R.L., *Deliver us from evil: the radical underground in Britain, 1660–1663* (Oxford, 1986).

Greengrass, Mark, ed., *Samuel Hartlib and universal reformation: studies in intellectual communication* (Cambridge, 1995).

Gunning, Henry, *Reminiscences of Cambridge,* selected and ed. D.A. Winstanley (Cambridge, 1932).

Haller, W., ed., *The arraignment of persecution* (1645), in *Tracts on liberty in the Puritan revolution* (Columbia, 1934), Vol. 3, pp.211–12.

Hamesse, J., 'Le Vocabulaire de la transmission orale des textes', *Vocabulaire du livre* (Louvain-la-Neuve, 1989).

Hassall, Christopher, *The prose of Rupert Brooke* (London, 1956).

Hermans, J.M.M. and Marc Nelissen, eds., *Charters of foundation: early documents,* Coimbra Universities Group (Leuven, Belgium, 2005).

Heyck, T.W., *The transformation of intellectual life in Victorian England* (New York, 1982).

Heywood, J., *Early Cambridge University and college statutes in the English language* (London, 1855).

Heywood, James and Thomas Wright, eds., *Cambridge University transactions during the Puritan controversies of the sixteenth and seventeenth centuries* (London, 1854).

Hicks, Carola, *The King's Glass* (London, 2007).

Higher education in London, Parliamentary papers (1889) (C.5709), XXXIX, 323.

Hilton, A.C., *The works of A.C. Hilton together with his life and letters,* ed. Robert P. Edgcumbe (Cambridge, 1905).

Hochstrasser, Tim, 'A college in the air': myth and reality in the foundation story of Downing College, Cambridge', *History of Universities,* 17(2001–2), 81–120.

Hofstetter, Michael, 'The classical Tripos and the Romantic movement at Cambridge', *History of Universities,* 19(2004), 221–39.

Hooper, John, *Early writings,* ed. Samuel Carr, Parker Society (Cambridge, 1843).

Hudson, A., *The premature reformation* (Oxford, 1987).

Hunter, Michael, *Robert Boyle, 1627–1691, scrupulosity and science* (Woodbridge, 2000).

Huxley, T.H., *T.H. Huxley on education,* ed. Cyril Bibby (Cambridge, 1971).

Huygens, R.B.C., *Accessus ad auctores* (Leiden, 1970).

Johnson, Thomas, *Quaestiones* (Cambridge, 1735).

Kamm, Josephine, *Hope deferred* (1965).

Kilgour, Alexander, *The Scottish universities and what to reform in them* (Edinburgh, 1857).

Kingsley, Charles, *Alton Locke* (Nelson, 1924, first published 1850).

Kingsley, Charles, *The water babies* (London, 1863).

Kneale, W. and M., *The development of logic* (Oxford, 1962), pp.298–9.

Knowlson, James, *Universal language schemes in England and France, 1600–1800* (Toronto, 1975).

Kusukawa, Sachiko, 'Law and gospel: the importance of philosophy at Reformation Wittenberg', *History of Universities,* 11(1992), 59–74.

Lander, Jesse M., *Inventing Polemic: religion, print and literary culture in early modern England* (Cambridge, 2006).

Lawrence, Alfred Henry ('O.C.'), *Reminiscences of Cambridge life* (London, 1889).

Leader, Damian R., 'Philosophy at Oxford and Cambridge in the fifteenth century', *History of Universities,* 4(1984), 25–46.

Lewis, Rhodri, 'A Babel off Broad Street: artificial language planning in 1650s Oxford', *History of Universities*, 21(2005), 108–46.

Ligota, C.R. and J.-L.Quantin, eds., *History of scholarship* (Oxford, 2006).

Lister, Irene, *Cambridge characters* (Cambridge, 1978).

Lubenow, W.C., *The Cambridge Apostles, 1820–1914* (Cambridge, 1998).

Luther, Martin, *Werke*, Weimar Ausgabe (1883), 127 vols., Vol. 39.

Lynch, Michael, *Art and artefact in laboratory science: a study of shop work and shop talk in a research laboratory* (London, 1985).

Lysons, Daniel and Samuel, *Magna Britannia: Cambridgeshire* (Wakefield, 1808).

Macaulay, Thomas B., *Letters*, ed. Thomas Pinney (Cambridge, 1974–81), 6 vols.

Macaulay, Thomas B., *The letters of Thomas Babington Macaulay*, ed. Thomas Pinney (Cambridge, 1974).

MacQueen, Daniel, *Letters on Hume's history of Great Britain* (1756, reprinted), with an introduction by John Valdimir Price (Thoemmes, 1990).

McKitterick, David, *Cambridge University Library* (Cambridge, 1986), Vol. II.

McLaughlin, R. Emmet, 'Universities, scholasticism, and the origins of the German Reformation', *History of Universities*, 9(1990), 1–43.

Melanchthon, Philip, *De corrigendis adulescentiae studiis*, CR, 11, pp.15ff., *The Reformation in its own words*, ed. and tr. Hans J. Hillebrand (London, 1964).

Melanchthon, Philip, *Locorum theologicorum...quibus et Loci Communes P. Melanchthonis explicantur* (Basle, 1599).

Melanchthon, Philip, *On Christian doctrine: Loci communes*, 1555, tr. and ed. Clyde L. Manschreck (New York, 1965).

Meyer, Carl S., 'Thomas More and the Wittenberg Lutherans', *Concordia Theological Monthly*, 39(1968), 246–56.

Mill, John S., *Collected works of John Stuart Mill*, xv, ed. F.E. Mineka and D.M. Lindley (Indianapolis, 1972).

Mill, John S., *Essays on ethics, religion and society*, ed. John M. Robson (Toronto, 1969), p.36.

Mill, John S., Inaugural address delivered to the University of St. Andrews, 1867, *Essays on equality, law and education*, ed. John M. Robson (Toronto, 1984), pp.217–57.

Milton, John, *Of education, works*, ed. Frank A. Patterson (New York, 1931), Vol. IV.

Minchamp, Georges, *Le Cartésianisme en Belgique* (Brussels, 1886).

Monchamp, Georges, *Galilée et la Belgique* (Brussels, 1892).

Montagu, Basil, *Enquiries and observations respecting the University Library* (Cambridge, 1805).

More, Henry, *A collection of several philosophical writings* (London, 1662).

More, Thomas, *Complete works* (Yale, 1990).

Morrell, Jack and Arnold Thackeray, *Gentlemen of science* (Oxford, 1981).

Muir, J., *Reasons for the establishment of a Sanskrit Chair in the University of Edinburgh* (Edinburgh, 1860).

Narrative of the days of the reformation ... with two contemporary biographies of the Archbishop Cranmer, ed. John G. Nichols (London, 1859).

Neild, Robert, *Riches and responsibility: the financial history of Trinity College* (Cambridge, 2008).

Nève, Félix, *La Renaissance des lettres en Belgique* (Leuven, Belgium, 1890).

Newton, Isaac, *The correspondence of Isaac Newton*, ed. H.W. Turnbull (Cambridge, 1959), 1.

Notker Hammerstein, 'The University of Heidelberg in the early modern period: aspects of its history as a contribution to its sextenary', *History of Universities*, 6(1986–7), 105–33.

Oates, J.C.T., *Cambridge University Library* (Cambridge, 1986), Vol. I.

Oberman, Heiko A., 'Luther and the Via Moderna: the philosophical backdrop of the Reformation breakthrough', *Journal of Ecclesiastical History*, 54(2003), 641–70.

Oberman, Heiko A., 'Via Antiqua and Via Moderna: late medieval prolegomena to early reformation thought', *Journal of the History of Ideas*, 48.1(January–March, 1987), pp.23–40.

Otterspeer, Wille, 'The mediating role of the University: Leiden University, its structure and function during the first two centuries of its existence', *History of Universities*, 18(2003), 147–95.

Paine, Thomas, *The writings of Thomas Paine*, ed. Moncure D. Conway (New York, 1894), vol. I, pp.20–5, originally published in the *Pennsylvania Magazine*, February 1775.

Paris, Matthew, *Historia Anglorum*, ed. F. Madden, Rolls Society (London, 1869).

Parker, Matthew, *Correspondence of Archbishop Parker*, ed. John Bruce, Parker Society (Cambridge, 1853).

Pattison, Mark. 'Address on education', published in *Transactions of the National Association for the Promotion of Social Science* (London, 1877), pp.61–2.

Pattison, Mark, *Suggestions on academical organization* (Edinburgh, 1868).

Peacock, Thomas L., *Letter to Thomas Forster*, February 1811, *Works*, ed. Nicholas Joukovsky (Oxford, 2001).

Philatheles, *A letter to the rector of Lincoln College*, by Philalethes (1807), G.A. Oxon b.19 (356), 383, p.8.

Playfair, Lyon, 'Industrial competition and commercial freedom', Discussion at the National Liberal Club, April 1888.

Piltz, Anders, ed., *Studium Upsalense: Specimens of the oldest lecture notes taken in the mediaeval University of Uppsala*, (Uppsala, 1977).

Porter, Roy, 'The natural sciences tripos and the "Cambridge School of Geology", 1850–1914', *History of Universities*, 2(1982), 193–216.

Powys, A.R., *From the ground up* (London, 1937).

Powys, John C., *Autobiography* (New York, 1934).

Priestley, Joseph, *A course of lectures on the theory of language* (Warrington, 1762).

Priestley, Joseph, *Experiments and observations, etc., in three volumes* (Birmingham, 1790).

Priestley, Joseph, *Heads of lectures on a course of experimental philosophy, particularly including chemistry, delivered at the New College in Hackney* (Dublin, 1794).

Querela Cantabrigiensis (Cambridge, 1647).

Rait, Robert S., *The Universities Commission: a review* (Banff, 1898).

Rashdall, Hastings, *The history of Europe in the Middle Ages*, ed. F.M. Powicke and A.B. Emden (1936), II.

Raverat, Gwen, *Period piece: a Cambridge childhood* (Bath, 2003).

Rawle, Tim, *Cambridge architecture* (London, 1993).

Records of Convocation VII, Canterbury, 1509–1603, ed, Gerald Bray, Church of England Record Society (Boydell, 2006).

Reeve, F.A., *The Cambridge that never was* (Cambridge, 1976).

Reeve, F.A., *The Cambridge nobody knows* (Cambridge, 1977).

Reid, David A., 'A science for polite society: British dissent and the teaching of natural philosophy in the seventeenth and eighteenth centuries', *History of Universities*, 21(2006), 117–58.

Reid, David A., 'Technical knowledge and the mental universe of the early cotton manufacturers', *Canadian Journal of History*, 36(2001), 284–304.

Rennie, James, *The menageries: Quadrupeds described and drawn from living subjects* (London, 1829–31).

Report of the Committee on Higher Education (Robbins) (London, 1963).

Report of the Public Schools Commission (London, 1864), I.

Ridley, Nicholas, *Works*, ed. Henry Christmas, Parker Society (Cambridge, 1841).

Robbins, Lord, *Higher education revisited* (London, 1980).

Roderick, G.W. and M.D. Stephens, 'Scientific studies at Oxford and Cambridge, 1850–1914', *British Journal of Educational Studies*, 24(1976), 49–65.

Roger of Wendover, *Flores Historiarum*, ed. H.G. Hewlett, RS 84 (London, 1886 9), Vol. II.

Roy, Lyse, 'University officers and the universities' institutional crisis: Caen (1450–1549)', *History of Universities*, 15(1997–9), 103–122.

Roye, William, *A Brefe Dialoge bitwene a Cristen Father and his stobborne Sone*, ed. Douglas H. Parker and Bruce Krajewski, tr. of Capito's original (Toronto, 1999).

Sanderson, Michael, 'The English civic universities and the "industrial spirit". 1870–1914', *Historical Research*, 61(1988), 90–104.

Sanderson, Michael, *The universities and British industry (1850–1970)* (London, 1972).

Sanderson, Michael, ed., *The universities in the nineteenth century* (Routledge, 1975).

Sanderson, Robert, *Logicae Artis Compendium*, ed. E.J. Ashworth, *Instrumenta rationis* (Bologna, 1985), Vol. II.

Scott, Sir Walter, *The heart of Midlothian* (London, 1818).

Searle, W. G., *The history of the Queens' College, 1446–1560*, Cambridge Antiquarian Society (Cambridge, 1867).

Secord, James A., 'How scientific conversation became shop talk', *Transactions of the Royal Historical Society*, Sixth Series, 17(2007), 129–56.

Sedgwick, Adam, *A discourse on the studies of the university* (1833 version), introduced by Eric Ashby and Mary Anderson (London, 1969).

Sharpe, Richard, 'The English bibliographical tradition from Kirkestere to Tanner', *Britannia Latina: Latin in the culture of Great Britain from the Middle Ages to the twentieth century*, ed. Charles Burnett and Nicholas Mann, Warburg Institute Colloquia, 8 (London, 2005), pp.86–128.

Sharpe, Tom, *Porterhouse Blue* (London, 2002).

Simon of Tournai, *Disputationes*, ed. J. Warichez, *Spicilegium Sacrum Lovaniense*, 12 (1932).

Sinclair, Andrew, *In love and anger: a view of the sixties* (London, 1994).

Sitwell, Edith, *The English eccentrics* (London, 1933).

Smahel, F. 'The Kuttenberg Decree and the withdrawal of the German students from Prague in 1409: a discussion', *History of Universities*, 4(1984), 153–61.

Smithsonian Institution, Washington, Dibner Collection, Burndy MS 16.

Southern, R.W., *Medieval humanism* (Oxford, 1970).

Southey, Robert, *New letters of Robert Southey*, August 1794, ed. Kenneth Curry (New York, 1965), Vol. I.

The Spectator, 197, 16 October 1711, ed. Donald F. Bond (Oxford, 1965), Vol. II, pp.271–2.

The Spectator, 239, ed. Donald F. Bond (Oxford, 1965), Vol. II.

The Spectator, 518, ed. Donald F. Bond (Oxford, 1965), Vol. IV.

Stern, F., *Gabriel Harvey, his life, marginalia and library* (Oxford, 1979).

Stevenson, David, ed., *Letters of Sir Robert Moray to the Earl of Kincardine, 1657–73* (Ashgate, 2007).

Stone, L., 'The Oxford student body', *The University in Society*, ed. L. Stone (Oxford, 1975), 2 vols.

Stray, Christopher, 'From oral to written examinations: Cambridge, Oxford and Dublin 1700–1914', *History of Universities*, 22.2(2005), 76–130.

Summit, Jennifer, *Memory's library* (Chicago, 2008).

Supplementa Melanchthoniana (1510–28), ed. O. Clemen (Leipzig, 1926), Vol. I.

Swift, Jonathan, *Gulliver's travels*, ed. Colin McElvie (London, 1976).

Syllabus of classes and examinations for the session 1873–4 with the results of the examinations and the examination papers of the year 1873 (London, 1874).

Ted Mott's Cambridge: a portrait of the city in old photographs (Norfolk, 1991).

Tennyson, Alfred Lord, *The letters*, ed. Cecil Y. Lang and Edward F. Shannon (Oxford, 1982), Vol. I.

Thackeray, William M., *The letters and private papers*, ed. Gordon N. Ray (Oxford, 1945), 4 vols.

Thackeray, William M., *Pendennis*, ed. Peter Shillingsburgh (New York, 1991).

Thompson, Joseph, *The Owens College: its foundation and growth; and its connection* (Manchester, 1886).

Thompson, Martin, 'The lure of landscape', *CAM*, 55(2008), 14–17.

Thomson, D.F.S., tr., *Erasmus and Cambridge: the Cambridge letters of Erasmus* (Toronto, 1963), p.188.

Todhunter, Isaac, *William Whewell* (London, 1976), 2 vols.

Took, Horne, *Diversions of Purley* (London, 1798 and 1805).

Tracts ... containing new experiments touching the relation betwixt flame and fire (London, 1672).

Twigg, J. D., 'The Parliamentary visitation of the University of Cambridge, 1644–1645', *The English Historical Review*, 98(1983), 513–528.

Twigg, John, 'The limits of reform: some aspects of the debate on university education during the English Revolution', *History of Universities*, 4(1984), 99–114.

Twigg, John, *The University of Cambridge and the English Revolution* (Cambridge, 1990).

Urkundenbuch det Universitat Wittenberg, I, 1502–1611, ed. W. Frieensburg (Magdeburg, 1926), pp.267ff.

Valla, Lorenzo, *Opera Omnia*, 1 (Basle, 1540, reprinted Turin, 1962).

Vanpaemel, Gert, 'Experimental physics and the Natural Science Curriculum in eighteenth century Louvan', *History of Universities*, 7(1988), 175–96.

Vaughnan, Thomas, *The magical writings of Thomas Vaughan*, ed. A.E. Waite (London, 1888).

Vickers, Ilse, *Defoe and the new sciences* (Cambridge, 1996).

Vitalis, Orderic, *Historia Ecclesiastica* (Oxford, 1969), Vol. IV.

Weber, Christoph F., 'Ces grands privileges: the symbolic use of written documents in the foundation and institutionalization processes of medieval universities', *History of Universities,* 19(2004), 12–62.

Webster, John, *Academiarum Examen* (London, 1963).

Weiss, R., *Humanism in England during the fifteenth century* (Oxford, 1967).

Whewell, William, *History of the inductive sciences* (London, 1837).

Whewell, William, *History of the inductive sciences from the earliest to the present time* (1837, third edition, London, 1857).

Whewell, William, *Novum Organum Renovatum* (London, 1858).

Whewell, William, *On the principles of English university education* (London, 1929).

Whewell, William, *The philosophy of the inductive sciences* (London, 1840), Vol. I.

Whitaker, William, *A disputation on Holy Scripture against the Papists,* Parker Society (Cambridge, 1849).

Whitgift, John, *Works of John Whitgift,* ed. John Ayre, Parker Society (Cambridge, 1851).

Wilkins, John, *An essay towards a real character and a philosophical language* (Menston, Yorkshire, 1968).

Williamson, Raymond, 'The plague in Cambridge', *Medieval History,* 1(1957), 53–4.

Willis, Robert, *The architectural history of the University of Cambridge* (Cambridge, 1886), 3 vols.

Wilson, Daniel, *Prehistoric annals of Scotland* (London, 1863).

Winstanley, D.A., *Later Victorian Cambridge* (Cambridge, 1947).

Winstanley, D.A., *Unreformed Cambridge* (Cambridge, 1935).

Winstanley, Gerrard, 'The law of freedom in a platform', *The law of freedom and other writings,* ed. Christopher Hill (Cambridge, 1973).

Woolf, Leonard, *Sowing: an autobiography of the years 1880–1904* (London, 1967).

Woolf, Virginia, *The early journals,* ed. Mitchel A. Leaska (London, 1990).

Woolf, Virginia, *A room of one's own, works* (London, 1929), Vol. I.

Woolgar, Steve. *Laboratory life: the social construction of scientific facts* (Beverly Hills, 1979).

Wordsworth, William, *Ecclesiastical sonnets* (1821–2), 43, Inside of King's College Chapel, Cambridge.

Wordsworth, William, *Ode on the installation of His Royal Highness Prince Albert as Chancellor of the University of Cambridge* (1847).

Wordsworth, William, *The Prelude,* ed. Stephen Charles Gill (Cambridge, 1991).

Yates, James, *Thoughts on the advancement of academical education in England* (London, 1826).

Zurich letters, ed. Hastings Robinson (Cambridge, 1842).

INDEX

Index

Index

Index

Index